Sinoglossia

Sinoglossia

Edited by
Andrea Bachner, Howard Chiang, and Yu-lin Lee

HKU PRESS
香港大學出版社

Hong Kong University Press
The University of Hong Kong
Pok Fu Lam Road
Hong Kong
https://hkupress.hku.hk

© 2023 Hong Kong University Press

ISBN 978-988-8805-71-6 (*Hardback*)

All rights reserved. No portion of this publication may be reproduced or transmitted in any form or by any means, electronic or mechanical, including photocopying, recording, or any information storage or retrieval system, without prior permission in writing from the publisher.

British Library Cataloguing-in-Publication Data
A catalogue record for this book is available from the British Library.

Digitally printed

Contents

List of Figures and Table   vii
Acknowledgments   viii
List of Contributors   ix
Introduction   1
    Andrea Bachner, Howard Chiang, and Yu-lin Lee

Part I. Corporeality

1. Inspecting Bodies, Crafting Subjects: The Physical Examination in Republican China   19
Jia-Chen Fu

2. Therapeutic Humanism in Hou Chun-Ming's Art: Queer Mimesis, Subaltern Souls, and the Body as Vessel in Sinoglossiac Taiwan   37
Howard Chiang

3. What Does an Open Body Say? The Body and the Cold War in the Early 1980s Theater of Taiwan   55
Chun-yen Wang

Part II. Media

4. Landscape of Words: *Romance on Lushan Mountain* (1980) and Sinoglossia as Delimitation   73
Paola Iovene

5. Sinopop: The Case of Namewee/Wee Meng Chee   91
E. K. Tan

6. Chinese Writing, Heptapod B, and Martian Script: The Ethnocentric Bases of Language   110
Carlos Rojas

7. The Techne of Listening: Toward a Theory of "Chinese" Sound   128
Junting Huang

Part III. Translation

8. Eileen Chang at the Intersection of the Sinophone and the Anglophone — 147
   Ping-hui Liao

9. The Frontier of Sinophone Literature in Syaman Rapongan's Translational Writing — 157
   Yu-lin Lee

10. The Promise and Peril of Translation in the Taiwan Literature Award for Migrants — 173
    Tzu-hui Celina Hung

Part IV. Conclusions: Theoretical Interventions

11. Sinophone States of Exception — 201
    David Der-wei Wang

12. The Inherent Contradiction of Sinoglossia — 212
    Ien Ang

13. Kingston beyond Orientalism — 220
    Colleen Lye

14. Demolishing Script: China and 拆那 (*Chai-na*) — 225
    Carlos Rojas

15. Sinotopias — 229
    Andrea Bachner

Bibliography — 237

Index — 261

Figures and Table

Figures

Figure 1.1: Cover image of *National Health Journal of China* (中華健康雜誌)	24
Figure 1.2: Appleton's physical examination	28
Figure 2.1: "Pleasure Seeking Picture," first installment of *Erotic Paradise* (1992)	38
Figure 2.2: Hou performs *tuina* on an interviewee	40
Figure 2.3: The *Male Hole* exhibition at the 2016 Taiwan Art Biennale (台灣美術雙年展)	41
Figures 2.4a and 2.4b: "Dog Slave" (2016)	43
Figures 2.5a and 2.5b: "Narcissus" (2016)	45
Figures 2.6a and 2.6b: "Lotus That Does Not Come" (2016)	48
Figures 2.7a and 2.7b: "Exotica Ahkong" (2014)	50
Figure 4.1: Zhou Yun and Geng Hua for the first time close to one another (*Romance on Lushan Mountain*, 13'52")	87
Figure 4.2: Geng Hua still reluctant to accept Zhou Yun's offer of friendship (*Romance on Lushan Mountain*, 15'32")	87
Figure 4.3: A long shot of Zhou Yun and Geng Hua within the doorframe decorated by an inscription (*Romance on Lushan Mountain*, 16'14")	89
Figure 4.4: Zhou Yun retraces the lower strokes of the character *lin* carved on the rock (*Romance on Lushan Mountain*, 25'12")	89

Table

Table 3.1: Three techniques, four directions, and five categories of Wu Jing-jyi's training	59

Acknowledgments

We would like to thank the many friends and colleagues from different universities around the world who made this book possible, especially also Chien-hsin Tsai, who held a conference at the University of Texas, Austin, in 2014, that helped shape the idea of Sinoglossia; the term "Sinoglossia" is actually his coinage. We also want to acknowledge the Chiang Ching-Kuo Foundation, as well as the Ministry of Science and Technology and Ministry of Education of Taiwan, for funding a conference held in Taiwan that enabled follow-up discussions on the topic in 2015. Special thanks go to Shu-Mei Lin and Tianyi Shou, who helped with formatting and other innumerable (yet important) details. And, finally, thanks to the staff of Hong Kong University Press for their patience and support of this project.

Contributors

Ien Ang is Distinguished Professor of Cultural Studies at Western Sydney University's Institute for Culture and Society, of which she was the founding director. Born in Indonesia of Chinese parentage and educated in the Netherlands, she relocated to Australia in the 1990s. She is one of the leaders in cultural studies worldwide, her wide-ranging interdisciplinary work focusing on cultural diversity and globalization, Asia-Australia relations, migration and urban change, and the politics of cultural institutions. Her books include *Watching Dallas* (Methuen, 1985), *Desperately Seeking the Audience* (Routledge, 1991), *On Not Speaking Chinese: Living Between Asia and the West* (Routledge, 2001), and most recently the coauthored *Chinatown Unbound: Trans-Asian Urbanism in the Age of China* (Rowman & Littlefield, 2019).

Andrea Bachner is professor of comparative literature at Cornell University. Her research explores comparative intersections between Sinophone, Latin American, and European cultural productions. She has published two books to date: *Beyond Sinology: Chinese Writing and the Scripts of Culture* (Columbia University Press, 2014) and *The Mark of Theory: Inscriptive Figures, Poststructuralist Prehistories* (Fordham University Press, 2017). She is currently working on two projects: the first, *Uncomparison: China, Latin America, and the Politics of Sameness*, reflects on the limits of comparison through an exploration of the history of cultural contact, exchange, and affinity between Latin American and Chinese cultures; the second, *Membranicity*, constitutes a critique of the deployment of surface metaphors in contemporary theory.

Howard Chiang is associate professor of history at the University of California, Davis. He is the author of *After Eunuchs: Science, Medicine, and the Transformation of Sex in Modern China* (Columbia University Press, 2018), which received the International Convention of Asia Scholars Humanities Book Prize and the Bonnie and Vern L. Bullough Book Award from the Society for the Scientific Study of Sexuality; and *Transtopia in the Sinophone Pacific* (Columbia University Press, 2021), a Lambda Literary Award in LGBTQ Studies finalist and winner of the Bullough Book Award and the Alan Bray Memorial Book Award Honorable Mention from the Modern Language Association. Between 2019 and 2022, he served as the founding chair of the Society of Sinophone Studies. His recent work focuses on the historical and conceptual foundations of the human sciences, especially psychoanalysis, cultural psychiatry, and racial science across the Sinophone Pacific.

Jia-Chen Fu is associate research fellow at the Institute for Modern History at Academia Sinica in Taipei, Taiwan. Her research focuses on the history of science and medicine in modern China, especially in relation to the body, nutrition, and food. Her book, *The Other Milk: Reinventing Soy in Republican China* (University of Washington Press, 2018), explores the construction of the Chinese diet as a deficient one that led to the reinterpretation, rediscovery, and reassignment of social and scientific meanings to the soybean in twentieth-century China.

Junting Huang is a college fellow in the Department of Comparative Literature at Harvard University. He received his PhD in comparative literature at Cornell University. His teaching and research interests include contemporary Sinophone art, cinema, and media culture as well as Chinese diasporic culture in the Caribbean, with additional interests in sound studies, new media studies, and digital humanities. His work has appeared in *ASAP/Journal*, *Journal of Contemporary Chinese Art*, *Journal of Chinese Cinemas*, and *Sounding Out!*

Tzu-hui Celina Hung is an independent scholar trained in comparative literature. Prior to 2022, she was assistant professor of literature at NYU Shanghai, where she also co-directed the Center for Global Asia in 2020–2021. In 2018, she was a Luce/ACLS postdoctoral fellow. Hung's research centers on Sinophone literature and culture, Chinese migration and its cultural networks, postcolonial Southeast Asia, Anglophone literature, and the discourses of creolization and multiculturalism. Some of her works on the cultural politics about Southeast Asian migrants in Taiwan include "Documenting 'Immigrant Brides' in Multicultural Taiwan" (in *Asian Video Cultures*), "Translator" (in *Keywords of Taiwan Theory*), and "Fishers, Captives, and Storytellers in Taiwan's Transnational Fishing Industry" (forthcoming in *Transpacific, Undisciplined: Intimating Current(s)*). She is completing a book project titled *Creolizing the Sinophone Pacific*, which examines the multilingual articulations of creolization by Baba, Chinoy, and Peranakan public figures from Southeast Asia. Her articles related to this issue include "'There Are No Chinamen in Singapore': Creolization and Self-Fashioning of the Straits Chinese in the Colonial Contact Zone" (in *Journal of Chinese Overseas*) and "Sinophone Studies through the Lens of Creolization" (in *Sun Yat-sen Journal of Humanities*).

Contributors xi

Paola Iovene is associate professor of modern Chinese literature in the Department of East Asian Languages and Civilizations at the University of Chicago. She is the author of *Tales of Futures Past: Anticipation and the Ends of Literature in Contemporary China* (Stanford University Press, 2014) and co-editor of *Sound Alignments: Popular Music in Asia's Cold Wars* (Duke University Press, 2021). Her current research projects include 1970s–1980s Chinese cinema; the intersections of literature, labor, media, and social mobility; and contemporary speculative fiction.

Yu-lin Lee is research fellow at the Institute of Chinese Literature and Philosophy at Academia Sinica, Taiwan. His research interests include literary theory, modern Taiwan literature and cinema, translation studies, environmental studies, and Deleuze studies. His recent publications include *Liminality of Translation: Subjectivity, Ethics, and Aesthetics* (Bookman Books, 2009) and *The Fabulation of a New Earth* (National Taiwan University Press, 2015). He has edited *Ten Lectures on the Sinophone* (Linking Publishing, 2020), *Translating Deleuze* (Academia Sinica Institute of Chinese Literature and Philosophy, 2022), and has co-edited *Cyborg and Posthumanism* (Airiti Press, 2013), *Deleuze and Asia* (Cambridge Scholars Publishing, 2014), and *The Empires on Taiwan* (National Taiwan University Press, 2015). He is also a Chinese translator of *Deleuze on Literature* (Rye Field Publishing, 2006) and *Deleuze on Music, Painting, and the Arts* (Rye Field Publishing, 2016). He is completing a book project titled *The Digital Phantasms*, which explores the issue of digital archivization in the current Taiwanese cultural production.

Ping-hui Liao is Chuan Lyu Endowed Chair Professor in Taiwan Studies and founding director of the Taiwan Studies Center at the University of California San Diego. He has published critical essays on subjects including postcolonial theory, music, and culture, and modern Taiwan literature and film. Among the books he has co-edited with friends and colleagues are *Comparatizing Taiwan* (Routledge, 2015) and *Taiwan under Japanese Colonial Rule* (Columbia University Press, 2006). He is completing a book manuscript on travels in modern East Asia.

Colleen Lye is associate professor of English at the University of California, Berkeley. She is the author of *America's Asia: Racial Form and American Literature, 1893–1945* (Princeton University Press, 2009) and the co-editor of *After Marx: Literature, Theory and Value in the Twenty-First Century* (Cambridge University Press, 2022). She is on the editorial boards of *Representations*, *Inter-Asia Cultural Studies*, and *Postmodern Culture*.

Carlos Rojas is professor of Chinese cultural studies, gender, sexuality and feminist studies, and cinematic arts at Duke University. He is the author of *The Naked Gaze: Reflections on Chinese Modernity* (Harvard University Press,

2008), *The Great Wall: A Cultural History* (Harvard University Press, 2010), and *Homesickness: Culture, Contagion, and National Transformation in Modern China* (Harvard University Press, 2015). He is also the co-editor of eight volumes, including *Writing Taiwan: A New Literary History*, with David Der-wei Wang (Duke University Press, 2007); *Rethinking Chinese Popular Culture: Cannibalizations of the Canon*, with Eileen Cheng-yin Chow (Routledge, 2009); *The Oxford Handbook of Modern Chinese Literatures*, with Andrea Bachner (Oxford University Press, 2016); and *Reading China Against the Grain: Imagining Communities*, with Meihwa Sung (Routledge, 2020); and the translator of sixteen volumes of literary fiction and critique. He is the co-editor of the Duke University Press's Sinotheory book series and the associate editor-in-chief of *PRISM: Theory and Modern Chinese Literature*.

E. K. Tan is associate professor of comparative literature and Sinophone studies in the Department of English, and chair of the Department of Asian and Asian American Studies at Stony Brook University. He received his PhD in comparative and world literature from the University of Illinois at Urbana-Champaign. He specializes in modern and contemporary Chinese literature, Sinophone studies, the intersection of Anglophone and Sinophone literature and culture from Southeast Asia, queer Asian studies, film theory, cultural translations, and postcolonial and diaspora theory. He is the author of *Rethinking Chineseness: Translational Sinophone Identities in the Nanyang Literary World* (Cambria Press, 2013). He is currently working on two separate projects titled *Queer Homecoming: Translocal Remapping of Sinophone Kinship* and *Mandarinization and Its Impact on Sinophone Cultural Production*.

Chun-yen Wang is assistant professor of cultural and performance studies at National Taiwan University. He received his PhD in theater arts from Cornell University. He is the recipient of multiple accolades including the S-AN Aesthetics Award, Taiwan Merits Scholarships, and a Fulbright Scholarship. Wang's research interest lies in contemporary Taiwanese theater, cultural translation, and the relationship between epistemology and aesthetics. His essays have appeared in *Chung-Wai Literary Quarterly*, *Taiwan: A Radical Quarterly in Social Studies*, *Inter-Asia Cultural Studies*, and others.

David Der-wei Wang is Edward C. Henderson Professor in Chinese Literature and Comparative Literature at Harvard University. His recent publications include *The Lyrical in Epic Time: Modern Chinese Intellectuals and Artists through the 1949 Crisis* (Columbia University Press, 2014), *Harvard New Literary History of Modern China* (ed., Belknap of Harvard University Press, 2017), and *Why Fiction Matters in Contemporary China* (Brandeis University Press, 2020).

Introduction

Andrea Bachner, Howard Chiang, and Yu-lin Lee

This volume proposes the concept of Sinoglossia as a lens for a more capacious, more heterogeneous approach to objects that are precariously described by labels such as "Chinese" or "Sinophone." At stake here is the acknowledgement of, and thereby an intention to overcome, three distinct limitations in existing theorizations of Chinese culture: their focus on ethnicity or language at the exclusion of thinking in terms of embodiments or styles; their limited attention to mediation and mediality; and their continual deferral of translational issues, challenges, and problems. Sinoglossia functions as a supplement to the paradigm of Sinophone studies. It introduces an alternative but complementary theory that is defined by cultural formations not overdetermined by Sinitic linguistic ties in the way that the Sinophone has been typically framed around the social life of language systems (whether by linguistic governance or political resistance). The concept of Sinoglossia thus combines a heteroglossic (Bakhtin) and a heterotopian (Foucault) approach to the critical study of mediated discourses of China and Chineseness. This enables a more flexible conceptualization of Chinese culture as an array of polyphonic, multi-discursive, and multilingual articulations, as well as one whose place or topos is composed of different flexible, at times frictional, positionalities. Since both Sinoglossia and Sinophone contain the prefix "Sino-," one of the recurring motifs that suture both theoretical frameworks is their consistent bind to, as well as resistance against, the symbolic seduction of "Chineseness." This friction brings to light the productive power of Sinoglossia as a platform for transmedial possibilities, such as for translating and reading different types of embodiment across languages and regimes of cultural production. In the spirit of the concept we propose in this volume, we have opted not to transform our distinct perspectives and conceptual contributions into a univocal text. Instead of a conventional introduction, a multi-vocal dialogue, then:

1. Why Sinoglossia?

AB: Do we really need another neologism with and about "Sino-," in the moment in which Sinophone has barely become established? While drawing on Sinophone, Sinoglossia and Sinophone are not the same. I see Sinoglossia as an intervention, an irritation, an interruption, an opening of ground. There will be no new discipline called Sinoglossic studies, nor should there be. The term maintains its allegiance to things "Sino-," while pairing it with "glossia." The multiple meanings of "glossia" invoke language (from "glotta," "language"), but also corporeality ("glotta" also means "tongue"), thus wedding signification and materiality and drawing attention to a question of media and mediation. The term resonates with Mikhail Bakhtin's term "heteroglossia," thus borrowing a whiff of multiplicity and heterogeneity by means of this echo. Its second part also marks the term "Sinoglossia" as a method—a way of glossing or conceptualizing. The term's unfamiliar combination invites us to reflect anew on our practices of naming, categorizing, theorizing with and beyond naturalized and conventional boundaries but also marks the possibility of thinking anew precisely by revisiting other formations. For me, the term does not come out of a gesture of rupture for rupture's sake, or newness for newness's sake. Rather, it sets itself up to serve as target of critique, a caveat also against traditional ways of marking disciplinary interventions, claiming theoretical newness, or marking a conceptual turn.

YL: I would like to emphasize the multiplicity and heterogeneity that the term "Sinoglossia" connotes. Sinoglossia, first of all, highlights the linguistic aspect of the Sinophone practice. Echoing the Bakhtinian concept of heteroglossia, Sinoglossia underscores the multilingualism in the Sinitic language "family" and further specifies a minor/minority discourse that opposes the major/majority one, similar to the conception of Sinophone. In this regard, Sinoglossia brings the awareness that the Sinophone can be regarded as a broad category that refers to all literature written in Sinitic languages on the one hand, for example, those produced by the linguistic and ethnic minority groups in the Sinophone world. On the other hand, Sinoglossia connotes minor/minority literatures against the backdrop of major/majority literature, for example, Malaysian Sinophone literature vs. Malaysian literature, and Sinophone Chinese-American literature vs. American literature. Moreover, when Sinoglossia is considered as a method, that is, a way of glossing, Sinoglossia highlights a transformation of a language and a society, as befits the paradigm of "minor literature" set by Deleuze and Guattari, where minorities produce their "minor" literatures by using major languages, thereby invoking a transformation of their societies. In the process, the means of translation becomes essential and deserves further investigation.

HC: Within the formulation of Sinoglossia lies an intrinsic contradiction, and I would like to suggest that this inherent contradictory nature represents the most theoretically powerful and promising aspect of Sinoglossic inquiries. If the prefix "Sino-," for all intents and purposes, continues to raise the specter of homogeneity (whether in relation to a "Chinese" family or aiming to represent all things related to "Chinese" broadly construed), the "glossia" part of the word draws attention to the possibility of difference and resistance to coherence. Language, after all, is a form of communication, but communicative ideals—especially after the Habermasian model—are premised on the rhetorical necessity of synthesizing difference in matters of opinion and concern. As such, Sinoglossia provides a framing rubric to unify forms of analysis or types of cultural texts that are not normally considered together. Like Andrea and Yu-lin, I share the view that Sinoglossia denotes a mode of intervention that privileges the epistemic status of heterogeneity and multiplicity. It therefore extends certain agendas of Sinophone studies to reconceptualize minor-to-major relationality and the historical and conceptual foundations of global identities in the twenty-first century. It also departs from it, though, by broadening out to consider the normative and subversive regimes of mediality, translation, and corporeality. In a debate on the public sphere, sociologist Richard Madsen predicted that it is precisely at the periphery of what Tu Wei-ming calls "cultural China," where the most exciting new stories about civil society may be told. Sinoglossia exemplifies such a topos of re-narration.[1]

2. What does/do your specific discipline(s) and theoretical background(s) contribute to the study of Sinoglossic articulations? What do different institutional contexts and cultural positionalities contribute to Sinoglossia?

HC: While we might agree that making a distinction between Chinese and Sinophone studies is important, we often overlook the fact that judicious historical studies weigh differently in these two fields. With this statement I am referring to several phenomena. First, Chinese history is an established and respected scholarly discipline, but there is no comparable field called Sinophone history. This is crucial, because if Chinese literary and cultural studies continue to be informed by historical scholarship (for example, we need the history of wartime China to contextualize the writings of Eileen Chang), what kind of history does Sinophone studies draw on? Up to this point, most Sinophone scholars have not

---

1. Richard Madson, "The Public Sphere, Civil Society, and Moral Community: A Research Agenda for Contemporary China Studies," *Modern China* 19, no. 2 (1993): 183–198; Wei-ming Tu, "Cultural China: The Periphery at the Center," *Daedalus* 120, no. 2 (1991): 1–32.

been trained in history, but they often shoulder the burden of explaining the history of how Sinophone communities and cultures have matured over time. Shu-mei Shih, for instance, has pointed to Qing continental colonialism, Han settler colonialism, and migration as three of the most important historical vectors in Sinophone history. Second, as a postcolonial intervention, Sinophone studies differs from Anglophone and Francophone studies most tellingly with respect to the centrality of historiography to the latter two field formations. Whether we are reading Gayatri Spivak, Dipesh Chakrabarty, Frantz Fanon, or Edouard Glissant, history matters because the work of these authors *already rewrites* history. But there is no Sinophone historiography to speak of; consequently, the growing body of scholarship in Sinophone studies does not rethink history as much as merely relying on history (whose history?) for ethical and political purposes. In this volume, we draw on the cultural history of the body, mediality, and translation as points of entry to enrich the prospect of placing Sinophone and Sinoglossic studies on a par with other postcolonial inquiries. That is, by launching the rubric of Sinoglossia, this book argues that the relation between new field formations and established areas of scholarly inquiry must always already critically attend to historical analysis and thereby devise new, creative ways of relating the past to the present. Sinoglossia rewrites history by displacing the hegemonic status of "China" and by creolizing methods that address the questions of mediation, multilingualism, and polyphonic corporeal practices.

YL: It is worth noting the etymological meaning of the term "gloss," interpretation, as Sinoglossia is considered a way of glossing. It is in the same vein that translation can be brought into the study of Sinoglossic articulations. It is true that Sinophone literatures are often accomplished through translation. Further, it is equally important to note that translation means not only transporting a word and its meanings from one language and culture to another but is also an act of repetition in interpretation. There are a great number of bilingual and multilingual authors in the Sinophone world whose writing undertakes an inevitable process of translation. From this perspective, Sinoglossia can also be seen as an act of redefining the so-called Chineseness that constitutes a process of aesthetic creation by traversing the linguistic thresholds within the language.

AB: To link "Sino" and "glossia" represents a call for a more flexible, interdisciplinary engagement with things to which we can append the label "Sino-." The different disciplinary backgrounds of our contributors and of us editors are a first attempt at imagining an even more radical inter-, and indeed, transdisciplinary stage for this kind of work. This also means to work productively with and beyond the limitations of our own fields. My own formation in (Western) critical theory and comparative literature in a European and American academic context is a case in point. To think conceptually and comparatively has allowed me to inhabit as well as to escape the boundaries of Chinese literary and cultural studies. My work is always about how a certain, culturally specific case helps us conceive of a whole set of phenomena and concepts differently; it always strives toward such conclusions by appreciating specificities and shared traits through a comparative perspective. My work with "Sino-" material and the concomitant problem of paying attention to cultural specificity while not falling prey to essentializing and while stepping carefully with and around the politics involved has sharpened my comparative and conceptual perspectives. It has also made me more sensitive to the theoretical blinders imposed by disciplinary limits and institutional contexts. After all, terms such as "Sino-" and their disciplinary valence change radically depending on where we stand as we label and analyze them. Consequently, to achieve a Sinoglossic perspective means to be open to other disciplines and other positionalities, to enrich and help shape such dialogic interactions instead of rigidly policing their boundaries.

3. Sinoglossia still marks itself as "Chinese" (Sino-) and as pertaining to things related to language (glossia, via "glotta"). Is this a limitation? (How) Can Sinoglossia reach beyond what it designates as a term and speak to other cultural/linguistic contexts and objects?

AB: The component "Sino-" is only a limitation if we abide by the logic imposed on area studies by Western-centrism or if we conjugate it only according to Sinocentric definitions. The latter pitfall, i.e., an overly limited understanding of "Sino-," has been mainly disarmed by Sinophone studies, since "Sino-" can no longer be used as a synonym of "Han" without contestation. The former pitfall, that of thinking of "Sino-" objects only as part of their own bounded territory is still alive and kicking in spite of multiple critiques. This forces us to spend more time and energy on clarifying the conceptual valence of what we understand as "Sino-" objects. Only within a mindset in which phenomena from a non-Western culture are merely examples but cannot generate their own theoretical impulses does a label such as "Sino-" become an obstacle. Once we contest the privilege of things European and North American to claim the status of theory, while phenomena from the rest are either representative of or exceptions to such theories forged at the center, work with culturally and linguistically specific material from elsewhere also sheds its fake conceptual boundaries. Of course, we cannot (and do not want to) be oblivious to the complex processes of translation, dialogue, contestation, and change that happen when conceptual thought travels. But since our understanding of what makes certain phenomena

"Sino-" is already temporary, flexible, and relational, instead of fixed or based on essentialist categories, a movement of adaptation, friction, or even complete rupture is already in place in a Sinoglossic approach. The component "glossia" is a slightly different matter. If we read it as merely descriptive of our objects of study, i.e., those related to language, the term would indeed curtail critical engagement—even in spite of the multiple significations of the term. However, I take glossia to describe a method rather than merely a trait of the examples with which such a method concerns itself. And such work, while attentive to objects far beyond the reach of language and textuality, functions with textual and linguistic media to communicate its findings. Since Sinoglossia does not designate a fixed and delimited disciplinary field but takes into account that culturally and linguistically specific phenomena are in flux, it can communicate its insights beyond its scope (which is always situational and temporary to begin with). As such, it happily shares its work with other methods and recognizes that its objects mingle with phenomena from other cultural and linguistic contexts.

HC: It may be useful to return temporarily to the field of Sinophone studies, for it has had to deal with the specter of language, as the "phone" part of the word lends itself easily to critiques of linguistic, scriptic, or textual centrism. Does the substitution of glossia resolve such tensions? I would argue that, through its connection to materiality and the body, glossia highlights the stakes of taking the physical markers of Chineseness and their mediation seriously. At the very least, what is being generated here is a theory of decentering any assumed equivalence between "China" and forms of Sino-representation. This is not a plea to abandon language altogether; as we will see in the third part of the volume, a more systematic interrogation of the technology of translation contributes to this decentering of assumed equivalence. This book, then, expands Sinophone studies to relate the transgression of linguistic boundaries to other material and conceptual forms of border crossing. In this way I consider Sinoglossia an analytical force of contradiction, and in so doing, the "Sino-" and "glossia" parts of the word promise to denaturalize one another continuously.

YL: Sinoglossia emphasizes the linguistic variation and the social transformation that follows, which offers an alternative way of viewing the Sinophone community as a linguistic and cultural unit. Deleuze and Guattari have argued that minor literature is political and often takes on a collective value.[2] In a similar fashion, Sinophone writers likely induce a transformation of the Sinophone community through their literary practice. In addition, with reference to Bakhtin's concept of heteroglossia, Sinoglossia marks a centrifugal tension existing within language

---

2. Gilles Deleuze and Félix Guattari, *Kafka: Toward a Minor literature*, trans. Dona Polan (Minneapolis: University of Minnesota, 1986), 17.

and its multiple dimensions in society. In this regard, Sinoglossia describes the transformation of the Sinophone community informed by linguistic hybridity. As the Sinophone community continues to change, it confronts the other from either the inside or the outside. There are many linguistic, cultural, and ethnic minorities within the Sinophone world; the Sinophone also encounters such communities as the Anglophone and the Francophone. Therefore, Sinoglossia describes a process of linguistic transformation in a global world. As a result, Sinoglossia does not close in on itself but rather it opens itself up to the world. That is to say, the minor, or the other, constitutes its subjectivity and invents a new society by inaugurating a transformation through language. In addition, this linguistic practice as an aesthetic creation does not necessarily base itself on the logic of center-periphery antagonism; rather, it opens itself toward the future by denouncing the authenticity of language and the loyalty to an idea of authentic language.

4. Does Sinoglossia describe a set of objects, a methodology, or both? What is the relationship it establishes between examples and methods?

YL: A Sinoglossic approach seeks neither a true definition of Chineseness nor any specific minority discourse against China-centrism. I would argue that the proposal of Sinoglossia aims to point out a new ethical-aesthetic mode and a new politics concerning the relationship between the local and the global. This effect can be evidenced by minority groups within the Sinophone world and by diasporic authors who have attempted to voice their unique linguistic and cultural heritage despite its close relationship with the Chinese.

AB: Sinoglossia is a work in progress. In flux, its definition remains open, subject to different perspectives. Hence a volume that dialogues with Sinoglossia from different vantage points, hence a "theory" section that showcases a multi-planar engagement rather than synchronicity, hence an introduction that underlines the specific voices of us co-editors rather than constructing a coherent version of Sinoglossia that we all subscribe to. It invests in tension, friction, overlap, and supplemental energy rather than setting up a doctrine. Sinoglossia can designate a set of objects as well as a method. In fact, I would argue (but other voices here and elsewhere might see this differently, of course) that we cannot (and should not) dissociate both. In consonance with Sinophone, Sinoglossia designates a set of objects that, while claiming the label "Sino-" in fact constantly push the boundaries of this very label. At the same time, it insists that groups of objects do not stand still and that the categories that form the basis for our work are also constantly in need of scrutiny and open to being redefined. Sinoglossia as a method has to remain flexibly open to evolve and question itself precisely because its objects are in flux. It sets out to trouble established categories rather than cementing them or imposing new disciplinary boundaries. In fact, Sinoglossia is a way of drawing attention to the complex feedback loops between objects and methods to begin with. To maintain critical openness, we cannot tie methods and objects into tautological loops, where each just confirms the other in its stability. However, methods and examples cannot be completely disconnected either. There is no method independent from its object, nor objects without a (however basic) methodological or conceptual framework. Sinoglossia reminds us also that we have to continue to link methods and objects anew, hearkening to the new impulses that come from the frictions between them.

HC: This book proposes three objects *as* methods in turning Sinoglossia into a new theoretical and interdisciplinary venture: body, medium, and translation. Although each of these objects of study may seem abstract at first, the various chapters give them concrete depth and cohesion by unveiling their signification of a contested and embedded claim to Chinese culture. In this sense, whether we are addressing the epistemological foundation of corporeality, engaging with the polyphonic ruminations of genre, or following the ways in which ideas and words cross the boundaries of time and space, our approach to defamiliarizing the Chineseness of a given case study simultaneously infuses it with a dose of Sinophonic aura and color. This constant ambiguation, always intentional, connects examples to methods and objects to methodology via a self-reflexive procedure in which synthesis and plurality collide. I would argue that rather than presenting one particular approach, this volume should be more appropriately taken as a flexible toolkit, with a common thread of acknowledging how the construction and refraction of Chineseness always contains its own seeds of undoing.

Part I. Corporeality

This part considers the body as the ground for comprehending the uneven normative claims laid by cultural forms to the signifier China. Traditionally, race and ethnicity have been closely scrutinized for phenotyping the biological expressions of Chineseness. Our aim, however, is to expand those inquiries by incorporating other modes of embodiment that overlap with race/ethnicity but are not confined by its conceptual criteria. For instance, the expressivity of the body in the performing arts oftentimes refigures at once the biopolitics and the geopolitics of Chinese culture, routed through distinct frames of localized universality. The recent work on the global history of acupuncture and "Chinese" medicine outside China, for instance, attests to the immense flexibility of the body for packaging alterity and tradition as new global commodities in the neoliberal age. Such practices tend to proceed across vastly different language systems and punctuate dispersed historical genealogies that provincialize the centripetal gravitation of China and Chineseness. Similarly, photographic and filmic productions of diseased embodiment over time perpetuate the global circulation of the ideological portrayals of certain polities (civilization, empire, nation, state, etc.) as intrinsically dead, pathological, or liminal.

Although there is a growing measure of scholarly thought and analysis on the materiality of literature and its social networks and conditions, this part of the project calls attention to a different type of materiality—the materiality that envelops and defines the soma as a corporeal assemblage through which language translates, media interact, experience is reconfigured, and meanings become transformed. For all the attention we pay to scripts and texts, it is particular body parts that execute their production and comprehension; for all our appeal to sound and image, it is bodily labor that conditions their realization and from which their value emanates. In this sense, corporeal practice itself captures the collision of the different geopolitical arrangements (and governance) of space, place, territory, region, and area. Moreover, somatic utterances often rely on the support of material objects—where they appear, how they are positioned, and why they exist in the first place. The matrix of materiality surrounding the body thus highlights the unpredictable ways in which moral economies mutate across time and space. Sinoglossia's take on corporeality focuses on bodily gestures, body modification practices, and processes of embodiment as the natal site of world making and social transformation.

Jia-Chen Fu's chapter, "Inspecting Bodies, Crafting Subjects: The Physical Examination in Republican China," brings us back to the variegated efforts to standardize the physical construction of the modern Chinese body in the early Republican period. Specifically, Fu explores how the practice of physical examination (*tige jiancha* 體格檢查) came to constitute a central focus of modernizing elites to build a strong and abled nation. Though seemingly placing an emphasis on the materiality of the body, the standardization of physical examination nested a larger aim of inculcating a fit and healthy mind—a modern and robust Chinese subjectivity—especially at a time when the Nanjing-based Nationalist government increasingly felt the entwined pressure from the Communist Party and the Japanese in the 1930s. This form of subjectivity helped to cultivate a refracted sense of self and other, thus always producing individual consciousness through the making of corporeal form and revealing the possible ways whereby one integrates into the larger social order/body. In this sense, Fu's chapter provides an important origin story in the history and epistemological foundations of Sinoglossia: how the technologies of generating normative bodily metrics contributed to the flexibility and biological expressions of Chineseness.

Howard Chiang's chapter, "Therapeutic Humanism in Hou Chun-Ming's Art: Queer Mimesis, Subaltern Souls, and the Body as Vessel in Sinoglossiac Taiwan," continues our investigation of Sinoglossic corporeality by turning to avant-garde art in contemporary Taiwan. In 2014, the highly acclaimed Chiayi-born artist Hou Chun-Ming 侯俊明 began his *Body Image* project, which involves interviewing people from all walks of life about their personal life. Aiming to uncover the deepest desires of the interviewees, these sessions normally last two days and begin with Hou and the interviewee stripping off their clothes. On the first day, the interviewee shares memorable autobiographical moments and the most intimate stories about past sexual experiences. On the second day, following a *tuina* massage by Hou, the naked protagonist paints an image of the body deemed most representative of his or her true self. After a period of reflection on the session, Hou responds by painting a separate drawing while naked. Chiang's chapter discusses a portion of these paired paintings that form the "Male Hole" subcollection of *Body Image*. Each of these pairs represents a unique subject position in the Taiwanese gay male community. Chiang argues that Hou's art, centering on the dialectic mechanisms of concealment and revelation, constitutes a form of queer psychotherapy in which the dynamic scripts of transference and counter-transference reciprocate between the interviewed subject and the work of art, between the body corporeal and the body visualized, and, above all, between the secrets and the fulfillment of the soul. From a Sinoglossic viewpoint, with its explicit utilization of queer bodily affects, Hou's art leverages an alternative genealogy of psychoanalytic governance in Sinophone Taiwan.

Chun-yen Wang's chapter, "What Does an Open Body Say? The Body and the Cold War in the Early 1980s Theater of Taiwan," historicizes the 1980s as a significant turning point in the history of modern theater in Taiwan. Rather than focusing on the reinvention of Chinese theatrical traditions, Wang's chapter looks into the connotations and denotations of the West in Taiwan's "theatrical renaissance." In the late Cold War context, an "open body" (開放的身體) on stage was highly praised and sought after among theater practitioners during this period. By historicizing the West in tandem with the notion of the open body, this chapter calls attention to the socio-historical and the geopolitical aspects of the Cold War in Taiwan's "theatrical renaissance." An important architect of the "open body" form was Wu Jing-ji 吳靜吉, who led a series of workshops and training courses in "Lan-Ling Theater Workshop" (蘭陵劇坊). Leading Taiwanese actors and actresses whose career came of age in this period, such as Lee Kuo-hsiu 李國修, Liu Jing-min 劉靜敏, Liu Rou-yu 劉若瑀, Jing Shi-chieh 金士傑, and Lee Tien-ju 李天柱, were all trained and influenced by the new "open body" performing method. The magnificent production of the play *Hezhu xinpei* (荷珠新配, Hezhu's New Match) in 1980 was a landmark exemplar that followed the method of "open body" in performing. Following the spirit of this volume to examine Sinoglossic cultural formations from the vintage point of corporeal politics, Wang's chapter explains the ways in which the modern "open" Taiwanese body is simultaneously imbricated in relation to geopolitics, area studies, progress, and modernity that the United States invents, leads, and develops throughout the Western bloc in the Cold War era and beyond.

Part II. Media

The term "Sinoglossia" puts particular pressure on questions of mediality, as it probes the connection between Chineseness ("Sino-") and mediation ("glotta," tongue or language). While the term "Sinophone" implies and implicates the question of mediality, it also limits—both in cultural and medial terms—what falls under its purview, i.e., what forms part of the Sinophone field. After all, Sinophone studies uses one aspect or medium of language—speech and sound—as the basis for a redefinition of its object of study. Meanwhile, much of Chinese media studies, a vibrant subfield of Chinese studies, similarly builds on preexisting assumptions of the links between media and Chineseness. In contrast and as a supplementary turn, the Sinoglossic approach we map and model here does not tie a specific medium to a definition (or redefinition) of Chineseness. Instead, it investigates how different media and mediascapes end up being defined as Chinese and indeed how Chineseness itself is being constructed. In other words, by paying attention to the mediation of Chineseness, Chineseness is no longer understood as an essence (being Chinese) or as a property (having Chineseness), nor as a linguistic category (speaking or writing in Chinese) or a context of production (made in Chinese places, by ethnic Chinese or speakers of Chinese). Instead, Chineseness can be understood as the outcome of acts of performance, representation, and mediation, as the product of repetitions of cultural scripts that create the impression of a stable category but also lend themselves to different reactivations that can trouble and redefine the limits of Chineseness.

To espouse such a theory of Chinese mediality, one that pays attention to how Chineseness is imagined and performed, implies a multi-perspectival approach from two different, yet complementary, vantage points. On the one hand, it involves thinking about medium specificity, the differences but also interactions between different media. Scrutinizing specific "Chinese" media allows for a comparative understanding of how "Chinese" mediascapes are scripted, introducing subtle medium-specific styles and aesthetics as particular ways of expressing and constructing cultural and national identities. On the other hand, such an approach will not only scrutinize Chinese media articulations and analyze their claim of Chineseness but also take into consideration how Chineseness is imagined and mediated from the outside or the margins of Chinese cultural spheres. Such a perspective on Chinese media, and indeed, the mediation of what counts as or is imagined as Chinese, thus allows for the theorization of Chineseness as a multiply contested ground that constantly renegotiates national nostalgias, orientalist dreams, regional and transregional interests, global networks, and cultural politics.

Paola Iovene's chapter, "Landscape of Words: *Romance of Lushan Mountain* (1980) and Sinoglossia as Delimitation," presents one example of how Chineseness is being renegotiated through an analysis of Huang Zumo's film *Romance of Lushan Mountain*. In the film, the landscape of the Lushan Mountain, a natural site multiply marked by different moments in Chinese culture, becomes the context for a romance that taught viewers how to fall in love with love, with the Chinese landscape, with tourism, with family, and ultimately with cinema itself. Iovene's attention to the filmic medium as is iconizes Chineseness-as-landscape as well as to the double inscription—the filmic recording of inscriptions at Lushan—allows for a reflection on the links between medium and Chineseness. As Iovene argues, multiplicity, diversity, and change themselves can be the defining characteristic of Chineseness and as such will be subjected to a fixing that limits the sliding movement of "glossia" and contains the scope of the "Sino-."

E. K. Tan's chapter, "Sinopop: The Case of Namewee/Wee Meng Chee," analyzes the multimedia work of Sinophone Malaysian artist Namewee (Wee Meng Chee) as a basis for a reflection on the possibilities and limits of Sinophone critique. For Tan, the term "Sinopop" designates popular music from marginal Sinophone communities that describes and represents localized expressions. Namewee's controversial work scrutinizes ethnic power constellations in Malaysia by underlining Malaysia's multilingual and multicultural wealth. As an example of Sinopop, Namewee's work showcases the productive intersections between different cultural and linguist traditions while also allowing for a critical perspective vis-à-vis the circulation of work from peripheral Sinophone communities within the Sinosphere.

In "Chinese Writing, Heptapod B, and Martian Script: The Ethnocentric Bases of Language," Carlos Rojas reframes the question of ethnocentrism and Chinese writing through an analysis of Ted Chiang's 1998 short story "Story of Your Life" and its screen adaptation as Denis Villeneuve's 2016 film *Arrival*. This analysis starts with a scrutiny of ethnocentric uses of the Chinese script but widens the conceptual questions involved by reflecting on the inescapable link between ethnocentrism and language. Quine and Derrida are brought into dialogue for an unusual critique of Derrida's use of Chinese characters: rather than faulting Derrida for his own ethnocentrism, Rojas reflects anew on the inescapability, and indeed, necessity, of what some call "ethnocentrism." The Chinese script enters this chapter peripherally, and thus, ultimately, centrally: as a question that leads us to critique conventional notions of writing and language themselves and thus also as a caveat against universal, non-ethnocentric definitions of language.

This part concludes with Junting Huang's chapter, "The Techne of Listening: Toward a Theory of 'Chinese' Sound." Rather than contenting himself with the idea of a Sinophonicity that limits the "phone" under scrutiny to language (the Chinese language family), Huang asks what it would mean to theorize "Chinese" sound by way of a Chinese techne of listening. This does not mean to essentialize some kind of sound or way of listening as Chinese. By looking at Sinophone sound artists such as Hsia Yu, Yan Jun, and Qiu Zhijie, Huang analyzes the dialogue between Chinese reflections on listening, for instance, Wang Jing's concept of "affective listening," and Western concepts, such as Pierre Schaeffer's notion of "reduced listening." For Huang, these examples allow us to think toward a Sinophone critique that situates language in the greater context of cultural practices and to investigate its technical operations and media infrastructure. How we understand sound as a medium, regardless of its particular shape, is also how we mediate the diverse traditions of a given culture. Theorizing "Chinese" sound must be seen as part of such a process.

Part III. Translation

This section treats the recent development of Sinophone studies from the perspective of translation. Ping-hui Liao's chapter, "Eileen Chang at the Intersection of the Sinophone and the Anglophone," explores the borderline where Sinophone and Anglophone articulations meet. After her sojourn in Hong Kong, Eileen Chang went to the US and published her well-known novels, including *Rice-Sprout Song*, *Naked Earth*, and *The Rouge of the North*. The three English novels brought her great fame in the Sinophone world despite the fact that they were not well received in the US. Not surprisingly, Chang's English novels are often considered a "translation" project, which embodies a process of negotiation between the past and her residence in the new world. In addition to these English novels, Liao examines further this "translation" project by looking at Chang's other works written during her stay in the US. Liao discovers in these works a "late style," developed through rewriting or retranslation of her early novels and characterized by her diasporic experience in relation to Hong Kong and Shanghai. With a focus on the Hollywood traces in Chang's *Father Takes a Bride* (*xiao ernu*), Liao argues that Chang's late work should not simply be considered a nostalgia for her homeland but rather constitutes an effort made by a Sinophone writer to accommodate the Anglophone. That is to say, Chang's experiment with a new genre and media, in particular Hollywood comedy and musicals, is in fact a "multilingual and polyphonic project" aiming to connect to the new world while reinventing a new image of "home," albeit a conflicting and dissonant one.

In a similar fashion, Yu-lin Lee's chapter, "The Frontier of Sinophone Literature in Syaman Rapongan's Translational Writing," examines the linguistic, ethnic, and cultural boundaries of the Sinophone. If the Sinophone always points to an irreducible tension that exists between linguistic, cultural, and ethnic articulations, the Taiwanese indigenous writer Syaman Rapongan's writing no doubt demonstrates that tension and pushes it to its extreme. Just as Syaman's Tao culture is a part of Austronesian culture, the Tao language belongs to the family of the Austronesian languages and has little to do with Sinitic languages. However, as a minority writer, Syaman is forced to use Chinese as his medium, and consequently, his writing undertakes an inevitable process of translation. Using Syaman's translational writing as an example, Lee's chapter addresses some key controversial issues central to Sinophone studies. Lee argues that Syaman's writing embodies a minor Sinophone articulation that inaugurates a linguistic transformation, characterized by orality as an uncharted field that is intersected by both articulation and signification. Lee further labels this uncharted field as the "frontier" of Sinophone literature and argues that, by discovering this linguistic uncharted field, Syaman is able to envision a possible territory of existence for himself and his entire culture as well.

Tzu-hui Celina Hung's chapter, "The Promise and Peril of Translation in the Taiwan Literature Award for Migrants," attests to the translingual practice of the Sinophone in the context of Taiwan by looking at the development of the emerging genre of migrant literature in Taiwan, in particular that of Southeast Asian marital and labor migrants—a literature that is written in Vietnamese, Thai, Indonesian, Filipino, and Burmese languages but translated for Sinitic-language readers. Language use is of course a crucial issue in this kind of literary expression. However, Hung does not limit her investigation to linguistic translation as a necessary vehicle for literary expression but extends her focus to the troubled politics of cultural translation. Accordingly, Hung examines not simply the migrant writings' storytelling patterns but looks into the award's grassroots history and organization, its selection process, and its implication for community formation. Drawing on translation studies, Hung explores a new frontier of Sinophone literature to rethink the frameworks, standards, and uses of literary criticism.

Part IV. Conclusions: Theoretical Interventions

In lieu of a conclusion, *Sinoglossia* closes with a series of short essays: David Der-wei Wang's "Sinophone States of Exception," Ien Ang's "The Inherent Contradiction of Sinoglossia," Colleen Lye's "Kingston beyond Orientalism," Carlos Rojas's "Demolishing Script: China and 拆那 (*Chai-na*)," and Andrea Bachner's "Sinotopias." Shuttling back and forth between different disciplinary and conceptual perspectives, these pieces reinforce the experimental character of this volume in the form of theoretical and methodological reflections. They approach the problems raised in this volume from different disciplinary vantage points, using different vocabularies and methodologies. Rather than establishing Sinoglossia as a univocal, fixed concept, we want to allow the frictions and consonances among these shorter essays to highlight the fluidity and flexibility inherent in our proposal to think through a Sinoglossic lens.

Part I

Corporeality

1
Inspecting Bodies, Crafting Subjects
The Physical Examination in Republican China

Jia-Chen Fu

To assess the health of a child, it is imperative to conduct a physical examination. By the late 1930s, this line of reasoning had become commonly accepted by medical professionals and popular writers throughout Republican China. In books like Zhang Renhua's *The Health of the Child* (兒童之衛生, 1924) and Zhou Shang's *The Care and Education of Children* (兒童保健與教師, 1948), in popular journals like *Health* (衛生) and *Family Weekly* (家庭星期), and in local-, municipal-, and provincial-level health fairs and competitions, the physical examination (體格檢查) afforded experts and laypeople alike the possibility of directly engaging in the construction of a modern Chinese body.

We can think of a physical examination as a general concept of inspecting some or many aspects of the physical body for a specific diagnostic purpose. This definition is both expansive and general. It could include, for example, an examination like the "four examinations" (四診) that has been an essential component of traditional Chinese medical diagnosis, or it could denote the more general concept of inspecting some aspect(s) of the physical body for a specific diagnostic purpose.[1] For this chapter, the "physical examination" is primarily preoccupied with what we might call "THE physical examination" as a feature of public health and biomedicine and involves a quantitative inspection of the body for the purposes of diagnosing a reported malady, as well as assessing the non-suffering body by a quantified set of bodily norms.[2] This physical examination emerged during the nineteenth century in conjunction with the rise of medical science in the United States and Europe. Its development in Republican period China

---

1. The four methods of examination in Chinese medicine are: looking, listening/smelling, asking, and palpating.
2. Roy Porter, "The Rise of Physical Examination," in *Medicine and the Five Senses*, ed. W. F. Bynum and Roy Porter (Cambridge: Cambridge University Press, 1993), 179–197.

was also closely interrelated with the global development of medical science as well as ideas about race, scientific knowledge more generally, and national sovereignty, which this chapter will only cover schematically.[3]

Instead, my interest in the physical examination will unfurl along a different plane—one more attuned to how the act of inspecting bodies worked to produce modern Chinese subjectivities.[4] The modern subjectivity Chinese educators sought to instill through the physical examination arose from a cultivated consciousness of one's corporeal form.[5] It was not enough to have a body; a modern subjectivity nursed a refracted sense of self and other, of the naturalized categories of comparison (height and weight) that both individuated one's specific bodily form while also denoting one's integration in a larger social order. It is in this sense of probing the body-subjectivity connectivity that this chapter contributes to the larger aim of this volume to rethink the biological expression of Chineseness and the tools needed to both evaluate and make such Chineseness manifest. Chinese educators identified this body-subjectivity connectivity as a crucial characteristic of being modern and Chinese. That this form of embodied subjectivity could also be construed as something broader and part of a more global, medicalized form of modern subjecthood neither negated nor undermined the Chineseness that was implicitly at stake. Put differently, the celebration and advancement of the physical examination by Chinese educators in constituting this body-subjectivity connectivity cannot be separated from the more pathological ways in which the Chinese political identity came to be in

---

3. For a more expansive exploration of how the sifting terrain of ideas and practices associated with health and disease produced what Ruth Rogaski has called "hygienic modernity," see her book, *Hygienic Modernity: Meanings of Health and Disease in Treaty-Port China* (Berkeley: University of California Press, 2004).
4. For discussion of heightened sensitivity to the perils of posture and its relation to school hygiene in Japan, see Izumi Nakayama, "Posturing for Modernity: Mishima Michiyoshi and School Hygiene in Meiji Japan," *East Asian Science, Technology, and Society* 6 (2012): 355–378.
5. For more on how Chinese corporeality as cultural practice has shifted over time, see Charlotte Furth, "Concepts of Pregnancy, Childbirth, and Infancy in Ch'ing Dynasty China," *Journal of Asian Studies* 46, no. 1 (1987): 7–34; Charlotte Furth, "From Birth to Birth: The Growing Body in Chinese Medicine," in *Chinese Views of Childhood*, ed. Anne Behnke Kinney (Honolulu: University of Hawai'i Press, 1995), 157–191; Charlotte Furth, *A Flourishing Yin: Gender in Chinese Medical History, 950–1665* (Berkeley: University of California Press, 1999); Shigehisa Kuriyama, *The Expressiveness of the Body and Divergence of Greek and Chinese Medicine* (New York: Zone Books, 1999); Fran Martin and Ari Larissa Heinrich, eds., *Embodied Modernities: Corporeality, Representation, and Chinese Cultures* (Honolulu: University of Hawai'i Press, 2006); Andrew Morris, *Marrow of the Nation: A History of Sport and Physical Culture in Republican China* (Berkeley: University of California Press, 2004); Yi-Li Wu, "Ghost Fetuses, False Pregnancies, and the Parameters of Medical Uncertainty in Classical Chinese Gynecology," *Nan Nü* 4, no. 2 (2002): 170–206; and Angela Zito and Tani Barlow, *Body, Subject, and Power in China* (Chicago: University of Chicago Press, 1994).

global discourses of race and health.[6] That Chinese educators emphasized the productive and positive ways in which bodily objectification and quantification could make young Chinese modern subjects should alert us to the multifaceted and multivalent ways in which discourses of Chinese deficiency worked, thereby offering insight into the historical and epistemological foundations of Sinoglossia.[7] The history of expertise about the physical examination deepens the scholarly literature on the interrelated historiographies of the body, modern science, and Sinophone geopolitics.

For many Chinese intellectuals, the physical examination provided the means by which objective facts about Chinese children could be obtained. Reports on disease incidence, patterns of physiological development, anthropometrics—these were all artifacts of the physical examination that both denoted the Chinese affinity for scientific rigor and esteem for objectivity and justified the value of the examination itself.[8] But this alone did not account for Chinese enthusiasm for the physical examination. The very process and procedures of examination elicited strong approval from Chinese educators especially, who saw the physical examination as a tool for inculcating modern subjectivities. In their estimation, the physical examination exemplified concrete action in defiance of traditional proclivities toward abstraction and book learning. To examine, and perhaps counterintuitively to be examined, were forms of doing, ways of being bodies that moved, sounded, and acted as modern bodies. Their insistence that the physical examination could effectuate modern subjectivities highlights the importance of treating the physical examination—its specific techniques and equipment used—as technology in the manner advanced by the anthropologist Francesca Bray. As Bray has so compellingly shown, technology can be a powerful force for cultural stability, because "it creates material forms that embody shared values and beliefs, tying people into orthodoxy through their everyday practices." When we ask why it matters how the Chinese understood and under what conditions they implemented the physical examination, we are attempting to limn the contours by which a new technology was learned, adopted, and

---

6. Howard Chiang, *After Eunuchs: Science, Medicine, and the Transformation of Sex in Modern China* (New York: Columbia University Press, 2018).
7. See, for example, Chiang, *After Eunuchs*, and Jing Tsu, *Failure, Nationalism, and Literature: The Making of Modern Chinese Identity, 1895–1937* (Stanford, CA: Stanford University Press, 2005). On a related note, the pairing of language and corporeality, as evident with "Sino-" and "glossia" (from "glotta," as "language" and as "tongue") is especially apt when we consider how Chinese educators relied on both textual and corporeal ways for demonstrating the significance of the physical examination for understanding the Chinese young.
8. For an analysis of anthropometrics and its expression of Chinese agency, see Jia-Chen Fu, "Measuring Up: Anthropometrics and the Chinese Body in Republican Period China," *Bulletin of the History of Medicine* 90 (2016): 643–671.

transformed into a form of *concrete ethics*—a material habitus that naturalizes social relations and moral principles.[9]

In presenting the physical examination as tool for inculcating modern subjectivities, Chinese educators navigated an alternate current, broadly conversant with but still different from the patient-physician dynamic that has shaped the physical examination's place in Western medicine or biomedicine. The history of the physical examination in biomedicine can be summarized as follows. Up until the nineteenth century, when a physician attempted to diagnose a patient, he largely relied on patient narrative with minimal physical contact. This was partly because of social convention, issues of class, and niceties regarding the etiquette of men and women. By contrast, the rise of the physical examination in the nineteenth century, its emphasis on tactile examination, use of instruments, and diagnostic testing, marked a shift in the relationship between patient and physician. The patient history that had been so important to the physician became less so. Disease was increasingly seen as an ontological, as opposed to a physiological, object of scientific inquiry. The disease itself became the primary focus of interest—with its own past progressions and forward-marking trajectories. The patient, by contrast, became the lesser of concerns. And their idiosyncrasies and habits might lead to distractions that might prevent the physician from truly understanding the disease in question. An ontological conception of disease, especially with the rise of germ-theory, led to a de-emphasis of the language-based, patient-generated format of diagnosis common among Western physicians prior to the nineteenth century. New technologies like the stethoscope enabled increased acuity of the physician's senses, and by permitting the physician to more directly access a locus of complaint, they also diminished the degree to which the patient's own subjectivity contributed to the diagnosis process.[10] The patient-physician relationship was refracted by the introduction of the patient's body as somehow distinct from the patient.[11]

The objectification of the human body through the physical examination yielded positive and negative ramifications. The historian of medicine Edward Shorter has argued that the development of the physical examination added a

---

9. Francesca Bray, *Technology and Gender: Fabrics of Power in Late Imperial China* (Berkeley: University of California Press, 1997), 369.
10. Other inventions include the thermometer, pulse counters, X-ray, and the electrocardiograph. Though diagnostic technology like the stethoscope may have improved a physician's diagnostic skill, its acceptance by both practitioner and patient alike was by no means assured. See, for example, Malcolm Nicolson, "The Introduction of Percussion and Stethoscopy to Early Nineteenth-Century Edinburgh," in *Medicine and the Five Senses*, ed. W. F. Bynum and Roy Porter (Cambridge: Cambridge University Press, 1993), 134–153.
11. The main complaint so often heard of contemporary medicine is its apparent disregard for the patient and their subjective experiences. See Edward Shorter, *Bedside Manners: The Troubled History of Doctors and Patients* (Harmondsworth, UK: Viking, 1986), 211–240.

hands-on dimension to the doctor-patient relationship. For many patients, past and present, this sensorial dimension conveyed an impression of *giving* care. It fortified the psychological bond between the physician and the patient and demonstrated the physician's authority and credibility to treat and cure the patient. The objectification of the body—in entirety or by parts—as the locus of organic disease displaced the individual, and collective, experiences of being ill. Now within the history of biomedicine, understanding this shift has been critical to how the field has talked about a whole range of topics, from use of technology in diagnosis to patient rights.[12] It may not be surprising then that this history of the physical examination is and has often been visually represented by three key elements: the physician, the patient, and the stethoscope, all in a single frame.

By contrast, Chinese understanding and adoption of the physical examination unfolded along a different path according to different constraints and needs.[13] This is not to suggest that the Chinese imputed no medical value to the physical examination. Indeed, as I will discuss below, Chinese intellectual elites, especially educators, were quick to adopt the physical examination as a constituent element of modern health and education. But the primary route by which large swathes of the Chinese population, especially infants and children, in the early twentieth century became familiar with the physical examination was not in private patient-physician relationships. Instead, the growth and development of health education, especially in modern schools and through community health campaigns, became the predominant forum within which the physical examination was deployed and young Chinese examined. Instead of the stethoscope per se, Republican images tend to feature scales or the act of measuring height and weight; instead of the white-jacketed physician, we are more likely to encounter a teacher (Figure 1.1).

Health Education, Children, and the Primacy of Doing

The physical examination was introduced to China as a critical component of modern health education. In the late nineteenth century, health education was

---

12. See, for example, Mary Fissell, "The Disappearance of the Patient's Narrative and the Invention of Hospital Medicine," in *British Medicine in an Age of Reform*, ed. Roger French and Andrew Weir (London: Routledge, 1991), 92–109; Michel Foucault, *The Birth of the Clinic*, trans. A. Smith (New York: Vintage, 1975); Jonathan Gillis, "The History of the Patient History since 1850," *Bulletin of the History of Medicine* 80, no. 3 (Fall 2006): 490–512; Iago Gladston, "Diagnosis in Historical Perspective," *Bulletin of the History of Medicine* 9, no. 4 (April 1941): 367–384; J. D. Newson, "The Disappearance of the Sick-Man from Medical Cosmology, 1770–1870," *Sociology* 10 (1976): 225–244; and Charles E. Rosenberg, "The Tyranny of Diagnosis: Specific Entities and Individual Experience," *The Milbank Quarterly* 80, no. 2 (2002): 237–260.
13. I will not be considering the role and forms of meaning-making associated with physical examination in traditional Chinese medicine in this chapter.

Figure 1.1: Cover image of *National Health Journal of China* (中華健康雜誌). Source: *National Health Journal of China* (中華健康雜誌) 1, no. 2 (1939).

directed primarily at infrastructural concerns at new-style schools: for example, creating bathing facilities and infirmaries, instituting a sick policy for students, hiring a school physician.[14] Within a few years after the establishment of the Chinese republic in 1912, articles about the physical examination, what it consisted of, and its efficacy in identifying developmentally abnormal or diseased children, began to appear in Chinese medical and educational journals. Whereas prior to the 1880s, Protestant missionaries had exerted considerable influence on the shape and content of scientific and medical translation projects, by the end of the nineteenth century, Chinese authors—many of whom had benefited educationally from study at Qing arsenals, Christian mission schools, or study abroad in Japan—assumed a more prominent role in the translation and compilation of books on medical and scientific knowledge.[15] Although many of these Chinese works drew both inspiration and form from Western sources, Japanese sources were also very popular. Between 1900 and 1950, approximately 200 books on medical topics ranging from pediatrics to experimental surgery were translated

---

14. Zhang Danhong 張丹紅 and Zhang Sumeng 張蘇萌, "19 Shiji houye 20 shiji qianye Zhongguo de xuexiao jiankang jiaoyu" 19世紀後葉20世紀前葉中國的學校健康教育 [Health education in Chinese schools during the late nineteenth century and early twentieth century], *Zhonghua yishi zazhi* 中華醫史雜誌 [Chinese journal of medical history] 29, no. 3 (July 1999): 168.
15. See, for example, Zhang Zhongmin 張仲民, "Wan Qing chuban de shengli weisheng shuji ji qi duzhe" 晚清出版的生理衛生書籍及其讀者 [Books of physiology published in the late Qing dynasty and their readers], *Shilin* 史林 4 (2009): 20–36.

from Japanese into Chinese.[16] The bulk of these (sixty-four books between 1911 and 1937; thirty-five books between 1938 and 1950) appeared on the market as textbooks for middle schools and teachers' colleges after the establishment of the Chinese republic in 1912. In addition to translated books, Chinese translations of Japanese source materials on health, measurement, and the physical examination appeared in popular and specialist journals and newspapers.

These early writings reflect a diversity of opinion about what constituted the physical examination and for what purposes the examination served. A 1914 translation by Zhang Jiehou for *Journal of Chinese and Western Medicine* (中西醫學報) described the physical examination as a series of highly technical acts of measurements for identifying a "no-good youth" (不良少年)—someone whose mind (精神) was abnormal (異常) and degenerate (變質).[17] Degeneracy, which was evidenced by an asymmetrical physique (e.g., humped back, dove chest, extra digits on the hands and feet), persistent maladies like anemia (貧血症), or sallow complexion, arose from impeded, obstructed, and abnormal physical growth and development—all of which could be verified through precise measurement. Zhang's discussion of the physical examination reflected the deep anxiety felt by Chinese intellectuals about racial integrity in a Social Darwinian world. But this characterization of the physical examination as a tool for identifying and confirming degeneracy was only one of many.

Other commentators, like Fang Qing, the editor of *Journal of Medicine* (醫藥學報), identified the physical examination as an essential predictor of national health, because an individual's physique framed in miniature what was happening to the country at large. Fang, who had received his medical training in Japan, insisted that the extent to which a person could fulfill his or her civic duties depended on whether or not the person was strong in body.[18] He was particularly concerned about the prevalence of tuberculosis, and he argued that a comparison of height to chest girth would indicate breathing capacity and by extension the presence of tuberculosis.

For all the differences separating Zhang Jiehou's emphasis on degeneracy and Fang Qing's keenness for a diagnostic to determine tuberculosis, neither man associated the physical examination with the hospital. Indeed, many of

---

16. Tan Ruqian 潭汝謙, ed., *Zhongguo yi Riben shu zonghe mulu* 中國譯日本書綜合目錄 [Comprehensive catalog of Japanese books translated into Chinese] (Hong Kong: Zhongwen daxue chubanshe, 1980), 130–180; and Benjamin Elman, *On Their Own Terms: Science in China, 1550–1900* (Cambridge, MA: Harvard University Press, 2005), 396–421.
17. Zhang Jiehou 張介候, "Buliang shaonian tige jiancha shang zhi zhuyidian" 不良少年體格檢查上之注意點 [Key points to pay attention to when making a physical examination of a no-good youth], *Zhongxi yixue bao* 中西醫學報 [Journal of Chinese and Western medicine] 4, no. 9 (April 1914): 1–5.
18. Fang Qing, "Lun tige jiancha zhi biyao" 論體格檢查之必要 [On the necessity for physical examinations], *Yiyao xuebao* 醫藥學報 [Medicine] 3 (1914): 1.

these early expositions on the physical examination focused on the quantitative aspects of inspection, which depended less upon a specific institution than on the appropriate, and calibrated, tools. In Yu Sun's multipart essay, "How to conduct a physical examination" (體格檢查法), for example, the issue of wearing clothes while being weighed occupied more textual space than did where one might be weighed.[19] That the physical examination constituted a flexible form of inspection untied to the hospital freed it for inhabitation in other institutional spaces and as an essential feature of public health education and community-directed health campaigns.

Schools were clearly identified as a critical site for implementation. Christian missionaries helped institutionalize this association by introducing regular, annual physical examinations in mission schools.[20] Because missionary doctors represented a large proportion of the Western-trained physicians working in China in the early twentieth century, their influence shaped broader, more national campaigns to improve Chinese health and bodies. The China YMCA was among the most active of the missionary societies and organizations to incorporate health education into its social reform and service programs and established a Health Division in 1913 to oversee the production and distribution of a variety of public health educational materials (e.g., disease prevention and germ theory), as well as provide public lectures and talks on scientific subjects ranging from bodily temperature, personal and national health, and aeronautics.[21] In March 1916, the YMCA worked with the Chinese Missionary Medicine Association (CMMA) and the National Medical Association of China (NMAC), which had been formed by Chinese physicians of Western medicine, to establish the Joint Council on Public Health Education. With the American public health physician William Wesley Peters (known as W. W. Peters, 1882–1959), who had been serving as the secretary of the YMCA in charge of daily operations and launching health campaigns across the provinces, the council became the first non-governmental organization to lead a nationwide health education campaign.[22]

---

19. Yu Sun, "Tige jiancha fa" 體格檢查法 [How to conduct a physical examination], *Zhonghua jiaoyu jie* 中華教育界 [Chinese educational world] 5, no. 10 (1916): 1–6.
20. A byproduct of the institutionalization of the physical examination at mission schools was the purported use of the gathered statistics for scientific advancement. See, for example, E. M. Merrins, "Anthropometry of Chinese Students," *China Medical Journal* 24 (1910): 318–324; G. D. Whyte, "Height, Weight, and Chest Measurements of Healthy Chinese," *China Medical Journal* 32 (1918): 210–216, 322–328; and W. W. Cadbury, "Height, Weight, and Chest Measurements of the Chinese," *National Medical Journal of China* 8 (1922): 158.
21. Liping Bu, "Public Health and Modernization: The First Campaigns in China, 1915–1916," *Social History of Medicine* 22, no. 2 (2009): 306–307.
22. The council was renamed the Council of Health Education in 1920.

The council represented the views of Chinese and Western medical professionals who believed that good health began with children, and schoolchildren should be the primary focus of health education. As Liping Bu has shown, teachers and students, joined by government officials, Chinese doctors of Western medicine, YMCA secretaries, and businessmen, were key local organizers of these campaigns.[23] Preschool child welfare, school hygiene, and student health education ranked especially high on the council's list of targets, and the council worked hard to promote public knowledge of each endeavor through a combination of education and propaganda.[24] The council produced and distributed health materials, conducted surveys of health conditions in Christian schools, launched special health campaigns in cities throughout China, and organized health conferences for missionaries and teachers. Most importantly, the council also dispatched physicians to conduct physical examinations at local schools—both mission schools and public schools.[25]

Vivia B. Appleton (1879–1978), who can be seen on the far-left side of Figure 1.2 using a stethoscope to listen to a student's chest, spent a significant portion of her three-year tenure in China traveling from school to school and conducting physical examinations on behalf of the Council of Health Education (Figure 1.2).[26] A graduate of Johns Hopkins University School of Medicine, Appleton traveled to the Practice School of the Jiangsu Second Provincial Government (江蘇省立第二師範學校) in May 1922, to undertake a "systematic inventory of [the students'] health."[27] The original caption for this image detailed each activity taking place: a boy on a scale having his weight taken and recorded; a boy whose height was being measured; a "small squad of learners in a toothbrush drill"; and another boy having his vision tested. Each component of the physical examination involved a choreographed exchange of gestures and responses that underscored its mediation of multiple agencies. This may seem less apparent when the examined child stands bare-chested and still as Dr. Appleton uses her auscultatory faculty to discern meaning from murmurs. Yet, the importance of child agency and performativity is still hinted at, especially with the "squad

---

23. Bu, "Public Health and Modernization," 310.
24. Liping Bu, "Cultural Communication in Picturing Health: W. W. Peter and Public Health Campaigns in China, 1912–1926," in *Imagining Illness: Public Health and Visual Culture*, ed. David Serlin (Minneapolis: University of Minnesota Press, 2010), 24–39. For an analysis of the failure of missionary public health education work to supply practical solutions for the creation of a modern health care system in China, see Ka-Che Yip, "Health and Society in China: Public Health Education for the Community, 1912–1937," *Social Science & Medicine* 16 (1982): 1197–1205.
25. Vivia B. Appleton, *A Doctor's Letters from China Fifty Years Ago* (Honolulu [publisher not identified], 1976).
26. For further discussion of the role of American New Women missionaries in propagating modern science, see Motoe Sasaki, *Redemption and Revolution: American and Chinese New Women in the Early Twentieth Century* (Ithaca, NY: Cornell University Press, 2016), chap. 2.
27. "Taking an Inventory of Health," *Weisheng* 衛生 [Health] 1, no. 1 (1924): 11.

Figure 1.2: Appleton's physical examination. Source: *Health* (衛生) 1, no. 1 (1924): 11.

of learners" duly mimicking the physical gestures of brushing one's teeth—a learned somatic utterance connotative of modern hygienic values.

What examinees could learn through the physical examination was not bracketed by age. As the photo's original caption noted, "The man behind the toothbrush is the teacher who is just as interested as any of his pupils. Picture this dignified person looking into a mirror at his first opportunity to see his own teeth. Probably he also took his own weight and height and tested his own vision. But of course, he would only do these things when there was no one else around to watch him."[28] The tone of the caption was likely only partially tongue-in-cheek. The presumed exclusivity of countenance and demeanor of "this dignified person" was, as the caption suggested, only a façade. The teacher was no less susceptible to the transformative allure evoked by the physical examination. But in contrast to the overt, compulsory spectacle of children being examined, adult participation necessitated some allowance for privacy.

As Margaret Mih Tillman has shown with the introduction and indigenization of better baby contests in China, Christian interest in Chinese children was part of a broader transnational effort to "save children" in light of the high infant mortality rates around the world in the early twentieth century.[29] These child-focused endeavors amplified domestic currents of concern and fascination for and about children, childhood, and child development among Chinese reformers, and what often began as Christian-led or -inflected activities assumed new affordances in light of the New Culture and May Fourth Movements in 1915 and 1919 and the rise of Chinese nationalism. New academic disciplines (child

---

28. "Taking an Inventory of Health."
29. Margaret Mih Tillman, "Measuring Up: Better Baby Contests in China, 1917–1945," *Modern Asian Studies* 54, no. 6 (2020): 1749–1786.

psychology and educational psychology) emerged and actively constructed childhood as a site of scientific and democratic improvement.[30]

New organizations dedicated to child welfare and promoting child health and education cropped up in urban areas. The National Child Welfare Association of China (中華慈幼協會), for example, which was established in 1928, operated a series of programs, which included welfare homes, nurseries, child sanitariums in Shanghai and Nanjing; the publication of a monthly magazine, *Modern Parents*, and a series of books on proper methods of child disciplining and parent training; and radio broadcasts of lectures on child welfare.[31] Scientific and practical knowledge about the nature of children and childhood development circulated to an eager and engaged reading public. Fascination with the figure of the child also permeated cultural criticism and literary discourse, especially between the advent of the New Culture Movement in 1917 and the outbreak of full-scale war with Japan in 1937. Whether in the form of new literary and musical works for Chinese children or the development of mass-market magazines like *Children's World* and *Little Friend*, discursive interest in the child fueled the burgeoning Shanghai culture industry. As Andrew Jones has argued, "The child, it seems, was as indispensable financially as it was discursively and ideologically, not only to a new world of vernacular knowledge, but also to the rise of a literature in the vernacular."[32] For its part, the Nationalist government sought to capitalize on popular enthusiasm by inaugurating a National Children's Day in 1932.[33]

This cultural fascination with the literal and the figurative child helped establish the physical examination as a technology for the self that extended beyond urban areas and gained political backing as the Nationalist Party established

---

30. More work remains to be done on these new sciences of the child in Republican-period China, but key texts that must be mentioned include: Limin Bai, *Shaping the Ideal Child: Children and Their Primers in Late Imperial China* (Hong Kong: Chinese University Press, 2005); Maura Cunningham, "Shanghai's Wandering Ones: Child Welfare in a Global City, 1900–1953" (PhD diss., University of California, Irvine, 2014); Susan R. Fernsebner, "A People's Playthings: Toys, Childhood, and Chinese Identity, 1909–1933," *Postcolonial Studies* 6, no. 3 (2003): 269–293; M. Colette Plum, "Orphans in the Family: Family Reform and Children's Citizenship during the Anti-Japanese War, 1937–45," in *Beyond Suffering: Recounting War in Modern China*, ed. James A. Flath and Norman Smith (Vancouver: UBC Press, 2011), 186–208; and Margaret Mih Tillman, *Raising China's Revolutionaries: Modernizing Childhood for Cosmopolitan Nationalists and Liberated Comrades, 1920s–1950s* (New York: Columbia University Press, 2018).
31. "National Child Welfare Association of China," 1928, Box 4, Folder 8, China Child Welfare, Manuscripts, Archives and Rare Books Division, The New York Public Library.
32. Andrew F. Jones, *Developmental Fairy Tales: Evolutionary Thinking and Modern Chinese Culture* (Cambridge, MA: Harvard University Press, 2011), Kindle, chap. 3, loc. 1310.
33. The Shanghai branch of the National Child Welfare Association launched the first children's day on March 7, 1931, and it petitioned the Ministry of Education to adopt the calendrical designation for the entire country. Jia Ruzhong, Wei Huimin, and Liu Guiyu, "Ertong jie jinian de qingxing ji banfa" 兒童節紀念的情形及辦法 [A commemoration of children's day], *Shida yuekan* 師大月刊 13 (1934): 187–255.

control over the country after 1927.³⁴ Newly established municipal departments of public health hosted better baby contests and wellness campaigns for children, which typically included physical examinations as part of the campaign's events. Many of these campaigns were timed to coincide with Children's Day, a holiday originally launched by the Shanghai branch of the National Child Welfare Association (NWCA) on March 7, 1931. The NWCA later petitioned the Ministry of Education to adopt April 4 as Children's Day for the entire country. Seeking to capitalize on popular enthusiasm and Christian-led efforts, the Nationalist government inaugurated a National Children's Day in 1932.³⁵ As Chieko Nakajima has shown, these health and hygiene campaigns predated Nationalist involvement, but once the Nationalist government took over, these campaigns developed into "political events that connected the physical health of individuals and their mundane practices to larger social and national issues."³⁶ An integral component of these campaigns, the physical examination served a variety of purposes. It was often introduced to the participating public as a component of modern health and hygiene and represented visually on informational posters and popular lectures. The physical examination was also a tool for ascertaining well-being. Infants and young children were measured and examined in health contests with prizes for the winners.³⁷

In 1936—four years after the official proclamation by the Nationalist government to make April 4 of each year "Children's Day," and quick upon the heels of China's first "Children's Year,"³⁸—Shenghuo shudian published a book of essays entitled *Today's Children* (今日之兒童). The thirty-odd contributors represented some of the most prominent Chinese intellectuals active in the study and promotion of children's issues in China. Addressing a variety of themes including the arts, science, health, and physical culture (體育) under the heading of education reform, each contributor stressed the national imperative of tackling head-on the problems facing Chinese children. The book, which had been organized through the efforts of the Association for Children's Culture (中國兒童文化協會), was intended to serve as a reference point for parents and

---

34. Tillman points out that Chinese reformers introduced their "own political and cultural goals to better baby contests" and by working with James Yen's Mass Education Movement extended the reach of such contests into the countryside. Tillman, "Measuring Up: Better Baby Contests in China, 1917–1945," 1752.
35. Jia, Wei, and Liu, "Ertong jie jinian de qingxing ji banfa," 187–255.
36. Chieko Nakajima, *Body, Society, and Nation: The Creation of Public Health and Urban Culture in Shanghai* (Cambridge, MA: Harvard University Asia Center, 2018), 131.
37. For a more detailed discussion about how these contests and examinations introduced new ideas of scientific child-rearing and construed good health as a measurable phenomenon, see Tillman, "Measuring Up: Better Baby Contests in China, 1917–1945."
38. The central government determined the specific dates bracketing "Children's Year" (兒童年) to be August 1935 through July 1936.

teachers. The renowned Chinese educator, Tao Xingzhi, wrote in his preface for the book, "There are many parents and teachers who really want to learn more about children's issues, but can't, because the research materials on the matter have not been collected and collated. Finding even a handful of books that can satisfy the reader's interest is difficult." But in assembling a collection of essays that addressed both conceptual and practical plans for improving the lives of Chinese children, the Association for Children's Culture, Tao argued, had done a great service for parents and teachers. The book, in short, was intended to serve as an instructional guide with one simple and clear message: the very sanctity and health of the nation depended upon practical interventions for the betterment of China's children.

The emphasis upon children as the keepers of the nation's fate was an idea gaining tremendous currency in wartime China.[39] According to Tao, "The world of the past belongs to adults [大人], but the world of the future belongs to children [兒童]."[40] In his appraisal, the task at hand was to destroy that adult world rife with lies and fears, injustice, depravity, and hedonism, and on its ruins, to create a children's world that prized truth and honesty, innovation and intellect. In this new world, there would be no people above or below; all would stand on the same plane, and no one would a slave (奴隸). Books would be useful rather than simply read. For such a world to exist, children must be liberated to build it with their heads and hands. Drawing upon the sing-song rhymes of another song, Tao wrote,

人生兩個寶，	The two treasures of your life
雙手與大腦。	are your mind and body.
用腦不用手，	To use your head without your hands,
快要被打倒。	quickly will you be knocked down.
用手不用腦，	To use your hands without your head,

---

39. M. Colette Plum, "Unlikely Heirs: War Orphans During the Second Sino-Japanese War, 1937–1945" (PhD diss., Stanford University, 2006). Plum focuses upon the emergence of the Chinese child as "war orphan" at both an institutional and a discursive level. Her dissertation makes a forceful case for how the "war orphan" gained social and cultural potency as a symbol possessed with "its own distinctive clarion call infused with nationalist ideology." Institutionally, this shift in attention and value to the plight of the "war orphan" was accompanied by the widespread development of state-run wartime children's homes that served the dual purposes of caring for and educating the children in the mold of modern citizens (iv, 15).
40. Tao Xingzhi 陶行知, "Ertong de shijie" 兒童的世界 [The world of children], in *Jinri zhi ertong* 今日之兒童 [Today's children] (Shanghai: Shenghuo shudian, 1936), 1. These two lines stand as the opening of a song generally sung during Children's Day festivities. Tao provides additional lyrics following his assertion that the world of adults had so presumptuously assumed dominance over everything that even children were their "private property" (大人的私產). Whether or not the additional lyrics, which raises the rhetorical question of which, a girl or a pig, will garner more money for a mother to buy a fatter pig, are from the same song cannot be determined from the text alone.

飯也吃不飽。	never will your stomach be full.
手腦都會用，	[But only by] using both your mind and body,
才算是開天闢地的大好老。	will you do great things.⁴¹

Change could only be wrought through the joint efforts of both the head and hands. Tao's emphasis upon both intellectual and physical transformation is important. As an admirer of Dewey's philosophy for education, he adapted Dewey's ideas with a "half somersault," arguing instead for "life as education" (生活即教育) and "society as school" (社會即學校). Tao stressed the essential, if not primary, role of doing as part of learning.⁴²

For Tao's colleagues seeking to build up health education for Chinese children, this focus upon doing redefined not only the role of bodily experience but also the physical body, in the contemporary discourse of education reform and national advancement. Books, particularly books stuffed with antiquated learning of the past, were insufficient and perhaps even detrimental to the needs of the day. As the song above describes, learning from books alone would be as if one were to use only one's head without one's hands. Standing metonymically for the body as a whole, "two hands" (雙手) gestured toward an educational system that prioritized practical, physically minded learning that was also grounded in the lessons and activities of everyday life. This insistence upon building up the body as a necessary precursor and counterpart to teaching the mind translated into substantive changes in how children's bodies were viewed and treated by school officials, teachers, and parents. Advocates for health education in schools, like Zhou Shang and Ma Chonggan, insisted that children's bodies be taken seriously. They called for the implementation of regular health examinations, improvement of school facilities, and the rectification of student diets. But in identifying the appropriate techniques and metrics of evaluation, health educators had to confront questions of authority and specialization. Zhou Shang, in the preface to his 1939 handbook, *Care and Education of Children* (兒童保健與教師), remarked, "Many people think that health and hygiene education (衛生

---

41. Tao Xingzhi, "Ertong de shijie," 5.
42. Even Tao's name, "Xingzhi" (行知), which he had changed several times in the past, reflected his commitment to doing. Initially arranged as "Zhixing" (知行) in reference to a quote by Wang Yangming, the Ming dynasty philosopher: "Zhi shi xing zhi shi, xing shi zhi zhi cheng" (知是行之始，行是知之成, knowing is the beginning for doing; doing is the end result of knowing), Tao flipped the order in order to highlight his reassessment of the importance of doing for knowing; hence his name, "Xingzhi" rather than "Zhixing." Tang Min 唐民, "Wei Zhongguo jiaoyu xunmi shuguang: renmin jiaoyujia, Tao Xingzhi" 為中國教育尋覓曙光：人民教育家，陶行知 [Seeking the dawn for education in China: People's educator, Tao Xingzhi], in *Minguo Nanjing: Xueshu renwu zhuan* 民國南京：學術人物傳, ed. Zhang Xianwen 張憲文 (Nanjing: Nanjing daxue chubanshe, 2005), 382.

教育) is a matter for doctors, but in fact, the main subject [for bringing about health education] are teachers."

Their enthusiasm for the physical examination derived in part from their criticism of certain latent tendencies that had apparently arisen in the health education movement. Professional groups like the Council on Health Education and, increasingly through the 1930s, the Nationalist government promoted health education through all sorts of materials. Health instructional materials in the form of books, periodicals, and pamphlets; classroom posters and charts; postcards; plasticine models; radio health talks; and lantern-slides and moving pictures were all employed for the purposes of instilling and developing a sense of good health among students. For educational proponents of the physical examination, these physical materials—books, pamphlets, posters—were all well and good but rather missed the point. Critics argued that such materials perpetuated the textual tradition of *jiao* (教) and if taken alone failed to create the embodied forms of consciousness proper to modern health. Only the physical examination could bridge this divide. The educator Ni Xiying contended,

> For most schools, they consider their responsibility for children only in terms of instruction [教] such that even if schools possess hygienic facilities [衛生的設備], they only hide behind the pretext of new learning [替新教育裝裝幌子而已]. Because teachers still conform to the traditional notion of "teaching" [教書] and stuff children's heads with dead knowledge [死知識], the best student for most teachers remains the student strong in character and scholarship [品學兼優] or like a "learned gentleman" [文質彬彬].[43]

What good, Ni Xiying queried, was achieved if learning about health and physical wellness resulted in dead knowledge neatly captured in the student's mind but not practiced through the body? The child constituted by such stilted pedagogy was sure to be refined and cultured (斯文) but also weak (衰弱). Ni reproved, "Today, most school curricula include health education (衛生教育) but in name only. One need not scruple to say that in reality [i.e., in practice] there is no health education."[44]

The fundamental challenge of health education was how to transform book learning into everyday practice and habit. Ni's main criticism of health education lay in its failure to consider the question of physicality and the necessarily embodied state that health knowledge ought to assume. Another educator, Zhou Shang, characterized this failure of recognition as a deception and a kind of betrayal of the teacher's duty. Drawing a comparison to music instruction, Zhou

---

43. Ni Xiying 倪錫英, "Jinri zhi ertong shengli weisheng shishi" 今日之兒童生理衛生實施 [A health plan for today's children], in *Jinri zhi ertong* 今日之兒童 [Today's children] (Shanghai: Shenghuo shudian, 1936), 198.
44. Ni, "Jinri zhi ertong shengli weisheng shishi."

asked, how different was it from a violin teacher (教梵啞鈴教師) withholding instruction of the instrument's unique structure or the principles behind tuning the violin?[45]

At its most basic level, the critique levied by these educators concerned the scholastic importance of doing (action) and experience in modern education, and in this respect, the physical examination represented the vital link between health education in name alone and health education embodied. From the perspective of the would-be examiner—generally a physician, but, in the opinion of health education proponents, just as likely a teacher—the physical examination cultivated the examiner's observational skills (觀察力). Instead of relying upon other people's abstractions, the examiner refined their powers of perception and observation and directly engaged with the health of the child.

For the child, the physical examination reproduced the ideal relationship one ought to have with one's body. Having been weighed and measured, indeed poked and prodded, the child gradually became aware of the proportions of their physical being—their physical aptitude, their carriage and bearing, their propensity for disease, etc. Moreover, the child acquired conceptual units by which to evaluate the pattern of their growth and development, and in turn, assess those around them. If health was, as Zhou Shang claimed, a criterion of the model citizen, then civic duty lay both in the inculcation of health habits in children and the mutual reinforcement of such habits through a heightened sense of observation and inspection.

Measuring height, weight and chest girth, testing vision, checking for dental caries, and others has no antecedent in China and was practically alien in its composition, but Zhou insisted that the physical examination was analogous to what people already do regularly, every day. The difference lay not in kind but in degree. The physical examination relied upon and promoted a heightened sense of observation and inspection. Consider, for example, how Zhou Shang explained the function of the physical examination through an analogy of common habits.

> In practice, we like to appraise [估量] people's general physique [一般體格情形], particularly, when meeting a person for the first time—for example, reflecting upon the person' age, whether he's tall or short, nimble or slow, or strong or weak. [We wonder about] whether he looks well or poorly nourished, if his skin looks healthy or bears the tinge of illness. Whether or not a person has received specific training [in making a physical examination], this kind of common assessment is basically the same in all cases.[46]

---

45. Zhou Shang 周尚, *Ertong baojian yu jiaoshi* 兒童保健與教師 [The care and education of children] (Shanghai: Shangwu, 1939), 4.
46. Zhou, *Ertong baojian yu jiaoshi*, 7.

Rather than positing an ontological difference between these activities, Zhou aligned the physical examination along a spectrum that began with the everyday tendency to "look a person up and down." Measuring height and weight were extensions of the natural inclination that dealt in qualitative terms: tall, short, heavy-set, thin, robust, frail, etc. Zhou's insistence that the physical examination operated alongside our more common impulses for curiosity and comparison set the stage for his next claim, which came in the form of an unattributed quote: "If you go and measure a child's height, then you'll easily become the child's lifelong friend" (假使你去測量一個兒童的高度，那你很容易成了他的終身的朋友).[47]

The reasoning behind his assertion of devotion and platonic tenderness lay in the ways that the physical examination promoted the formation of relationship bonds between the examiner and examinee, the teacher and the child. "By taking the child's height," Zhou emphasized, "you have expressed interest in the child's body and in this way begun to pave the road by which to care for the child's body and ensure the child's good health. But more importantly, [by taking their height], you have stoked the flames of their own interest in the mechanics of their own body."[48]

This sense of assurance gained from the teacher's interest became the bedrock of improved health, and even increased weight and height. "Although a child may discern that his weight cannot rival that of another child of the same age," Zhou argued, "they will nonetheless continue to think they are growing (發育) [because the act of measurement implies there is something worth measuring] and [by this thinking] will increase and improve their height and weight."[49]

If the physical examination served to heighten and refine an examiner's sense of perception and responsibility, for the child, the physical examination became the key for a metaphysical transformation. Not only would the child become interested in his or her own health, but this interest would promote the growth and development so earnestly desired. By emphasizing the subject-forming dimensions of the physical examination, these educators denuded the examination of its foreign connotations. They cast it as a hyperextension of already existing, everyday behavior, but with the power to shape and reshape individual consciousness. Both the examiner and the examinee could be remade through the physical examination, as each performed the expectation and aspirations of modern health.

---

47. Zhou, *Ertong baojian yu jiaoshi*, 8.
48. Zhou, *Ertong baojian yu jiaoshi*, 8.
49. Zhou, *Ertong baojian yu jiaoshi*, 8.

Conclusion

This chapter has infused critical inquiries of "Chineseness" with a history of science perspective through a specific episode of corporealist-diagnostic inception: the consolidation of the physical examination and its attendant apparatuses of cultural authorization. The modern Chinese subjectivity Chinese educators sought to achieve through the physical examination participated in its own formation. Being examined and examining were twinning processes crucial to proper development and maturation, whose effects operated both psychically and physiologically. By being subject to a physical examination, one learned the proper metrics and categories of analysis for assessing one's own body. Height and weight would become intimate extensions of one's consciousness as one learned to embody a modern body. As one child health guidance tract indicated, to achieve a strong physique, one needed first to know what constituted a strong physique, i.e., the height, weight, and other bodily measurements signifying health and strength.[50] Such numbers relied upon a technology of doing—the lengthening of the measuring tape (or a malleable belt if a measuring tape is unavailable), the straightening of one's posture, eyes forward, heels against the wall. Even the examiner could not escape the psychic and somatic effects of the physical examination. Through the physical examination, examiner and examinee were knitted together as affective partners in the mutually entangled project of crafting modern Chinese subjectivities.

---

50. Zhang Renhua 張任華, ed., *Ertong zhi weisheng* 兒童之衛生 [Child health and hygiene] (Shanghai: Shangwu yinshuguan, 1924), 2.

2

Therapeutic Humanism in Hou Chun-Ming's Art

Queer Mimesis, Subaltern Souls, and the Body as Vessel in Sinoglossiac Taiwan

Howard Chiang

Can Chinese therapeutic massage work alongside anthropology and psychoanalysis? In what ways do art, text, and therapeutic governance collide or conjoin? How does the body conceal, mimic, or stage the secrets of the soul? What forms of medium, cultural and historical resources, and strategies of simulation enable the subaltern agent to be heard? Can avant-garde art produced for the sake of expressiveness be at once about artistic creation, curative science, queer resistance, postcolonial healing, social survival, political refraction, regimes of selfhood, scriptive aesthetics, and the authorization of futurity? This chapter shows the converging possibility of these otherwise disparate injunctions in the art of 侯俊明 Hou Chun-Ming (b. 1963).

My choice of this Chiayi-born artist is perhaps not surprising. When his 搜神記 *Soushenji* (*Anecdotes about Spirits and Immortals*, 1993) was sold for HK$2.64 million at Christie's in Hong Kong in 2008, Hou rose to international acclaim after many years of relative obscurity.[1] Apart from his fame, though, I have chosen to focus on Hou's art because it speaks to the most pressing concern of this volume: the way that the Mandarin Chinese writing system interacts with—and even morphs into/from—other genres of cultural expression and, ultimately, styles of social critique.[2] Hou's work captures the highly transmedial nature of Sinoglossiac cultural production in three distinct ways: first, the visuality of his art assigns textual and scriptural elements to a preeminent role so that

---

1. Chun-Ming Hou 侯俊明, *Soushenji* 搜神記 [Anecdotes about spirits and immortals] (Taipei: China Times, 1994).
2. On the role of textual inscription in Hou's art, see Chi-Lin Hsu 許綺玲, "Chutan Hou Chun-Ming yishu zuopin zhong de wenben shengcheng lichen" 初探侯俊明藝術作品中的文本生成歷程 [A preliminary genetic observation of texts in the art works of Hou Chun-Ming], *Sun Yat-sen Journal of Humanities*, no. 37 (2014): 133–160.

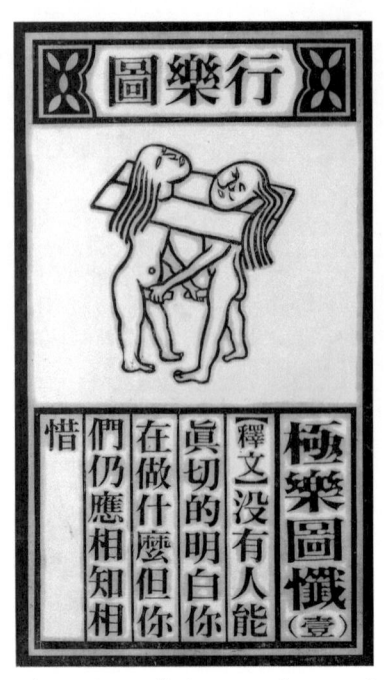

Figure 2.1: "Pleasure Seeking Picture," first installment of *Erotic Paradise* (1992). Courtesy of Hou Chun-Ming.

the artistic value is inseparable from the vital work of Sinitic characters; second, his signature of creativity accentuates body politics through its very embodiment in the sense that corporealism routinely commands the spotlight of his artistic imagination; and thirdly, Hou often sanctions these two structural commitments through an explicit representation of sexuality. These intertwined strategies of a highly erotically charged Sinoglossiac production have formed a central motif throughout his work ever since the appearance of the now canonical 極樂圖懺 *Jile tuchan* (*Erotic Paradise*, 1992) if not earlier (Figure 2.1).

Another reason to focus on Hou's art is that his work took a decisive "psychoanalytic turn" immediately after his reputation peaked circa 2008. This turn built on an important legacy of his oeuvre: a Freudian interest in investigating and revealing the deep-seated deposits of sexual repression. For Hou, not only is the sex drive the most basic design of human instinct, but it can be best uncovered through the biological urge to draw and narrate. Embodying the clinical utility of analysis, aesthetic art in Hou's abstraction provides a liminal space to articulate the unconscious sediments of irrationality—even madness—where reality necessitates the ontology of otherwise. Arguably, Hou's ultimate patient has been himself all along. As the literary scholar Pin-Wen Ke notes, since 2000

Hou has decidedly liberated his work from the superficial bind of "need" (需要) and "demand" (需求) and gravitated toward the accumulated attention on the fluid nature of "desire" (慾望). What has surfaced as a result is an "incarnated subject" (復生的受訪者)—a metonymy of self-desire summoned by Hou.[3]

Meanwhile, the psychoanalytic turn of his work also ventured in two distinctively new directions. First, inspired by a fractured relationship with his own father, Hou became obsessed with cataloging and visualizing the variety of configurations assumed by a father-son relationship across different Asian societies. This ethnographic impulse resulted in the 亞洲人的父親 *Yazhouren de fuqin* (*Asian Fathers*, 2008–present) project, for which Hou has interviewed men from Japan, Taiwan, Thailand, and Hong Kong about their impression and understanding of their father.[4] Each "case" resulted in a drawing, adding up to what one critic has labeled a "visual archival documentary" (視覺檔案的紀錄).[5] This empirical archive embodies the growing appeal to Oedipal and reparative dynamic explorations in Hou's art. Second, the psychoanalytic turn of his work is undergirded by Hou's personification of what Carl Jung has called a "wounded healer."[6] Hou often renders the curative function of his work *as* the art of healing precisely from the viewpoint of a therapist who has been impaired.[7] As Hou divulges about the conditional source of his inspiration, "the majority of my creative output is related to the kind of illness and pain my body has experienced."[8]

---

3. Pin-Wen Ke 柯品文, "Shentitu de zhaohuan yu jiushu: Lun Hou Chun-Ming Nandong shenti yuwang de keneng zhishe" 「身體圖」的招喚與救贖：論侯俊明《男洞》身體慾望的可能指涉 [The summon and redemption of "Body Images": Possible references to bodily desire in Hou Chun-Ming's *Male Hole*]," *Taiwan Fine Arts* 112 (2018): 72.
4. Chun-Ming Hou 侯俊明, *Yazhouren de fuqin: Hengbin* 亞洲人的父親：橫濱 [Asian fathers: Yokohama] (Taipei: L'Orangerie International Arts Consultant Co., 2008); Chun-Ming Hou 侯俊明, *Yazhouren de fuqin: Taiwan* 亞洲人的父親：臺灣 [Asian fathers: Taiwan] (Taipei: L'Orangerie International Arts Consultant Co., 2009).
5. Kai Sheng 盛鎧, "Hou Chun-Ming Yazhouren de fuqing Zhong de dang'an yishu yu duihua meixue" 侯俊明《亞洲人的父親》中的檔案藝術與對話美學 [Visual archive and dialogical aesthetics in Chun-Ming Hou's *The Asian Fathers Interview Project*], *Journal of Art Studies* 14 (2014): 102.
6. Carl G. Jung, "The Psychology of the Transference," in *Practice of Psychotherapy*, 2nd ed., trans. R. F. C. Hull (Princeton, NJ: Princeton University Press, 1966), 163–320.
7. Viewing medicine as a form of art, I borrow from anthropologist Judith Farquhar's insight that non-biomedical styles of healing culture afford us the opportunity to experience the "presence of the vastness of an unfamiliar world." Judith Farquhar, *A Way of Life: Thing, Thought, Action in Chinese Medicine* (New Haven, CT: Yale University Press, 2020), 111. It is in this sense that I maintain a close affinity between the study of medical pluralism and the interest in alterity in queer theory. On the relation of the foreignness of alternative healing systems to the scientific understanding of the mind, see Howard Chiang, "Contested Minds Across Time: Perspectives from Chinese History and Culture," *Integrative Psychological and Behavioral Science* 56, no. 2 (2022): 420–425.
8. Chun-Ming Hou 侯俊明, *Shentitu fangtan chuangzuo: 2014–2017* 身體圖訪談創作：2014–2017 [Male hole: 2014–2017] (unpublished pamphlet in Mandarin Chinese), 44.

In order to accord Hou the status of a bona fide Sinoglossiac artist, this chapter focuses on his 身體圖 *Shentitu* (*Body Image*) project. Starting in 2014, Hou has interviewed sexual minorities with a diverse sociodemographic background about their personal life. Aiming to expose their deepest libidinal secrets, these sessions normally last two days and begin with Hou and the interviewee disrobing with consent. On the first day, the interviewee shares memorable autobiographical details and the most intimate stories from past sexual encounters. On the second day, following a *tuina* (推拿) massage performed by Hou, the naked protagonist paints an image of the body deemed most representative of his true self (Figure 2.2). After a sustained period of introspection reflecting on the interview and the interviewee's self-drawing, Hou responds by painting an independent image—often with him naked during the process.

This chapter closely examines four of the nineteen pairs of these paintings that make up the 男洞 *Nandong* (*Male Hole*) subcollection of *Body Image* (Figure 2.3). Produced with oil pastel on paper and in the format of 55 × 237 cm × 2 pieces, each of these sets represents a unique index of subjectivity derivative of the Taiwanese gay male community. Why invoke the trope of "hole" in such a gendered context? Hou explains the premise of his project as follows:

> 洞，是關於慾望、匱乏與追尋。[Hole is about desire, lack, and pursuit.]
> 洞，是關於記憶、秘密與窺視。[Hole is about memory, secret, and peeking.]
> 身體，是慾望的載體，記憶著個人的生命故事，乃至家族、社會文化的制約。[Body is the carrier of desire, remembering one's individual story and even the constraints of the family, society, and culture.]⁹

Figure 2.2: Hou performs *tuina* on an interviewee. Courtesy of Hou Chun-Ming.

---

9. Hou, *Male Hole*, 5.

Figure 2.3: The *Male Hole* exhibition at the 2016 Taiwan Art Biennale (台灣美術雙年展). Courtesy of Hou Chun-Ming.

By treating the non-normative agent, its imagery, and its corporeal history as an intertwined vessel, the *Male Hole* project thus offers a window into the emotions and experiences of queer life in a region that has been depicted as an "orphan of Asia."[10]

I argue that Hou's art, centering on the dialectic mechanisms of concealment and revelation, constitutes a form of queer psychotherapy in which the dynamic scripts of transference and counter-transference reciprocate between the interviewed subject and the work of art, between the body corporeal and the body visualized, and, above all, between the secrets and fulfillment of the soul. *Male Hole* pinpoints the nuance of therapeutic humanism that has come to underpin Hou's "psychoanalytic turn," which posits a new homeostatic-defense mechanism of the psyche: mimesis. The tensions that emerge out of the contrast among each pair of the *Male Hole* installments bestow the central message that what we see in others is ultimately our own projection and imitation. In mirroring and resolving unconscious conflicts as such, Hou's art encapsulates a series of "mimesis of the self"—from the self of the queer analysand to that of the *tuina* psychotherapist—to leverage an alternative genealogy of psychoanalytic governance in Sinophone Taiwan.

---

10. See Chien-hsin Tsai, *A Passage to China: Literature, Loyalism, and Colonial Taiwan* (Cambridge, MA: Harvard University Press, 2017), 251–280.

Labeling Deviance: Pleasures of the Body

A portfolio of the diverse gay male subjectivities that define contemporary queer life in Taiwan, *Male Hole* assigns a label to each of the interviewed subjects. For each interview, Hou draws on the information he had culled to formulate a nickname that he considers best captures the subject's personality. Each installment in the project is thus marked by a dual identity: the subject's own pseudonym and a nickname invented by Hou. On a general level, this labeling technique in Hou's art ingests the spirit of empirical classification that has anchored the Enlightenment project to decode nature through scientific interrogation.[11] But more specifically, Hou's project reinscribes the analyst-analysand interplay and the modern sexologist's impulse to tabulate new sexual vocabularies that corresponded to—through the systematic decoding of—the nature of the relationship between bodily experience, erotic desire, and sexual subjectivity.

While sexual connotations underwrite nearly all of the labels, a subgroup of them specifically designate a taxonomy of sexual deviance. The case of "Dog Slave/Chris" (犬奴／克里斯) is a striking example in this regard. The thirty-two-year-old Chris holds a graduate degree and works as an administrator in a non-profit organization. The only subject in *Male Hole* who self-identifies as an active member of the bondage, discipline, sadism, and masochism (BDSM) community, Chris fulfils his erotic fantasy by playing the submissive role of a "dog slave" in sex. This stands in stark contrast to his strong leadership and superb organizational skills at work. In his words, "being a dog slave is stress-relieving" (當犬奴，好舒壓).[12] Chris likes men to tramp on his face, slap him in the face, and piss on him. He enjoys licking the toes of other men, drinking their urine, and turning his body into an object that can be abused by them.

Chris's sexual fantasy emblematizes how some gay men practice sadomasochism as an eroticized insinuation of power play. Upon meeting a "master" through an online dating app, Chris turns this fantasy into a reality by manipulating the pleasurable pursuits of his own body. The master trains Chris's physical fitness, progressively taming him so as to mimic a real dog. Instructed by the master, Chris wears a dog tail, a dog collar, a gag, an oxygen-reducing mask, a chastity belt, and a horse eye rod (urethral expansion). He also shaves his pubic hair, learns to bark like a dog, and uses a dog bowl to drink soy milk and piss. Infatuated with the unconditional love that the master confers upon him through physical torment, insult, derogatory discipline, and punishment, Chris declares that "master loves me, understands me" (主人愛我，懂我).[13]

---

11. Michel Foucault, *The Order of Things: An Archaeology of the Human Sciences* (New York: Vintage, 1994 [1966]).
12. Hou, *Male Hole*, 35.
13. Hou, *Male Hole*, 35.

Notable similarities can be discerned from juxtaposing Hou's "Dog Slave" painting (Figure 2.4a) with Chris's self-drawing (Figure 2.4b): the two white spots on the face that represent the light specks on a dog's eyes, the circular rhythm of the corporeal blueprint, the razor-sharp paw nails, the vertical asymmetry of the body, and so forth. Yet Hou's drawing adds a distinct web-like coating (an inference to bondage) to "capture" Chris's personality, as if the image both crystallizes Hou's impression of Chris and projects his own desire to record the darkest secrets of the soul from an ostensibly neutral, objective viewpoint. In the textual exposition of the work, Hou traces the roots of Chris's sexual fantasy to a growing resentment toward his father since adolescence. Chris himself represents this discontent by drawing a blue eye and several teardrops near the torso, followed by the remark: "father, why do you have to be like this" (爸爸／

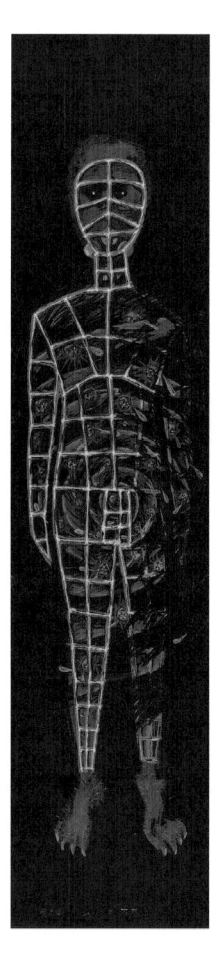

Figures 2.4a and 2.4b: "Dog Slave" (2016). Courtesy of Hou Chun-Ming.

為什麼你要這樣).[14] It is as if Chris's deviant fantasy to be dominated, controlled, disciplined, and even punished by other men resolves his universal—however untenable it seems to him—desire to be a sufficiently masculine and filial son. As the only work in *Male Hole* that thematizes BDSM, "Dog Slave" visualizes a mechanism of eroticization whereby the kinship and quotidian relations of gay men become deeply saturated in the fabrics of power.

Another installment is labeled "Narcissus/Hao Hua" (納西瑟斯／皓華), referencing the famous Greek mythology figure known for adoring his own beauty and pining away for knowing that the object of his love cannot love him back. By referencing the origin of a psychoanalytic condition popularized by Freud—narcissism—this entry univocally proclaims the uncovering of such a case in the Taiwanese queer community. Interestingly, similar to Chris's self-perception, the twenty-six-year-old Hao Hua oftentimes sees himself as a dog waving his tail to different sexual partners in search for a sign of affection. Yet if Chris incorporates the play of domination/subservience into BDSM practice, Hao Hua's sexual fantasy should be more appropriately aligned with the psychopathology of excessive self-love. Hao Hua admits that whenever he has cam sex, his attention is fixated more on the projection of himself at the corner of the computer screen than on the digital image of his partner. Although he enjoys seeing the virtual display of another person's body, he derives even greater erotic pleasure from showing his naked body to others.

In admitting to his narcissistic obsession, Hao Hua distinguishes his psychological desire from his biological needs. What he truly falls in love with is the way others perceive him. During webcam sessions, random partners would request to see different parts of his body, and Hao Hua complies with their various demands, including the demand that he "self-penetrates" (自插肛門).[15] He enjoys giving vulgar and slutty performances to casual strangers he meets online. But that is different from masturbating while staring at himself in the mirror, a habit that he has developed since high school. Hao Hua explains that whenever he masturbates to his mirror reflection, he always imagines the image to be the body of someone else. Nevertheless, to Hao Hua, masturbation is a regular pursuit: whenever his body clock triggers the signal, he masturbates to fulfill the biological need. Cam sex, by contrast, speaks to his true desire—a performance that satisfies his psychological appetite.

The pair of drawings that constitute the "Narcissus" installment in *Male Hole* can be interpreted as a response to Hao Hua's parting question: "An erected penis is a lie detector. People always say that they have an erection because they have

---

14. Hou, *Male Hole*, 35.
15. Hou, *Male Hole*, 29.

feelings for me. But which part of me exactly do they have feelings for?"[16] Recall that the true object of love for Hao Hua is the way other people perceive him. His self-drawn image (Figure 2.5b), then, can be understood less as a mere representation of the self than as a *solicitation* for others to paint a sexualized image of him. In this way Hou's painting (Figure 2.5a) symbolizes Hao Hua's ultimate lust, unlocking the darkest truths of his desire.

Yet Hou's painting also departs from Hao Hua's self-drawing in significant ways. Whereas the former works to "record" Hao Hua's personality type by visualizing the clinical category of narcissism, the latter narrates a chronology of psychosexual development that underwrites a corporealism from head to toe:

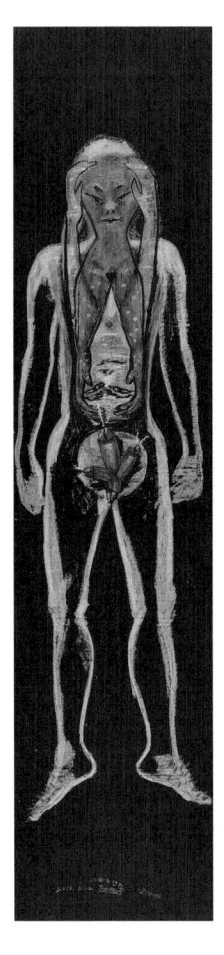

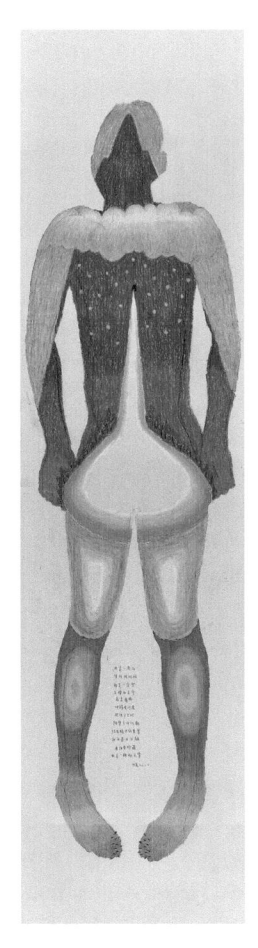

Figures 2.5a and 2.5b: "Narcissus" (2016). Courtesy of Hou Chun-Ming.

---

16. Hou, *Male Hole*, 29.

我是一座山 [I am a mountain]
等待被征服 [waiting to be conquered]
我是一朵雲 [I am a cloud]
支撐那天空 [supporting the sky]
我是瀑布 [I am a waterfall]
沖積成河床 [giving rise to a riverbed]
肥沃了土地 [enriching the soil]
經歷了冰河期 [surpassing the ice age]
結出碩大的果實 [resulting in strong fruitification]
就永遠不分離 [then will never be separated]
有誰來珍藏 [who will come and cherish]
我是一隻仙人掌 [I am a cactus][17]

Each of the entities described in Hao Hua's poem maps onto a separate constituent of the body he draws of himself from top to bottom, the mountain representing his head and the cactus representing his feet. Yet if the analysand's drawing resists the temptation to locate his identity in a singular physical marker, the analyst's art moves in the exact opposite direction by revealing the face and sexual organ of the narcissistic analysand. Whereas the invisible mirror—the narcissist's symbolic source of pleasure—splits Hao Hua's image into two vertical halves, Hou's painting turns the mirror by ninety degrees and fastens this new horizontal plane to the narcissist's chest region so as to divulge the subject's psychopathological identity in manifest terms.

The theme of narcissism is picked up in another entry, "Lotus That Does Not Come/Ahlong" (不洩蓮華／阿隆). Yet in contrast to the case of Hao Hua, Ahlong's condition is depicted more as an idealized manifestation of universal human existence than as a pathological obsession peculiar to a minority population. The forty-one-year-old partnered Ahlong holds a graduate degree and is now a brand manager. Despite having established this seemingly stable and successful life, he was deliriously immersed in hook-ups and short-term relationships for a period of time. For example, he used to date only foreigners, because part of their appeal came from their mandated departure: leaving Taiwan was inevitable once their residential permit expired. Within the framework of this anticipated outcome, Ahlong felt at ease to express his deepest lust and passion with these short-term boyfriends. Similarly, as it became easier to hook up through using the new online dating apps, Ahlong enjoyed sleeping around with different partners on a frequent basis. He found excitement in, quoting Ahlong himself, "standing behind the front door [at a stranger's place], not knowing

---

17. Hou, *Male Hole*, 28.

what will happen next."[18] Yet Ahlong eventually brought closure to this ostensible preference for a quick turnover of sexual partners. According to Hou's interpretation, Ahlong is not dispositioned to trying something new constantly; instead, Ahlong believes that the most sublime form of sex comes from the union of minds. He believes that it is possible to achieve better sex only with the same individual.

This vision of sex par excellence ultimately defines Ahlong's eroticization of his own self and body. Over time, Ahlong turns himself into a master of acquiring sexual satisfaction with the same individual—himself. Extending from his yearning for stability and control, he frequently finds sexual fulfillment in nonsexual activities. For instance, Ahlong acquires sexual gratification when practicing Ashtanga yoga. Doing yoga *is* having sex with himself, because in these ninety-minute sessions, his very existence becomes tangible through painful stretches and intense poses, allowing him to locate his senses within his own bodily being and thereby attending closely to his bodily needs. Similarly, he finds fulfillment in Buddhist Vipassana meditation, because it provides illuminating "insight" into his bodily-sexual energy. This type of energy circulates within and gives life to every cell of his body. This alternate type of orgasm defies the conventional erotic orgasm that exhausts and takes life away from an individual. As such, Ahlong no longer feels the need to delight in sexual fulfillment through engaging with the world external to his corporeal being. He claims that "as long as one possesses extreme sensitivity, one can have sex with the entire world."[19]

Drawing on Ahlong's experience, Hou's "Lotus That Does Not Come" offers a distinct caricature of narcissism that grounds its origin in the work of Mother Nature and not the outcome of abnormal psychology. Ahlong's exaltation of engaging in sexual intercourse with himself is clearly depicted in his body art (Figure 2.6b). On top of his head, he "showers [himself] with love."[20] From below his waist sits an erected penis that ejaculates into his body. According to his own textual annotation,

性能量不外洩時，回返自身 [when sexual energy does not leak, it returns to the body]
感受覺知自己，就是與自己做愛 [when one is self-aware, he is making love to himself]
根植大地，接原始能 [rooted in the earth and receives primordial energy][21]

---

18. Hou, *Male Hole*, 33.
19. Hou, *Male Hole*, 33.
20. Hou, *Male Hole*, 32.
21. Hou, *Male Hole*, 32.

In between the constant showering of love from above and the unabated circulation of orgasm from below sits a brightly colored, healthy lotus—the protagonist of this metabolic system that epitomizes a monogamous romance with oneself. This lotus is where the name of this installment derives and, by extension, what Hou's response-drawing represents (so the absence of a lotus denotes its very presence in Figure 2.6a). In order to draw attention to Ahlong's spiritual journey, Hou multiplies the Vipassana meditational eye (which was singularly present in Ahlong's original drawing) and saturates Ahlong's upper body with these proliferated eyes. Hou accentuates the earth's firm support and nourishment of the lotus by artistically blending the meditational eyes with the tree stems that aggregate into Ahlong's sturdy legs (a rhetorical technique borrowed directly from Ahlong's original painting). Unlike the narcissist, Ahlong indulges in a distinct sexual appetite for himself without the fatal preoccupation with how others

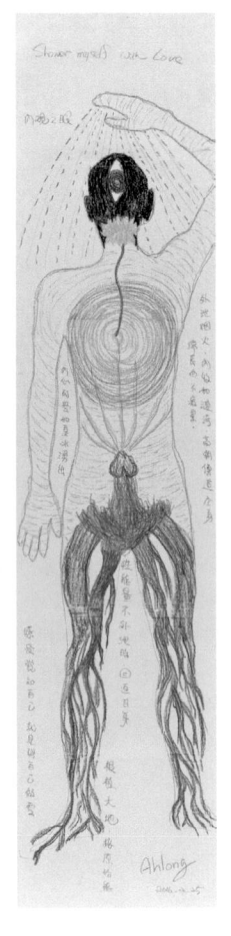

Figures 2.6a and 2.6b: "Lotus That Does Not Come" (2016). Courtesy of Hou Chung-Ming.

perceive of him. His unconventional desire is solidly rooted in its connection to the natural—not the mentally deviant—world.

Overindulgence of sex does not stop at oneself, of course. Among the gay male subjects interviewed by Hou, many blatantly confess that they are addicted to sex. The most startling example is the case of "Exotica Ahkong/Kong" (異物阿空／阿空). The twenty-nine-year-old Kong is in fact a well-known public figure in the Taiwanese sex industry. Yet if sex work and pornography conjure up the stereotypical preeminence placed on erotically charged bodies, Kong's story—from its narration during his interview with Hou to its materialization in the "Exotica Ahkong" installment—turns this popular imagery on its head. First, Kong's biography embodies the value of the mind. Proudly claiming that his intelligence sits at the top one percentile in the nation, Kong describes his brain as an "ecological orbit" (生態球) that generates as soon as it absorbs ideas.[22] Kong holds degrees from some of Taiwan's most prestigious institutions, including a bachelor's degree in computer science from National Tsing Hua University and a graduate degree in music from National Chiao Tung University. He has also been enrolled in graduate studies in the Department of Law at Fu Jen Catholic University. His interest in studying law stems from his commitment to improving the legal conditions of sex work in Taiwan. The meeting of his body and mind finds its foremost expression in the pursuit of knowledge and social transformation.

Yet for Kong, intellectual attainment remains meaningless without routing the energy it entails to sex and bodily pleasure (and vice versa). He concedes to have trained himself in penile enlargement regimens. With an 18-cm phallic organ, he wishes to become a pornographic actor one day and regrets having "discovered" sex so late in life. As such, he identifies as a "sex addict" (性愛成癮的男人) who could potentially have sex—with intermittent rest—for twenty-four hours straight in his apartment.[23] In gay sex, he prefers to be the top, because an erotically fulfilling sense of dominance emerges from this sexual position. Kong construes his penis as a baton that orchestrates the staging and rhythms of a sex scene, and this is apparently related to his commitment to pushing the legal boundaries of sex work. According to Kong, selling his body for money reflects more on the rebellious nature of his personality than anything else. The merging of his educational desire and addiction to sex materializes most tellingly in his decision to work with the Taiwan-based sex toy manufacturer Exotica, to produce a commercial dildo based on a clone of his penis. For every dildo sold, Exotica donates 3.5 percent of the profit to a volunteer organization called Hand Job TW. Founded in 2013, Hand Job TW is the first non-profit organization that

---

22. Hou, *Male Hole*, 17.
23. Hou, *Male Hole*, 17.

comprises "sex volunteers" (性志工) who provide sexual service to queers with disabilities. In inscribing to his intimate labor a legitimate means to push the limits of sexual knowledge and acceptable sexual expression, Kong refuses to distinguish his bodily deeds from epistemological needs and the potent symbolism of his sexuality from the promise of social activism.

The syncretism of Kong's intellectual and sexual addictions provides an explanatory framework for comparing the two paintings that constitute the "Exotica Ahkong" installment of *Male Hole*. Similar to the aforementioned cases, Hou's drawing (Figure 2.7a) and Kong's representation of himself (Figure 2.7b) relate to one another in a dialectical manner. Whereas Kong presents the image of his body as a declaration of "self-de/construction" (his appended signature at the bottom and an unambiguous valorization of post-structuralist

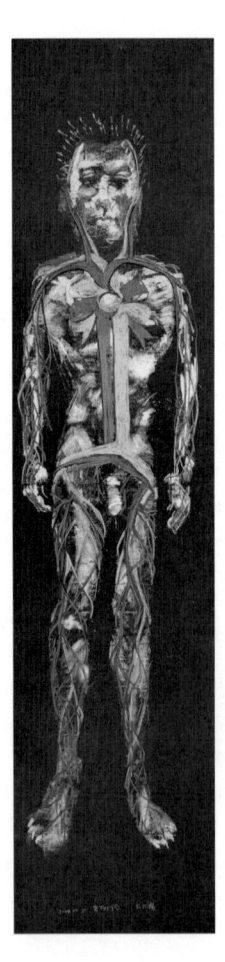

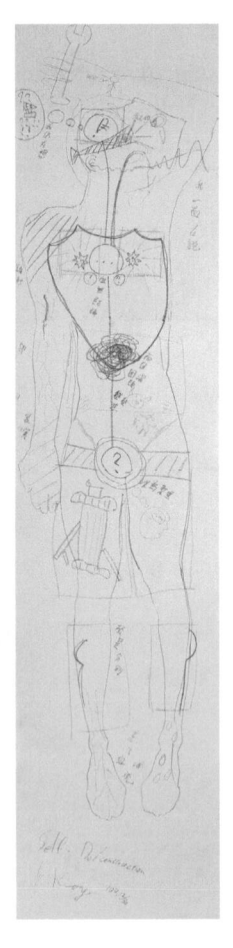

Figures 2.7a and 2.7b: "Exotica Ahkong" (2014). Courtesy of Hou Chun-Ming.

thinking),²⁴ Hou's response piece eliminates all of the detailed "deconstructed" components of Kong's body and furnishes instead a holistic painting of a flesh-colored body. As if to reflect the labor he had put into the making of the Exotica dildo, Kong intentionally places a question mark over his growing area, followed by these words: "以為聚焦 *yiwei jujiao* [Assumed spotlight] / 於是分割 *yushi fenge* [therefore splits] / 忘了血流（淚流）*wangle xieliu (leiliu)* [forgets to shed blood/tears]."²⁵

Rather than continuing to second guess what the question mark conceals, Hou's drawing, in contrast, unveils Kong's genitalia (alongside his facial features) and thereby turns the most valuable organ of his body decidedly inside out (value is invoked here also in the Marxian economic sense). Hou utilizes a number of artistic techniques to accentuate the fixation and fetishization of Kong's phallus, and the most notable of these may be the wrapping of Kong's body as a gift by using his own veins as ribbons (an allusion to Kong's self-proclamation that contempt and defiance are written in his blood). If Kong's self-representation transposes his performative labor onto a visual matrix of deconstruction that is intended to prompt incessant questioning, we might say that its counterpart—Hou's image—counter-transfers the affective components of the very same labor into a concrete materialization of Kong's embodied self.

Therapeutic Instrumentation: Art as Clinical Encounter

Although sex is an omnipresent theme in the works examined above, the ultimate principle of Hou's art is not to represent sex—thus defying *ars erotica* in the Foucauldian sense.²⁶ The kind of dialogic interplay between Hou and the agents of queer subalternity reveals a *psychodynamic* therapeutic approach that valorizes libidinal drive as the most innate form of human desire and sex as its most natural expression. The *Male Hole* installments capture both Hou's and the various protagonists' mimesis of the self by painting implicit codes that substitute the sexual instinct. The interviews conducted by Hou resemble sites of clinical encounter. In this regard, my reading of Hou's art differs from the way that critics have typically explored the relationship between psychoanalysis and modern art: they either psychoanalyze pieces of art to try to understand what

---

24. Hou, *Male Hole*, 16.
25. Hou, *Male Hole*, 16.
26. Michel Foucault, *The History of Sexuality, Vol. 1: An Introduction*, trans. Robert Hurley (New York: Vintage, 1990). For a critique of the *scientia sexualis* and *ars erotica* distinction from the angle of East Asian history, see Gregory M. Pfulgfelder, *Cartographies of Desire: Male-Male Sexuality in Japanese Discourse, 1600–1950* (Berkeley: University of California Press, 1999), 6–7; Leon Antonio Rocha, "Scientia sexualis and ars erotica: Foucault, van Gulik, Needham," *Studies in History and Philosophy of Biological and Biomedical Sciences* 42 (2011): 328–343.

the artist attempts to accomplish at an unconscious psychological level, or shed light on how artistic images aim to visualize Freudian ideas.[27] In contrast, the psychoanalytic turn of Hou's art that I have diagnosed cannot be reduced to the representational register, but it furnishes the very *enactment* of psychodynamic transference and counter-transference. Moreover, this reading effect also valorizes the indisputable role of art—visual, textual, corporeal, or otherwise—in the regimes of scientific knowledge production. The former can no longer be relegated to a "subsidiary" role that only helps to convey—rather than embody—the very epistemic authority of Science.[28]

Hou's drawings are not mere representations of clinical transference. Rather, their mode of production works to mediate the processes of transference and counter-transference. This analytic mediation proceeds in four crucial steps. First, the pre-drawing interview sessions put Hou in the role of the analyst and the interviewee in the role of the analysand. The procedural design of these sessions allows Hou to collect background information—to build a "case" history—about the subject and gives the latter an opportunity, too, to highlight the most memorable moments and pertinent details of his life.[29] In the second step, the dynamic of analysis is injected with a dose of Chinese healing practice, whereby the *tuina* massage that Hou performs on the interviewee transforms the latter's thoughts and feelings into corporeal sensation. Hou considers this a necessary preparatory step congenial to eventual bodily expression.

In the third, definitive step where transference occurs, the subject expresses himself through drawing. His body serves as a conduit for translating ideas and feelings into an image accompanied by a set of explanatory texts. A therapeutic product of what I have been calling mimesis, this image (and set of texts) of the self becomes a gesture of appreciation, a token of affection, and evidence of sacrifice. The act of offering this token to Hou denotes a psychoanalytic transference. However, rather than directing the emotions entirely to Hou, the self-drawn image works as a "surrogate" that contains those affective feelings and thereby neutralizes any potential conflicts the subject may feel toward Hou. In essence, the surrogate token encapsulates the material instrumentation of therapeutic entanglement. In the fourth and final step, counter-transference takes place as Hou absorbs the meanings and emotions interpellated by the token and then counter-transfers them to a newly produced image, which now functions as *both*

---

27. See, for example, George Hagman, *The Artist's Mind: A Psychoanalytic Perspective on Creativity, Modern Art, and Modern Artists* (New York: Routledge, 2010).
28. For a remarkable treatment of this problem, see Ari Larissa Heinrich, *Chinese Surplus: Biopolitical Aesthetics and the Medically Commodified Body* (Durham, NC: Duke University Press, 2018).
29. On reasoning in cases in psychoanalytic science, see John Forrester, *Thinking in Cases* (Cambridge, UK: Polity, 2017).

a sign of reciprocity *and* a projection of Hou's own desire (revelation through, again, mimesis of the self).

The focus on transference as a key therapeutic mechanism of Hou's art sheds light on the competing orderings of knowledge in which Taiwanese culture has encountered psychoanalysis. Whereas other critics have analyzed Hou's art from the perspectives of its broader resonance with the evolving political context of Taiwan,[30] its artistic sophistication and refinement over time,[31] and its representational strategies,[32] my reading is intended to shed light on the nature of its psychotherapeutic attainment. In lieu of an empirical catalog in the sense of a late Victorian prescriptive sexological manual, *Male Hole*—and *Body Image* more generally—should be more accurately interpreted as a (queer) affective compendium—an intersubjective product of the mimesis of the self. This recasting of the *Body Image* project as a kind of "vernacular sexology" provides a cultural history of science perspective distinctively missing from the current scholarly literature on Hou's oeuvre.[33] It deepens a growing historiography on the global reception and production of psychoanalysis by turning to an unlikely region and an unusual epistemic medium.[34]

A subaltern psychotherapeutic reading of *Male Hole* further complicates the cultural genealogies summoned by Hou. On the one hand, his art draws on the rich historical resources of Chinese culture from the May Fourth "diary" genre

---

30. Jow-Jiun Gong 龔卓軍, "Roushen gongxiang: Hou Chun-Ming de seqing haofei yu jianchi zhuji" 肉身共享：侯俊明的色情耗費與賤斥註記 [Sharing the flesh: Hou Chun-Ming's pornographic consumption and abject notations], *Modern Arts* 144 (2009): 38–51.
31. Ming-E Yang 楊明鍔, "Yongbao zhizhuo: Hou Chun-Ming de mili huanjing" 擁抱執著：侯俊明的迷離幻境 [Embracing perseverance: Hou Chun-Ming's blurred fantasy], *Modern Arts* 115 (2004): 46–55; Mei-ling Shih 石美玲, "Xingtian fuhao bianyan: Taiwan huajia Hou Chun-Ming xifang huafeng shiren" 刑天符號變衍：台灣畫家侯俊明戲仿畫風試論 [Transformation of the symbol of Xing Tian: On Taiwanese artist Hou Chun-Ming's parody style], *Chung Hsing Journal of Humanities* 48 (2012): 187–210.
32. Kai Sheng 盛鎧, "Fansixing zhuti de fansi: Hou Chun-Ming zuopin zhong de zaixian celüe zhutiguan yu shehui pipan" 反思性主體的反思：侯俊明作品中的再現策略、主體觀與社會批判 [Reflection on reflexive subjectivity: The representational strategy, subjective view, and social critic in Chun-Ming Hou's work], *Journal of Art Studies* 7 (2010): 213–250.
33. I borrow the notion of vernacular sexology liberally from Benjamin Kahan, *The Book of Minor Perverts: Sexology, Etiology, and the Emergences of Sexuality* (Chicago: University of Chicago Press, 2019); and Charu Gupta, "Vernacular Sexology from the Margins: A Woman and a Shudra," *South Asia: Journal of South Asian Studies* 43, no. 6 (2020): 1105–1127.
34. Mariano Ben Plotkin, *Freud in the Pampas: The Emergence and Development of a Psychoanalytic Culture in Argentina* (Stanford, CA: Stanford University Press, 2002); Ruben Gallo, *Freud's Mexico: Into the Wilds of Psychoanalysis* (Cambridge, MA: MIT Press, 2010); Eli Zaretsky, *Political Freud: A History* (New York: Columbia University Press, 2015); Dagmar Herzog, *Cold War Freud: Psychoanalysis in an Age of Catastrophe* (Cambridge: Cambridge University Press, 2017); Omnia El Shakry, *The Arabic Freud: Psychoanalysis and Islam in Modern Egypt* (Princeton, NJ: Princeton University Press, 2017); and Howard Chiang, "Translators of the Soul: Bingham Dai, Pow-Meng Yap, and the Making of Transcultural Psychoanalysis in the Asia Pacific," *Psychoanalysis and History* 23, no. 2 (2021): 161–185.

that exposes a modern subject's inner thoughts, volitional desires, and feelings about an interiorized self to the late imperial Chinese leisure/travelogue albums (行樂圖 *Xinletu*) and the ancient compilations of hearsay concerning the supernatural world (搜神記 *Soushenji*).[35] On the other hand, Hou's art is structurally and methodologically underwritten by the principles of psychodynamic therapy originating from fin-di-siècle Europe.[36] Yet the ethnographic focus of *Male Hole* revolves around the marginalized sexual subjects typically overlooked by the mainstream society of post–Martial Law Taiwan.[37] Not only does the queer subalternity of Hou's art subvert the strict protocols of art therapy and *tuina* medicine (Hou's body massages are never intended to be an end in itself but simply a catalyst of transference), but it also resists conforming to the hegemonic scientific principles of humanist psychology (the *Male Hole* sessions do not lay its claim of legitimacy or originality on the methodological standards of behavioral science). Precisely due to its multidirectional legacies and transmedial effects, the Sinoglossiac humanism of Hou's art disrupts any chain of equivalence that works to suture and authorize a global therapeutic governance of the human mind.

Acknowledgments

I wish to thank Hou Chun-Ming for his generosity in providing me with the unpublished pamphlet documenting his work, *Male Hole*, and the relevant textual and visual files associated with his *Body Image* project. I have greatly benefited from dialogues with Chien-hsin Tsai, Andrea Bachner, and Yu-lin Lee on the concept of Sinoglossia. Research for this project was supported by a Research Grant (RG001-A-19) from the Chiang Ching-kuo Foundation for International Scholarly Exchange.

---

35. For an example of the May Fourth "diary" genre dealing with sexual subjectivity, see Tani Barlow and Gary J. Bjorge, eds., *I Myself Am a Woman: Selected Writings of Ding Ling* (Boston, MA: Beacon Press, 1989).
36. See, for example, George Makari, *Revolution in Mind: The Creation of Psychoanalysis* (New York: HarperCollins, 2008).
37. For a recent critical reappraisal, see Howard Chiang and Yin Wang, eds., *Perverse Taiwan* (London: Routledge, 2016); and Howard Chiang, *Transtopia in the Sinophone Pacific* (New York: Columbia University Press, 2021).

3

What Does an Open Body Say?

The Body and the Cold War in the Early 1980s Theater of Taiwan

Chun-yen Wang*

> On the Jingju [京劇] stage, we see that there is nothing that cannot be signified and interpreted by bodily performance. Based on this belief, Li Ang [李昂] and I trained actors to imagine and represent a world using/through their bodies. For what we want is to let them use their bodies more openly and freely.
>
> —Wu Jing-jyi 吳靜吉, *Lanling jufang de chubu shiyan* 蘭陵劇坊的初步實驗[1]

> Wu Jing-jyi is a psychologist, who knows completely how shy and introspective Chinese people are. He thinks that it is not that we do not know how to use our bodies; instead, our bodies are "rotten." It is because we have an oppressive personality. As such, he tried hard to free the actors of their mental obstacles. The body can be released like a cat only through opening one's mind and trusting other people. To be open and trusting is the lube to a rotten body.
>
> —Zhuo Ming 卓明, *Lanling jufang de chubu shiyan* 蘭陵劇坊的初步實驗[2]

---

* An earlier version of this chapter appeared in *Inter-Asia Cultural Studies* 19, issue 4 (December 2018). It has been rewritten to engage the theoretical concept of "Sinoglossia," the theme of this edited volume.
1. Jing-jyi Wu 吳靜吉, ed. *Lanling jufang de chubu shiyan* 蘭陵劇坊的初步實驗 [The first experiment of Lan-ling Theater Workshop] (Taipei: Yuan-liou Publishing, 1982).
2. Ming Zhuo 卓明, "Dang women zaiyiqi: Jieshao Lanling jufang de peitai gengxin shiyan jutuan" 當我們在一起：介紹蘭陵劇坊的胚胎耕莘實驗劇團 [When we are together: An introduction to an experimental embryo troupe Lan-ling Theater Workshop], in *Lanling jufang de chubu shiyan* 蘭陵劇坊的初步實驗 [The first experiment of Lan-ling Theater Workshop], ed. Jing-jyi Wu (Taipei: Yuan-liou Publishing, 1982), 19–26.

In April 1980, the Lan-ling Theater Workshop was founded. Theatre scholar Chung Ming-der hailed this event as the "renaissance of modern Taiwanese theater," which "launched the little theater movement in 1980s Taiwan."[3] The origin and development of many popular theaters in Taiwan today, such as U-Theatre, Performance Workshop, and Godot Theatre, date from this "renaissance" of the 1980s. Concerning this critical formative period in modern Taiwanese theater, scholars Ma Sen and Chung Ming-der offer different interpretations of its indebtedness to "the West" and "the avant-garde." Ma argues that scholars who returned from studying in Europe and North America brought about "the second Western tide"—a renaissance in the drama that gave birth to a new form of Chinese modern theater that distinguished it from the earlier "Pseudo-realist" drama dating from the 1930s.[4] Chung suggests that most of Lan-ling's productions, under Wu's direction, absorbed Western avant-garde theater in toto, both in content and spirit.[5] Both scholars are of the view that the new wave and renaissance of modern Taiwanese theater spearheaded by Lan-ling are inextricable from the impact of "the West."

Situated in contraposition to the West, China or Taiwan can be seen as the enunciating subject of the genealogy of modern theater. The West vs. China/Taiwan exemplifies yet another relationship between modernism and nativism that serves as two factors in the postwar Taiwan cultural production, to take a cue from Chiu Kuei-fen's concept of cultural translation.[6] In other words, the dichotomy provides an epistemology, in the form of Sino or modern, East and West, or native versus foreign, regarding Edward Said's term "contrapuntal discourse,"[7] that articulates and understands Taiwan modern theater practices since Lan-ling. The contrapuntal reading of culture is made possible on the premise of implying that the West cannot be the same as the East while the foreign is different from the native by supposing a cultural authenticity.

The articulation in which East and West or native vs. foreign are recognized formulates a mechanism that provides a way to distinguish the West or Euro-America from Chinese/Taiwanese or the native although it also helps to explain

---

3. Ming-der Chung 鍾明德, *Taiwan xiaojuchang yundongshi 1980–89: Xunzhao linglei meixue yu zhengzhi* 台灣小劇場運動史1980–89：尋找另類美學與政治 [The little theater movement of Taiwan (1980–89): In search of alternative aesthetics and politics] (Taipei: Yang-Chih Book Co., 1999), 32.
4. Sen Ma 馬森, *Zhongguo xiandai xiju de liangdu xichao* 中國現代戲劇的兩度西潮 [The two Western tides in Chinese modern theater] (Taipei: UNITAS Publishing, 2006), 15.
5. Chung, *The Little Theater Movement of Taiwan* [The little theater movement of Taiwan], 40.
6. Kuei-fen Chiu 邱貴芬, "Fanyi qudongli xia de Taiwan wenxue shengchan" 翻譯驅動力下的台灣文學生產 [Taiwanese literary production driven by translation], in *Taiwan xiaoshuo shi lun* 台灣小說史論 [Taiwan literary history], ed. Hu Jin-lun 胡金倫 (Taipei: Rye Field Publishing, 2007), 197–273.
7. Edward. W. Said, *Culture and Imperialism* (London: Vintage, 1993), 64–67.

how Taiwan's modern theater is *influenced*. Yet, it may be also the mechanism that hinders reading Lan-ling's performance from its complexity about body and geopolitics by remaining an authentically cultural or aesthetical imagination. This chapter tries to rearticulate a historical and material relationship between "the West" and Chinese/Taiwan on the one hand and reflects on the contrapuntal reading of modern Taiwan theater on the other.

Said's reflection on and critique of the contrapuntal culture provides me with a materialist reading of Lan-ling's aesthetics. Here what I mean by materiality is to examine culture by paying attention to social processes and concrete historical development during an exchange of signs. Cultural materialism is not simply equated with political, social, or cultural change, or a historicist investigation in the social sciences. Instead, it echoes a Foucauldian discursive reading of power that is formed through knowledge and an analysis of the body as knowledge in which a contested field is constructed. This chapter contributes to the theorization of Sinoglossia, with a special attention on cultural materialism, by examining the complexity of the body in modern Taiwan theater. It emphasizes that the so-called "Sino-body" is a cultural performance materially situated in both the understanding and the problematics of Chinese/Chineseness. Any representation of the body "Sino-," in the codified form of race, nation, culture, or tradition, will be revealed in discursive formation through the lens of a historicized reading.

Lan-ling is often considered a highly successful model of modern Taiwanese theater through the merger of the West and the local. My question is then: Under what historical-material condition and discursive discourse did this merger take place? What kinds of body practices are implicated in the formation of modern Taiwanese theater? To be specific, how do we examine Lan-ling's body performance? Can we locate it in Taiwan's Cold War history? What can we glean from investigating Wu's training in the postwar US avant-garde theater?

Building on the genealogical investigations in the last two chapters, my exploration of Taiwanese theater renders the Sinoglossiac body as a vessel for rekindling and remaking historical meanings for the present. That the politicization of a corporeal form is intimately connected to the ebb and flow of a major stream of Taiwanese art is precisely what is at stake. By using the production "Hezhu xinpei" (literally, "Hezhu's New Match") directed by Chin Shih-chieh as a case study, this chapter attempts to address the historical condition in which Lan-ling performed its experimentations. How do we read Lan-ling's experiment in the name of the "open body" in the discursive context of postwar Taiwan? What bodily prototypes are being performed in the modern Taiwanese theater since the 1980s? How are the problematics of the Sino-body of modern Taiwan theater during the Cold War hidden under the concept and claim of the so-called "openness"? How does the theoretical critique of Sinoglossia, which invokes language as well as corporeality, provide a rearticulation between spoken drama and the Lan-ling experiment?

Lan-ling: A Bodily Turn from Language

At the first experimental theater exhibition in 1980, Lan-ling's artistic director, Wu Jing-jyi, inaugurated the renaissance of modern Taiwanese theater with the introduction of the theater group. Wu obtained his doctoral degree in educational psychology at the University of Minnesota and has taught at Yeshiva University and City College in New York. Between 1968 and 1972, he participated in LaMaMa E.T.C at Off-Off-Broadway and performed in productions such as "Wonton Soup," "Cranes and Peonies," and "Five Flower Ghettos."[8] After returning to Taiwan, he taught in the Department of Psychology at National Chengchi University. Chin Shih-chieh, the leader of Lan-ling, invited Wu to become the supervisor of 耕莘實驗劇團 T'ien Experimental Drama Club, which later became Lan-ling. Li Ang, who got her MA degree in drama and theater from the University of Oregon, co-supervised Lan-ling in directing and acting. Before the group's debut in 1980, Wu developed stage performance techniques to train the actors, particularly with a focus on the body and voice, for two years. For instance, he asked every actor to feel his voice, body, and emotion by opening himself and trusting others. Li Ang, also introduced drama and theater theories, for example, epic theatre and Jingju, collective improvisation.[9] Wu concludes his training during the period by offering "three techniques, four directions, and five categories" (Table 3.1).

The doctrines of the "three techniques, four directions, and five categories" seem to confirm what Chung concludes: we find no exclusive advocacy or theory. "All members aim for no specific goal except being open, open to oneself and all theater art, knowledge, and training."[10] Nevertheless, I posit three particular theses regarding the doctrines of Lan-ling. The first concerns a contrapuntal reading of theater art and aesthetics in the form of East and West or native versus foreign. Secondly, experimental theater is the theater that Lan-ling pursues, and openness is the core. Thirdly, Lan-ling's performance is both an individual and a collective practice.

I will examine these three theses through the lens of cultural materialism, historicizing Lan-ling about postwar American avant-garde theater amid the global Cold War. The main question I hope to address is: Is it possible that the openness/open body is itself a discourse under certain historical and material

---

8. Chung, *The Little Theater Movement of Taiwan*, 36.
9. Chung, *The Little Theater Movement of Taiwan*, 37.
10. Chung, *The Little Theater Movement of Taiwan*, 39.

Table 3.1: Three techniques, four directions, and five categories of Wu Jing-jyi's training

Three techniques	1. the artistic achievement and development in the East and the West
	2. knowledge of the Chinese performance tradition
	3. knowledge of the development and experimentation of experimental theater
Four directions	1. to fill everyone with a sense of creative passion, ability, and achievement
	2. to see every performance as a collective production, where each member contributes his or her intellect and ideas
	3. to incorporate life experience and stage language of all traditions, Chinese or foreign, in the theater creation
	4. to learn from scholars of modern theater and experts in related fields
Five categories	1. regular training
	2. improvisational material
	3. knowledge of traditional Chinese theater
	4. observation and participation of relevant art
	5. experience of the everyday life

conditions? In other words, to be open is itself a position and statement. As such, Lan-ling's case should not be seen as exclusive but merely as a starting point to reexamine modern Taiwanese theater.

Lan-ling changed the tradition of modern Taiwanese theater, which had been dominated by spoken drama since the Kuomintang's retreat to Taiwan in 1949. From the name "spoken drama" we know that language matters in this performance genre, which contrasts itself with traditional Chinese theater, *xiqu*, in which songs, lyrics, and dance serve as the core aesthetics. Strictly speaking, spoken drama stands in opposition to *xiqu*, which was considered a decadent and obsolete form of theatrical art during the late Qing period, when China was undergoing domestic and international turmoil. For the late Qing Chinese intellectuals, *xiqu* needed to be reformed and modernized. By contrast, since its inception during the drama reformation, modern Chinese theater relies heavily on speech. To put it differently, we can say that a performance that features speaking is regarded as modern while that with singing and dancing is traditional. Not until Lan-ling advocated an alternative aesthetic—coined "experimental theater"—did spoken drama lose its "modern" position in Taiwanese theater.

Body Performance in *Hezhu xinpei*

Wu's training focuses on an open body by eradicating the use of language in performance. According to Wu, his training regime consists of the following:

> Twice a week the actors train with me. My preparatory and warm-up activities include relaxing and massaging exercises for actors who hold full-time jobs during the day. By releasing their anxiety and fatigue I hope to free their imagination. Bodily movements are rarely used in our traditional spoken drama. It is not that we *cannot*, but we have hardly tried and never experimented. On the Jingju stage, there is nothing that **cannot** be interpreted using the body. Based on this belief, Li Ang and I trained actors to imagine and represent a world by using / through their bodies. To free up their bodies, we developed many warm-up exercises before class, for instance imitating animals or plants, imagining lifeless objects such as tables and chairs via human emotions, and incorporating and stimulating the inner voice and movements.[11] [emphasis added]

As can be seen, Wu emphasizes corporeal training, which spoken drama lacks, paying particular attention to openness and freedom as the basis of an imaginative world in performing. In other words, the development of the body with an emphasis on being open and free is Lan-ling's aesthetical principle.

The aesthetical principles were implemented in the production of *Hezhu xinpei*, which later won Lan-ling's great reputation in the renaissance of modern Taiwanese theater. Although *Hezhu xinpei* was only one of many plays on the list of the first experimental theater exhibition in July 1980, it won critical appraisal from theater scholars and intellectuals alike, on top of being in demand to stage extra performances by the major newspaper, *United News*. In the following year, it toured all the major cities in Taiwan in addition to being invited to perform in Singapore.[12]

Hezhu xinpei is a comedy adapted from the Jingju *Hezhupei*. Most critics, artists, performers, scholars, and researchers tend to regard *Hezhu xinpei* as a work of modern drama that pays tribute to Jingju and hence is a rebirth of traditional Chinese heritage. This interpretation also signifies identity recognition by showing how Chinese drama is modernized. In other words, *Hezhu xinpei* was seen as a perfect combination of modernity and nationality, progression and tradition.

Deriving from *Hezhupei*, a comedy of role and identity reversal, *Hezhu xinpei* also implicitly touches upon an identity crisis issue. Hezhu, who by accident finds that the missing daughter "Jinfeng" of President Qi Zixiao is her age, reunites with her father by pretending to be the daughter. Yet, Qi's family

---

11. Wu, *The First Experiment of Lan-Ling Theater Workshop*, 6–7.
12. Chung, *The Little Theater Movement of Taiwan*, 50–63.

manager, Zhao Wang, later sees her real identity. An important conversation between Zhao Wang and Hezhu with regard to the question of how to be oneself ensues:

Hezhu:	Ugh . . . do people's names belong to themselves?
Zhao Wang:	Of course, people's names are theirs.
Hezhu:	My previous name "Hezhu" is given by others. I don't like it. "Jinfeng" is a name I give to myself, and I like it. Tell me, am I doing anything wrong?
Zhao Wang:	Well . . . you are right, and I am wrong. But I am warning you that your identity as Qi's daughter in disguise is under my control. If I want to keep your identity, you will. If I don't want to, you will not.

This conversation brings up a critical issue of identity: Can a person determine who she or he wants to be? Can Hezhu be Jinfeng at her own will? Here, the implication seems to be that whether Hezhu can be "herself" depends on others' recognition when all the roles are interconnected. This implication is a good metaphor for how Lan-ling seeks its own identity as modern Chinese/Taiwanese theater. While Lan-ling takes for granted its adaptation of the Jingju *Hezhupei* into a modern drama, *Hezhu xinpei*, how a piece comes to be accepted as modern is never easy and without the recognition of modernity. In other words, modernity plays a crucial role in Lan-ling's theater praxis. Wu's training of "opening the body," which is derived from American avant-garde theater, happened to play a key role in assisting Lan-ling in its quest for modernity.

After *Hezhu xipei*'s debut, theater scholars started to focus on Lan-ling's body experiment. For example, in his essay "The Past and the Future of Spoken Drama: From *Hezhu xinpei* Onwards," Ma Sen mentions that a seasoned actor knows full well how to perform with his body and Lan-ling has since established an ideal regimental model for actor training, particularly in the aspect of muscle control and emotional governance.[13] Essayist Lin Ching-hsuan also notices the significance of the performance and points out that "Liu Ching-min, playing the role of Hezhu, Li Tien-zu, the role of Laobao, Lee Kuo-hsiu, the role of Zhao Wang, all of whom are tremendously talented and have reached their acting potentials." Critic Yin Shi-ying finds that the actors' performance was relaxed and smooth and attributes "their success to be based on hard work and advanced preparation."[14] Wang Hsi-lian appraises the performance by saying that "audiences burst into laughter as soon as the actors enter the stage. Zhao Wang impresses me most with his walking in a small suit. He is so hilarious

---

13. Wu, *The First Experiment of Lan-Ling Theater Workshop*, 99.
14. Wu, *The first experiment of Lan-ling Theater Workshop*, 142.

when ridiculing Jingju's gestures with a mysterious expression on his face.... Li Tien-zu in the role of Laobao is funny, too. It's a typical comedic cross-dressing role in Jingju. This is exaggerated acting that satisfies the audiences' needs."[15]

In my viewing of the VHS recording of *Hezhu xinpei*, Hezhu's and Zhao Wang's performances provide a good example of how the open body merges with "traditional" gestures. The acting is successful in its naturalized movements imitating a "modern" person by inserting easily recognizable Jingju gestures. The bodily movements' seeming naturalness also embodies a sense of reality and modernity. As Chung suggests, "Derived from Jingju, *Hezhu xinpei* is a play that demonstrates innovation in which the contemporary Taipei people's bodies, voices, and senses are intermingled with traditional Jingju acting."[16] The temporality and spatiality of contemporary Taipei, which *Hezhu xinpei* embodies, arouses a connection with both actors and audiences. For them, theatricality of the play provides all participants whose identities are interpellated with the feeling that "I/my body will be the same if I am on the stage." It is the creation of the theatricality, instead of codes or signs of Jingju, that calls for commonality and a sense of connection.

The *Hezhu xinpei* performance emphasizes freedom and openness in the actors' bodies, which allows the characters they portray to achieve a high sense of reality. Lan-ling's other productions, "Xuansiren" [A Puppet Person] and "Maode tiantang" [A Cat's Paradise] are two such examples. The former is a silent play where all the actors perform the role of puppets. The latter is a story of cats, and all the actors are cats on stage. No matter what roles they play—animals, puppets, or human beings—the actors feel and employ their bodies as the characters' bodies; there are no differences between the two.

Why Do Open Bodies Matter? Free Camp and Geopolitics in the Cold War

How can we read the open body via the lens of cultural materialism? What does the open body have to do with historicity in postwar Taiwan and the increasingly neoliberal world? The open body seems to denote apolitical and ahistorical neutrality by opening the body to welcome any sort of theory and aesthetics. Scholars tend to argue that Lan-ling is a group of formalism, which is only concerned with acting styles instead of touching upon critical, ideological, and political agendas,

---

15. Xi-liang Wang 王錫蓮, "Hezhu xinpei" 荷珠新配 [Hezhu's New Match], in *Lanling jufang de chubu shiyan* 蘭陵劇坊的初步實驗 [The first experiment of Lan-ling Theater Workshop], ed. Jing-jyi Wu 吳靜吉 (Taipei: Yuan-liou Publishing, 1982), 135.
16. Chung, *The Little Theater Movement of Taiwan*, 86.

which some would argue accounts for its popularity among the middle-class.[17] Yet, my intervention here is to question if Lan-ling is indeed apolitical and ahistorical. On the contrary, I argue that Lan-ling is political and historical and is particularly connected with Taiwan's development within the postwar Free Camp in the Cold War. As critic Wang Mo-lin suggests, "If ideology is metaphysical, then bodily movements are a materialistic representation of ideology."[18] In my reading, Lan-ling too is ideologically motivated in its welcoming of an open body. As is the case with spoken drama in displacing *xiqu* in its pursuit of Chinese drama modernization, Lan-ling embraces a free and open body through its claim to modernity in Cold War Taiwan. In the postwar period, democracy for Taiwan is represented and defined by the US while Taiwan sees itself as a member of the democratic campaign in the Free World. The US-led postwar modernization theory during the Cold War is particularly welcome among East Asian nations and states—Japan, South Korea, Hong Kong, Singapore, and so on—and Taiwan is no exception.

When World War II concluded, the onset of the Cold War played an instrumental role in reshaping the world order. At the end of 1949, the Chinese Communist Party took over China, and the government of the Republic of China (ROC) retreated to Taiwan. To prevent Communism from further expansion, the ROC and the US governments signed the Military Assistance Agreement that shaped the Cold War in East Asia. The US sent the Seventh Fleet to protect the ROC from Communism at the outbreak of the Korean War while assigning the Military Assistance Advisory Group (MAAG) to upgrade the ROC's military strength in 1951. Scholar Shan Te-hsing, in his discussion of Taiwan literary translation during the Cold War, argues that in addition to an arms race the US and the USSR were competing over ideology and culture: "The US was trying hard to make itself the leader of the Free World, the frontier of democracy, and the leader of the knowledge production."[19] Shan examines the Cold War through the perspective of culture politics by analyzing magazines and books that advocate scientific knowledge, political thought, social and intellectual beliefs, as well as literature and art. These reading materials connect with/influence our everyday life in subtle and popular ways. As such, East Asia was positioned as an area where knowledge needs to be modernized by accepting advanced values of democracy, freedom, law, and science imported from advanced countries, in

---

17. Wei-jan Chi 紀蔚然, "Tansuo yu guibi zhijian: Dangdai Taiwan xiaojuchang de xiexu fengmao" 探索與規避之間：當代台灣小劇場的些許風貌 [Between exploration and evasion: On recent developments of Taiwan's little theater], *Chung wai literary quarterly* 中外文學 31, no. 6 (2002): 44.
18. Mo-lin Wang 王墨林, *Dushi juchang yu shenti* 都市劇場與身體 [Urban theater and the body] (Taipei: Dao-xiang Publishing, 1992), 55.
19. Te-hsing Shan 單德興, *Fanyi yu mailuo* 翻譯與脈絡 [Translations and contexts] (Taipei: Bookman Books, 2013), 120–121.

particular, the US. Critically speaking, it is due to the Cold War that established US democracy, freedom, law, and science as important values for the ROC, which henceforth defined the power/knowledge relation between Taiwan and the US. Thus the discursive formation of modernity in the Cold War perpetually upheld the US as an advanced model of learning by Taiwan. Chiu also talks about how US aid ideologically had an impact on postwar Taiwanese literature by equating Westernization with modernization, that is, Americanization.[20] Petrus Liu's critical reading of East Asia and Free China (Taiwan) about liberalism under the Cold War further accentuates this point. He argues that the miraculous economic performance and industrial development of the Asian Tigers during the period secured the East Asian firewall led by the US by being the exemplary model to prove that "the newly industrialized countries of Asia, unlike most countries in South-east Asia, Latin America, and Africa, have somehow escaped the laws of colonial underdevelopment, which in turn shows that the real cause of poverty in the third world is not the history of Western imperialism, but the economically backward countries' lack of willingness to modernize." In other words, as long as the newly industrialized Asian countries are willing to adopt democracy and market capitalism, like the ROC, they will become modern societies. Liu's critical insight points out that East Asia during the Cold War was set "to deny that racism and colonialism have any lasting effects on those determined to succeed."[21]

Open to Modernity: American Avant-Garde Theater and Taiwan

Tracking Wu Jing-jyi's theater experience in New York, I find that LaMaMa Experimental Theatre Club was part of a series of avant-garde and alternative theaters in postwar America, such as the Open Theatre, the Living Theatre, and the Performance Group. Contemporary American avant-garde playwrights, directors, and actors, such as Sam Shepard, Lanford Wilson, Philip Glass, Robert Wilson, Harvey Fierstein, Blue Man Group, and David and Amy Sedaris, for instance, were participants in LaMaMa.[22] These theater groups break away from realism, challenge the "playwright-actor-director" hierarchy as well as subvert the "performer-spectator" relationship by working collectively with an ensemble. Action, movements, and rituals, instead of the text, serve as the core of the performance. Performance, politics, and social issues are highly interconnected.[23]

---

20. Chiu, *Taiwan Literary History*, 208.
21. Petrus Liu, *Queer Marxism in Two Chinas* (Durham, NC: Duke University Press, 2015), 114–115.
22. LaMaMa, "Mission+History" (2008), *LaMaMa*, http://lamama.org/about/mission-history/.
23. Martin Banham, *The Cambridge Guide to Theatre* (Cambridge: Cambridge University Press, 2000), 364–366.

Art is not separate from life.²⁴ In short, the theaters proclaim an intertwined relationship between life and society by deconstructing rules and authority.

The 1960s New Left and Counter Culture during the Cold War provided the theaters with important resources and ideas. The Students for a Democratic Society (SDS), a New Leftist activist group, for instance, fought against a government under the control of capitalist and military groups, as well as world economics that was manipulated by America's anti-communist policy. Instead, it advocated a kind of economic socialism to equally distribute property and resources by supporting local communities and common people while advocating that the US should stop intervening in other counties.²⁵ Participatory democracy echoed/promoted during the Counter Culture is found in the theaters where all members work with equality. The avant-garde and alternative theaters push for "power to the people" and stress the equality between art and other communities. They reject playwrights who have been placed on the pedestal as gods of creation.²⁶

Openness is significant in postwar American theater. Theater should be open to art creativity, collectivity, people, politics, and society. Theater establishes democracy by restoring people's power. The concept and proclamation of openness are made ideally as a collective practice where individuals participate. The civil rights movement in the 1960s is an example describing the relationship between the collective and the individual. All individuals are managed as part of the collective according to their nature. An absolute relationship between the individual and the collective is thus reinforced. Let me try to differentiate between two relationships, the individual and the collective. The former is a relationship that relies on a materialist and socialist principle. The individual must be a part of the collection due to certain economic and social conditions. Laborers belong to the first relationship, which is mandatory according to socialism. A collective identity emerges with the laborers' materiality. The latter is a relationship that relies on human nature, such as nationality or ethnicity. For example, anyone with Black ancestry belongs to the Black community. The latter is different from the former, for the former is in lacking reconfirmation of materiality and may be ignorant of complicated social and historical change. It is the second, not the first, that plays a significant role in the Cold War in East Asia while the concept of openness is being introduced to Taiwan.

The avant-garde theater's openness derived from the Counter Culture and New Left signifies a different denotation across the Pacific Ocean. While Taiwan

---

24. Theodore Shank, *American Alternative Theatre* (London: Macmillan, 1982), 93.
25. Judith Ellen Rieser, "The American Avant-Garde Ensemble Theaters of the Sixties in the Historical and Cultural Context" (PhD diss., Northwestern University, 1982), 35–36.
26. Rieser, "The American Avant-Garde," 122–124.

was under martial law (1949–1987), all activities of socialist intent were prohibited. The openness is transformed as a representation of American modernity in correspondence with the ROC and the US regimes in the name of the Free World. That is to say that a modern theater has to be an open theater. The American open theater once again contrasts itself with Chinese (and) spoken drama—which is yet to be modern in the eyes of modernization. The idea of openness in favor of action and practice ironically represents the regime of civilizational difference in Cold War Taiwan.

Know Yourself and Develop Yourself: Epistemology of Area Studies and Sinoglossia as Critique

If modernization theory provides a disposit of temporality in which the US is leading the Free Camp during the Cold War, then area studies is a spatial mapping of the world that is explained by the US. From its name, area studies seemingly aims to provide local knowledge in understanding various cultures and customs, for example, East Asian studies, Southeast Asian studies, or Africana studies. Yet, there is no denying that the genesis of area studies is a result of American geopolitical arrangement during the Cold War.[27] To take East Asia as an example, when area studies corresponds to the Containment Policy—which was best known as the Cold War policy to contain the spread of communism by the US and its allies—the US government and NGOs, be it directly or indirectly, provided much funding and resources to encourage extensive research in the same area. For example, because Japan and South Korea were allies of the Free World while China and North Korea were treated as enemies, research on the former focuses on modernization theory and the latter on communism.[28]

Besides conspiring with US diplomatic policy, area studies idealizes, and thus essentializes and simplifies, history and culture. Ban Wang argues that area studies either idealizes a long tradition of Chinese cultural heritage or mostly contains narrative accounts of harrowing experiences of living in contemporary.[29] Take Chinese studies as an example:

> This paradigm is the modernization discourse or the tradition versus modernity approach. It posits Chinese culture as being devoid of real history and stuck in its timeless, immutable tradition until it was jolted out of its age-old sleep by the impact of the imperialist West. It defines modern changes in China by how

---

27. Bruce Cumings, "Boundary Displacement: Area Studies and International Studies during and after the Cold War," *Bulletin of Concerned Asian Scholars* 29, no. 1 (1997): 6–26.
28. Cumings, "Boundary Displacement," 8.
29. Ban Wang, "The Cold War, Imperial Aesthetics, and Area Studies," *Social Text* 20, no. 3 (2002): 45.

well or miserably the Chinese can make the grade in catching up with the West in economic modernization.[30]

Wang's observation may well apply to how openness defines modernity in postwar Taiwan theater, and in particular the Lan-ling theater renaissance. The representation of modernity is an anxiety discourse in which the national culture desires to become modern. This self-conscious need to modernize is symptomatic of Lan-ling's desire for a modern Chinese theater: a theater that is *both* Chinese *and* modern.

In addition to modernization theory and area studies that contextualize Lan-ling's openness in a material sense, I find that the quest for cultural self-representation is reinforced by the connection between the individual and the collective. As mentioned, nationality can be seen as a relationship between the individual and the collective void of materiality. The Lan-ling experiment is one such example that explains how each actor (re)turns to a national imagination while seeking an open body on stage by representing a modern Chinese theater. The doctrine of three genres, four directions, and five categories serves as an example as far as China/Chinese is concerned. A kind of New Leftist social and political practice thus turns out to be a quest for modernity in national culture during the Cold War. Despite the fact that artistic director Wu says, "Don't think about performance. All you have to do is develop yourself and express yourself at will,"[31] the "self" is never free and open, even though it is meant to be so. Instead, the self is a collective representation, usually nationality, as Naoki Sakai reminds us.[32]

The Cold War is a restarting point to reconsider/reevaluate Lan-ling's significance. During the Cold War, Taiwan in the name of Free China, along with Japan, South Korea, and East and Southeast Asia, all belonged to the US-led Western bloc that opposes the communist Eastern Bloc. Seen from this cultural materialist perspective, Taiwan and the US underwent a similar historical moment during the Cold War. This chapter has contextualized Lan-ling in the cultural-materialist condition in lieu of cultural essentialism that predetermines the national body. In other words, I posit that we need to discard reading Lan-ling from a "native versus foreign," "Sino versus modern" or "East versus West" dichotomy while repositioning the group about Taiwan and the world in the postwar period. By examining what lies in Lan-ling's doctrine and training about the West, this chapter hopes to unveil some of the key origins of Lan-ling's open body discourse.

---

30. Wang, "The Cold War, Imperial Aesthetics, and Area Studies," 57.
31. Wu, *The First Experiment of Lan-Ling Theatre Workshop*, 28.
32. Naoki Sakai, *Translation and Subjectivity: On "Japan" and Cultural Nationalism* (Minneapolis: University of Minnesota Press, 1997), 14.

Since *Hezhu xinpei* stemmed from the Jingju *Hezhupei*, it has both inherited elements of traditional Jingju drama and presented a new contemporary Taiwanese drama with its open mind and body.[33] The tremendous success of the play ignited much social attention that prompted the press *United News* to hold a forum titled "The Future of Chinese Experiment Theatre" to further discuss the phenomenon. Forum participants included actors, directors, scholars, and intellectuals, who expressed an interest in how *Hezhu xinpei* is a modern response to traditional Jingju and who were keen on learning more about Chinese theater, traditional culture, and acting.[34] Jingju has been engaged as a signifier of the experiment of modern Chinese theater since the late Qing, indicating that any trials on the modernization of Chinese theater and performance are imagined within the limited understanding of race and nationality. It is also to say that any national image of the theater of the future is racial.

Yet, this chapter argues that the cultural politics that Lan-ling embodied may be overlooked if we only pay attention to aspects of tradition and modernity or the cultural renaissance that the troupe brought about. By examining the historical and material conditions in which the troupe derived its acting concepts, this chapter has probed the discursive formation of "the open body" in the context of Cold War Taiwan, which differentiates it from spoken drama.

As far as this chapter is concerned, the examination of the "openness" challenges the authenticity and authority of Jingju adopted in the modern Chinese/Taiwan theater. Furthermore, it provides an intervening and interrupting reading of the complexity of the connotations and denotations of the "Sino-" and the Sinoglossiac body. Any cultural representation of the so-called Chinese performance or body tells a complicated story well beyond the imagination in the engagement of historicity and materiality.

For artistic director Wu Jing-jyi, Lan-ling's open body is a practice brought about by postwar American avant-garde theater. By viewing through the lens of cultural materialism, this chapter reexamines how Lan-ling is positioned in the historicity of the Cold War and how it gave rise to the open body, which is different from that of American avant-garde theater. Failure to contextualize Lan-ling in postwar Taiwan's cultural-political discourse may therefore reinforce a conspiracy that area studies has created hand in hand with liberalism in the name of freedom and democracy. It may further hinder us from examining how the open body discourse, by representing modernity, formulates modern Taiwanese drama along with the epistemology of area studies. In this regard, the exploration of a modern Chinese/Taiwanese body is yet to be finished even though Lan-ling has supposedly parted from spoken drama and its immature acting.

---

33. Wu, *The First Experiment of Lan-Ling Theatre Workshop*, 261.
34. Wu, *The First Experiment of Lan-Ling Theatre Workshop*, 237–267.

Unpacking Lan-ling with a critical reading of Cold War modernity provides a more robust reappraisal of contemporary Taiwanese theater since the 1980s and its corporeal imagination.

Part II

Media

4
Landscape of Words
Romance on Lushan Mountain *(1980) and Sinoglossia as Delimitation*

Paola Iovene*

> Viewed horizontally a range; a cliff from the side,
> It differs as we move high or low, or far or nearby.
> We do not know the true face of Mount Lu,
> Because we are all ourselves inside.
> —Su Shi, "Written on the Wall of the Temple of West Woods"[1]

"The term 'Chinese' is ambiguous and contentious for both conceptual and political reasons, and the meaning of Chineseness has been hotly debated within the field of Chinese cultural studies for decades." Thus writes Song Hwee Lim, in an essay that rethinks, once more, the signifier "Chinese" and along with it the framework of national cinema.[2] Indeed, reconsidering Chineseness within cinema studies means to join a plethora of scholars who have come up with alternatives to the national cinema model, for Chineseness, Chinese identity, and Chinese nation appear interchangeable whenever they are under question. It is by now a truism that China is not some unchanging national essence one might find reflected in a movie but rather an image that is "contested and construed in different ways."[3] Cinema was a transnational formation from the start,

---

* I am grateful to everyone who offered comments on previous versions of this chapter, including Andrea Bachner, Kristine Harris, William Carrol, Pao-chen Tang, Panpan Yang, and Zhiyan Yang. Many thanks to Lilian Kong for her prompt help with images.
1. As translated in Zhang Longxi, "The True Face of Mount Lu: On the Significance of Perspectives and Paradigms," *History and Theory* 49, no. 1 (Feb. 2010): 58–70.
2. Song Hwee Lim, "Six Chinese Cinemas in Search of a Historiography," in *The Chinese Cinema Book*, ed. Song Hwee Lim and Julian Ward (London: Palgrave MacMillan on behalf of the British Film Institute, 2011), 35.
3. Chris Berry and Mary Farquhar, *China on Screen: Cinema and Nation* (New York: Columbia University Press, 2006), 14, quoted in Song, "Six Chinese Cinemas," 35.

emerging from intersections between localities and flows occurring across, as well as within, the geopolitical boundaries of nation-states.[4] Many have argued that the nation is by no means the only or even most relevant framework for the study of cinema, especially when approaching Taiwan or Hong Kong films, contemporary transnational productions, or the works of authors who might have a Chinese name but whose life experiences attaches them simultaneously to different languages and locations.

Why, then, does the nation persist? Lim's chapter outlines six approaches to Chinese cinemas that have emerged from book-length publications over the last twenty years. He points out that, in spite of stated goals, the nation continues to function as the "organizing principle" in four of them.[5] The fifth and sixth models he discusses, "diasporic cinema" and "Sinophone cinema," explicitly challenge the national cinema model but in his view hardly go far enough. Lim finds "diasporic cinema" problematic because "it is essentially China-centric and assumes that Chinese migrants and their descendants necessarily possess a relationship with China,"[6] and criticizes the Sinophone because

> [it] does not so much decenter the China-centrism that [Shu-mei Shih] challenges; rather it replaces one form of essentialism with another. For what is the 'Sino-' in the Sinophone? In Shih's construction, the Sinophone is defined 'not by the race or nationality of the speaker but by the languages one speaks', but isn't this lingua centrism itself a form of essentialism that denies access to one's cultural production and cultural identity via a language that is presumably not one's own?[7]

Drawing on Deleuze and Guattari's concept of minor literature, Lim proposes a "minor Chinese film historiography that can account for films made in

---

4. On transnational approaches to Chinese cinema, see, for instance, Sheldon Hsiao-peng Lu, *Transnational Chinese Cinemas: Identity, Nationhood, Gender*, ed. Sheldon Hsiao-peng Lu (Honolulu: University of Hawai'i Press, 1997); Yingjin Zhang, "Chinese Cinema and Transnational Film Studies," in *World Cinemas, Transnational Perspectives*, ed. Nataša Durovicová and Kathleen E. Newman (New York: Routledge, 2010), 123–136; Yingjin Zhang, *Cinema, Space, and Polylocality in a Globalizing China* (Honolulu: University of Hawai'i Press, 2010); and Jeremy Taylor, *Rethinking Transnational Chinese Cinemas: The Amoy-Dialect Film Industry in Cold War Asia* (London: Routledge, 2013).
5. See also Sheldon H. Lu, "Genealogies of Four Critical Paradigms in Chinese-Language Film Studies," in *Sinophone Cinemas*, ed. Audrey Yue and Olivia Khoo (London: Palgrave Macmillan, 2014), 13–25.
6. Lim, "Six Chinese Cinemas," 37.
7. Lim, "Six Chinese Cinemas," 38. The Sinophone, however, is a more contested and heterogeneous concept than Lim makes it out to be. See, for instance, Shu-Mei Shih, *Visuality and Identity: Sinophone Articulations Across the Pacific* (Berkeley: University of California Press, 2007); Jing Tsu and David Der-wei Wang, eds., *Chinese Global Literature: Critical Essays* (Leiden: Brill, 2010); Audrey Yue and Olivia Khoo, eds., *Sinophone Cinemas* (London: Palgrave Macmillan, 2014); and Shu-mei Shih, Chien-hsin Tsai, and Brian Bernards, eds., *Sinophone Studies: A Critical Reader* (New York: Columbia University Press, 2013).

any corner of the world that challenge the concept of Chinese-language cinema and that refuses to privilege national identities."[8] Lim's invitation is twofold: first, to definitely disconnect the "minor Chinese" from any specific locality and accent and make it the realm of the hybrid and the impure; and second, to foreground cinema's role as a polyphonic medium that gives voice to alternative sexual and gender identities and subaltern or displaced subjects who lack a stable sense of belonging. His critique represents a compelling effort to dislodge the national framework in Chinese cinema studies. And yet, Chineseness is still in some ways there at its center, perhaps inevitably, for the value of a minor Chinese film historiography is that it gives voice to what is ultimately a certain Chinese condition, or an aspect of Chinese culture, however unmoored from stable signifiers and modes of identification. This assumption justifies the very effort of coming up with such a historiography—what makes the "minor" relevant is that it complicates what it is to be Chinese. Paradoxically, it seems that every questioning of Chineseness also gives it new life. Changing the *objects* to which the term refers, opening up Chineseness to encompass a variety of hybrid expressions is a welcome but ultimately insufficient move, for hybridity and marginality per se do not "guarantee the effectivity of any cultural practice or determine in any final sense its aesthetic value."[9]

The field of Chinese cinema and media studies has, meanwhile, seen the flourishing of a variety of approaches, and much innovative work has been done by bracketing Chineseness in favor of historical and theoretical inquiries into the medium of cinema.[10] And yet, many debates still revolve around identity, which might indicate that these issues continue to matter. The question of Chineseness continues to be taken up mostly in efforts to engage media ecologies that cut across and confound the boundaries of diverse ethnicities, territories, languages, and media, and that stand in complex relation with centers of political power. As the field seems to be decentering cinema to encompass a wider range of media practices, such terms as "Sinophone" and "Sinoglossia" help make space for heretofore marginalized communities and representations, for which neither the

---

8. Lim, "Six Chinese Cinemas," 40. Lim's proposal of a minor cinema also echoes an early article by Tom Gunning even though Gunning's concept of the minor refers to the emergence of a new avant-garde that self-consciously engages mainstream forms of cinema rather than to the shaping of alternative identities. Tom Gunning, "Towards a Minor Cinema: Fonoroff, Herwitz, Ahwesh, Klahr and Solomon," *Motion Picture* 3 no. 1/2 (Winter 1989–90): 2–5.
9. Here I am borrowing Stuart Hall's words on blackness. See Stuart Hall, "Race—The Sliding Signifier," in Stuart Hall, *The Fateful Triangle. Race, Ethnicity, Nation* (Cambridge, MA: Harvard University Press, 2017), 76–77.
10. For instance, Weihong Bao, *Fiery Cinema: The Emergence of an Affective Medium in China, 1915–1945* (Minneapolis: University of Minnesota Press, 2015); Victor Fan, *Cinema Approaching Reality: Locating Chinese Film Theory* (Minneapolis: University of Minnesota Press, 2015); and Jason McGrath, *Chinese Film: Realism and Convention from the Silent Era to the Digital Age* (Minneapolis: University of Minnesota Press, 2022).

connection with mainland China nor dominant notions of Chinese ethnicity, race, or culture play a determinant role.

Nonetheless, despite many thought-provoking propositions, any attempt at broader inclusion also risks reifying the concept of identity over again. Rather than pushing for broader inclusion, this chapter proposes that it is the very relationship between mediation and identity formation that ought to be rethought. I realize this is nothing new. This is indeed a direction already alluded to at the end of Lim's essay, when he invites us to see cinema as an "artifice," as a process of image-construction "made possible by a certain conjunction of economy and capital . . . rather than . . . as merely providing *representations* of the nation and its multiple subjects."[11] But my contention is that if we take seriously the notion that cinema is a collaborative process of producing images that do not preexist the film in the form in which they are delivered, the debates contrasting national, diasporic, and Sinophone lose some of their edge. Even a controversial term such as "diasporic" might actually make sense, allowing us to put into dialogue a variety of films made at different locations. Not because Chinese migrants and their descendants are innately fixated on China but rather because certain films mediate China in a way that performs such fixation, independently of who made them and where. The film I examine in this chapter, *Romance on Lushan Mountain* (廬山戀 *Lushan Lian*), could be called diasporic because it aims to elicit a diasporic attachment in audiences, even if it was produced by the Shanghai Film Studio and therefore does not originate in an actual diasporic condition.[12] In this vein, I engage the term Sinoglossia not to replace or debunk previous terms but to help rethink what is "Sino-," building on the premise that such terms as "Sino-," "nation," and "diaspora" are images that are constantly remediated.

What Is the Sino- in Sinoglossia?

I have qualms about the term "Sinoglossia" as a catchall to be applied to a variety of processes of mediation: the suffix "glossia," after all, means tongue or language, and there is a gap between language and mediation—unless we take glossia to mean whatever we want it to mean. Sinoglossia echoes Bakhtin's notion of heteroglossia, which, in Stuart Hall's rendering, means "the culture of

---

11. Lim, "Six Chinese Cinemas," 41. Emphasis added. Lim draws on Rey Chow, "A Phantom Discipline," *PMLA* 116, no. 5 (Oct. 2001): 1393.
12. *Romance on Lushan Mountain* anticipates the theme of return to the mainland, explored in films of the Chinese diaspora such as Peter Wang's *A Great Wall* (1986). See Gina Marchetti, "Cinemas of the Chinese Diaspora," in *The Chinese Cinema Book*, 26–34. For an argument on the relevance of the category of diasporic cinema, see Felicia Chan and Andy Willis, "British Chinese Short Films: Challenging the Limits of the Sinophone," in *Sinophone Cinemas*, 169–184.

many intersecting languages, the cultural politics of which creatively exploits the multiaccentuality of meaning and the carnivalesque properties of enunciation."[13] There is, in the notion of heteroglossia as well as in Sinoglossia, a faith in the subversive potentials of creolized and hybridizing tendencies—a trust in the destabilizing power of non-conformist expressive forms, which does not sufficiently account for the mechanisms that keep neutralizing and appropriating them.

Moreover, any neologism risks reifying previous terms (in this case, Sinophone), reducing and overly simplifying their richness and heterogeneity. One way to work with Sinoglossia, nonetheless, might be that of considering it as an elastic term foregrounding the contradictory effects of mediation, in turn understood as a process that both subjects meanings to closure and opens them up for rearticulation. In other words, I suggest that we take Sinoglossia as an approach to the "Sino-" that considers both differentiation and fixing as complementary poles in the process of mediation.[14] While "glossia" evokes plurality of languages and centrifugal fragmentation, "Sino-" forces us to consider what it is that gets defined as Chinese at different historical moments, reminding us of the centripetal movement of national identification and of the aesthetics and technologies of subjectification that keep it going. In the remaining part of this chapter, I examine such a dialectics of differentiation and fixing in *Romance on Lushan Mountain*, an extremely popular movie released in 1980. In my analysis, which revolves around landscape, weather, and the use of the Chinese script in the film, I take Sinoglossia as an opportunity to examine the "historical forms of knowledge"[15] that make some elements legible as Chinese, and the material conditions and legacies that shape their performance and intelligibility. What this chapter sets out to investigate, then, are the ways in which Lushan, considered as a largely foreign place in the nineteenth century, is remade into a recognizable icon of China. I am interested in Lushan's relations with cinema and in the histories of its mediation: in "how cinema gets embedded in, attached to, particular places," and in how various processes of mediation "transform both place and cinema, binding each to each in contingent and unpredictable ways."[16] Dwelling on the role of cinema in the process of place-making, I suggest, may help further our understanding of how China continues to appeal as a source of attachment.

---

13. Hall, "Nations and Diasporas," in *The Fateful Triangle*, 169.
14. My usage of "fixing" is inspired by Stuart Hall, "Race—The Sliding Signifier." But see also Corey Byrnes, *Fixing Landscape: A Techno-Poetic History of China's Three Gorges* (New York: Columbia University Press, 2018).
15. Hall, "Race—The Sliding Signifier," 53.
16. John David Rhodes and Elena Gorfinkel, eds., *Taking Place: Location and the Moving Image* (Minneapolis: University of Minnesota Press, 2011), xvi.

Love, Cinema, and a Landscape in Motion

Considered the first movie to show a kiss on the Chinese screen since 1949, the "love dictionary" that taught young people "how to fall in love,"[17] and "an iconic example of Chinese cinema from the Reform era,"[18] *Romance on Lushan Mountain* tells the story of Zhou Yun 周筠, the daughter of a KMT general exiled in the US, and Geng Hua 耿樺, the son of a Chinese Communist Party (CCP) general, who meet and fall in love in Lushan. Directed by Huang Zumo 黃組模 (1921–2011) for the Shanghai Film Studio and based on a script by Bi Bicheng 畢必成 (1941–1993), who hailed from Pengze 彭澤 County (about 100 kilometers from Lushan), the film was mostly shot on location in autumn 1979, employing several local performers as extras. The gorgeous landscape of Lushan—its waterfalls, peaks, and clouds celebrated by such poets as Li Bai 李白 and Su Shi 蘇軾—as well as its historical sites underscore the growing affection between the protagonists and convey a not-so-subtle vision of cultural nationalism in which love for the motherland and for ancient Chinese culture replace party loyalty as markers of Chineseness in the early post-Mao era. The film premiered at the Lushan East Valley movie theater on July 12, 1980, where it was still screened when I visited Lushan in November 2016.[19]

Romance on Lushan Mountain has been discussed for its focus on love (a thematic novelty shared with several other movies released at the turn of the 1980s), for being one of the earliest films to reintroduce the US to Chinese viewers, and for its nationalist message.[20] If the film taught viewers "how to fall in love" with

---

17. The first kiss in movie-related media was a still from the British Musical *The Slipper and the Rose* (1976), published in *Mass Cinema* in May 1979. See Huang Pujiang 黃浦江, "Xin Zhongguo diyi bu wenxi *Lushan lian*" 新中國第一部吻戲《廬山戀》 [New China's first movie with a kiss scene, *Romance on Lushan Mountain*], *Jiangxi yule wang* 江西娛樂網, November 17, 2008, http://ent.jxnews.com.cn/system/2008/11/17/010000160.shtml.
18. Michael Berry, "The Absent American: Figuring the United States in Chinese Cinema of the Reform Era," in *A Companion to Chinese Cinema*, ed. Yingjin Zhang (Hoboken, NJ: Wiley-Blackwell, 2012), 555.
19. The film was released nationally and was one of the most successful films of the early 1980s. According to lead actress Zhang Yu, "Tickets at that time cost 2.5 mao, and *Romance on Lushan Mountain* made over a billion yuan already in the first week of release." A sequel of the film directed by Zhang Yu herself was released in 2010. Huang Lei 黃蕾 and Feng Ming 馮明, "Zhang Yu: 30 nian hou zaixu Lushan lian" 張瑜：30年後再續廬山戀 [Zhang Yu: Remaking *Romance on Lushan Mountain* thirty years later], *Shenzhen wanbao* 深圳晚報, September 28, 2012, http://www.zgnfys.com/a/nfrw-9380.shtml.
20. On the treatment of love in the film, see Chris Berry, *Postsocialist Cinema in Post-Mao China: The Cultural Revolution after the Cultural Revolution* (London: Routledge, 2008), and a brief mention in Yomi Braester, *Witness against History: Literature, Film, and Public Discourse in Twentieth-Century China* (Stanford, CA: Stanford University Press, 2003). See also Li Xigeng 李錫賡, "Ping *Lushan lian* suo xie de aiqing" 評《廬山戀》所寫的愛情 [On love in *Romance on Lushan Mountain*], *Dianying yishu* 電影藝術 (October 1980): 16–19; Li Jingyang 李景陽, "Aiqing zenme xie—dianying *Lushan Lian* gei women de qishi" 愛情怎樣寫——電影《廬山戀》給我們

a person of the opposite sex, it also taught them how to fall in love (again) with China, for what the protagonists find in one another is not only mutual attraction but also a shared love for their country, synecdochally represented by the landscape of Lushan. As Michael Berry put it:

> [T]he lovers' . . . relationship is punctuated by countless shots of Lushan's idyllic trickling streams and mountain backdrop, which functions almost as a cinematic version of a traditional Chinese landscape painting. Lushan's variety of historical identities is highlighted throughout the film, from Buddhist retreat to political meeting place in modern China. Huang Zumo takes great pleasure in displaying the bold calligraphy carved into majestic mountainside rocks and embellishing poetic lines from Tang masters Li Bai and Bai Juyi commemorating their own visits to Lushan. Collectively these elements help establish Lushan as a site firmly branded with quintessentially Chinese local identity.[21]

Michael Berry argues that the Lushan landscape conveys "an elaborate multileveled construction of Chinese nationalism," which is, in his view, finalized at mitigating the allure of the US.[22] That a new form of what we could call "Americanophile Chinese nationalism" is the main ideological goal of this 1980 film is especially obvious in a scene in which the protagonists repeat: "I love the morning of the motherland!" facing the rising sun. Geng Hua pronounces these words in English and is then joined by the female protagonist, Zhou Yun, the overseas returnee who teaches him the correct pronunciation. The rising sun, previously a symbol of Mao, is now hailed as the motherland, in English. The identification of China with socialism that characterized the cinema of the previous decades is thus reoriented toward a potentially less stable chain of associations. China denotes the territory with its awe-inspiring beauty, of course, but transcends mere territory and is redefined as a transcontinental, bilingual community including overseas Chinese as well. China is the people sharing memories, histories, culture, and love. And while the Chinese language is the

---

的啟示 [How to represent love: Lessons from *Romance on Lushan Mountain*], *Dianying pingjie* 電影評介 (December 1980): 18; Yang Gang 楊崗, "Wo zhande laoyuan laoyuan de kan ni—cong *Lushan Lian* de aiqing miaoxie tanqi" 我站得老遠老遠地看你——從《廬山戀》的愛情描寫談起 [I look at you from very far away: Starting from the depiction of love in *Romance on Lushan Mountain*], *Dianying pingjie* 電影評介 (February 1981): 21; and Xiao Ming 曉銘, "Zenyang tuchu 'lian'—*Lushan lian* de yishu tese" 怎樣突出"戀"——《廬山戀》的藝術特色 [How to foreground love: The artistic characteristics of *Romance on Lushan Mountain*], *Dianying pingjie* 電影評介 (February 1981): 20.
21. Berry, "The Absent American," 555–556.
22. Berry, "The Absent American," 556. *Romance* was released only a few months after the official reestablishment of diplomatic relations with the US in January 1979. The Shanghai Communiqué (February 1972), which occurred during Nixon's visit to China and expressed both nations' commitment to the normalization of their relations, is mentioned in the film as taking place a year before Zhou Yun's first visit, which is set in 1973. She returns to look for Geng Hua five years later; therefore, the present of the film is 1978.

medium of communication and culture, learning English is fundamental to the protagonists' self-identification as modern citizens.

That Lushan appears, in the film, as a "quintessentially Chinese" site is the result of a century-long process of remediation. In the late nineteenth century, Lushan "was very much like an international concession though without the name."[23] The town of Guling 牯嶺, or, as it was romanized at the time, Kuling (a pun on "cooling" due to its cool climate) was a popular summer resort for foreigners, who leased land, built villas and churches, and even established their own administrative office (Guling Estate) and police force. Yajun Mo reports that "Staying at the Guling resort during her 1917 visit to Mount Lu, Lü Bicheng, an acclaimed woman poet and writer, depicted an essentially foreign space where the only Chinese presence was sedan chair carriers and the local woodcutters."[24] Guling Estate was taken over by the Nationalist government in 1927, and throughout the 1930s and 1940s was promoted as an all-year-round travel destination for Chinese and foreign tourists alike. A 1936 bilingual brochure released by the China Travel Service advertised steamer and bus trips from Shanghai, Nanjing, and Hankou.[25] Prices ranged from $7 to $58 (depending on the company, vessel, and class), which included steamship fare to Jiujiang 九江, bus, and chair transfer—four coolies would carry each traveler to destination.[26] The attractions of Lushan, meanwhile, were celebrated in the media. One of the earliest landscape documentaries released by Commercial Press, *Lushan Vistas*

---

23. Jianlang Wang, *Unequal Treaties and China*, Vol. 1 (Honolulu, HI: Enrich Professional Publishing, 2015), 189. There were 1,731 foreigners living in Kuling in 1917. "Holiday makers came from Shanghai and the Yangtze ports . . . to occupy the 500 houses and bungalows and scores of hotel and guesthouse rooms. The facilities, for which they paid a modest charge, included tennis, swimming, hiking, a public library, and an auditorium. There were hospitals, British and American schools, churches, a dairy, and branches of several Hankow (Hankou) and Shanghai stores. Kuling became both a summer and winter resort, and some people chose to retire there permanently." Robert Nield, *China's Foreign Places: The Foreign Presence in China in the Treaty Port Era, 1840–1943* (New York: Columbia University Press, 2015), 150.
24. Yajun Mo, *Touring China: A History of Travel Culture, 1912–1949* (Ithaca, NY: Cornell University Press, 2021), 29.
25. *Lushan youcheng: Zhong-ying duizhao* 廬山遊程：中英對照 [Lushan Tours/Kuling through Traffic: In English and Chinese], Shanghai: Zhongguo luxingshe, 1936, microfilm, National Library of China. The Chinese section offers an extensive introduction to the sites of Lushan, whereas the English section only includes price lists of various transportation companies and recommended itineraries of one to seven days. While to Chinese readers Lushan was primarily presented as a preferred destination of eminent poets and literati, to English readers it was just promoted as a beautiful resort to escape the summer heat. Nonetheless, an American who traveled to Lushan in the 1970s called it "a place that evokes thoughts of eras past," adding that "many centuries ago, poets and painters began coming here in search of inspiration." Ross H. Monro, "Lu-shan: Quiet Retreat for China's Poets and Politicians," *The Christian Science Monitor, Weekly International Edition*, August 1, 1977, quoted in Roderick MacFarquhar, *The Origins of the Cultural Revolution: Volume II, the Great Leap Forward 1958–1960* (New York: Columbia University Press, 1983), 191.
26. In Jiujiang, travelers could stay at the China Travel Service guesthouse, one of the eighteen that the travel agency managed all over China.

(*Lushan Fengjing* 廬山風景, 1919) depicted its natural beauty and historical sites in order to elicit feelings of national pride.[27] Articles in travel journals in the 1940s and early 1950s, often titled after famous classical poems, drew connections between the travelers of the past and those of the present.[28]

Lushan also became known as the favorite residence of politicians and the site of important political meetings. It was from Lushan that Chiang Kai-shek announced his plan to resist Japan in July 1937, and two decades later, Mao Zedong spent a good part of his summers there. Important CCP meetings took place in Lushan in summer 1959, 1961, and 1970, which not only added new political dimensions to the locality but also associated it with Mao's poetry and Jiang Qing's love for photography. Mao wrote a poem titled "Climbing Lushan" (*Qilü: Deng Lushan* 七律・登廬山) in July 1959, and Jiang Qing (under the pseudonym Li Jin 李進) shot many photographs there, two of which, one portraying the chairman in a wicker chair and the other titled "The Fairy Cave on Lushan" (*Lushan Xianrendong* 廬山仙人洞), were widely reprinted in the press. Mao also wrote a poem inspired by his wife's photograph, titled "On a Photograph of the Fairy Cave Taken by Comrade Li Jin" (*Qijue: Wei Li Jin tongzhi ti suo she Lushan Xianrendong zhao* 七絕・為李進同志題所攝廬山仙人洞照, 1961). Both the photograph and the poem were published in *People's Daily* (Renmin ribao 人民日報) and in *China Photography* (Zhongguo Sheying 中國攝影) in 1964, and in *New Photography* (Xin Sheying 新攝影) in 1968. The photograph "Fairy Cave" was also republished in *People's Pictorial* (Renmin huabao 人民畫報) and *PLA Pictorial* (Jiefangjun huabao 解放軍畫報) in 1971, while the last verse of Mao's poem was carved on badges featuring his profile.[29] In the commentaries that accompanied the photograph and the poem, the classical tropes of Lushan such as the pine tree and majestic peaks were reinterpreted as symbols of the

---

27. Landscape documentaries often served as a means to express concern for national salvation. See Fang Fang 方方, *Zhongguo jilupian fazhang shi* 中國紀錄片發展史 [Historical development of the Chinese documentary] (Beijing: Xiju chubanshe, 2003), 23–25. On the film production by Commercial Press, see also Matthew Johnson, "Regional Cultural Enterprises and Cultural Markets in Early Republican China: The Motion Picture as Case Study," *Cross-Currents: East Asian History and Culture Review E-Journal*, no. 16 (September 2015): 103–138.
28. See, for instance, Chen Qiying 陳其英, "Lushan mianmu xin renshi" 廬山面目新認識 [Knowing Lushan anew], *Lüxing zazhi* 旅行雜誌 (July 1947): 43. An article published in the same journal in August 1950 and titled after the famous verse from Su Shi's poem (quoted in the epigraph at the opening of this essay) reemployed the time-honored trope of the difficulty of knowing Lushan. Lu Danlin 陸丹林, "Lushan zhenmian" 廬山真面 [The true face of Lushan], *Lüxing zazhi* 旅行雜誌 (August 1950): 55.
29. On Jiang Qing's picture-taking at Lushan, see Xu Dagang 徐大剛, "Yizhang zhaopian qi bolan" 一張照片起波瀾 [A photograph causes a stir], in *Lushan lao xiangce, 1895–1987* 廬山老相冊, 1895–1987 [Old photos of Lushan, 1895–1987], Vol. 2, ed. Chen Zheng 陳政 (Nanchang: Jiangxi meishu chubanshe, 2003), 125–29. On Mao badges, see Helen Wang, *Chairman Mao Badges: Symbols and Slogans of the Cultural Revolution* (London: British Museum Press, 2008), 46.

indomitable revolutionary spirit of Chairman Mao and of the Chinese people. Thus Lushan came to represent a socialist paradise.[30]

Compared to other spectacular locations portrayed in classical painting and poetry, then, by the 1970s Lushan was more directly associated with China's global interactions and with its history of foreign subjugation, with the history of both the Nationalist Party and the Communist Party, and with the cultural lives of Mao Zedong and Jiang Qing. How exactly was its landscape rendered as "quintessentially Chinese" by the cinematic medium at the turn of the 1980s? Which aspects and moments of its history were selected, and which ones were left out of the frame at this transitional moment?

Landscape of Words

Romance on Lushan Mountain leads the viewer through a myriad of historical sites, temples, and scenic spots, capitalizing on two characteristic features of the Lushan landscape: stone inscriptions, and mountains and waterfalls swathed in clouds and mist. Throughout Chinese history, characters were carved onto rocks to commemorate the visit of eminent travelers, underscore morphological similarities between certain rocks and real or mythical figures or objects, celebrate the beauty of the landscape, and point to feats of engineering nearby. By way of writing, moreover, specific locations were repurposed as "an environment for ritual or meditation set apart from the domains of ordinary experience."[31] Hundreds of such calligraphies can be found in Lushan, ranging from poems finely carved on the walls of a grotto to a gigantic "dragon" (*long* 龍) inscribed on a cliff.[32] As these texts are interwoven in the film narrative, they acquire new functions and meanings. An inscription may help express a certain mood or provide clues to overcome the obstacles that stand in the way of the fulfillment of romance. As mentioned, Michael Berry has suggested that the textual abundance

---

30. See Guo Moruo 郭沫若, "Taohuayuan li ke gengtian—Du Mao zhuxi xin fabiao de shici 'Qilü: Deng Lushan'" 桃花源裡可耕田——讀毛主席新發表的詩詞〈七律・登廬山〉 [Plowing in Peach Blossom Spring: Reading Chairman Mao's new poem "Climbing Lushan"], *Renmin ribao* 人民日報, February 2, 1964; and "Wuxian fengguang zai xianfeng—Du Mao zhuxi 'Qi jue: Wei Li Jin tongzhi ti suo she Lushan xianrendong zhao'" 無限風光在險峰——讀毛主席〈七絕・為李進同志題所攝廬山仙人洞照〉 [Boundless beauty among perilous peaks: Reading Chairman Mao's poem "Fairy Cave: Inscription on a photograph taken by Comrade Li Chin"], published together with the photograph in *Renmin ribao* 人民日報, April 11, 1964. In the first article, Guo Moruo addresses Lushan in the second person, recounting its history and calling it "Lushan of the people" and emphasizing that Lushan was a microcosm of socialist China and not a Shangri-la outside of it.
31. Robert E. Harrist Jr., *The Landscape of Words: Stone Inscriptions from Early and Medieval China* (Seattle: Washington University Press, 2008), 111.
32. Tao Yongqing 陶勇清, *Lushan lidai shike* 廬山歷代石刻 [Lushan stone inscriptions through the centuries] (Nanchang: Jiangxi meishu chubanshe, 2010).

of this film "help[s] establish Lushan as a place firmly branded with a quintessentially Chinese local identity." In a different context, Andrea Bachner has argued that the Chinese script (and writing in general) always presents multiple meanings due to the plurality of media involved in its reproduction. As she puts it, "a single embodiment of a writing system always invokes a multiplicity of meanings and symbolic values. Rather than symbols of any identitarian essence, languages and their scripts are embodied in multiple, changing media." Hence, any instantiation of writing is not easily reducible to "a univocal expression of national identity."[33] Is it possible to reconcile Berry's and Bachner's contrasting claims—the first suggesting singularity and fixity, and the second multiplicity and change? A closer look at the ways in which graphic elements function in select scenes of the film will help tackle this question and illustrate the dialectics of differentiation and closure that I wish to associate with the term "Sinoglossia."

After an opening sequence composed of static wide-angle shots, tilts, and pans of the mountainous landscape, the film narrative proper begins with Zhou Yun in the back seat of a car, absorbed in recollections as she approaches Lushan. Close-ups of her eyes followed by flashbacks suggest that her trip is as much a voyage inward as it is the pursuit of someone she has encountered there in the past. Like many of the films released at the turn of the 1980s, *Romance on Lushan Mountain* is structured around the contrast between before and after the momentous events of 1976. Five years have passed since her last visit [in 1973], Zhou Yun says in voice-over. The Gang of Four has been arrested and Chinese people abroad are happy. She looks at the photo album she has brought with her: in a point-of-view shot, the camera zooms in on a photograph of a young man standing on a rock, which then dissolves into an extended flashback of their first encounter. Zhou Yun is walking briskly, holding the map that her father has drawn for her, while her father's voice urges her to visit the White Deer Grotto Academy.[34] In front of it, says the father, you will find Zhenliu Bridge, under which lies a rock with the characters *zhenliu* 枕流 (literally, pillow flow) carved on it. On that rock the philosopher Zhu Xi 朱熹 used to sit and read. Her father's words resonating in her mind, Zhou Yun walks toward the site and points her Polaroid at the rock. The inscription is shown from her point of view, the film frame coinciding with that of her instant camera. In the exact moment in which Zhou Yun presses the shutter button, Geng Hua breaks into her frame. As Zhou Yun shifts her gaze from the photograph she has just taken back to the rock, she

---

33. Andrea Bachner, *Beyond Sinology: Chinese Writing and the Scripts of Culture* (New York: Columbia University Press, 2013), 13.
34. The White Deer Grotto Academy (*Bailudong* shuyuan 白鹿洞書院) has been considered as the "prototype of the Neo-Confucianist academy." Zhu Xi revived and expanded it in 1179. Carsun Chang, *The Development of Neo-Confucian Thought* (New Haven, CT: College and University Press, 1963), 66.

sees him sitting there, absorbed in his book. Next, an image of Zhu Xi repeatedly intercuts with that of Geng Hua.

The characters carved on the rock mark a specific place, for sure, but also mark the person who sits next to them. Even before Geng Hua is properly introduced, the carved inscription suggests he might be a present-day Neo Confucian. The characters themselves refer to the shape of the rock, similar to a big pillow, but they may also bring to mind the idiom *shushi zhenliu* 漱石枕流, which means to conduct a reclusive life so as not to compromise one's principles, which is what Geng Hua is doing when they first meet. Chinese writing thus serves as a prop that defines the circumstances of the male protagonist as an upright literatus in exile.

Perhaps no other medium than cinema can so vividly represent the process of recollecting within a recollection: the mental echo of a remote voice or image reverberating within the reverie of a more recent past. Zhou Yun's flashback, to repeat, is induced by a photograph, which was in turn spurred by her father's wish that she visit the academy and by his first mention of the stone inscription. The father's words in the voice-over constitute a flashback within the flashback, linking the lovers' first encounter to the parental recommendation to visit that historic site. Indeed, Zhou Yun might not have noticed Geng Hua had her father not mentioned the rock inscription to her. The inscription constitutes a material trace conjoining different moments and media—media that include her father's voice, his hand-drawn map of Lushan, the photograph she takes, and the filmic representation of her reverie. The flashback within flashback produces a simultaneous sense of connection and break between different technologies of inscription (from hand drafting to photography), in which the very effort to recall and reconnect paradoxically reinforces a sense of rupture. The remediation of Chinese writing binds past and present but also punctuates the gap in between, just like a bridge that makes us aware of the distance between the two banks of a river. At the level of narrative, what the inscription does for Zhou Yun is to introduce Geng Hua to her and thus initiate the romance. Secondly, the stone inscription represents her object of desire, the cipher of the paternal cultural order from which she is still partly excluded and which she tries to appropriate through her camera lens. Altogether, the inscription helps convey a harmonious view of intergenerational relations and suggests full compatibility between romantic love, respect for the parents' will, and the endurance of Chinese culture despite political upheavals and diasporic rifts.

Chinese script partakes of the physical world of the film, thus corresponding to what Michel Chion has defined as "diegetic writing."[35] Chion proposes a

---

35. Michel Chion, *Words on Screen*, ed. and trans. Claudia Gorbman (New York: Columbia University Press, 2017), 2.

distinction between an "inclusion," to indicate writing that is "part of the setting, in the diegetic space, but is not meant as the central element or the subject of the shot," and "the [diegetic] insert," which "as its name indicates, is a close-up shot of a detail between two other shots."[36] Most of the stone inscriptions found in *Romance* are inclusions rather than inserts, and they have a utilitarian function: they signal where the characters are. Toponymic references, however, do not just help identify the sites and attest to their authenticity: they valorize and advertise them as well. In a film that is also meant as a travelogue introducing Lushan's touristic attractions, the inscriptions single out the places that viewers should visit on their own. The map that Zhou Yun's father has drawn by hand and has given to his daughter prior to her departure thus functions as a mise-en-abyme of the film, in so far as both map and film propose a sightseeing itinerary linking a series of inscribed locations. Over the years, viewers probably used the film as a visual map to Lushan, subsequently capturing the same scenic spots with their cameras.

The inscriptions that appear in *Romance* are generally to be read silently, or at times they are merely to be looked at—when reading is not vocalized, the boundary between looking and reading is unclear. Especially when the calligraphy is not fully decipherable by audiences (because it is barely lit, or it is shown only in fragments), its significance lies more with the iconic connotations of Chinese characters than on whatever information the script itself may convey, and whether it comes to mean anything more depends on the extent to which its implications are verbalized by the protagonists. One instance in which the protagonists translate barely visible characters to viewers occurs when they run into one another in the Yubei pavilion (*Yubeiting* 御碑亭), a historical building dating to the Ming dynasty. In this scene, the story carved on the walls of the pavilion is not readable but is interwoven with the skirmishes between the soon-to-be couple, breaking the ice between them and allowing them to become closer. By this point, Zhou Yun and Geng Hua have only run into one another briefly, and the latter appears reluctant to befriend such a bold and outgoing young woman—one who sports high heels, red bootcut pants, and miniskirts.[37] He is initially uneasy, his mistrust underscored by the intensification of the rain, which plays a central role in the film. In *Cinematic Weather*, Kristi McKim writes,

---

36. Chion, *Words on Screen*, 5.
37. On fashion in the film, see Wang Suhong 王素紅, "Tan Zhou Yun de fuzhuang bianhua" 談周筠的服裝變化 [On Zhou Yun's change of clothes], *Dianying pingjie* 電影評介 (February 1981): 20. For a critique of Zhou Yun's "exotic clothes," see Li Xigeng, "Ping *Lushan lian* suo xie de aiqing."

rain makes characters do something, whether finding and opening an umbrella, seeking shelter, or passionately refusing shelter. In many examples, rain manifests otherwise latent desire; the sound and image of rain accelerate the pacing and intensify the sensation of the scene.[38]

The expressive potential of the whimsical Lushan weather is discussed at length by the cinematographer, Shan Lianguo, and the assistant director, Bao Qicheng, both of whom emphasize that they utilized its mercurial quality to reflect the protagonists' psychological upheavals.[39] A sudden gush of rain underscores a turning point in the narrative, as dark clouds gather and Zhou Yun seeks shelter in the Yubei pavilion, densely carved with Chinese characters. Seemingly amused by the impromptu detour, she briefly glances at the inscribed wall. Next, an over-the-shoulder tracking shot shows her in profile, sitting against the carvings, drying her face with a handkerchief, and checking her appearance in a compact mirror. She does not appear interested in the writing. Hurried steps are heard, and the film cuts to a frontal shot showing her in the foreground and Geng Hua entering from the same doorframe behind. Finding her there, he makes a brief attempt to escape, but she grabs his arm and holds him back, noting that it is "pouring cats and dogs outside" and making him realize that he is trapped. Here they appear for the first time close to one another, in a two-shot within the doorframe, the characters 壁雲山 *bi yun shan* visible on the right (Figure 4.1).

These characters are a fragment from the couplet "Surrounded by cloudy mountains and paddling on the Nine Rivers / a pavilion in mist and rain, amidst ravines and pines" (*Si bi yun shan jiu jiang zhao / yi ting yan shui wan he song* 四壁雲山九江棹 / 一亭煙水萬壑松), a 1919 inscription attributed to Luo Xiaxian, a nationalist intellectual who sojourned in the area. After a quick point-of-view shot of the rainy landscape, the film cuts back to the framed couple. Geng Hua looks at her hand holding his arm, and with an embarrassed smile she loosens her grip and steps back into the pavilion.

By entering the pavilion first, Zhou Yun transforms the historical location into a feminine and sensual place. For a few minutes, the couple is relegated to a different spatio-temporal dimension, separated from the external world by rain, writing, and stone. Initially, they stand with their back to one another,

---

38. Kristi McKim, *Cinema as Weather: Stylistic Screens and Atmospheric Change* (London: Routledge, 2013), 91.
39. Bao Qicheng 包起成, "*Lushan lian* waijing paishe diandi" 《廬山戀》外景拍攝點滴 [Shooting on location *Romance on Lushan Mountain*, bit by bit], *Dianying pinglun* 電影評論 (May 1980): 14; Bao Qicheng 包起成, "Renzao yunwu he dongyong—*Lushan lian* shezhi shiling" 人造雲霧和冬泳——《廬山戀》攝製拾零 [Artificial fog and winter swimming—tidbits on the production of *Romance on Lushan Mountain*], *Dazhong dianying* 大眾電影 (June 1980): 26; and Shan Lianguo 單聯國, "Zhuazhu 'jiaohua' zuo wenzhang—*Lushan lian* sheying xinde" 抓住"交化"做文章——《廬山戀》攝影心得 [Fussing over capturing "change"—What I learned from shooting *Romance on Lushan Mountain*], *Dianying yishu* 電影藝術 (March 1981): 52–58, 61.

Figure 4.1: Zhou Yun and Geng Hua for the first time close to one another (*Romance on Lushan Mountain*, 13'52")

Figure 4.2: Geng Hua still reluctant to accept Zhou Yun's offer of friendship (*Romance on Lushan Mountain*, 15'32")

and when he lights a cigarette, she coughs and reprimands him for his lack of manners, as if continuing her task of civilizing him (following up on her first attempt to teach him the proper English pronunciation of "I love the morning of my motherland"). "Don't you know that tobacco is harmful and smoking is forbidden all over the world?" As he continues to smoke, flaunting indifference, she grabs his cigarette and throws it out in the rain. The pavilion is, at this point, a divisive space. Two shots of them in separate doorframes alternate with one shot medium close-up of each of them. The sense of separation, however, is not there to last. A medium close-up of Geng Hua shows him visibly pleased that this unknown young woman shows interest in his health, and yet in the next shot they are still pacing back and forth, each within a different doorframe.

The rain prevents them from leaving this refuge, but they do not dare to share it either and remain on the threshold, as if suspended between two equally inhospitable spaces inside and outside of it. In a film that is generally accompanied by an emphatically sentimental soundtrack, this scene stands out because it is only accompanied by the continuous sound of the rain, hinting at larger scales of separation and incommunicability, and momentarily transcending the vicissitudes of this young couple. Eventually, Geng Hua throws away his packet of cigarettes and she walks closer to him. They are momentarily united in a two-shot as she stretches her hand and proposes that they become friends, the characters *bi yun* featured again on the right side, but he is still reluctant to accept her offer of friendship (Figure 4.2).

Obviously, Zhou Yun is the propelling force of their romance while Geng Hua is, at least for the first half of the film, exclusively focused on his professional aspirations (learning English and becoming an architect to build a modern country). Next, the camera shows her again in the foreground, her hand leaning on the carved wall as if to verify its solidity or seek support from it, and asking him if he knows the history of the pavilion. While Geng Hua recounts how the founder of the Ming dynasty, Hongwu (Zhu Yuanzhang), had the pavilion built in honor of a Lushan monk who had helped him during his rise to the throne, she looks at the wall as if reading the characters carved on it, and then the camera cuts to a barely lit shot of the character imperial (*yu* 御) of "Yubeiting." The history carved on the pavilion's interior walls contains a lesson for Geng Hua: she suggests to him that just as the emperor had been grateful to the monk, he should be grateful to her because she taught him how to pronounce "I love the morning on my motherland" in English. However ridiculous her comparison may sound, it successfully dispels his distrust. Finally, a long shot shows them both within the doorframe decorated by the couplet, five characters now visible on each side (Figure 4.3).

As the camera zooms in and they shake hands, the off-screen call of a pigeon announces the end of the rain, the sky clears up, and the extra-diegetic music announces the beginning of their romance. I have dwelled on this sequence to show how the Chinese script initially serves as a cultural icon that viewers could interpret in different ways, but eventually the protagonists extract a story from it, a fable of gratitude that allows them to move closer to one another and hence advance the romantic plot, thereby reducing its semantic possibilities.

Some other scripts featured in the film do not serve to advance the plot. Rather, they momentarily pause or transcend the narrative to invoke an idea, or a concept, which simultaneously reminds viewers of the context in which the film was produced and presents them with an argument about China's recent history. During Zhou Yun's flashback of her first visit in 1973, the couple exchange a promise to reunite and work together as architects, in front of the characters "The moon shines on the pinewood" (*Yue zhao song lin* 月照松林), a famous inscription carved by Feng Zushu, a military officer stationed in Lushan during the second Sino-Japanese War in the late 1930s.[40] It is by now clear that Zhou Yun's father was a Nationalist general whose "entire life was shaped by Lushan," and Geng Hua recounts that his father too is attached to Lushan because it is there that he began his revolutionary path, fighting in the war. And while her US-based father cannot return to China because of his political past, Geng Hua's father is being persecuted despite being a loyal communist, so they are both patriotic outcasts. While Geng Hua tells her that his father has not yet been

---

40. He Wei 賀偉, ed., *Shike li de gushi* 石刻裡的故事 [Stories in stone inscriptions] (Nanchang: Jiangxi jiaoyu chubanshe, 2016), 135. Situated along a small path between pinewoods, the inscription is another of Lushan must-see attractions and is now considered a favorite dating spot for moon viewing for young couples during Mid-autumn Festival.

Figure 4.3: A long shot of Zhou Yun and Geng Hua within the doorframe decorated by an inscription (*Romance on Lushan Mountain*, 16'14")

Figure 4.4: Zhou Yun retraces the lower strokes of the character *lin* carved on the rock (*Romance on Lushan Mountain*, 25'12")

"liberated" (*jiefang* 解放), presumably from prison or from a labor camp, her finger retraces the character *lin* 林 carved on the rock (Figure 4.4).

She appears to caress it casually, but the parts of the character that she retraces are the two lower diagonal strokes, drawing the character "human" (*ren* 人), a common trope in the literature of the late 1970s lamenting the dehumanizing effects of the Cultural Revolution. Her partial retracing reanimates the script and intensifies the feeling of an absence, contrasting the moment in which the calligraphy was first inscribed to the year in which the scene is set, 1973, and suggesting a distinction between a "humane" war (the War of Resistance to Japan that brought Nationalists and Communists together) and a conflict-ridden present in which humanity is crushed.

Zhou Yun returns to this site during her second trip in 1978, searching for Geng Hua, whose whereabouts are now unknown. This time around, her finger traces the "sun" radical in the character "shine" (*zhao* 照)—possibly an allusion to the "morning sun" of the motherland. Her words from their past conversation ("I believe you will surely become a successful architect") and his response ("at that point, together we . . .") echo in her mind, while a high-angle zoom on her frowning eyes underscores the intensity of her daydreaming alternating with despair. These instances of tactile engagement with the Chinese script could be read as instances of automatic writing, as if the strokes engraved decades earlier provided a clue to find someone, or something, temporarily lost, inviting viewers to partake in a séance.

Delimitations of Sinoglossia

At the turn of the 1980s, *Romance on Lushan Mountain* taught viewers how to fall in love with love, with family, with tourism, with China, and ultimately with cinema itself, for it showed that only the moving image could convey the beauty of love and the beauty of landscape in ways that powerfully resonated with one another. In this film, the remediation of the Chinese script acquires different connotations in relation to its physical surroundings, to the protagonists, and to viewers. Much of it is filtered through Zhou Yun's perception and serves narrative purposes, advertising a location, intensifying a mood, or advancing the plot. However, at times the script suspends the narrative and spectators themselves can activate writing according to their knowledge of the historical world from which it emerged, for "writing imposes binds such that in the act of viewing, the spectator is forced to work in various directions at once."[41] In this perspective, the filmic remediation of the Chinese script can be related to the oscillatory movement of Sinoglossia, if we understand the latter as a tension between the pole of fixing and the pole of differentiation resulting in an act of delimitation. It is this tension, this oscillatory movement, and ultimately this act of delimitation that ensures that categories such as the nation continue to persist. What *Romance* shows is that multiplicity and change themselves are the defining characteristic of Chineseness. There is no unique essence here, but at the same time, multiplicity and change are subjected to a fixing that delimits the sliding movement of "glossia" and contains the scope of the "Sino-."

Romance on Lushan Mountain presents multiple aspects of Chinese history and culture spanning from antiquity to the late 1930s, but apart from the bleak setting of 1973, it leaves the Lushan of the socialist period completely out. If we think of locality itself as a palimpsest in which new images are constantly covering previous ones, we might conclude that *Romance on Lushan Mountain* erased as much as it recreated Lushan. The love *in* and *for* the landscape featured in this film remade the place into a signifier of Chineseness—one characterized by openness, multiplicity, and change—by evacuating the residual presence of Mao Zedong and Jiang Qing.

---

41. Tom Conley, *Film Hieroglyphs* (*With a New Introduction*) (Minneapolis: Minnesota University Press, 1991), 1.

5

Sinopop

The Case of Namewee/Wee Meng Chee

E. K. Tan

In July 2007, a twenty-four-year-old Sinophone Malaysian student studying mass communications at Ming Chuan University in Taiwan posted a rap video titled "Negarakuku" (我愛我的國家) on YouTube.[1] Meant to be a parody of the Malaysian national anthem "Negaraku," which means "My Country," the video is a rap song about life in Malaysia portrayed from the point of view of a Sinophone Malaysian. Wee Meng Chee (also known as Namewee), the producer of the song and video, titled the song "Negaraku**ku**," which means his own version of the national anthem, or "My 'Negaraku.'"[2] Yet, for those who know Bahasa Malay, *kuku* means crazy. It is also a euphemism for the male genitalia. Seemingly, Wee had produced the rap video to create a controversy from the beginning, starting with the song title. Wee probably did not expect his video to attract 400,000 viewings within a month of posting it on his YouTube channel; neither did he expect to be threatened with jail time in Malaysia under the Sedition Act.[3] But in fact, several police reports were filed against him, accusing him of provoking racial and religious conflicts and of inciting hatred among the various racial groups in Malaysia. One such accusation claimed that Wee had insulted Islam by referring to the Muslim Azan 5 a.m. prayers as his daily morning call: "5 o'clock in the morning / there is always a morning call to wake me up / Sometimes a few different mosques will begin to recite together / They sound like they are singing a duet" (早上五點還有morning call會叫我起床／有時幾間一起唱／聽起來好像

---

1. Namewee, "Namewee 黃明志 Controversial Song [Negarakuku 我愛我的國家] @2007," dir. Namewee, December 22, 2015, music video, 5:45, https://youtu.be/g0moet-jLw8.
2. The additional syllable "ku" means "my" in Malay.
3. Deborah Loh, "Student May Face Music Over 'Negaraku' Rap Video," *New Straits Times*, August 8, 2007, 8. For details on the act, see "Laws of Malaysia: Act 15—Sedition Act 1948" (*Malaysia: The Commissioner of Law Revision and Malayan Law Journal*, 2006).

情歌對唱).⁴ He also compared the morning prayers to R&B songs: "Sometimes their voice gets twisted like R&B" (聲音拗來拗去像唱R&B一樣) and claimed that the prayers sounded like the crowing of a rooster: "Some of them sound like a rooster / but are up earlier than the rooster" (有些聲音像公雞 / 可是比公雞早起床). In addition, Wee's music video attracted the attention of the Malaysian authorities for thematizing the corruption of the police force and the lack of efficiency of civil servants—professions predominantly held by Malays:

我們的警察叫做MATA
因為他們的眼睛很亮
新年一到他們就很努力
拿住筆可是很少會跟你開單
因為他們口很渴需要喝茶
還有kopi O要不要加糖
如果加糖他嘴巴會甜甜跟你微笑

Our police are called Mata
Because their eyes are very sharp
When the new year comes, they tend to work very hard
They take out their pens but rarely issue violation tickets
That is because they are very thirsty for tea
And also black coffee. "Want some sugar?"
If you add sugar, they will put on a sweet smile for you.⁵

Of course, Wee was at least partly aware of the possible consequences of his actions. He ended the video with a disclaimer in Malay: "*Jangan sue saya, saya takde duit*" (Don't sue me, I don't have money). The Malaysian Communications and Multimedia Commission (MCMC) launched an investigation on Wee shortly after receiving the reports from government officials and community leaders. Wee was asked to give a public apology before August 31, by Culture, Arts and Heritage Minister Datuk Seri Dr. Rais Yatim. However, the police were only able to question Wee a year later upon his return to Malaysia on August 29, after he graduated from college.

Malaysia's Deputy Youth and Sports Minister Datuk Liow Tiong Lai explained that even if Wee was trying to reflect on the social issues in Malaysia out of his love for the country, as Wee claimed, he should have protected the honor of his country by respecting the national anthem, the very symbol of national pride. To emphasize this point, Liow stresses that "If [Wee] had used another song instead of 'Negaraku,' nobody would be criticizing him."⁶ This statement seems

---

4. My translation.
5. My translation.
6. Loh, "'Negaraku' Rap Video," 8.

contradictory, because it calls for Wee and Malaysian citizens to show blind faith in the Malay government and its national symbols. This and similar responses to Wee's controversial piece indirectly confirm the racial inequalities and the privileges enjoyed by the Malays as "natives" to the Malay Peninsula. By calling Wee's self-expression unpatriotic despite its attempt to reflect the everyday experience of Sinophone Malaysians, the authorities publicly silence the voice of this particular ethnic group. Critical of the stance of the Malaysian government with regards to the Wee controversy, *New Straits Times* journalist Bryan Yap suggests that Malaysians regard Wee's example as a reminder for them to speak up for themselves. He asks who has the right to speak for Malaysians. Is it political figures that use race and religion as their political tools, or students filled with angst like Namewee, whose YouTube videos have sparked national debates on racial and religious issues? Yap recognizes that Malaysians are speaking up more and urged them to do so more aggressively instead of allowing political figures and organizations or hip-hop artists like Wee to speak on their behalf. Especially in the year 2007, when Malaysia celebrated its fiftieth Merdeka (Independence or National Day), Yap argued that the nation should embrace the multiple voices and opinions of the people.[7] Aside from the controversy and debates on whether Wee was guilty of sedition, the sudden popularity of his rap video brought to light the fact that interethnic relations and racial harmony in Malaysia cannot be taken for granted.

In a phone interview, Wee claimed that the rap video was meant to be a satirical commentary on the social life in Malaysia from the point of view of an ethnic Chinese. It was not meant to insult Islam or the Malays. He also explained that the things he rapped about were things Malaysians often talk about in situations such as daily conversations in a coffee shop. The scenarios depicted were all based on his hometown experience in Muar. Wee also stated that his other intention was to depict the life and experience of Sinophone Malaysians for ethnic Chinese in China and Taiwan as a way to show them the reality of the Sinophone Malaysian experience, which they know little of.[8] This, in an interesting way, casts a subtle Sinophone critique on how overseas Chinese experience is often seen as mere extension of the proto-identity of Greater China. By claiming this geopolitical tension of the identity formation of Sinophone Malaysian not simply within the discourse of the Chinese diaspora but also vis-à-vis that very same discourse, Wee simultaneously challenges the stable notion of "Chineseness," a Han-centric identity category, as well as the racial politics in Malaysia. In a sense, Wee's controversy reveals the contradictory nature of Malaysianness as an identitarian category. On the one hand, the Malay government promotes

---

7. Bryan Yap, "Stand Up and Speak Up If You're Malaysian," *New Straits Times*, August 15, 2007, 27.
8. David Yeow, "Namewee: I Did Not Mean to Insult Malays," *New Straits Times*, August 10, 2007, 6.

identification with the nation among its citizens regardless of race, gender, or religion; on the other hand, the very essence of Malaysianness is racially and religiously tied toward Islam and the Malays despite the cultural and linguistic diversity in the Malay Peninsula. The state discourse, only superficially accepting of racial and cultural diversity and acceptance, undercuts the significance of local differences. Wee's work resists this cooptation of local Chinese identities by celebrating in his work the heterogeneity of local identities, be it Malay, Chinese, or others. Apart from "Negarakuku," this is evident, for instance, in his music video "Muar's Mandarin" and his multicultural and multilingual feature film, *Nasi Lemak 2.0* (2011). By extension, Wee's promotion of racial and cultural diversity in Malaysia questions state-sanctioned Malaysianess and critiques the institutional racism of the Muslim state.[9]

Using Wee Meng Chee's "Negarakuku" controversy as entry point, I hope to examine Wee Meng Chee's work as a challenge to concepts such as "Chineseness" and "Malaysianness" by the multilingual and multicultural characteristics of a specific genre of cultural productions I call "Sinopop." Unlike more descriptive concepts like Mandopop and Cantopop, I coin Sinopop as a critical term used to represent and analyze localized popular cultural expressions such as those produced by marginal Sinophone communities, like Wee's work. As a critical category, Sinopop engages with anti-hegemonic ideologies that speak to power centers in order to deconstruct uniform representations and to celebrate marginal voices. I see Wee's music as an example of such expressions since it articulates the cultural diversity and the interethnic relations of communities such as that of Malaysia.

Sinopop: The Concept

I propose Sinopop as a critical approach to the study of Sinophone popular cultural expressions that refuses to give in to hegemonic structures and systems of oppression. First, such a concept needs a critical edge; if not, the purpose of inventing a new concept would be nothing but futile. Second, the concept must resist uncritical celebrations of difference and heterogeneity, for example,

---

9. Interethnic relations are complex in Malaysia. The Malays make up the majority, approximately 50 percent of the population, the Chinese, approximately 22.6 percent, the Indian, 6.6 percent, and a small population of aborigines often known collectively as the Orang Asli (information collected by the 2010 census). Despite the fact that the Malays are the majority and run the government, they believe the natives or "sons of the soil," the *bumiputras*, enjoy privileges in addition to their majority status. Resentment among the other ethnic groups surfaces from time to time, especially among Sinophone Malaysians, who feel discriminated against by policies regulating access to higher education, career opportunities, etc. Some of these resentments are reflected in Wee's work. For more, see Timothy P. Barnard, ed., *Contesting Malayness: Malay Identity Across Boundaries* (Singapore: National University Press, 2004).

state-sanctioned forms of multiculturalism. Only by adhering to such an agenda can a generative concept facilitate our examination of the Sinoglossic features of communities outside or on the margins of China. It can also remind us that, aside from China or China-centric discourses, there are other forms of hegemony and power that Sinophone communities face. Sinoglossia, which, for me, emphasizes the multiplicity and heterogeneity of linguistic and cultural contexts, seems neutral as a term; yet it comes with a political charge due to the complex relations between Sinitic languages (and beyond). Language is power. Hence, Sinoglossia is profoundly political. It is under this premise that I want to highlight the political nature of the term "Sinopop." The lack of a critical concept to assist our investigation of Sinophone pop culture ends up perpetuating the misconception of pop culture as low culture, with nothing to offer to social and political consciousness among the people. Yet, renowned cultural theorists such as Walter Benjamin, Theodor Adorno, and Max Horkheimer have theorized the power of pop culture in reaching out to the masses since the turn of the twentieth century, even before cultural studies became a field of its own. I do not intend to replace Mandopop or Cantopop with Sinopop though categorically the concept could potentially act as an umbrella term for popular music or culture produced in Sinitic languages. Instead, I aim to bring into play different cultural expressions that have historically been subsumed under categories like Mandopop. Wee Meng Chee's works, for instance, are an example of Sinoglossic articulations that cannot be contained and described by uncritical, classificatory terms. In this chapter, I will reflect on the connection between Sinophone studies and popular culture via the concept of Sinopop by focusing on three different aspects of Wee Meng Chee's work: the lyrics, their music, and their visual media aspect.

As an entry point for my theorization of Sinopop and my analysis of Wee Meng Chee's work, I draw on the concept of "Pop Culture China" first proposed in 2001 by cultural studies scholar Chua Beng Huat.[10] In his essay, Chua proposes the concept "Pop Culture China" as a term critical of identity categories such as the Chinese diaspora or overseas Chinese. He argues that these categories point to mainland China as the unchallenged homeland and place of origin for ethnic Chinese around the world.[11] He especially takes issue with Weiming Tu's concept of "Cultural China," a uniform global Chinese identity Tu formulated with the assumption of Confucianism as the foundation of the everyday experience of

---

10. Beng Huat Chua, "Pop Culture China," *Singapore Journal of Tropical Geography* 22, no. 2 (2001): 113–121. A version of this essay was later included in his book *Structure, Audience and Soft Power in East Asian Pop Culture* (Hong Kong: Hong Kong University Press, 2002), 31–50.
11. See Chua, *Structure, Audience and Soft Power*, 31.

the Chinese diaspora.¹² Instead, by focusing on the production and circulation of popular culture from and among Chinese communities from various locales, from Taiwan to Hong Kong to Singapore, for Chua, Pop Culture China forms a network of cultural affinities among ethnic Chinese via films and popular music produced in and circulated to different places. Although this alternative to a centralized concept of ethnic identity rejects a homogeneous system of identification to embrace the multiplicity of Chinese identity, it does not necessarily address the perpetuation of Chineseness as a myth that interpellates ethnic Chinese across the globe into believing in a shared cultural experience and identity, one that is defined by Pop Culture China. Can we or should we assume that, despite Pop Culture China's proposal of a common ethnic identity based on a range of local variations as production centers, popular culture is void of ideological and political implications regardless of whether pop culture consumers are aware or oblivious to these implications? Are issues relating to the cultural hegemony of an essentialized Chineseness, reinforced by the rise of China as a global power, addressed when we substitute Confucianism or transnational business with popular culture in the form of a pluralistic common identity among ethnic Chinese? How is Pop Culture China different from Tu's Cultural China, except for the difference in the object of study? Why argue for an alternative model that ends up reproducing a system of identification very similar to the one against which it argues, one ultimately mapped onto the rise of China as a geopolitical center for cultural production in the twenty-first century? Would it not be more productive to engage in a dialogue to examine how the myth of Chineseness, regardless of whether it is tied to neo-Confucianism, transnational business, popular culture, or academia, continues to be reproduced and conveniently reinforced? Dissatisfied with Chua's proposal of Pop Cultural China for its lack of critical potential to address the questions I raise above, I propose Sinopop as an alternative concept that would allow for a broader discussion of the relationship between popular culture and Sinophone identities with regard to specific local politics and sociality.

Consumers of popular culture are not apolitical subjects regardless of how politically disengaged they seem in their everyday life. Although Chinese popular culture, as Chua suggests, was and has been historically produced in multiple centers, I believe that it is not simply the production and circulation processes that condition and define these products. The desires and socio-political backgrounds of the consumers are equally important to understand the relationships

---

12. Chua, *Structure, Audience and Soft Power*, 33. Even though I am critical of Tu's "Cultural China," the lack of an institutionalized structure of Confucianism in the everyday life of ethnic Chinese (Chua uses Singapore as example) does not mean that Confucianism is not part and parcel of the belief system of ethnic Chinese.

between popular culture, different communities, and individuals. When pop culture from production centers such as Taiwan and Hong Kong is circulated throughout Asia and beyond, it experiences transformations and acquires different forms of representations and meanings. At times, local uniqueness is celebrated while there are also instances when these products are subsumed under the myth of Chineseness. It is not that cultural producers are insincere in their promotion of difference and diversity among the global Chinese community; it is simply that artists sometimes fail to see the complicity of their work when they adopt certain essentialized cultural symbols that circumscribe the nostalgia for a Chinese identity. This self-exoticization, conscious or not, inevitably reproduces an essentialist notion of identity. Chineseness, in such cases, is often reproduced via various affective structures shaped by specific genres, media, contents, or other choices adopted by Sinophone cultural producers.

Chua's proposal of Pop Culture China shares an intellectual concern with Shu-mei Shih's critique of the concept of diaspora in Sinophone studies.[13] For example, when mentioning the resistance of scholars like Allen Chun, Aihwa Ong, or Ien Ang to Sinocentrism by referring to the hegemonic power as "Chinese chauvinism" instead of "Chinese nationalism," Chua cautions that the use of the concept "Chinese diaspora" to describe ethnic Chinese living around the world is problematic. After all, it perpetuates the ambiguous identification of a home and nation defined by the myth of consanguinity among ethnic Chinese.[14] Yet, Chua avoids directly engaging in dialogue with the concept of the Sinophone, except in a passing question: "to which Chinese language does the 'Sino-' in 'Sinophone' refer?"[15]

Chua's Pop China Culture and Shih's concept of the Sinophone overlap in their belief that ethnic Chinese or Sinophone identities focus on the cultivation of local characteristics and politics.[16] In addition, both Chua and Shih understand

---

13. Shih argues that diaspora has an end date. See Shu-mei Shih, "Against Diaspora: The Sinophone as Places of Cultural Production," in *Global Chinese Literature: Critical Essays*, ed. Jing Tsu and David Der-wei Wang (Boston, MA: Brill, 2010), 45. In a different essay, she explains that there are two dimensions to diaspora: first, there is diaspora as history, which involves the actual dispersal of peoples; and second, diaspora as value, which is how one perceives his or her being in the world. It is the latter that perpetuates nostalgia, which in return endorses the myth of Chineseness.
14. Chua, *Structure, Audience and Soft Power*, 34.
15. Chua, *Structure, Audience and Soft Power*, 34–35.
16. Chua claims that "[the term diaspora] is now seldom a term of self-identity but more often than not is imposed on individuals by others for the latter's own self-identity but more often than not is imposed on individuals by others for the latter's own self-interest as the cultural definition of Chineseness has been unavoidably and increasingly marked by local politics" (*Structure, Audience and Soft Power*, 34); but Shih argues that "the definition of the Sinophone must be place-based and it must be sensitive to time" because "[p]lace matters as the grounding where the Sinophone acquires its valance and relevance." Shu-mei Shih, *Visuality and Identity: Sinophone Articulations Across the Pacific* (Berkeley: University of California Press, 2007), 34.

ethnic Chinese or Sinophone cultures as heterogeneous by stressing the need to pay attention to the linguistic plurality of these communities. Chua focuses on the notion of "being Chinese" as a pluralistic experience by describing the linguistically diverse everyday life of societies such as Taiwan and Singapore.[17] Shih takes a step further to emphasize how the array of accents present in Ang Lee's *Crouching Tiger, Hidden Dragon* (2000) challenges the monolithic and essentialist image of China as "the Middle Country" in which "authentic" Chinese culture and identity reside.[18]

While I question the utility of a concept like Pop Culture China and caution against its potential danger of reinforcing a geopolitical power play centered on China despite Chua's claim that the concept does not privilege any center, I want to note that Chua does admit that he is merely introducing an under-examined area to be explored by scholars in the field.[19] He sees Pop Culture China as a phenomenon, not necessarily an approach.[20] In fact, in the conclusion of his chapter on Pop Culture China, Chua affirms that this paradigm is a descriptive and prescriptive one, not exactly a critical or analytical one.[21]

What Pop Culture China does as a proposal is identify and delineate the patterns of circulation of popular culture produced in various locales by Chinese communities. The significance of this gesture lies in its attempt to initiate a change in direction for scholars who work on Sinophone cultures around the world via the production and circulation of popular culture from multiple sites. First, it encourages scholars to treat popular culture as an important phenomenon for the study of a pluralistic *huaren* (overseas Chinese) identity that consists of a web of flow and exchange among cultural producers and consumers of an array of backgrounds; second, it reminds us of the potential richness in research materials accessible to scholars, by resisting an essentialist and centralist research methodology.[22]

My proposal of Sinopop builds on Chua's Pop Culture China by adding an analytical and critical dimension to the study of popular culture in Sinophone

---

17. Chua elaborates his point: "differences, heterogeneities, and difficulties manifest themselves in the everyday life of every sizable ethnic Chinese community, including urban populations in contemporary China, not only in terms of frequently and mutually incomprehensible languages but also in other large and small ways, right down to the variation of daily foods. In this sense no individual ethnic Chinese would ever presume 'being Chinese' means a 'singular/mono' anything and a self-proclamation of 'being Chinese' is always a vague claim which is only substantiated contextually, depending on which, among the array of possible cultural elements, is called forth to substantiate the claim." *Structure, Audience and Soft Power*, 35.
18. Shih, *Visuality and Identity*, 2–4.
19. In Chua's words: "The configuration of Pop Culture China is materially and symbolically without center," *Structure, Audience and Soft Power*, 39.
20. Chua, *Structure, Audience and Soft Power*, 38.
21. Chua, *Structure, Audience and Soft Power*, 50.
22. Chua, "Pop Culture China," 121.

communities. I use Sinopop to describe popular music written in a Sinitic language (or languages) that captures multicultural and multilingual characteristics. Sinopop is thus a Sinophone expression with strong local features. Sinopop takes the "neglected terrain, which awaits analysis by interested scholars who reside within the dispersed ethnic Chinese population" by adopting the challenge of marginal Sinophone projects "with a desire to mine the richness of different cultural experiences."[23] More importantly, Sinopop takes this "desire" and turns it into actual action by challenging and undermining the powers that oppress various kinds of Sinoglossic experiences in order to give voice to local expressions often subsumed under hegemonic discourses.

Wee Meng Chee's Work as Sinopop

On September 28, 2010, Wee Meng Chee held an event at the Chinese Assembly Hall to launch his debut album, *Ho Ho Yeah* (*hou hou ye* 好好野),[24] which means "Good Stuff" in Cantonese, a dialect almost as commonly spoken as Mandarin is among Sinophone Malaysians. About fifty Perkasa members appeared at the venue to protest the launch.[25] Without any knowledge of the album's content, this Islamic organization insisted on boycotting and suppressing a voice of difference by invoking the rhetoric of racial harmony under the pretense of ethnic elitism.

Realizing the need to explain his position on the racial politics of Malaysia to those who saw him as a threat to the supposed racial harmony of the nation, in 2010, Wee openly supported Prime Minister Datuk Seri Najib Razak's 1Malaysia initiative, a national campaign to build a unified Malaysia by promoting interethnic relations.[26] He proposed to meet with the prime minister to discuss the possibility of promoting the principles of 1Malaysia in his work.[27] Even though Najib did not grant his wish, Wee released his directorial debut, *Nasi Lemak 2.0*,[28] the following year. The film is a Sinophone musical that promotes the 1Malaysia initiative of ethnic diversity and multiracial harmony. The film follows the journey of a Sinophone Malaysian chef as he undergoes various ordeals to learn how to make the best *nasi lemak* (coconut rice), a Malaysian national dish. Along the journey, he encounters several historical figures in Malaysian history that help him figure out the recipe for the dish. As the film concludes, he finds out that to

---

23. Chua, "Pop Culture China," 121.
24. Namewee, *Ho Ho Yeah* 好好野, Prodigee Media PDG 2010A, 2010, compact disc.
25. Perkasa is a non-governmental organization formed by conservative, extreme-right, ethnic Malays, convened in the aftermath of the Malaysian general elections in 2008. "Perkasa Disrupts Rapper's Do," *New Straits Times*, September 29, 2010, 20.
26. The campaign was officially launched on September 16, 2008.
27. Anis Ibrahim and Elvina Fernandez, "Rapper to Sing 1Malaysia Principles," *New Straits Times*, December 10, 2010, 20.
28. Namewee, dir., *Nasi Lemak 2.0*, Prodigee Media, 2011. DVD.

make good *nasi lemak*, he needs to come to terms with his Malaysian identity by weaning himself of the nostalgia for his cultural belonging to China.

The film uses food as a metaphor for interethnic connections, and the musical numbers in the film are products of the diversity in Malaysian society. Some of these musical numbers are songs from Wee's debut album and several are new songs written specifically for this film. "Rasa Sayang 2.0,"[29] the theme song of *Nasi Lemak 2.0*, appears at the end of the film. An example of Sinopop, the song takes a conciliatory tone rather than a controversial one, partly because of the film's attempt at interpreting and promoting the principles and agenda of Najib's 1Malaysia initiative. The song is a rendition of the popular Malay folk song "Rasa Sayang" (A Loving Feeling). Wee rewrote the song into "Rasa Sayang 2.0" to echo the basic beliefs of 1Malaysia in forging interethnic relations and understanding. The song is what we call a *rojak* (literally an Indian salad, but used commonly to refer to a mix) of languages, from Mandarin to Malay to English to Sinitic dialects. The lyrics repeatedly reference *Satu Malaysia* (1Malaysia), which has, since its introduction to the public, become a popular catch phrase in contemporary Malaysia, alongside *Malaysia boleh* (Malaysia can do it), to emphasize the unique diversity in Malaysia where ethnic groups learn to live in harmony, just like the variety of Indian, Malay, and Chinese cuisines available everywhere in the country.[30] 1Malaysia aims at promoting national unity regardless of racial background and religious belief. The 1Malaysia initiative believes that in order for the nation to benefit from its ethnic and cultural diversity, its people have to first come together to build a set of common values, such as equality, peace, and harmony. The government's role is important in helping build these values in Malaysia's multiethnic society.[31] No doubt a lot more effort is needed to repair the interethnic tensions that have a long history in Malaysia.[32] And in fact, rather ironically, instead of unifying its citizen by addressing issues of inequalities and exploitations, the 1Malaysia initiative downplays the historical context of racial

---

29. "Rasa Sayang 2.0," Apple Music, track 12 on Namewee, *Asia Most Wanted*, Warner Music Taiwan, 2013.
30. "Satu" means "one" in Bahasa Malay.
31. Some practical initiatives put forth by the government involve the building of the 1Malaysia health clinics, where Malaysians of any ethnic background can receive medical treatment for any condition for merely one ringgit (one Malaysian dollar), which is a version of universal healthcare, the 1Malaysia Housing Programme designed to help middle-income families become homeowners, and the building of low-cost grocery stores. For specific initiatives involving 1Malaysia, see Najib Razak, "The 1Malaysia Concept Part 1," NajibRazak.com, June 15, 2009, https://najibrazak.com/the-1malaysia-concept-part-1/.
32. Despite its call for equality and unity, to its critics, the 1Malaysia proposal harbors discriminatory regulations and rhetoric toward those who are not considered *bumiputras*. Even though the "true" *bumiputras* are the ethnic minorities or indigenous cultures such as the Orang Asli, the Malay symbolically appropriate the status of "natives." Needless to say, as majority natives, the concerns of the Malays are very different from those of the underrepresented groups.

and gender inequalities in the country to promote a brand of national identity built on meritocracy and elitism.[33]

On the one hand, the multiculturalism in Wee's "Rasa Sayang 2.0" compromises with the official version of interracial discourse championed by the state-sponsored 1Malaysia initiative and promotes the kind of conciliatory multiculturalism Wen Jin critiques in *Pluralist Universalism*.[34] On the other hand, the song does offer a critical edge in addressing power relations that suppress local identities, which I find necessary for a discussion of Sinopop. The fact that the song resists the nostalgic calling of ancestral cultures of all ethnic groups in Malaysia by emphasizing a return to local identities is the kind of critical and generative energy that is needed to encourage us to think beyond state power and the empty promises of multiculturalism: "No matter where you grandfathers are from, setting your heart on this land, is what 1Malaysia means."[35]

Before turning to the next example of Wee's work, I want to address an aspect of Sinopop that deals with a crucial element of Sinophonicity that has thus far been neglected by Sinophone scholars. While scholars are starting to pay more attention to the aspect of sound in Sinophone studies, such discussions tend to focus mainly on multilingualism or the difference between spoken language (in films) and written scripts (in literature). But what challenges does Sinophone studies face when it comes to the study of nonverbal and nonlinguistic sound, for example music? Have we been privileging linguistic sound and script by treating nonlinguistic sonic expressions as mere servants? Because the concept of Sinopop engages directly with music, it possesses the potential to scrutinize sound broadly understood, including nonlinguistic expressions. My proposal of the concept of Sinopop adds to and expands on this under-examined sonic aspect of Sinophone studies. The term is necessary, as its underscores the significance of a subfield or category affiliated with Sinophone studies that cannot be easily explained away with a general concept of the Sinophone. Wee's Sinopop, besides dealing with multilingual themes and content, appropriates different culturally coded musical genres to address issues of multiculturalism and interethnic harmony. The choice of transposing the Malay folk song "Rasa Sayang" into a multilingual and multicultural Malaysian national song of sorts throws the question of Sinophonicity into high relief. The melody of the song is familiar to the various communities in Malaysia regardless of ethnic or linguistic background, thus creating an affective interethnic connection among Malaysians, above and beyond the different languages of "Rasa Sayang 2.0." Beyond its ethnic specificity,

---

33. See Sheela Jane Menon, "Rakyat Malaysia: Contesting Nationalism and Exceptional Multiculturalism" (PhD diss., The University of Texas at Austin, 2016).
34. Wen Jin, *Pluralist Universalism: An Asian Americanist Critique of U.S. and Chinese Multiculturalisms* (Columbus: Ohio State University Press, 2012).
35. The line appears in the rap lyrics of "Rasa Sayang 2.0."

the genre of the Malay folk song has become a locally shared cultural expression, gaining new meanings for Malaysian society as a whole beyond linguistic and ethnic boundaries. We could take issue with Wee's reproduction of "Rasa Sayang" as a gesture of subsuming minority cultures to the dominant Malay culture. And yet, in so doing, we would also undermine the process of localization of the folk song through decades of interethnic cultural exchange and influence and thus empty out its significance to Malaysia at different stages of the country's history. Or, we can produce a strong reading of Wee's appropriation of the familiar Malay folk song to underline shared local features, casting an inclusive version of multiethnic Malaysia in support of the 1Malaysia initiative and thus resisting the nationalistic interpellation of the discourse of Chineseness in the diaspora. We can also read Wee's "Negarakuku," with which I opened this chapter, through a similar lens: as a song that contests hegemonic discourse and national ideologies. "Negarakuku" renders Malaysia's national anthem in the hip-hop genre, thus framing its satirical portrayal of interethnic tensions and racial inequalities within the genre's transgressive connotation as a subculture.

In March 2013, Wee rereleased his debut album in Taiwan with Sony Music under a different title: *Asia Most Wanted* (*Yazhou tongji* 亞洲通緝).[36] In addition to the songs collected in his debut album released in Malaysia, the album includes songs from *Nasi Lemak 2.0*, such as "Rasa Sayang 2.0." The album opens with "I Am Who I Am" (*Wo haishi wo* 我還是我),[37] a song about Wee's "Negarakuku" controversy. Yet, the prime example of what I would consider Sinopop is the song "Muar Love Song" (*Mapo de qingge* 麻坡的情歌).[38] The love theme in "Muar Love Song" is merely a foil as the linguistic plurality in Malaysia becomes the central topic of the song. The song, though written mainly in Mandarin, incorporates Malay, English, and the Hokkien dialect throughout. Wee suggests that Muar, the Malaysian state in which he grew up, has a version of Mandarin that is unique to the state and distinct from other versions such as those in Taiwan, China, and other states in Malaysia. This song proposes the possibility to conceptualize different versions of Mandarin similar to the debates about global Englishes. If different Sinophone communities speak their own versions of Mandarin, should the discussion of Mandarin in Sinophone studies not pay close attention to local versions of Mandarin while resisting the hegemony of *Putonghua*, standard Mandarin? "Muar Love Song" seems to propose this. But anyone who knows and follows Wee on his blog and YouTube page knows that "Muar Love Song" is a toned-down version of an earlier music video Wee posted

---

36. Namewee, *Asia Most Wanted*, Warner Music Taiwan, 2013, Apple Music.
37. Namewee, "Wo hai shi wo" 我還是我 [I am who I am], track 1 on *Asia Most Wanted* 亞洲通緝, Warner Music Taiwan, 2013, Apple Music.
38. Namewee, "Mapo de qingge" 麻坡的情歌 [Muar love song], track 11 on *Asia Most Wanted* 亞洲通緝, Warner Music Taiwan, 2013.

on YouTube in October 2006. This music video, "Muar Mandarin"³⁹ predates his controversial "Negarakuku":

語言沒有標準性 只有地方性
我不相信 你很了解這個道理
不然為什麼去KL 學人家講廣府話
……
不要害怕自己的文化 沒有定義
潮州粿條 福建炒蝦面
這就是我們的style 我們的定義
大聲講出來 這就是麻坡的華語

Language has no standard traits, only local features
I don't believe you truly understand this logic
If not, you would not be learning Cantonese in KL [Kuala Lumpur]
. . .
Don't be concerned about defining your own culture
Teochew Rice Noodle, Hokkien Fried Shrimp Noodle
That is our style, our definition
Say it loud and proud, "This is Muar Mandarin"

This excerpt from the song resonates with Shu-mei Shih's definition of the Sinophone by proclaiming that there is no essential standard of a language, except local versions of it. In a colloquial Mandarin marked by the local accent from Muar, Wee's hometown, the lyrics comment on how some Chinese from Muar fail to understand the significance of their local identity, especially with regard to language. Wee criticizes those who obsess over standard language by mocking them for moving to Kuala Lumpur to learn Cantonese, a dialect that has almost similar status as Mandarin in Malaysia. He reminds Muar Chinese that their cultural identity is defined by their local culture, such as food and their unique hybrid Mandarin, not the ideal of a standard language. Instead of pursuing a standard language, be it Malay, English, or a Sinitic language, Muar Chinese should be proud of their own local version of Mandarin rich in local characteristics. In other words, Wee uses his song to stress that each community defines its own language based on its local influence and usage; it is a matter of style, not a question of authenticity or standard. Hence, by comparing food culture to language in Muar, Wee declared the uniqueness of Muar's own version of Mandarin.

While I celebrate the uniqueness of local cultures in Sinophone societies as depicted in Wee's work, such as *Nasi Lemak 2.0* and "Muar Mandarin," I am

---

39. Namewee, "Namewee 黃明志 1st Music Video on YouTube [Muar Mandarin 麻坡的華語] @明志同名EP 2007," dir. Namewee, March 8, 2007, music video, 4:27, https://youtu.be/6M8fnjPLx6k.

aware of the politics involved in the seemingly innocent concept of multiculturalism. As discussed, Wee's embrace of multicultural Malaysia in his film *Nasi Lemak 2.0* is a compromise and a nod to the 1Malaysia initiative. In the end, such a conciliatory gesture fails to truly integrate and unify the Malaysian society. Contradictions that arise from discourses of multiculturalism like the above examples are what I hope a concept such as Sinopop could excavate. Another of Wee's songs, "Geebai People" (or "The Defeater," *Jibai ren* 擊敗人), will allow me to show what insights Sinopop can offer to our discussion of Sinoglossia and Sinophonicity.

Sinophonicity with a Postcolonial Twist: "Geebai People/Jibai Ren"

When Wee released a new song in the summer of 2017, "Geebai People," another controversy sprang up. The song depicts the confession of a man who was cheated on by his girlfriend. Feeling betrayed, hurt, and defeated, he describes the girlfriend as a defeater. The ballad reached one million hits within days of its release on YouTube.[40] Unlike his usual rap songs that openly include profanities, this ballad has a catchy tune and is soothing to listeners. Yet, Hokkien speakers or Malaysians who know some profane terms in Hokkien will not miss the double entendre of the title pronounced in pinyin as *Jibai ren*. The first two characters in the Mandarin pronunciation of the title sound exactly like the curse word for female genitalia in Hokkien. While Wee makes his fans speak vulgarities every time they sing along to his sad love song, the implications of *Jibai ren* are not just the product of word play. The defeater in the song is not just the girlfriend who cheated; in English translation, she is the f—ker who f—ks things up. The song references Wee Meng Chee or Namewee, since Wee had launched his YouTube channel under the name Namewee ten years before releasing the song. And Namewee, also almost sounds like a different Hokkien curse word for female genitalia. The song *Jibai ren* thus seems to commemorate Namewee's decade-long existence as an online personality and a constant nuisance to the Malaysian government. It only took a few days for the Malaysian public to react to Wee's new song. But this time most of the criticism came from the Sinophone community. A barrage of criticism of the song and of Wee started to surface in the Malaysian media, in mainstream newspapers, as well as radio and television stations. Politicians and celebrities chimed in to chastise Wee for negatively influencing young children by including profanity in this song. Some mainstream media even criticized him for casting a negative image of Malaysia as a Malaysian living abroad.

---

40. Namewee, "R-18! Namewee 黃明志 [Geebai People 擊敗人] @亞洲通吃 2017 All Eat Asia," dir. Namewee, July 1, 2017, music video, 7:10, https://youtu.be/yL1lr2gxRn4.

Again, Wee used his most familiar platform to response to this criticism. On July 8, 2017, he posted on his Facebook page a four-point response to his critics. First, he called out those who claimed to be protectors of moral values: "If young children do not even understand dialects, how would they pick up the homophonic meanings of profanity in the song title and the lyrics? Furthermore, if they already know some of these profanities, why should I be the one accused of contaminating them in the first place? Would they not have learned them somewhere else?" Second, he called the Malaysian mainstream media criticism ridiculous that he embarrassed his home country, Malaysia, by producing a vulgar song and releasing it abroad. As Wee pointed out, since he started uploading his music composition on YouTube, he had already released over 100 songs, but the Malaysian mainstream media had never aired any of them, except for "Stranger in the North" (*Piao xiang beifang* 漂向北方) a duet with pop-artist Leehom Wang (王力宏).[41] Even after five music albums, with a number of "healthy" songs, the media was only interested in reporting on his troubles with the Malaysian government, not in promoting his music. Only when he was nominated for the Taiwan Golden Melody Award (*Taiwan jinqu jiang* 台灣金曲獎) did mainstream media begin to report on him in a somewhat positive light as representing Malaysia. Additionally, he pointed out the hypocrisy of the Malaysian media: "you, the media would not support Malaysia-born artists and their works until they are acknowledged by the music industry abroad. And when they have a little accomplishment, you choose to beat them down with criticism of how they failed to represent Malaysia." Third, to his fellow artists in the entertainment circle in Malaysia, he put out a challenge: "For those who do not think that I deserve a nomination for an international award and am neither qualified to make music nor represent Malaysia, I truly hope that you would use your talent and accomplishment to beat me in representing Malaysia to the world. That would be much more positive and productive than to leave a bunch of online comments on the evening of the award ceremony to criticize and put me down." Last, he urged Malaysian politicians to stay out of the music industry and focus on their corrupted politics until their terms run out,[42] a reference to the criticism he made in "Negarakuku."

---

41. Namewee, "Piao xiang beifang" 漂向北方 [Stranger in the north], track 2 on 亞洲通車 *Cross Over Asia*, Avex Trax, 2016, Apple Music.
42. Namewee, "Zhe jitian yinwei 'jibairen' zhe shouge, wo bei malaixiya zhuliu meiti diantai baozhi zhengzhi renwu he yulequan de ren lunliu hongzha le yifan" 這幾天因為「擊敗人」這首歌，我被馬來西亞主流媒體電台報紙政治人物和娛樂圈的人輪流轟炸了一番 [Because of my song "Geebai People," I have been repeatedly bombarded by Malaysian mainstream media, politicians, and celebrities], Facebook, July 28, 2017, https://www.facebook.com/namewee/posts/10155189586673429.

I want to focus on Wee's first two responses to this controversy. First, on his second point, I think it is important to continue to examine why certain kinds of music are intentionally or unintentionally censored on mainstream media or on state-run media outlets. Why is Wee's music as a whole underappreciated at home unless it involves an internationally known artist like Leehom Wang? And why, then, is it appealing to audiences and media outside of Malaysia, for example the Taiwanese audience, but not in Malaysia? Furthermore, how has media censorship changed in this age when the circulation of various forms of media is seemingly less constricted? I envision Sinopop as a product of this transformation of the contemporary mediascape where transgressions to traditional systems of media production and regulations are made possible with the introduction of new platforms for cultural producers. Taiwan occupies an interesting position in this respect, especially when it comes to the politics of Chineseness and freedom of speech. Since the KMT took over Taiwan in 1949, Taiwan has adopted the other China discourse by opening its arms to overseas Chinese. Sinophone Malaysians have enjoyed the benefits of related policies by pursuing education and career opportunities in Taiwan for decades. What appears to be offensive to the Malaysian government and patriotic communities could appear as mere entertainment for Taiwanese audiences. In addition, Taiwan's perception of its society as frontrunner of democracy and civil rights in East Asia enabled Taiwanese audiences to come to Wee's defense when he was arrested and interrogated by the Malaysian government on charges of sedition. Hence, Wee earned himself the bad boy image and was able to maintain a significant fan base there, precisely because of these controversies. In a sense, Wee has benefitted from the ideological tug-of-war between Malaysian nationalism and international human rights via Taiwan. The changing mediascape in our globalized and technocratic world has allowed individuals living in and from authoritarian societies to locate alternate platforms for self-expressions beyond the scrutiny of state surveillance. Under such circumstances the traditional methodology of Area studies, which focuses predominantly on issues concerning specific nation states, requires the reconfiguration of our scholarly approach to identify and challenge the axes of power involved in the global circulation of popular culture today. The multidirectional approach of Sinophone studies and the concept of Sinopop as I propose it here pioneer the kind of methodology that addresses both issues at home and abroad as popular culture circulates in physical and cyber spaces across national boundaries.

Let me return to Wee's response to the criticism of his music video *Jibai ren* as an example of how he continues to toe the line with his controversial stance in Malaysian politics under the evolving mediascape of pop culture circulation. On Wee's first point, the issue of language and dialects comes into question. Though I am not advocating the use of profanity in any case, Wee's homophonic wordplay throughout the song *Jibai ren* is another example of Sinopop that reveals the Sinoglossic nature of multicultural communities with a Sinophone ingredient, like Malaysia. Unlike the direct handling of the theme of language plurality among Sinophone communities in "Muar Mandarin," the depiction of Sinophone cultures as heterogeneous through the inclusion of an array of languages, Wee makes a similar case in *Jibai ren* in a more subtle mode. While the song's lyrics are seemingly exclusively in Mandarin, profanities in several Sinophone languages are planted throughout. For instance, Hokkien words for "dick," "cry father,"[43] "f—k your mother," and "balls" appear in the following lines: "今天的天空很藍，叫我的心更不安／……／妳曾是我的依靠，被妳一再地灼傷／……／都怪我不夠勇敢妳釀的酒能取暖／……／曾經那麼燦爛，怕妳受傷" (The sky is blue today, I am feeling even more unsettled / . . . / You used to be my pillar, I am now repeatedly burnt by you / . . . / Because I lack courage, the wine you brew warms me up / . . . / Our love was once so splendid, I am afraid you will get hurt). Cantonese expletives such as "f—k your father" and "f—k your mother" can be found in the following: "愛情丟內樓道誰都不管／手裡淡淡的菸草裡痲痺我的憂傷" (Our love gets dumped in the inner corridor and no one cares / I immerse in the cigarette in my hand to numb my sadness). And there is also a homophone for the most commonly use expletive in English, "f—k" in "妳說妳沒辦法，可又心亂如痲" (You say you can't [love me] but you also can't help feeling distraught). Among those who recognize some of the languages embedded in the song, some might find the song offensive, while others might find it funny and entertaining instead.

Rather than only focusing on Wee's lyrics of the song, we also must take a closer look at the music video. It is hard not to wonder about the reasoning behind Wee's choice of a white woman as the female lead the defeater (or the Geebai person) and the choice of Malaysia as the backdrop.[44] The fact that Wee plays the male lead in the music video already suggests a colonial relationship of white woman versus Asian man. Furthermore, Wee is dressed in the typical East India Company colonial-style outfit, made with lightweight materials such as cotton, linen, and silk and designed for comfort and easy dressing to accommodate the tropical heat. To complete the colonial look, he wears a straw fedora throughout the music video. In this guise, Wee is akin to Homi Bhabha's "mimic man" in the music video, dressing up like and thus mimicking Malaysia's own oppressor from the past, the British colonialists in Malaya, while being caught up

---

43. This is an expression that could be translated as "what's the fuss?!" One would "cry father" when one's father is dead, so that is, in a sense, a curse word.
44. In the introduction to the music video, Wee approaches the woman who is supposedly vacationing in Malaysia, to star in his music video.

in an emotionally abusive unrequited relationship, as the lyrics suggest.[45] When the song and music video are regarded as a whole, and it should be treated so since Wee always premieres his works on YouTube as an audiovisual product, a latent colonial narrative and critique lies beneath the song. If the defeater as the white woman represents the desirable colonial promise couched in the discourse of "the white man's burden" (white woman perhaps, in this case), the unreciprocated relationship only ends up defeating him and leaving him abused and exploited. This could very well be summarized in the line where two sexual acts are camouflaged in the homophones for anal and oral sex (我才剛剛交出真心 妳卻扣繳我的真誠 I have just given you my true heart but you choose to discount my sincerity). Yet, the line is much more complex, as the homophones also work as homonyms to reinforce the colonial exchange as one that has left "I," the colonized, symbolically "f—ked in the a—," and the return payment from the British Empire as highly discounted (*koujiao* 扣繳), which is also a homophone for oral sex. To reinforce the subtle critique of the British colonization of Malaya, the title of the song as translated into English by Wee refers to Geebai people in the plural. Hence, the female lover in the song or white woman in the video could also be a stand-in for a group or nation (of colonizers, for instance).

Regardless of how controversial or low-brow these works are, I feel the need to think of a way to characterize them as a genre that would distinguish them from the solely descriptive category of Mandarinpop or Mandopop. Also, mandopop is too narrow in its common usage because it fails to capture Wee's multilingual work. Wee's works, in both music and film, are expressions of Sinoglossia. Describing these works as examples of Sinopop points beyond their Sinoglossic multiplicity to highlight their critical and transgressive nature. Sinopop as a concept hopes to amplify the critical potential of Sinophone studies to continuously challenge and question hegemonies of all forms.

Conclusion

The interest in Sinophone studies over the past decade offers Sinophone cultures from various locales ways to articulate their unique localized expressions outside the paradigms of Sinocentrism or diaspora. The Sinophone, as a critical category, rejects uniform representations circumscribed by hegemonic discourses within local societies, such as the ethnic policies in Malaysia. Even though Shih's work highlights Sinophonic dissonance as unique features of global Sinophone communities, her examples focus on the depictions of Sinophone heteroglossia in visual forms, such as cinema. This chapter has offered an examination

---

45. Homi Bhabha, "Of Mimicry and Man: The Ambivalence of Colonial Discourse," in *The Location of Culture* (New York: Routledge, 1994), 121–131.

of Sinophonic dissonance in popular music and culture using Taiwan-based Sinophone Malaysian artist Wee Meng Chee's work as a case study. I call this particular subgenre of music Sinopop to distinguish it from Mandopop and Cantopop, which are genres defined by the linguistic features of Mandarin and Cantonese respectively. Arguably, Sinopop could be regarded as a broader category that includes Mandopop and Cantopop; however, I propose it as a separate concept that can encompass popular cultural articulations of a Sinoglossic nature, especially the multilingual pop culture from marginal Sinophone communities, and propose to use the concept exclusively for marginal Sinophone expressions that reveal voluntarily or involuntarily tactics or rhetoric of resistance to cultural and political hegemony.

6

Chinese Writing, Heptapod B, and Martian Script

The Ethnocentric Bases of Language

Carlos Rojas

> The concept of Chinese writing thus functioned as a sort of European hallucination.
> —Jacques Derrida, *Of Grammatology*[1]

First published just over half a century ago, in 1967, Jacques Derrida's *Of Grammatology* is best known for its critique of what Derrida calls logocentrism—which is to say, an ontological orientation characterized by a systemic prioritization of the spoken word, while written text is treated as merely a second-order derivation of speech. Derrida contends that these assumptions inform a wide range of discourses and beliefs, particularly within what he identifies as a Western metaphysical tradition.

However, it is worth remembering that, after opening with three short epigraphs on writing taken from texts by Hegel, Rousseau, and two ancient Mesopotamian documents, respectively, Jacques Derrida begins *Of Grammatology* by referring first not to logocentrism but rather to ethnocentrism:

> This triple exergue is intended not only to focus attention on the *ethnocentrism* which, everywhere and always, had controlled the concept of writing. Nor merely to focus attention on what I shall call *logocentrism*: the metaphysics of phonetic writing (for example, of the alphabet) which was fundamentally—for enigmatic yet essential reasons that are inaccessible to a simple historical relativism—nothing but the most original and powerful ethnocentrism, in the process of imposing itself upon the world.[2]

---

1. Jacques Derrida, *Of Grammatology*, trans. Gayatri Spivak (Baltimore, MD: Johns Hopkins University Press, 1998), 86.
2. Derrida, *Of Grammatology*, 3, here and below, all emphases are from the original, unless otherwise noted.

Moreover, not only does Derrida introduce logocentrism through the lens of ethnocentrism, but he emphasizes that the function of his "triple exergue" (and, by implication, of the volume as a whole) is "not only to announce that the science of writing—*grammatology*—shows signs of liberation all over the world," but rather it is "above all" to suggest that "such a science of writing runs the risk of never being established as such and with that name."[3] The reason for this risk, Derrida contends, is that this science of writing, or grammatology, can only be imagined from within a preexisting logocentric framework—"within a world to which a certain concept of the sign (later I shall call it *the* concept of the sign) and a certain concept of the relationships between speech and writing, have *already* been assigned."[4]

In *Of Grammatology*, Derrida not only examines the nexus of ethnocentric and logocentric assumptions embedded within Western metaphysics, but he also points to the way in which (nominally) non-phonetic writing systems ranging from Mesopotamian cuneiform and Egyptian hieroglyphics to Chinese characters frequently functioned as a hallucinatory other within the European imagination and were tacitly used to reinforce the logocentric assumptions that have aggregated around the Western writing systems. In fact, at one point Derrida suggests (apparently in his own voice) that "massively nonphonetic scripts like Chinese or Japanese" function as "testimony of a powerful movement of civilization developing *outside of all logocentrism*"—thereby appearing to replicate the same logocentric gesture that he himself is ostensibly critiquing, by imagining Chinese and Japanese as occupying a status of radical alterity vis-à-vis Western logocentrism.[5] That is to say, by positing other writing systems as occupying a space radically *outside of all logocentrism*, Derrida is implying that human linguistic systems form a strict binary between thoroughly logocentric ones and categorically non-logocentric ones—which, ironically, further reinforces the *perception* of logocentrism as a homogenous and undifferentiated entity.

The distinction between popular *discourses about language* and *linguistic reality* is an important one, because while it is certainly true that the Chinese writing system is frequently *discussed* as though it represented a stark antithesis to the very nature of the Western alphabetic scripts, it is important to recognize that it is deeply misleading to characterize the Chinese and Japanese writing systems as "massively nonphonetic." Apart from the fact that the Japanese writing system is a hybrid of a syllabary (actually, two distinct syllabaries) and a character-based system, it is not even correct to characterize the *character-based* portion of the Japanese and Chinese writing systems as nonphonetic. Not only did most

---

3. Derrida, *Of Grammatology*, 4.
4. Derrida, *Of Grammatology*, 4.
5. Derrida, *Of Grammatology*, 90, emphases added.

Chinese characters (and their Japanese equivalents, known in Japanese as *kanji*) "includ[e] phonetic elements very early," as Derrida concedes, but many of those same elements continue to carry a phonetic function in the writing systems as they exist today (and this is particularly true of modern Chinese). Moreover, even in the absence of phonetic elements that reliably reflect the modern pronunciation of the character, it is still inaccurate to say that the Chinese character system (as it is employed in either the Chinese or Japanese scripts, or historically in other writing systems such as Korean and Vietnamese) is nonphonetic. As William Boltz observes in an essay on the emergence of writing in China, the claim that Chinese is nonphonetic ignores

> the very obvious fact that every Chinese character has a specific, concrete, recognized pronunciation . . . just as graphs in alphabetic scripts do, and that every literate Chinese speaker can read it (i.e., can give phonetic values to it), just as literate speakers of languages written with alphabets do.[6]

Instead, what Derrida and others actually *mean* when they use the term *phonetic* in this way is that lexical elements code for sound at the level of the individual phoneme or syllable. By characterizing the Chinese writing system as nonphonetic, accordingly, Derrida is not only replicating a logocentric view of language, but he is simultaneously promulgating a misleading and counterintuitive understanding of what it means for language to be phonetic in the first place.

My objective here, however, is not to rehearse Derrida's critique of logocentrism or his fascination with the Chinese script; instead, I follow his lead in approaching the question of language and writing through a set of concerns with community and ethnocentrism. For instance, it is important to note that even as Derrida uses the Chinese script as a strategic counterpoint to what he claims are the logocentric tendencies that underpin Western writing systems, his understanding of Chinese writing itself is mediated through a set of ethnocentric assumptions. Derrida, accordingly, is in fact correct when he states that *"logocentrism . . . was fundamentally . . . nothing but the most original and powerful ethnocentrism,"* though the ethnocentrism in question is actually his own. What role does ethnocentrism play in our understanding of the relationship between speech and writing, and of language itself? Is this sort of ethnocentrism necessarily a limitation, or is it instead a necessary precondition for language itself?

In the following discussion, I approach these questions through an analysis of a fictional work that uses a mediated version of the Chinese writing system to describe humanity's encounter with an extraterrestrial race. Ted Chiang's 1998 short story, "Story of Your Life," which was subsequently adapted for the screen

---

6. William Boltz, "Literacy and the Emergence of Writing in China," in *Writing and Literacy in Early China: Studies from the Columbia Early China Seminar*, ed. Li Feng and David Branner (Seattle: University of Washington Press, 2011), 55.

in Denis Villeneuve's 2016 film, *Arrival*, explores issues of language, culture, and ethnocentrism through a plotline that revolves around aliens whose language (and worldview) is radically different from our own. In this way, the work explores how our understanding of the world is mediated through language and what it might mean to radically reassess the underlying assumptions upon which these worldviews are predicated. I suggest that not only do these two works (Chiang's story and Villeneuve's film) reflect on a set of linguistic issues that are at the heart of the concept of Sinoglossia (in that the works indirectly reference a set of long-standing Western assumptions about the nature of the Chinese language while at the same time referencing more directly the challenge of establishing effective communication and forging communities within a heteroglossic environment), but furthermore they may be viewed as Sinoglossic texts in their own right (in that Ted Chiang is a member of the global Chinese diaspora, whose own views on the Chinese language offer an interesting counterpoint to those presented in his story).

Language and Meaning

In both Chiang's and Villeneuve's versions of the work in question, Earth is visited by a fleet of alien spacecraft that then hover above multiple locations around the world. Each of the spacecraft periodically sends down an elevator-like contraption to the earth's surface, permitting humans on the ground to enter the spacecraft and view the aliens, who resemble giant seven-legged octopi. The work's main plotline revolves around an American linguist named Louise Banks (played by Amy Adams in the film) and a theoretical physicist surnamed Donnelly (Jeremy Renner), who have been hired by the US Army to help decipher the aliens' language and figure out how to communicate with them. When Banks is initially recruited for this assignment, she is given a recording of sounds made by the aliens and is asked whether she can decipher it. She replies that it would be impossible to decipher the language without more context, and instead she must be given access to the aliens in order to be able to interact with them directly.

In Ted Chiang's original story, Banks proceeds to label the aliens' aural language "Heptapod A," and when Donnelly asks her what the "A" stands for, Banks replies that "it just distinguishes this language from any other ones the heptapods might use."[7] Later, Banks tries to communicate with the aliens using writing, and gradually realizes that their speech and their writing belong to two

---

7. Ted Chiang, "Story of Your Life," in Chiang, *Stories of Your Life and Others* (New York: Vintage, 2016).

completely different linguistic systems. She therefore dubs the writing system Heptapod B and treats it as a distinct language in its own right.

At one point in the story, Banks explains the relationship between Heptapod A and Heptapod B to Donnelly by writing the words *not allowed* on a whiteboard, and then drawing a circle with a diagonal line through it. She explains,

> "Linguists describe writing like this"—I indicated the printed words—"as 'glottographic' because it represents speech. Every human written language is in this category. However, this symbol"—I indicated the circle and the diagonal line—"is 'semasiographic' writing, because it conveys meaning without reference to speech. There's no correspondence between its components and any particular sounds."
>
> "And you think all of heptapod writing is like this?"
>
> "From what I've seen so far, yes. It's not picture writing, it's far more complex. It has its own system of rules for constructing sentences, like a visual syntax that's unrelated to the syntax for their spoken language."

The distinction between glottographic and semasiographic writing systems was popularized by Geoffrey Sampson in his 1985 volume, *Writing Systems*, and refers to the relationship between linguistic form and meaning.[8] A non-glottographic sign is one that conveys a meaning for which there is no *unique* analogue in oral speech though its meaning may be explained using speech. To take Banks's example, the sign Ø means "forbidden," "prohibited," "barred," and so forth, but this meaning can be expressed using a variety of linguistic formulations, and there is no single one-to-one correspondence between the sign and its oral articulation.

Banks's claim that "every human written language" is glottographic, meanwhile, is perhaps technically true—but only as an uninteresting tautology. That is to say, humans do in fact use many semiotic systems that are *not* glottographic (common examples include traffic signs, mathematical symbols, and even emojis),[9] and in principle these latter systems could also be considered "human languages," *unless* one's definition of a human language includes the additional specification that *the meaning of formulations produced by the semiotic system must have one-to-one correspondence with a corresponding formulation in a natural language*. If one's understanding of a "human language" does not include this additional stipulation, then non-glottographic semiotic systems could also be considered languages (and, indeed, we already frequently speak of computer or coding "languages," and refer to mathematics as the "universal language"). In addition, it is important to recognize that these latter systems are

---

8. Geoffrey Sampson, *Writing Systems*, 2nd ed. (Sheffield, UK: Equinox Publishing, 2015).
9. Xu Bing, for instance, wrote an entire book in emojis: Xu Bing, *Book from the Ground: From Point to Point* (Boston, MA: MIT Press, 2014).

not distinguished solely by the fact that they lack fixed equivalents in *oral speech*, because it is equally true that they lack fixed equivalents in any *written script* associated with a natural language. Accordingly, the real difference that the glottographic/non-glottographic distinction ultimately serves to address is really a distinction between the written forms of natural languages, and semiotic systems that are not considered natural languages (and, by extension, do not have fixed equivalents in *either* the oral *or* written forms of any natural language).

The term *glottographic*, accordingly, is arguably a (partial) logocentric misnomer, since it implies that oral speech is the only true form of a natural language, and all written (or other) forms of linguistic expression are merely "representations" of speech. (The root of *glottographic* is *glotto*, which is derived from the Greek term *glotta*, meaning "tongue," and therefore implies that language is fundamentally oral.) Moreover, even if we adopt a non-logocentric approach and specify that a non-glottographic language is one that does not have fixed equivalents in *either* the oral *or* written forms of any natural language, this simply raises the question of what counts as a "natural language" in the first place. A natural language is usually defined as a language that has developed autonomously, in contrast to a semiotic system that has been developed for a specific purpose. However, one could just as easily argue that many nonlinguistic semiotic systems (like math) develop organically over time, and, conversely, many elements of "natural languages" are deliberately formulated for specific purposes. Moreover, while it is often assumed that writing evolved naturally from representational pictures to pictographic systems to ideographic systems and, finally, to syllabic or alphabetic systems, this is a deeply logocentric perspective that implies that only syllabic or alphabetic writing systems are fully developed and that other writing systems (such as Chinese) are stuck in a state of arrested development (while also ignoring the degree to which even alphabetic languages frequently feature non-glottographic elements, such as punctuation marks).[10]

In Chiang's story, the heptapods use a "flat circular screen mounted on a small pedestal" to display their writing, which is described rather abstractly as resembling "fanciful praying mantids drawn in a cursive style, all clinging to each other to form an Escheresque lattice." In Villeneuve's film adaptation, however, the writing had to be displayed directly, and the task of figuring out what exactly the alien script should look like fell to Eric Heisserer, the screenwriter, who recalls that

> it was a long, arduous process for me. I started trying to describe the language textually in the script, but I was dissatisfied with my own descriptions. I was complaining to my wife about that at dinner, and she challenged me to draw for

---

10. For a summary and critique of this logocentric narrative, see James Elkins, *The Domain of Images* (Ithaca, NY: Cornell University Press, 2001).

her what it looked like. So I drew a circular symbol to connote the nonlinear orthography of the heptapods, and I added some accents and circles around the symbols. It was the first time I put visual things in a screenplay.[11]

Heisserer then passed his initial thoughts to the film's designer, Patrice Vermette, who came up with the idea of having the heptapods produce and display their writing not by using a digital screen but rather by generating puffs of dark globules, like squid ink. Vermettte oversaw a team that essentially invented the script from scratch, coming up with a "font" that would determine the script's basic appearance and then developing over a hundred distinct morphemic elements that could be combined to form each "logogram."

Heisserer incorporated the work of Vermette and his team as he was completing and revising the screenplay, and the final shooting draft describes the alien script as consisting of

> INK GLOBULES [that] float from the mist. Like oil in glycerine. Thousands of drops; horizontal black rain, but intelligent . . .
>
> They all start to form something against the partition:
>
> A brilliant LOGOGRAM. An inkblot coffee-cup stain with mesmerizing fractal embellishments.

In the film, the logograms are beautifully rendered as delicate, effervescent clouds that retain their intricate forms for a few seconds before dissolving, like ink dissolving back into water. Curiously, however, it was precisely in this transition from the story (in which Banks attempts to decode both heptapod languages simultaneously) to the film (in which she never really attempts to decode the oral language and instead focuses exclusively on the written one) that we simultaneously see a shift in the terminology used to refer to the heptapods' written characters. In particular, in the story, the characters are called *semagrams* (which is a term used to denote textual elements that have no direct counterpart in oral speech) while in the film they are instead called *logograms* (which technically refers to a written character that directly denotes a word or phrase, thereby implying that the alien language is, in fact, glottographic). In addition to dropping the story's use of the term *semagram*, the film drops the story's emphasis on the fact that Heptapod A and Heptapod B are two completely independent (and, hence, non-logocentric) linguistic systems. In other words, the film adaptation tacitly reintroduces a set of logocentric terminology and assumptions that Chiang's original story had carefully avoided.

---

11. Jordan Zakarin, "Arrival Invented a New, Insanely Complicated Alien Language," *Inverse*, https://www.inverse.com/article/23159-arrival-invented-new-complicated-alien-language.

As Banks, in the film, gradually learns the aliens' written language, she discovers that each logogram can be broken down into discrete lexical elements. At the same time, however, each logogram is shaped as a circle, with no fixed beginning or end—which implies, as Banks puts it, that the heptapods use a "non-linear orthography," to which Donnelly adds that this means "they'd actually have to think nonlinearly, then." A few scenes later, the film returns to this question of the relationship between language and thought, in response to the discovery that Banks has begun using some Heptapod B lexical elements that others in her team had not yet deciphered. Donnelly remarks, "All this focus on alien language. Look, I did some research and there's this idea that immersing yourself in a foreign language can rewire your brain," to which Banks responds, "The Sapir-Whorf hypothesis, yes. The theory that the language you speak determines how you think."

Not really a formal linguistic theory, the Sapir-Whorf hypothesis instead refers to a popular extrapolation of some elements of the work of Edward Sapir and Benjamin Lee Whorf, positing that language either influences or even determines thought. Many of the published discussions of *Arrival*'s treatment of language and linguistics note the film's allusion to this hypothesis though many proceed to point out that few professional linguists would support the strong version of the hypothesis as it is popularly understood (that language determines cognition) though many would accept a weaker version (that language, under some circumstances, may influence thought). Given that the popular understanding of the Sapir-Whorf hypothesis is not widely accepted by linguists, it is worth noting that, in the film, the hypothesis is introduced not by Banks (who is a professional linguist) but rather by Donnelly, who mentions that he ran across it while doing some independent research online. On the other hand, the film introduces the hypothesis precisely in the context of Banks's military superiors' suspicion that Banks—in the process of learning the heptapods' language—may in fact be starting to *think* like a heptapod. The work concludes with the revelation that, as a result of learning the alien language, Banks has in fact gained the ability to disengage herself from a strictly linear temporality and is able to perceive the past, present, and future simultaneously.

Although the Sapir-Whorf hypothesis is the linguistic model that is mentioned most explicitly in *Arrival*, the film also alludes indirectly to another well-known intervention in the philosophy of language—though this latter allusion appears to have received little or no attention from commentators discussing the work's linguistic implications. In particular, when Banks is initially trying to convince her military superiors to let her try to decipher the aliens' writing (rather than focusing only on their "speech," as she had been originally instructed), she offers a short anecdote to explain her request:

> In 1770, Captain James Cook's ship ran aground on the coast of Australia. He led a party into country and met the aboriginal people. One of the sailors pointed to the animals that hopped around with their young in pouches and asked what they were called. The aborigine replied "Kanguru." . . . It wasn't until later that they learned that "Kanguru" means "I don't understand."

This anecdote about the origins of the word kangaroo is a popular one though the film itself correctly notes that it is probably apocryphal.[12] The anecdote, however, closely resembles philosopher W.W.O. Quine's well-known thought play illustrating the difficulties of what Quine calls "*radical* translation, i.e., translation of the language of a hitherto unknown people."[13] The full version of Quine's thought play is not as succinct as Banks's Kanguru anecdote in *Arrival*, but it opens with a similar premise. Quine asks his reader to imagine an encounter between a linguist and his informant, wherein "a rabbit scurries by, the native says 'Gavagai,' and the linguist notes down the sentence 'Rabbit' (or 'Lo, a rabbit') as tentative translation, subject to further cases."[14] The premise of the thought play is that while deciphering the informant's utterance, the linguist has the opportunity to try out various stimulus-response exchanges to assess whether his interpretation of the native word is correct. However, as Quine carefully details, there are many points of conceptual indeterminacy where this would be difficult or impossible, based simply on an observation of the native's speech acts and his response to outside stimuli.

In particular, the native may have a very different ontological orientation, such that his very understanding of the world may be qualitatively different from that of the linguist:

> Who knows but what the objects to which this term applies are not rabbits after all, but mere stages or brief temporal segments of rabbits? . . . Or perhaps the objects to which "gavagai" applies are all and sundry undetached parts of rabbits . . . A further alternative likewise compatible with the same old stimulus meaning is take "gavagai" as a singular term naming the fusion . . . of all rabbits: that single though continuous portion of the spatiotemporal world that consists of rabbits.[15]

Quine proceeds to argue that the meaning of *any* utterance, if considered only within the specific context in which it is made, is radically indeterminate—since the act of specifying its meaning necessarily requires an attention not only to issues of language but also to the underlying epistemological and ontological

---

12. For a discussion of the etymology of the term, see Online Etymology Dictionary, "Kangaroo," http://www.etymonline.com/index.php?term=kangaroo.
13. Willard van Orman Quine, *Word and Object* (Cambridge, MA: MIT Press, 1960), 28, emphases added.
14. Quine, *Word and Object*, 29.
15. Quine, *Word and Object*, 51–52.

paradigms that the utterance necessarily presupposes. In some instances, these conceptual differences could perhaps be clarified through further observation, but in others the interpretive gaps may be so profound that they prove virtually impossible for the prospective interlocutors to bridge.

In the scenario featured in *Arrival*, meanwhile, the possibility of an ontological gap is particularly acute, given that the prospective interlocutors literally come from different worlds, and therefore there is no reason to assume that they have *any* shared "worldview." The attempt to learn each other's language, accordingly, necessarily involves not only an attempt to decipher a linguistic code but also to use that same linguistic interaction to investigate an underlying set of postulates on which the languages in question are grounded. At the same time, the extraterrestrial premise of *Arrival* merely dramatizes a set of concerns that are relevant to everyday language use. That is to say, given that we are rarely fully aware of the epistemological and ontological assumptions on which our language use is predicated, it is nearly impossible to know precisely whether our assumptions are shared by our interlocutors, or whether we are *really* talking about the same thing when we use language in similar ways.

The implication of the Kanguru/gavagai thought experiments, accordingly, is that a set of "ethnocentric" assumptions is a necessary precondition for meaningful communication, because at some point prospective interlocutors must make a leap of faith and assume that their counterparts share at least some of the ontological assumptions that underpin their own linguistic community. By showcasing a linguistic encounter in which none of these ethnocentric assumptions apply, meanwhile, the fictional example of the extraterrestrial heptapods points to an alternative possibility—suggesting that in the process of learning a truly alien language, one may simultaneously gain access to the language's corresponding ontology.

Language and Time

In Villeneuve's adaptation of Chiang's story, each of the twelve alien ships distributes a message to the nation over which it is positioned, and each nation races to decipher the missive. While each national delegation uses very different methodologies to communicate with the aliens (we are told, for instance, that the Japanese use cello music, a South American delegation use sign language, and the Chinese use mahjong),[16] they all end up making the same basic error—

---

16. This reflects the somewhat bizarre belief that, according to the "language expert" on the team advising the film's scriptwriter, "it would be nigh impossible for anyone to try to teach an alien race or even just a foreigner Mandarin in a compressed time. There are thousands of unique symbols and interpretation is tough." Zakarin, "Arrival Invented a New."

interpreting the heptapods' desire to offer humanity a "tool" as instead being an offer of a "weapon." Deciding that the aliens' visit has military implications, each of the twelve nations—which had previously been cooperating—immediately shut down lines of communication, and several prepare to launch preemptive military attacks against one another. Banks and Donnelly, however, eventually realize that the alien text that the US has received is only one-twelfth of the full message, and that in order to decipher the rest it would be necessary for the US to cooperate with the other eleven nations.

Fortunately, at the last moment—just as the US and China are about to initiate military actions against one another—Banks manages to get through to her Chinese counterpart and together they convince both nations to stand down and reopen lines of communication. The remaining ten nations are brought into the dialogue as well. It turns out, moreover, that the ultimate significance of the message lies not so much in its content, but rather in its *function*. That is to say, the message is designed to encourage the major nations of the earth to collaborate with one another and to gift humanity with the heptapods' own nonlinear relationship to time, thereby enabling humanity to see the future. The film explains that the heptapods, thanks to their own ability to see the future, know that humanity will help them out in another 3,000 years, which is why they are now giving humanity the gift of (their) language as an anticipatory expression of their gratitude. The heptapod message, accordingly, has a truly perlocutionary function, insofar as its significance lies not so much in the meaning that it conveys but rather in its ability to (re)constitute human communities.

Although Villeneuve's film concludes on an optimistic note, the heptapods helping humanity to bridge its existing ethnocentric differences and unite into a global community, Chiang's original story ends on a more ambiguous note, the aliens abruptly leaving Earth without having made their objective clear. Moreover, although the climax of Villeneuve's film revolves around a critical moment of collaboration between Banks and her Chinese counterpart, Chiang's original story is itself haunted by a moment of what may be perceived as anti-Chinese ethnocentric prejudice.

In particular, in May of 2016—just six months before the release of Villeneuve's adaptation of his story—Chiang published an essay in *The New Yorker* recalling the frustration he experienced trying to learn Chinese characters when he was young, and he goes on to speculate that the nature of the written language may have contributed to what he contends to be the general conservatism of Chinese culture. Chiang posits that "Chinese culture is notorious for the value it places on tradition" and argues that it may be precisely the Chinese script's non-phonetic nature that has helped historical texts (and the viewpoints they contain) to retain relevance in a contemporary world:

> One of the virtues claimed for Chinese characters is that they make it easy to read works written thousands of years ago. The ease of reading classical Chinese has been significantly overstated, but, to the extent that ancient texts remain understandable, I suspect it's due to the fact that Chinese characters aren't phonetic. Pronunciation changes over the centuries, and when you write with an alphabet spellings eventually adapt to follow suit. (Consider the differences between "Beowulf," "The Canterbury Tales," and "Hamlet.") Classical Chinese remains readable precisely because the characters are immune to the vagaries of sound. So if ancient Chinese manuscripts had been written with phonetic symbols, they'd become harder to decipher over time.[17]

What Chiang expresses here may be seen as a version of the Orientalist conviction that Asian societies are located in a state of temporal stasis, outside of linear history. Starting from the assumption that Chinese culture is backward-looking and rooted in the past, Chiang suggests that the specific nature of the Chinese writing system has played a causal role in helping perpetuate this orientation.

As Chiang himself acknowledges, however, the ease of reading classical Chinese can be overstated, and the stability of the Chinese written language is frequently exaggerated. To begin with, although in principle it may be true that the forms of Chinese characters tend to change more slowly than do the spellings of words in European languages, Chinese characters have undergone significant transformations over time. Most recently, in the 1950s, the People's Republic of China simplified the composition of over 2,000 characters, yielding a written form of the language that differs so much from the "traditional" form of the language still used in Hong Kong, Taiwan, and elsewhere, that readers familiar only with one variant often have considerable difficulty reading text written in the other. The Chinese writing system had undergone numerous other transformations prior to the twentieth century, and not only are the earliest forms of the written language (such as those found in the oracle bone inscriptions from approximately 3,000 years ago) virtually unintelligible to contemporary readers without specialized training, even texts written in the small seal script style developed after the Qin dynasty (221–206 BCE) script reform would be challenging to most contemporary readers, not to mention the pre-reform script of all of the now-canonical Warring States period texts (including all of the works subsequently canonized as the Four Books and Five Classics). When modern readers read these early Chinese texts, however, they usually read them with the characters "translated" into their modern forms—which would be the equivalent of reading Beowulf with the words rendered with their modern spellings.

---

17. Ted Chiang, "Bad Character," *The New Yorker*, May 16, 2016, https://www.newyorker.com/magazine/2016/05/16/if-chinese-were-phonetic.

Moreover, the degree to which the spelling of individual words or the rendering of individual Chinese characters has changed over time is only one factor contributing to the intelligibility of premodern texts, and others include changes in syntax, punctuation, and even the actual *meanings* of individual words or characters. Beyond the empirical question of how much the Chinese writing system has changed over time compared with alphabetical languages like English, however, there is also Chiang's underlying implication that the form of the written language *causes* a broader set of attitudes and beliefs. In fact, however, in this particular case it is more likely that the causality works largely in reverse—in that it is precisely the belief in the continued relevance of tradition that leads to efforts to make written language from earlier eras available and intelligible to the general public.

In his comments on the Chinese writing system, in other words, Chiang is implicitly proposing a version of Sapir-Whorfism that is the direct inverse of that which he foregrounds in his own story. Specifically, while the story revolves around the ability of Heptapod B semiagraphs to permit its users to become "unstuck in time,"[18] Chiang himself contended that Chinese characters had the effect of leaving Chinese culture and civilization figuratively "stuck in time." Although Chiang's linguistic claims are almost certainly incorrect (for the reasons detailed above), in *making* these claims Chiang simultaneously illustrated an alternative version of the Sapir-Whorf hypothesis. In particular, to the extent that Chiang is unwittingly reiterating a set of Orientalist prejudices about the ahistorical nature of Asian societies, he is demonstrating the power of those same ethnocentric *discourses* to transform the (sociocultural) worldview of individuals exposed to them—even when the individuals in question might otherwise be viewed as part of the extended community that is being targeted by those same discourses (as is the case with the Chinese-American Ted Chiang).

Language and Community

As noted, in Ted Chiang's original story, Heptapod B is expressed not via clouds of ink globules but rather by means of images on a digital screen. Although Chiang associates the Chinese written language with the weight of tradition and a hyperstability of cultural attitudes, digital text, by contrast, is arguably characterized by a high degree of flexibility and fluidity. On one hand, digital text can be erased with a single keystroke, and even under ideal circumstances the underlying technology tends to be significantly less stable than is text that is printed or

---

18. Kurt Vonnegut, *Slaughterhouse-Five*; quoted by Douglas Robinson, "Translating the Nonhuman: Towards a Sustainable Theory of Translation, or a Translational Theory of Sustainability" (unpublished manuscript).

inscribed on physical surfaces. On the other hand, however, the dynamism of the internet—and particularly its ability to bring together individuals separated by vast distances—has helped encourage the development of a wide range of linguistic permutations, some of which diverge quite radically from the "standard" versions of the corresponding languages.

One notable example of this phenomenon is the recent development of what is known as "Martian script" (*huoxing wen* 火星文), which is an internet variant of Chinese script in which characters are systematically substituted with other characters or symbols. Originally developed in Taiwan and subsequently adopted in mainland China, the script is particularly popular among young people but is regarded as rather alien by others. This script had a moment of notoriety in early 2006, after the administrators for Taiwan's national college entrance exams decided to include two questions involving Martian script phrases that students were asked to translate into standard Chinese. The phrases in question consisted entirely of punctuation marks and alphabetic letters and were likely to be self-evident to students who frequented internet chat rooms but unintelligible to others. The first question, for instance, asked students to translate the symbol ::>_<::, which is a visual representation of the act of crying (with teardrops running down one's cheeks). The second question offered students the phrase *3Q Orz*, which was a combination of a visual and translingual signifiers, the "3Q" portion being read as "san-Q" (i.e., the Chinese pronunciation of the numeral 3 and the English pronunciation of the letter Q), which yields a rough homonym of a Chinese-accented pronunciation of the English phrase "thank you," while the visual form of the letters *Orz* invokes an image of a person kneeling on the ground while facing left, to show appreciation. The full phrase "3Q Orz," accordingly, could be translated as meaning "thank you very much."[19] These exam questions precipitated a wave of protest, and two months later it was announced that these sorts of questions would be banned from future tests (though the results from the January test would not be recalculated).

The practice of calling this internet language Martian script reflects the perception that the youth cohort who developed it is radically distinct from mainstream society—to the point of being perceived as virtual aliens. At the same time, beyond the internet script's general connotations of exoticness, the specific reference to Martians invites a set of associations that bring us back to the concerns with language and communication at the heart of *Arrival*. In particular, the film's representation of the aliens as resembling giant seven-legged octopi builds on a long tradition of representing extraterrestrials—and Martians

---

19. "Martian Language Banned in Taiwanese College Entrance Exam," Taiwan.com.au, https://web.archive.org/web/20091024125942/http://www.taiwan.com.au/Scitech/Internet/Trends/20060306.html.

in particular—as cephalopod-like creatures. Most notably, in one of the most famous fictional depictions of Martians, H. G. Wells's *War of the Worlds*, the aliens are described as having "Gorgon groups of tentacles":

> Those who have never seen a living Martian can scarcely imagine the strange horror of its appearance. The peculiar V-shaped mouth with its pointed upper lip, the absence of brow ridges, the absence of a chin beneath the wedgelike lower lip, the incessant quivering of this mouth, the Gorgon groups of tentacles, the tumultuous breathing of the lungs in a strange atmosphere, the evident heaviness and painfulness of movement due to the greater gravitational energy of the earth—above all, the extraordinary intensity of the immense eyes—were at once vital, intense, inhuman, crippled and monstrous.[20]

Beyond the countless adaptations of Wells's novel, many subsequent science fiction works have similarly imagined aliens as tentacled creatures—examples ranging from H. P. Lovecraft's classic 1928 story, "The Call of Cthulhu," to the squid-like alien in the 2012 film *Prometheus*.

As popular science writer Christie Wilcox notes, there is probably a good reason why Martians and other aliens have been frequently rendered as cephalopods. Cephalopods have an anatomy and physiology that is radically unlike our own (they belong to the phylum of mollusks, which consists primarily of shelled animals like mussels and clams), yet they are surprisingly intelligent. Octopi, in particular, have a remarkably large number of neurons in their nervous system (approximately 500 million, which is close to the range of some mammals, such as dogs)—though, unlike mammals, most of octopus neurons are not located in their comparatively large brain (which is wrapped in a ring around their esophagus) but rather in their tentacles.[21] At a functional level, octopi are known to play, use tools, and solve puzzles, and in 2012 a consortium of scientists even included octopi on a list of animals that display a level of cognition that appears to be consistent with consciousness.[22]

Octopus intelligence, however, is radically unlike our own. From an evolutionary perspective, the lineages that yielded cephalopods and vertebrates diverged more than 500 million years ago, which is to say twice as long as it has been since the appearance of the earliest dinosaurs. As Wilcox explains, most other animals that we consider intelligent—from apes and dolphins to pigs and parrots—are relatively long-lived and highly social creatures, whose need to

---

20. H. G. Wells, *War of the Worlds* (Oxford: Oxford University Press, 2017).
21. Peter Godfrey-Smith, "The Mind of an Octopus," *Scientific American* (blog), updated January 1, 2017, accessed October 6, 2021, https://www.scientificamerican.com/article/the-mind-of-an-octopus/.
22. Katherine Harmon, "Octopuses Gain Consciousness," *Scientific American* (blog), August 21, 2012, https://blogs.scientificamerican.com/octopus-chronicles/octopuses-gain-consciousness-according-to-scientists-declaration/.

develop and maintain complex social relations is presumably an important driver behind the evolutionary development of their intelligence. Octopi, by contrast,

> live brief, antisocial lives. Even large species like the giant Pacific octopus last but a few years, and want little to do with other octopuses outside of copulation. Their minds didn't evolve to form social bonds or lasting relationships. We don't really know why they're so smart or what evolutionary pressures led to their relative brilliance, though some think it may have to do with adapting to a life without a shell. . . . Their intelligence, like their eight-legged, boneless bodies, is truly alien, even though both are from this world.[23]

To the extent that octopi may possess a form of intelligence that is fundamentally different from that of creatures like us, they offer a glimpse of a radical version of the Sapir-Whorf hypothesis. That is to say, while the hypothesis is typically framed by the question of how different languages may influence cognition, the cephalopod example instead invites us to consider a form of cognition that exists in the absence not only of language itself but even of the social imperatives that drive language development in the first place.

More recent research complicates Wilcox's narrative a bit, though only at the outer edges. For instance, although octopi are generally assumed to be solitary and asocial, a new study reveals that a certain species of shallow-water octopus known as the "gloomy octopus" communicate with one another by changing their skin color,[24] and other scientists have discovered two separate gloomy octopus communities—dubbed Octopolis and Octlantis—that are each inhabited by up to fifteen octopi at a time though even in these make-shift communities the octopi appear to do little more than fight with one another.[25]

In this serendipitous convergence of the social phenomenon of "Martian script" (together with the broader phenomenon of digital script) and the common practice of rendering imaginary Martians (and extraterrestrials in general) as octopus-like creatures, accordingly, we find two complementary commentaries on the relationship between language and community. In the first instance, new forms of community facilitated by the internet help generate the rapid evolution of innovative scripts, while in the second instance, our imagination of extraterrestrials takes inspiration from a terrestrial (or, to be more precise, aquatic) "alien" whose mode of cognition and communication may have evolved under

---

23. Christie Wilcox, "The Scientific Explanation for why Humans Are So Convinced that Aliens Look like Octopuses," *Quartz*, December 8, 2016, https://qz.com/857377/the-aliens-in-arrival-look-like-octopuses-because-humans-think-cephalopods-are-both-scary-and-smart/.
24. David Scheel, Peter Godfrey-Smith, and Matthew Lawrence, "Signal Use by Octopuses in Agonistic Interactions," *Current Biology* 26, no. 3 (February 2016): 377–382.
25. David Scheel et al., "A Second Site Occupied by *Octopus tetricus* at High Densities, with Notes on their Ecology and Behavior," *Marine and Freshwater Behavior and Physiology* 50, no. 4 (September 2017): 285–291.

very different conditions of sociality compared to those found among humans and other animals we typically regard as intelligent.

In the end, the key question raised by Chiang's story and its filmic adaptation is not so much what kind of intelligence octopi *actually* have but rather how the popular *perception* of octopi as anti-social loners intersects with the work's decision to feature octopus-like creatures in a plotline that revolves around alien attempts to give humanity the gift of their language and specifically to encourage the world's major nations to collaborate with one another. In other words, the heptapods signify not a radical *absence* of sociality and of language but rather the possibility of a form of sociality that is radically different from our own. In this way, the work invites a reassessment of the degree to which a certain form of sociality and social embeddedness—which is to say, a form of "ethnocentrism"— functions as a constitutive condition for the very possibility of language and linguistic communication itself.

Adrift on Neurath's Ship

While Derrida, as noted, opens *Of Grammatology* with a critique of ethnocentrism, Richard Rorty, in a 1989 article titled "Solidarity or Objectivity," instead offers an energetic *defense* of what he similarly calls ethnocentrism. Rorty posits that "there are two principal ways in which reflective human beings try, by placing their lives in a larger context, to give sense to those lives. The first is by telling the story of their contribution to a community. . . . The second is to describe themselves as standing in relation to a nonhuman reality."[26] Rorty labels those individuals who take the first approach "pragmatists" and those who take the second "realists," and suggests that both are, in principle, challenged by the question of how to respond to perspectives, ideologies, and even worldviews fundamentally different from their own. In particular, he contends that both approaches are haunted by the need to navigate between a Scylla of ethnocentrism and a Charybdis of relativism, and argues that pragmatists should simply "grasp the ethnocentric horn of this dilemma," contending that "we" (i.e., pragmatists) have no choice but to "privilege our own group, even though there can be no noncircular justification for doing so."

Although the preceding allusion to Odysseus sailing between Scylla and Charybdis is my own, later in the same paragraph Rorty himself introduces a similar nautical reference, building on a well-known metaphor proposed by philosopher Otto Neurath. Neurath, in his original formulation, was alluding to the old philosophical conundrum of whether the ship of Theseus would retain its identity if every plank were to be replaced with new ones, and he famously

---

26. Richard Rorty, "Solidarity or Objectivity," *Post-Analytic Philosophy*, ed. John Rajchman and Cornel West (New York: Columbia University Press, 1986), 3.

concludes, "like sailors are we, who must rebuild their ship upon the open sea, never able to dismantle it in dry dock or to reconstruct it there from the best materials."²⁷ Rorty, meanwhile, gives this metaphor a political twist, suggesting that "we can *understand* the revolutionary's suggestion that a sailable boat can't be made out of the planks which make up ours, and that we must simply abandon ship. But we cannot take his suggestion seriously" (emphasis in the original). In other words, Rorty is arguing that while a pragmatist can understand, in principle, the suggestion that one must fundamentally rethink the foundational postulates on which one's sociopolitical worldview is grounded, in practice, this cannot be accepted as a viable option, because "we want to be able, so to speak, to justify ourselves to our earlier selves."²⁸

Quine also cited the same ship metaphor repeatedly throughout his career, but whereas Neurath originally proposed the metaphor in the context of a discussion of scientific discourse, and Rorty borrowed it to think through a set of ideological and sociopolitical concerns, Quine instead primarily applied it to a set of epistemological and ontological concerns. For instance, he opens *Word and Object* with an epigraph citing the metaphor, and elaborates the metaphor in his first chapter, positing that "our boat stays afloat because at each alteration we keep the bulk of it intact as a going concern. Our words continue to make passable sense because of continuity of change of theory: we warp usage gradually enough to avoid rupture." Although Quine is nominally speaking here about philosophical discourse, his point is equally relevant to ordinary beliefs and conventional discourse: that it is possible to revise our perspective and worldview, but only incrementally, such that what Quine elsewhere calls our "web of belief" remains fundamentally intact.

This metaphor of Neurath's ship concisely captures Derrida's contention that a radically non-logocentric grammatology can only be imagined from within the space of a logocentric perspective and by extension from within the ethnocentric locus on which that perspective is grounded. In the end, *Arrival* also arrives at a similar conclusion that the alterity, or even *monstrosity*, represented by the aliens may indeed have the potential to catalyze a radical reassessment of one's existing worldview but only in such a way that one remains able, as Rorty puts it, "to justify ourselves to our earlier selves." Or, as Derrida puts it, the objective is a process "that is faithful and attentive to the ineluctable world of the future which proclaims itself at present"—to glimpse a "future world" "which breaks absolutely with constituted normality and can only be proclaimed, *presented*, as a sort of monstrosity.²⁹

---

27. Otto Neurath, "Protocol Sentences," in *Logical Positivism*, ed. A. J. Ayer, trans. George Schick (New York: The Free Press, 1959).
28. Rorty, "Solidarity or Objectivity," 12.
29. Derrida, *Of Grammatology*, 4–5, emphasis in the original.

7

The Techne of Listening

Toward a Theory of "Chinese" Sound

Junting Huang

Introduction

In 2013, the Taiwanese poet Hsia Yu received an unexpected gift from her friend Yan Jun, who is often regarded as the godfather of Chinese experimental music. The gift was a self-released CD with a humble yet unusual appearance: a disc that was carefully placed inside a plastic case with a piece of sandpaper. Its shape resembling a circular saw blade and its sharp teeth along the edge, it seemed glossy, heavy, and a bit intimidating. We do not know how exactly Hsia reacted upon opening the album, but she was at least curious enough to insert this disc into her MacBook, expecting a correspondingly novel listening experience. However, Hsia did not anticipate that this piece of metal was, in fact, a real saw blade found at a construction site. As a collaboration between Lao Yang and Yan Jun, the disc was released by their record label, Sub Jam (Saba jiemo 撒把芥末), as a conceptual artwork—it was never supposed to be played.[1]

And yet, it provided Hsia with an unusual listening experience. After hearing a loud buzzing sound, Hsia discovered that the disc was stuck inside the drive; it had damaged her computer. Hsia complained to Yan, "I thought it was supposed to be played and listened to!" In response, Yan suggested that perhaps only poets were supposed to play the disc and listen to it. When Yan told this story in *The Only Authentic Work*, he concluded that Hsia's response was, however, not the stupidity of the poet; on the contrary, he described it as an ideal relationship between the poet and the material world—it is intimate, straightforward, yet dangerous.[2] By engaging herself in the act of attentive listening, Hsia allowed the

---

1. Jun Yan, "Lao Yang, Untitled," *Sub Jam* (blog), May 6, 2013, http://www.subjam.org/archives/2528.
2. Jun Yan, *The Only Authentic Work: Fragments, for Lionel Marchetti's 23 Formes En Elastique* (Beijing: Sub Jam, 2003), 2.

sound to touch her, resonate with her body, and elicit an almost visceral effect from within. Nonetheless, we may be baffled by Yan Jun's ambiguous witticism on the act of listening. How exactly does a poet listen differently?

The reason is that sound, as an object of study, is ontologically ambiguous. The physical phenomenon is understood as an object, an event, and a relationship at the same time. It requires a distinctive mode of thinking that attends to its own medium specificity. Sound passes through us and escapes from us; the ephemerality of sound makes it difficult to examine its intrinsic texture, especially before the invention of sound reproduction technologies. Sound is an act, an unfolding process; the temporality of sound makes it hard to fully capture its ever-changing signifying process. Sound not only occupies a physical space but also corresponds to the boundless and directionless sensory world; the spatiality of sound makes it challenging for listeners to orient themselves in and navigate through the world of noises. In short, our perception of sound is overdetermined by its material medium. In order to interpret the significance of a sound practice, we first need to consider its medium specificity: the physical medium it travels through, the vibrational energies it carries, and its own ephemerality.

However, the ontology of sound is inseparable from the act of listening as a culturally contextualized practice. "It is 'music,' they say. Are bells and drums all that is meant by music?" *Yueyun yueyun, zhonggu yun hu zai* 樂云樂云，鐘鼓云乎哉—as noted in *The Analects of Confucius*, the cultural significance of sound lies beyond the domain of material apparatus. In other words, the signifying process of sound is defined by not only sounding objects themselves but also their cultural contexts. Despite a wide range of purposes for which music is performed—from religious ceremonies to weddings and funerals—the perceived sound is always located in a specific cultural milieu, bound to its site and locality. Sound production is, after all, a cultural practice. Despite the nonsensical noises that the metal disc makes, for example, its meanings ultimately derive from a situated listening practice by Lao Yang, Yan Jun, and Hsia Yu. Its origin from a construction site documents the material traces of the changing urban fabric of Chinese cities. Also, the deafening noise serves as a familiar critique of "music" as culturally codified sounds in conversation with classical Chinese aesthetics and philosophy. Yet is there a culturally specific understanding of sound—a "Chinese" sound? What are the implications when we ask such questions?

Sound has been an important form of cultural production in China. Thanks to the rise of sound studies, scholars have begun to reflect on sound cultures in relation to Chinese modernity. For instance, Andrew Jones, Jean Ma, Andreas Steen, Nicole Huang, and Xiaobing Tang have all shed light on the political or ideological valence of Chinese sound culture.[3] One common thread in their scholarship is an attempt to explicate a process through which Western sound technologies and sound cultures are Sinicized in modern China. In their discussions, a methodological tension between medium specificity and cultural specificity often arises. It is a methodological tension that was often seen in the area-based media studies.[4] Media studies often aspires to achieve a universal sense of media from a technological or an anthropological perspective, whereas the area focus also compels scholars to grapple with the demarcations of geopolitical entities.[5] In other words, while the studies of "media" aspire to transcend "area" as an organizing principle in academic knowledge productions, their theorizations also risk losing validity in specific cultural contexts. In this chapter, I do not intend to universalize a theory of sound from a technological or an anthropological perspective or to reveal specific geopolitical power struggles about a definition of "China." Instead, I argue that the meanings of a sound practice are a product of both cultural and technological mediations. To that end, I use examples from contemporary sound art to theorize sound not so much *in* the geopolitical entity of contemporary "China" but *through* the cultural and technological mediations that are often marked as "Chinese."

In what follows, I echo the volume editors' call to resist thinking of "Sino-" or "Chinese" as a shorthand descriptor of ethnicity or language. My attempt to theorize "Chinese" sound is not to prescribe clear-cut boundaries for cultural productions that fall under an ethnic or a linguistic category but to trace the dynamic interplay between materiality and signification in cultural practices associated with "Chineseness." In doing so, I provide an example of Sinoglossic inquiries. More specifically, in asking questions about how certain cultural practices could be marked as "Chinese," I provide a conceptual framework to analyze the act of listening in its cultural and media contexts. Although "to listen" simply means to channel one's attention toward a sound, the practice of listening is both culturally and technologically mediated. We engage ourselves in different modes of listening: we may "listen to" music, "listen for" an instruction, and "listen in" to

---

3. Andrew F. Jones, *Like a Knife: Ideology and Genre in Contemporary Chinese Popular Music* (Ithaca, NY: Cornell University Press, 1992); Andrew F. Jones, *Yellow Music: Media Culture and Colonial Modernity in the Chinese Jazz Age* (Durham, NC: Duke University Press, 2001); Jean Ma, *Sounding the Modern Woman: The Songstress in Chinese Cinema* (Durham, NC: Duke University Press, 2015); Xiaobing Tang, "Radio, Sound Cinema, and Community Singing: The Making of a New Sonic Culture in Modern China," *Twentieth-Century China* 45, no. 1 (2020): 3–24. In addition, Nicole Huang's forthcoming book is entitled *Late Mao Soundscapes: Auditory Culture and Daily Practice of 1970s China*.
4. See Ani Maitra and Rey Chow, "What's 'In'? Disaggregating Asia through New Media Actants," in *Routledge Handbook of New Media in Asia* (London: Routledge, 2015), 29–39.
5. See W. J. T. Mitchell and Mark B. N. Hansen, eds., *Critical Terms for Media Studies* (Chicago: The University of Chicago Press, 2010), xiii–iv.

a radio broadcast. All these listening strategies relate to how sound is perceived and understood in each context. We have learned to distinguish meaningful sounds from noise and interpret their meanings because the different modes of listening are mediated by the listener's cultural and technological environment; I call this process "the techne of listening."

The word "techne" is derived from Greek, referring to "art," "craft," "skills," as "a mode of doing." In "The Question Concerning Technology," Martin Heidegger famously contends that techne, the essence of technology, was once closely associated with *poiesis*, a poetic bringing-forth in the realm of truth revealing.[6] Despite its ontological weight, Heidegger's notion of techne is useful in thinking listening as an artful, skillful, and creative practice. Listening, as "a mode of doing," brings forth the hidden significance of sound. By "the techne of listening," I intend to emphasize two premises: 1) listening is a bodily technique that we must learn to practice, and 2) sound is a cultural artifact that was produced from technological apparatus. In a sense, it resembles what Bernhard Siegert calls "cultural techniques" (*Kulturtechniken*), in that the act of listening not only marks the interactions between humans and media but also participates in the construction of the semantics and aesthetics of a culture.[7]

In this chapter, I demonstrate the ways in which the techne of listening mediates our understanding of sound and listening. Since this process is both cultural and technological, I also provide a culturally specific understanding of media. In other words, I ask "how does a listening practice draw on 'Chinese' cultural and philosophical traditions?" with the assertion that such questions are not to encourage cultural essentialism but to illuminate a culturally specific contextualization of media theory. The reason is that I believe that the ontology of sound is intrinsically tied to the act of listening as a culturally contextualized practice. In my analysis, I draw from contemporary artists and cultural critics to trace the dynamic exchange between theorizations of sound and listening from China and the West. In what follows, I first focus on Wang Jing's concept of affective listening, which clearly approximates but diverges from Pierre Schaeffer's reduced listening in the West, as a uniquely "Chinese" practice. I then return to contemporary sound art practitioners—Yan Jun, Hsia Yu, and Qiu Zhijie—by examining their engagement with a theorization of media through Chinese language, culture, and philosophy. In conclusion, I point to a potentially productive space for thinking the relationship between sound and language within Sinophone studies.

---

6. Martin Heidegger, *The Question Concerning Technology and Other Essays*, trans. William Lovitt (New York: Garland Publishing, 2013), 12–13.
7. Bernhard Siegert, *Cultural Techniques: Grids, Filters, Doors, and Other Articulations of the Real*, trans. Geoffrey Winthrop-Young (New York: Fordham University Press, 2015).

Cultural Mediation: Reduced Listening, Affective Listening

In "Affective Listening as a Mode of Coexistence," Wang Jing proposes that China's contemporary sound art practice, represented by artists such as Li Jianhong, Lin Chi-Wei, Wang Fan, and Yan Jun, affords what she calls an "affective listening." According to Wang, affective listening embodies a mode of coexistence that acknowledges "somatic, relational, and spiritual relations among participants and the environment."[8] In this mode of listening, a listening subject learns to use their body (somatic) to channel their intentionality toward the world of sounds (relational) in search of an ideal of harmony (spiritual). By emphasizing "the intentional commitment" in affective listening, Wang suggests that this mode of listening is different from prominent listening practices in the West. Wang contends that, rooted in Chinese cultural and philosophical traditions, affective listening diverges from Pierre Schaeffer's reduced listening and John Cage's purposeless listening, both of which have downplayed the intentionality of a listening subject.

While Wang attempts to theorize affective listening as a uniquely Chinese practice, she is certainly familiar with the aesthetic and philosophical influences of the West on modern sound art. Wang begins her article by tracing a genealogy of sound art in the West.

> The Western history of sound art and experimental music often starts with such events as the futurist Luigi Russolo's manifesto, the sound poetry of the Dadaists, Marcel Duchamp's anti-retinal art, Pierre Schaeffer's *musique concrète*, and John Cage's 4'33". Also frequently cited in this history are Alvin Lucier's experimentations with the varied physical characteristics of sound, Murray Schafer's world soundscape project and acoustic ecology, and other variations of sound practice in the music and art worlds, including its aesthetic connections in experimental theater and American minimal art and land art, as well its sociopolitical connections with Fluxus and futurism.[9]

Luigi Russolo, Marcel Duchamp, John Cage, and Alvin Lucier. Futurism, Dadaism, *musique concrète*, and the Fluxus. Indeed, the origin of modern sound art is often traced to modernism in the West; its history is usually dominated by Western names and movements. As Wang points out, it is in "this history" that "these names" are frequently cited and carefully studied. The list therefore becomes not only an acknowledgement of influence but also a plea for intellectual reciprocity. "Like most of China's sound practitioners," Wang continues, "I learned about these names, movements, art practices, and concepts through

---

8. Jing Wang, "Affective Listening as a Mode of Coexistence: The Case of China's Sound Practice," *Representations* 136, no. 1 (November 1, 2016): 112.
9. Wang, "Affective Listening," 113.

books, articles, videos, online radio programs, and exhibitions."[10] In the following paragraphs, Wang begins to develop affective listening in comparison with Schaeffer's reduced listening: the former focuses on the intentionality of the listener as a subject (affective listening), whereas the latter concentrates on the concrete materiality of sound as an object (reduced listening). Wang suggests that Schaeffer's reduced listening has deprived listening of its imaginative elements, thereby foreclosing the spontaneous interplay between the listener and the sounding environment.[11] When situated in "the history of sound art," affective listening is therefore not only to rescue the listening subject and the auditory imagination from Schaeffer's influential legacy on modern sound art but also to articulate one epistemological difference between Chinese and Western listening practices.

Although Pierre Schaeffer does not represent the entirety of the listening practice of the West, his reduced listening—which was later developed by theorists such as Michel Chion—has certainly evolved into one of the most prominent schools of thought in the West.[12] In "The Three Listening Modes," Chion characterizes reduced listening as "the listening mode that focuses on the traits of the sound itself, independent of its cause and of its meaning."[13] This listening practice is not limited to a particular set of sounds—"verbal, played on an instrument, noises, or whatever"—but these sounds are to be examined as objects in themselves.[14] Regardless of the listeners' knowledge in acoustics or musicology, this mode of listening requires them to concentrate on the physical traits or material properties of sound. As Chion writes, "when we identify the pitch of a tone or figure out an interval between two notes," we reveal the intrinsic characteristics of the sounds and thus defamiliarize them.[15] As this listening practice was intended to disrupt established "lazy habits," it is both an understanding of sound (*episteme*) and a technique of the body (techne).[16] It is not a practice

---

10. Wang, "Affective Listening," 113.
11. Wang, "Affective Listening," 115.
12. For Pierre Schaeffer, there are originally four modes of listening. They are translated as (1) listening, which focuses on the cause of sound and its indexicality; (2) perceiving, the raw-sounding materials or sound object; (3) comprehending, the semantic meanings of sound; and (4) hearing, the selective perception of sounding materials. Of these four modes of listening, (1) and (2) are used for concrete sounds, whereas (3) and (4) are more on an abstract level; (1) and (4) focus on the object of perception, whereas (2) and (3) turn toward the listening subject. In Chion's conception, reduced listening is close to (2), perceiving. However, to avoid further theoretical complexity, I will use reduced listening to investigate the techne of listening and its cultural imprints. See "Table of Listening Functions," in Michel Chion, *Guide to Sound Objects*, trans. John Dack and Christine North (London: Monoskop, 2009), 21.
13. Michel Chion, "The Three Listening Modes," in *Audio-Vision: Sound on Screen* (New York: Columbia University Press, 1994), 29.
14. Chion, "The Three Listening Modes," 29.
15. Chion, "The Three Listening Modes," 30.
16. Chion, "The Three Listening Modes," 30.

based on daily routines or natural behaviors but rather a listening practice that demands labor and effort, a bodily technique that requires heightened awareness, attention, and involvement. As the listeners attend to the fine texture of the sound, their bodies are also readied for a privileged acoustic experience in its purest form.

By contrast, affective listening aims not to create a sound object but to affirm an intentional commitment from the listening subject. In order to distinguish the "Chinese" mode of listening from other listening practices, Wang elaborates on the notion of "intentional commitment" in affective listening as a relationship between the listening participant and the environment. More specifically, affective listening includes three important aesthetic rules: 1) still time or the "nowness," 2) poetic space, which she later specifies as *yijing* 意境, where meanings and feelings are invoked harmoniously, and 3) *qi* 氣, the flow of psychic and cosmic energy.[17] And these three rules are interestingly embodied in a philological analysis of *yijing*:

> The etymology of *yijing* contains two characters, *yi* 意 and *jing* 境. In the Chinese classic *Shuowen Jiezi* (Explaining graphs and analyzing characters) of the Han dynasty, *yi* 意 can be further divided into two characters, the upper part *yin* 音 (sound) and the lower part *xin* 心 (heart). *Yi* 意 means sound from the heart. It also means feelings and will. *Jing* 境 comes from the ancient character *jing* 竟, which means the end of a piece of music. It later evolves to mean boundaries of land, with an addition of *tu* 土 earth on the left side. In the Tang dynasty, *jing* 境 pertains to spatial and psychological connotations. According to the Chinese literature scholar Lian Duan, *jing* 境 is a word from Sanskrit, *visaya*, referring to one's reflection on what one sees and hears. *Yijing* now refers to a poetic space where the subjective and the objective coexist.[18]

In analyzing the etymology of *yijing*, Wang establishes a correlation between sound, space, and intentionality. Unlike musical hearing (*chronos*), in which the structure of sound unfolds in time, affective listening resorts to an "immeasurable" and "trans-spatial" still time. Thus this *yin* 音 (sound) is not bound to the flow of time but rather to the notion of *jing* 境 (space), an acoustic and immersive environment that is both physical and psychological. In addition, *yi* 意 (desire/meaning) consists of both *yin* 音 (sound) and *xin* 心 (heart). In *Shuowen jiezi* 說文解字 (Explaining graphs and analyzing characters), *yi* 意 denotes the idea of

---

17. Elsewhere, Wang also alludes to the affect of a listener's body. Drawing on Gilles Deleuze, Félix Guattari, Brian Massumi, and Jean-Luc Nancy, Wang articulates the ways in which sound touches the body. In regard to today's sound practices in China, especially the improvised sound practice, Wang argues that the listening participant is always responding to their sonic environment. Jing Wang, "To Make Sounds inside a 'Big Can': Proposing a Proper Space for Works of Sound Art," *Leonardo* 49, no. 1 (July 7, 2014): 38–47.
18. Wang, "Affective Listening," 118.

congxin congyin 從心從音 (following the heart, following the sound). As such, through classical Chinese philology an epistemological relationship between sound and intentionality is established, creating an imaginary space for psychic and cosmic energy. It is in this poetic space that the subjective and the objective modes/realms coexist.

Despite similar emphases on the listener's intentionality, reduced listening and affective listening could not be more different. Reduced listening is meant to create a sound object in its purest form, whereas affective listening is meant to redeem a listening participant; reduced listening focuses on the intrinsic characteristics of the sound in and of itself, whereas affective listening affords an imaginary relation beyond the sound that is to be heard. In fact, reduced listening originates from its own cultural and historical context, and its formation has been mediated by centuries-long philosophical and philological traditions in the West. By linking reduced listening (*l'écoute réduite*) to phenomenological reduction (*réduction phénoménologique*), for example, Schaeffer's sound object suspends judgments about the natural world and instead focuses on the analysis of experience, which follows Edmund Husserl's phenomenological tradition.[19] The sound object thus concerns not the ontology of sound but is reduced to a perceptual phenomenon. Even though Schaeffer had revised the theory of sound object after reading Husserl, he claimed that he had always been practicing Husserl's phenomenology even without knowing it. As such, Schaeffer's fixation on "the object" and his search for "the transcendence of the object" resonate little with Wang's advocacy of the affect from a listener. Simply put, the philosophical baggage in Schaeffer's theorization—not only Husserl's phenomenology, but also the Cartesian subject/object dualism at the core of modern Western philosophy—situates itself in a cultural context.[20]

Listening is a bodily technique that is also culturally inclined. As we have seen in both reduced listening and affective listening, listening practice is constantly

---

19. Husserl's notions of object and intentionality have greatly influenced Pierre Schaeffer. According to Brian Kane, Schaeffer's description of "the lived particulars" is essentially "Husserl's theory in miniature"; Schaeffer defines them as "the multiple visual, audible, tactile impressions which succeed one another in an incessant flux, across which I tend towards a certain object, I 'intend' it [je le 'vise'] and the diverse modes according to which I connect myself to this object: perception, memory, desire, imagination, etc." Brian Kane, *Sound Unseen: Acousmatic Sound in Theory and Practice* (New York: Oxford University Press, 2014), 20–21.
20. In *Sound Unseen*, Brian Kane further historicized Schaeffer's acousmatic imagination in the West. Kane regards reduced listening as an inadequate response to the Wagnerian notion of absolute music at the birth of German Romanticism—or the acousmatic phantasmagoria. Kane demonstrates that Arthur Schopenhauer's advocacy of a bodily technique, for example, is "designed to ready the listener for the experience of music's disclosure of profound metaphysical truth." Wagner's Bayreuth Festival Theater, as another example, hides performers from the audience in order to preserve the "transcendental power" of the music and of the subject. See Kane, *Sound Unseen*, 10.

mediated by cultural and philosophical traditions. The techne in listening opens up a space for a wide range of cultural practices, which in turn provide cultural protocols for what we listen to and how we listen. In comparing these two modes of listening, I illustrate an epistemological difference in the techne of listening. This is not to prescribe any "essential qualities" for the cultural systems from which they originate but to demonstrate the process of cultural mediations. When contextualized, both affective listening and reduced listening exemplify the culturally specific practice of listening. As such, affective listening illustrates what a "Chinese" mode of listening might entail.

Technological Mediation: Concrete Sound, Relational Sound

While the techne of listening is mediated by cultural traditions, it is also assisted by a wide range of media infrastructures. In fact, when reduced listening was first introduced by Pierre Schaeffer, it was considered an immediate response to the rapid developments of sound technology in the West in the first half of the twentieth century, when electronically reproduced sounds became more prevalent in everyday life. As Jonathan Sterne also reminds us, when sound reproduction technologies started to preserve the audible past, sound became an object of study.[21]

However, music that had experimented with electroacoustics was first received with great suspicion because, in Schaeffer's understanding, the electronically reproduced sound is split from its natural origin. When we hear the electronically reproduced sounds, we can hardly visualize their sources and relate them to their natural sonic environment. By focusing on the raw materiality of sound, however, reduced listening was supposed to ease the tension between the perceived sound and the absence of the visual; it was also supposed to teach us how to appreciate sounds in the age of electrical reproduction. As Michel Chion also points out, reduced listening is only attainable in the spirit of mechanical reproduction. In order to appreciate the fine details of each unique sound event and its raw material energy, we have to listen to the exact same sound over and over again. As such, reduced listening is not possible without the reproduced sound of the tape recorder.[22] In other words, reduced listening is closely associated with the acousmatic situation in the West around the turn of the twentieth century, where listeners often heard the sound without seeing its

---

21. Jonathan Sterne, *The Audible Past: Cultural Origins of Sound Reproduction* (Durham, NC: Duke University Press Books, 2003).
22. According to Chion, Schaeffer's notion of sound object is in fact derived from a number of technological situations: 1) two discoveries at the very origins of *musique concrète*—the closed groove and the cut bell, and 2) the growing awareness of the acousmatic situation in the age of mass media. Chion, *Guide to Sound Objects*, 11.

source. This acousmatic situation in the West is often traced to the Pythagorean school in ancient Greece, where students were required to sit behind a veil so that they could better concentrate on the speech of the master.[23] This veil was to help the listeners direct their attention to the sound of wisdom and of authority. It is a technique of screening and separation. In doing so, this listening practice also isolates the auditory experience from other sensory channels as it attempts to capture the sound in and of itself.

However, the contemporary sound art practice in China does not originate from the same history. In many cases, the acousmatic condition brought forth by the early sound reproduction technologies in the West is less of a concern to the artists' practice of listening in China. In affective listening, for example, the techne of listening is neither to isolate hearing from other sensory channels, nor to negotiate the conceptual tension of the acousmatic situation. As such, sound is not understood as a concrete material entity but rather as a relationship between perceptions. As Wang puts it, "The kind of listening suggested in these examples is different from John Cage's purposeless listening and Pierre Schaeffer's reduced listening—listening for the materiality of sound rather than its sources. Instead this kind of listening is based on relations of seeing, reading, interpreting, and imagining."[24] In other words, affective listening is never limited to the auditory because sound is never tied to a hidden source, and hearing is always apprehended in relation to other perceptions. To practice affective listening, we do not need to concentrate on the concrete materiality of sound, but we must instead vigorously relate the auditory experience to "seeing, reading, interpreting, and imagining," as the sound needs not to be heard but must be imagined.

In fact, many critics trace the beginning of Chinese sound art to Qiu Zhijie, whose works provided a similarly synthetic understanding of sound. In 2001, his exhibition "Sound of Sound" (*Shengyin de shengyin* 聲音的聲音) in Koshigaya, Japan, presented three silent "sound" works. According to Qiu, although the three multimedia installations are silent, "they are however centered on the notion of sound, especially how it is understood in traditional Chinese culture."[25] The installation piece *Lo Shu Square • Twelve-Pitch Scale* (*Jiugong, lülü* 九宮・律呂), for example, invites participants to walk on the floor, where their footprints

---

23. Michel Foucault also discussed the Pythagorean veil in his later seminars on "the hermeneutics of the self." In the first hour of the seminar on January 3, 1982, Foucault discussed the testing techniques in Pythagoreanism, including "listening to the music" as "the technology of the self." In the first hour of the seminar on March 17, Foucault mentioned the rules of silence in Pythagorean practices: "the pedagogical silence." Michel Foucault, *The Hermeneutics of the Subject: Lectures at the Collège de France, 1981–1982*, ed. Frédéric Gros, trans. Graham Burchell (New York: Picador, 2005).
24. Wang, "Affective Listening," 115.
25. Zhijie Qiu 邱志杰, "Zhongguo fasheng" 中國發聲 [Sounding China], *ArtLinkArt*, http://www.artlinkart.com/cn/artist/txt_ge/3a3avz/319hAxm.

leave the names of the musical notes in the twelve-pitch scale.[26] The participants are asked to wear Japanese clogs (*geta* 下駄). As they walk through the installation, the floor is covered with increasingly thicker paper, which eventually makes the sound of their footsteps inaudible. In a strange manner, this sound installation is a process of becoming "soundless." At first glance, Qiu's "silence" may resemble John Cage's notorious silence in 4'33," in which Cage instructs the performers not to play any musical notes but allows the audience to concentrate on the ambient noise. Unlike Cage, however, the absence of musical sound is not replaced by other concrete sounds in *Lo Shu Square*. Instead, the participants in Qui's sound installation read the Chinese characters, imagine their represented musical notes, and visualize their associated meanings. This silence is rather evocative of the synergy between a variety of senses; this silence refers not to the absence of sound but to an opening to a psychological space, where sound is in relation to other perceptions, feelings, imaginations, and interpretations.

The relational imagination of sound is also embodied in another installation at Qiu's exhibition. In the installation piece *Silent Bell* (*ya zhong* 啞鐘), a bell-shaped paper lantern is covered with transparent layers, on which multiple Chinese characters are written. Having the same radical mouth (口), these characters are all onomatopoeic words—"Ha" (*ha* 哈), "Ah" (*a* 啊), "Oh" (*o* 哦), "Wow" (*o* 喔), "Alas" (*yi* 噫). When the lantern spins, the audience sees waves of characters moving up and down, thus creating a unique acoustic imagination. In this installation, sound is once again not heard but rather visualized by the participants who are reading the words. Undoubtedly, the unique logographic construction of Chinese characters is at the heart of this acoustic imagination. Qiu says, "I cannot quite tell where my genuine interest lies, the sound or the Chinese characters. Of course, I could just quote the Chinese saying that 'great music is soundless' (*dayin xisheng* 大音希聲) or something like that on the metaphysical level, but there is always a however."[27] Similarly, in Yao Dajuin's web-based artwork, *A Study on the Kinetics of Mandarin Tones* (1997), the artist also uses Chinese characters to re-create a synesthetic experience of sound.[28] The piece requires its participants to read, instead of listening to, Chinese characters on screen. As these Chinese characters have similar tones but different semantic meanings, the participants repeat the same sounds in their heads while creating free associations of rich imagery. As such, sound is only in the mind of the reader.

---

26. Lo Shu is an emblem of Chinese mathematics, and the Twelve-Pitch Scale (*shi'er lü* 十二律) is the standardized gamut of Chinese music.
27. Qiu, "Zhongguo fasheng."
28. Dajuin Yao, "Revolutions Per Minute: Sound Art China," School of Creative Media, City University of Hong Kong, https://www.scm.cityu.edu.hk/event/37.

In these examples, the ontology of sound is mediated by technological apparatus, media infrastructure, and media environment. Just as reduced listening conceptualizes sound as a concrete and material entity in the age of electrical reproduction, affective listening calls for a relational harmony, a synthetic experience that derives from not only the materiality of Chinese language but also the age of new media and convergence culture, where a collision of senses and a mixture of media forms are commonplace. While the former contests the acousmatic situation in the West, the latter—often focusing on the spontaneous "live" sound rather than the reproduced sound—also reshapes the ways in which sound is understood in the age of new media. While the practice of reduced listening was considered an immediate response to the proliferation of electronically reproduced sounds in the West, these new sounds in China were also made possible by the circulation of affordable musical instruments and the rise of digital media, which continued to cultivate a community of sound practitioners.[29] As these emerging art practices promote new ways of listening using a wide range of new media technologies, they also mediate our understandings of sound.

The Washing Machine: Toward a Theory of "Chinese" Sound

In comparing affective listening and reduced listening, I reveal the cultural and technological mediations behind the techne of listening. To conclude, I want to return to Yan Jun and Hsia Yu's collaboration and analyze how one of their favorite figures, the sound of a washing machine, invites us to contemplate, negotiate, and theorize a "Chinese" mode of listening. In 2016, Sub Jam published a poetry collection: *7 Poems and Some Tinnitus* (*Qishou shi he yixie erming* 七首詩和一些耳鳴). In the postscript, Hsia included a poem about the washing machine.

> The poet catches a pile of clouds
> The installation artist puts the clouds into the washing machine
> The noise artist turns on the washing machine
> The washing machine emits the sound of concrete and crushed stones

---

29. For example, as Samson Young suggests, the making of the *Buddha Machine*, a portable device that generates musical loops of Buddhist music, is closely associated with the copyright infringement across different media platforms in mainland China. Young believes that FM3's *Buddha Machine*, therefore, is a genuine expression of "the Socialist China" because this artwork then becomes a response to "the tyranny of endless commodity refinement and technological advancement." Samson Young, "The Possibility of Authenticity: Sounding the Socialist China in FM3's Buddha Machine," in *Contemporary Music in East Asia*, ed. Hee Sook Oh (Seoul: University of Seoul Press, 2014), 267–283.

詩人捕獲一堆雲
搞裝置的人把雲堆在洗衣機裡
做噪音的人把洗衣機開關打開
洗衣機發出混凝土和碎石子的聲音³⁰

In a figurative language, Hsia depicts the process of artistic creation. Within these four lines, we see clouds quickly turned into crushed stones even though the two are associated with different sensibilities: the clouds are ethereal, delicate, and nebulous, hosting the imaginative powers of the poet, whereas the crushed stones are raw, robust, and concrete, making loud and harsh noises. In a sense, this poem may be read as a commentary on poetic writing itself, as the wildest abstract thoughts are always to be concretized in words and language.

However, within these four lines, there is also a story of artistic collaboration between the poet, the installation artist, the noise maker, and the machine. Based on the close relationship between Hsia and Yan, we may suspect that Hsia is the poet who chases after the clouds and that Yan is the noise artist who initiates a relationship with the washing machine. The art installation in the poem may also refer to a real sound artwork, an installation piece named *Was*.[31] The installation was created by Dutch artists Wessel Westerveld and Lydia van de Streek in 2010. It was supposed to re-create the sonic environment of a laundry room, which consists of the dripping sounds from the wet clothes and the rumbling noise from the washing machine. In the installation, these two sounds are thrown into a dramatic but interesting contrast—they operate as counterpoints as if in a piece of music composition: the natural water sound is clear, delicate, intermittent, and of the higher pitch, whereas the human-made machine sound is sonorous, full, constant, and of the lower note.[32]

At the tenth Shanghai Biennale in 2014, Yan returned to the figure of the washing machine. In an essay entitled "The Laundromat by the Sea" (*Haibian de xiyidian* 海邊的洗衣店), the artist uses the figure to put forth a theory of noise.[33] He begins by claiming that noise cannot and should not be defined; noise, as he suggests, is supposed to fail, to fail better, to return to an original chaos, and to resist any taxonomy that art galleries and cultural institutions have imposed

---

30. Jun Yan and Yu Hsia, 七首詩和一些耳鳴 *Qishou shi he yixie erming* [7 poems and some tinnitus] (Beijing: Sub Jam, 2016).
31. See also Min'an Wang 汪民安, "Lun xiyiji" 論洗衣機 [On washing machine], *Sub Jam* (blog), April 19, 2014, http://subjam.org/blog/28.
32. The washing machine is not foreign to the audience of modern and contemporary Chinese art. Over thirty some years ago, Huang Yongping's provocative installation—"Two-Minute Wash Cycle"—created a noise in the Chinese art world. Its original name, "The History of Chinese Painting and the History of Modern Western Art Washed in the Washing Machine for Two Minutes," represents a visual form of "noise."
33. See Jun Yan, "The Laundromat by the Sea," https://yanjun.org/archives/1286.

upon the listeners. The moment when "noise" is defined (such as with Japanoise in the 1990s), the act of definition forecloses a path to authenticity. Then, the artist suggests that the washing machine is a domestic space of noise and of resistance. On one hand, this technology always remains neutral and treats every duty equally; on the other hand, the machine exists not as an independent object entirely external to us but rather as a prosthetic extension to our body and mind.

While it may seem that Yan Jun is discussing the noise of a washing machine, he is in fact describing a mode of listening. For the artist, the washing machine has embodied the techne of listening not only because of the wide range of noises that the washing machine makes but due to the "neutral" and "prosthetic" relationship it establishes between the listener and their material environment. Just as the way the washing machine may treat all duties equally by severing the emotional connections between a person and their personal items (in comparison with the hand-washed clothes), this mode of listening treats all kinds of sounds with absolute neutrality by suspending the listener's emotional attachment to them. To clarify this point, the artist then quotes a philosophical paragraph from "Meditation on the Organ of Hearing" in *Śūraṅgama Sūtra*, a classical Buddhist text:

> At first by directing the organ of hearing into the stream of meditation, this organ was detached from its object, and by wiping out (the concept of) both sound and stream-entry, both disturbance and stillness became clearly non-existent.
>
> 初於聞中，入流亡所。所入既寂，動靜二相，了然不生。[34]

In this meditation, *Guanyin* 觀音—the "Goddess of Mercy" in English, or the one who "Perceives the Sounds of the World" in Chinese—found the path to Nirvana through listening. More specifically, Guanyin discovered this path through the practice of *ru liu wang suo* 入流亡所 (the flow of perception and the disappearance of phenomenon). According to C. T. Chen, this *ru* 入 (entry) is a Buddhist terminology referring to the phenomenon produced by the contact between the organ and the external world, in this context, the hearing perceived by the listening subject.[35] And this *liu* 流 (stream) refers to a state of mind in which all sensory entries "never stayed" and quickly "moved away." In other words, the listening subject acts as a filter through which sonic vibrations and disturbances can only pass but not stay. In this way, the referred or the perceived object (*suo* 所) is vanished (*wang* 亡). In Yan Jun's own words,

---

34. This is Charles Luk's translation. See Charles Luk, trans., *The Surangama Sutra* (London: Rider, 1966), 135–136.
35. C. T. Chen 沈家楨, *Shen Jiazhen jushi yanjiang ji* 沈家楨居士演講集 [Collection of lectures by C. T. Chen] (New Taipei City: Dharma Drum Institute of Liberal Arts, 2017), 112–113.

> They [Guanyin] cast away the interface between the listening subject and the sound object. With the movement of sound/listening, they enter every moment between life and death, where the continuity between one and another no longer exists. As these sounds are experienced in their basic material form, which is vibration, the sounds all disappear without differentiation.
>
> 他拋棄了聆聽主體和聲音客體之間的接觸界面,在聲音/聆聽的流動中,進入每一個方生方滅的瞬間,兩者的連續性都不復存在,它們被體驗為物質的基本形式,也就是振動,它們沒有分別地消亡了。[36]

The "interface" between the listener and the thing that is heard emphasizes the Buddhist notion of *ru* 入 (entry), and it is in the constant movement *liu* 流 (stream) that sound is experienced in its most basic material form before dissolving into the nothingness. This philosophical contemplation on sound reminds us of Ji Kang—a Daoist Chinese poet, musician, and philosopher of the Three Kingdoms period. The artist has also repeatedly rehearsed Ji's famous treatise of "On the Absence of Emotion in Sound" (*Sheng wu aile lun* 聲無哀樂論) by emphasizing that "the sound and the mind have different paths, and they could never intersect" (*ranze shengzhi yu xin, shutu yigui, buxiang jingwei* 然則聲之與心,殊途異軌,不相經緯) and that "the nature of sound is neutral and balanced, and the ways in which the world is perceived are always impermanent" (*shengyin yi pinghe weiti, er ganwu wuchang* 聲音以平和為體,而感物無常).[37]

This notion of neutrality, however, resembles affective listening because the free association of the affective is not achievable unless the emotional content is fully detached from the sound object. As such, the neutrality of sound, which is often articulated as *zhong* 中 (middle, neutral, and appropriate) and *he* 和 (harmonious, parallel, and mixed), is considered as a space of mediation that blurs the boundaries between *neng* 能 (self, subject, human) and *suo* 所 (other, object, technology), creating a space of coexistence. This mode of listening departs from reduced listening as well as the *musique concrète* tradition in that it does not create a sound object in its purest form, nor does it attend to the concrete materiality of sound. If Yan Jun's saw blade CD can be taken seriously, it demands a culturally specific listening practice that is in dialogue with cultural traditions as well as media environments. While this CD is not supposed to be listened to as a piece of music, it reflects on the techne of listening by insisting on the neutrality of sound. And as a poet, Hsia executed the action; she completed this art piece by (not) listening to it.

---

36. Yan, "The Laundromat by the Sea." This is my translation.
37. See Yao-Nong Tian 田耀農, "Lun Ji Kang de shengwu aile" 論嵇康的聲無哀樂 [Analyzing Jikang's "music being irrelevant to grief or joy"], *Zhongguo yinyue xue* 中國音樂學, no. 4 (2013): 20–24; Mingji Zhu 朱明基, "Guanyu shengwu aile lun zhong sheng de biaoshu fangshi tantao" 關於〈聲無哀樂論〉中 "聲" 的表述方式探討 [A discussion on the expressions of "sound" in "on the absence of emotions in sound"], *Yinyue tansuo* 音樂探索, no. 4 (1999): 39–42.

Postscript: Reflections on Sound in Sinophone Studies

Because language remains a central topic in Sinophone studies, sound is almost always synonymous with speech, or the linguistic sounds, in this context. In "The Sinophone Redistribution of the Audible," for example, Shih Shu-Mei alluded to the importance and multiplicity of the audible language; Shih borrowed from Jacques Rancière's notion to account for a radical audioscape of Sinophone cinema.

> The radical audioscape of Sinophone cinema, in all its audible differences and multiplicities, challenges the ways in which national communities are understood (heard, seen, etc.), and it is therefore transformative and possibly productive of not only a "different common world" but also "a different people," which would be the ultimate aim of politics for Rancière. What we understand through our sense of hearing Sinophone cinema, in conjunction with the other senses, intervenes into the distribution of the sensible and can thus fundamentally alter our way of viewing the world. This altering is the work of redistribution, beyond recognition, which I call here the Sinophone redistribution of the audible.[38]

For Shih and many other Sinophone cinema scholars, the audible is largely tied to the use of language. When Shih claims that Ang Lee's *Crouching Tiger, Hidden Dragon* is a Sinophone cultural product, the reason is that the actors' accents break the fourth wall, thus signaling a cultural politics behind the use of language on screen.[39] The emphasis on "speech" and "sound" in Sinophone studies is often manifested through the necessary combination of two parts—the "lingua-" and the "-phone." As such, the audible is either modified by or limited to its linguistic parameters: How does it sound in the language(s)? What does it mean to sound like that? In other words, sound is primarily referred to as the phonic varieties of Sinitic languages rather than as a wider collection of nonlinguistic sounds and their associated cultural practices. Because the notion of the Sinophone requires a language community, when it addresses the relationship between sound, nationality, and identity, it understandably focuses on the regulations of language usage, or what Jing Tsu calls "literary governance," in both written and verbal forms.[40]

"Sinophone studies as a whole," Shih writes, "is everywhere attentive to the specificity of time and place of its different objects of study."[41] In the domains of

---

38. Shu-Mei Shih, "The Sinophone Redistribution of the Audible," in *Sinophone Cinemas*, ed. Audrey Yue and Olivia Khoo (New York: Palgrave Macmillan, 2014), xi.
39. Shu-Mei Shih, *Visuality and Identity: Sinophone Articulations Across the Pacific* (Berkeley: University of California Press, 2007).
40. Jing Tsu, *Sound and Script in Chinese Diaspora* (Cambridge, MA: Harvard University Press, 2010).
41. Shu-Mei Shih, "Against Diaspora: The Sinophone as Places of Cultural Production," in *Global Chinese Literature*, ed. David Wang and Jing Tsu (Boston, MA: Brill, 2010), 29.

sound, how far can we go with the objects of study? How can we study extralinguistic sounds within the framework of the Sinophone? Shih confirms that the theoretical model is not explicitly about literature. However, the notion of the Sinophone is still oftentimes bound to literature, writing, and print culture. As Carlos Rojas also observes in "Danger in the Voice: Alai and Sinophone," "Even if approached in strictly linguistic terms, the linguaphone is grounded on an internal tension, in that etymologically it refers to spoken language (the suffix phone is Greek for "voice" or "sound"), though in practice is it used primarily to refer to written—rather than oral—texts."[42] Shih also noted the fact that the written medium was more effective in establishing China's colonial relations to the world: "When China was a cultural empire, the literary, classical Han script was the lingua franca of the East Asian world where scholars could converse by conducting so-called 'pen conversations' (*bitan* 筆談) through writing."[43] The reason is that many parts of East Asia used to share the Sinitic script even though their spoken languages are vastly different.

Since its conception, Shih's Sinophone model has generated numerous productive debates. It has provided a helpful framework for a focus on language and speech. Its emphasis on relationality has also helped us understand why Sinophone cultural productions have to be localized. Its advocacy of the "redistribution of the sensible" also reminds us of the ongoing struggles of the politically marginalized within the Sinophone world. However, we may also need other theoretical models to examine sound practices whose significance is beyond the domain of literary language. Yet this is certainly not to exclude language in the study of media. On the contrary, as these examples tell us, many of the artists drew their inspirations from the language. Instead, this is rather to situate language in the greater context of cultural practices and to investigate its technical operations and media infrastructure. This is not to claim a particular mode of listening as intrinsically Chinese either. As mentioned, how we understand sound as a medium, regardless of its particular shape, is also how we mediate the diverse traditions of a given culture. Theorizing "Chinese" sound could be seen as such a process.

---

42. Carlos Rojas, "Danger in the Voice: Alai and the Sinophone," in *Sinophone Studies: A Critical Reader*, ed. Shu-Mei Shih (New York: Columbia University Press, 2013), 296–303.
43. Shih, *Visuality and Identity*, 28.

Part III

Translation

8
Eileen Chang at the Intersection of the Sinophone and the Anglophone

Ping-hui Liao

"Art demands of us that we do not stand still."

—Ludwig van Beethoven, on the late quartets

"American publishers don't like my works . . . Among the current trends are to write on the life experiences of Asian Americans to their likes, or along the line of Orientalism and anti-Communism, to show a regressive China."

—Eileen Chang, letter to C. T. Hsia

Before her complete correspondences with such friends as C. T. Hsia and Stephen Soong were published to provide new perspectives about her years in the US, Eileen Chang (or Ailing Zhang, 1920–1995) had often been looked upon as a modern Chinese writer of short stories about Shanghai in the 1930s–1940s. Scholars tended to ignore her late works or even to fault her for failing to maintain productivity or to go on accomplishing more abroad. Employing a less-than-forgiving tone, Ye Zhaoyan, for instance, commented, "Eileen Chang escaped the mainland and should have plenty of free time to write, but she did not produce any good works."[1] Ye is joined here by quite a few of Chang's fans worldwide who continue to take issue with her posthumous works as they are brought to light.

In contrast to Ye, other critics have recently begun to turn attention to late works by Chang, especially with respect to her attempts during the almost forty-year stay (1955–1995) in the US at translating her own novels into English with improvisations or revisions, putting women on top in several of her film scripts for Hong Kong's Motion Picture and General Investment, struggling with global Cold War cultural politics and American Orientalism when she found her

---

1. Ye Zhaoyan, "Weicheng li de xiaosheng" [Laughter in the fortress besieged], *Shouhuo* no. 4 (2000): 149.

fictions in English to incur poor receptions, while battling all sorts of personal health and interpersonal emotional issues or financial crisis to reinvent her past in relation to the new home.

David Der-wei Wang is perhaps the most eminent reader after C. T. Hsia and Leo Oufan Lee to offer insightful, nuanced interpretive accounts of Chang's self-translation project in repetition and reinvention. Teasing out the warring forces between Chang's nostalgic obsession with the old Shanghai and the new political demand to denigrate the corrupt Communist Chinese regime, David Wang suggests that Eileen Chang had a tough time in the US. To him, anti-Communist novels by Eileen Chang (like *Rice-Sprout Song* and *Naked Earth*) only serve to reveal the author's "apolitical" inclinations and her unease with the subject matter. Accordingly, Chang's last novel in English, *The Rouge of the North*, is "a novel not of national politics but about politics as a daily practice of life," not only probing the reactionary meaning of "Chinese obsessiveness" but "a last imaginary refuge after [Chang] had taken political asylum in the US," in a new country where Chang found that "fictional experience had infiltrated lived experience, and that she herself might finally have become the embittered woman."[2]

Wang considers Chang's English fiction as part of her translation (and transgression) project, in which the novelist sets out to reinvent early stories and characters, renegotiate the "fates of Chinese women," rethink the significance of remembrance and repetition.[3] "Shifting back and forth on linguistic, cultural, gender, and temporal territories," he advocates, "Chang is able to find that 'between memory and reality an awkward disharmony frequently arises.'"[4] While a lot of what Wang said is true, he appears to be interested solely in Chang's novelistic discourse rather than her late works in prose and in multimedia. On Chang's choice of English as a way to escape and to start anew, Wang observes, "[a] foreign language was no more alien a medium than Chinese to transmit, or translate, her already alienated existence in the Chinese environment."[5] But this comment is made on a national, provincial rather than transnational perspective, not drawing on Eileen Chang's diaspora experience in light of its cross-cultural pollination. As a result, in spite of his meticulous and convincing analysis, David Wang neglects to mention Eileen Chang's other late works, prose prefaces, letters, journal entries, and especially her film scripts.

In fact, during her stay in the US, Eileen Chang was attracted to her new environment, particularly Hollywood's screwball comedy. Her American husband,

---

2. David Der-wei Wang, "Foreword," in *The North of the Rouge*, by Eileen Chang (Berkeley: University of California Press, 1998), vii.
3. Wang, "Foreword," xxvii.
4. Wang "Foreword," viii.
5. Wang, "Foreword," xi–xii.

Ferdinand Reyher (1891–1967), was a playwright, not only in collaboration with Bertolt Brecht but in touch with Hollywood industry, remaining a close friend to John Huston, who asked him to supply film scripts between 1931 and 1943.[6] Through Reyher, Chang became familiar with modern plays, musicals, and especially Hollywood romance comedies such as *Bringing up Baby* (1938) and *The Philadelphia Story* (1940). Reyher introduced her to the main trends of American cinema and entertainment industries of the time, often urging they watch movies together. Chang appears to have taken Hollywood themes and styles to heart, as indicated by her scripts in the late 1950s and early 60s, in which feminist motifs and melodramatic plots intertwine to attain happy endings, often giving female characters playful and even subversive roles that are rarely seen in her early novels set against the background of modern Shanghai.

Her late prose works reflect this sort of discrepant cosmopolitanism, mixing nostalgic memories of Shanghai with marvelous experience as a traveler and diaspora away from the homeland well lost. She wrote about all kinds of foods she had enjoyed, including not only homemade food back in Shanghai but also international and ethnic cuisines ranging from Spanish tapas to Japanese sushi, Italian pizza, and American steak. She documented her travel experiences and her change to a more receptive perspective. In other words, she developed a new style of writing, more prosaic in approach and oriented toward global popular culture or American musicals, to initiate a self-fashion project, so that her new modes of rewriting early works or, in the words of Adrienne Rich, "re-vision," of looking back with a fresh eye and feminist advantage point, might reconnect with China that had been radically transformed and caught in a great divide, as introduced by the new Cold War politics.

Fortunately, books and articles by Kam Louie, William Tay, Xiaojue Wang, and in particular, Yingjin Zhang's illuminating discussion of Chang's use of Hollywood screwball comedies, not to mention some of Chang's late novels and journals, all help shed a different light on Chang's Cold War days in the US. In this regard, Chang's late work is not just about "reminiscence" or about Shanghai and even China, as David Wang and Leo Ou-fan Lee duly noted. Rather, her multilingual and polyphonic project aims at piecing together the fragments of her life in a new home. Kam Louie draws on Chang's urban experience in Shanghai and Hong Kong, the two major westernized cities in China at the time, to point out that Chang has no difficulty operating in the "Chinese-Western binary," bridging "a variety of cultures and languages," "expressing innermost thoughts about her private life and the world around her," raising issues over Chinese patriarchal culture and traditional notions of masculinity.[7] Louie and

---

6. William Tay, ed., *Zhang Ailing de shijie* [The world of Eileen Chang] (Taipei: Yunchen, 1990), 34.
7. Kam Louie, ed., *Eileen Chang: Romancing Languages, Cultures and Genres* (Hong Kong: Hong

a number of critics have demonstrated convincingly how Chang's film scripts transcend the "conventional ideologies of motherhood and nationalism."[8]

In many ways, William Tay's essays on Eileen Chang mark important follow-ups to the seminal works by C. T. Hsia, Leo Lee, and many others, by calling attention to her late works in response to the Cold War and in their hybrid mode of fiction into film. As an editor of a leading Sinophone literary magazine *Unitas* and a friend of Chang among very few in whom she trusted, Tay publishes Chang's late novels and her letters. He is instrumental in urging scholars to appreciate what Chang did in light of Sinophone articulation, linking and reinventing Shanghai with Hong Kong and Hollywood, along with a long shadow cast by the Cold War led by the US. Xiaojue Wang's recent book chapter on Eileen Chang, Hong Kong, and the Cold War argues that Chang's translingual practices "not only questions the restraints of modern Chinese literary and political discourse but also bespeak the manipulative ideological and cultural control of the Cold War United States."[9] Her comments can serve as an important footnote to Tay's argument.

And it is Yingjin Zhang, whose article on Eileen Chang's gender performance has shifted our attention to the roles of Hollywood screwball comedy together with the impact American feminism had on her film scripts. Tracing "performance" as a recurring motif in Eileen Chang's writing, Zhang suggests a new way to consider her "conscientious navigation across the print-screen divide."[10] Perceived in such light, "In her screen world, genre issues take center stage while her signature gender critique has subsided considerably, and patriarchal values seem to rule her characters and leave little room for the kind of feminist subversion regularly attributed to her literary works." While largely on the right track, Zhang falters in highlighting continuity in Eileen Chang's changing modes of writing from fiction to film. Zhang also does not take into account Eileen Chang's diaspora experience in the US that actually contributes to the drastic transformation and revision in her late works. Zhang's main interest lies in "the specificities of media and genre" in film script writing and production: "Through repetition and regeneration, female performance continued to mediate her genre choice and gender questions."[11]

Kong University Press, 2012), 7.
8. Louie, *Eileen Chang*, 12.
9. Wang Xiaojue, *Modernity with a Cold War Face: Reimagining the Nation in Chinese Literature across the 1949 Divide* (Cambridge, MA: Harvard University Asia Center, 2013), 295.
10. Yingjin Zhang, "Gender, Genre, and the Performance in Eileen Chang's Films," in *Chinese Women's Cinema: Transnational Contexts*, ed. Lingzhen Wang (New York: Columbia University Press, 2011), 256.
11. Zhang, "Gender, Genre, and the Performance in Eileen Chang's Films," 256.

Zhang appears to have slighted the rupture and discontinuity that quite a few scholars suggested as informing Eileen Chang's "late style." Critics have employed the notion of the "late style" as advocated by Theodor W. Adorno and Edward W. Said to explain Chang's stylistic change in reworking her early novels. Adorno and Said draw on Beethoven's late piano sonatas, string quartets, and especially *Missa Solemnis*, to suggest that we might be better able to understand Beethoven in light of his disruptive and difficult style in the face of agonizing deafness, illness, and fear of death that torments the composer. Instead of accepting death in mature and dignified ways, Adorno argues, Beethoven "produced some extremely 'expression-less,' dispassionate compositions" as if in defiance. "His inner turmoil is not always associated with a resolve to die or with demonic humour, but is often simply enigmatic, discernible in pieces which have a serene, even idyllic tone."[12] Adorno describes Beethoven's late style as difficult, "archaistic,"[13] "fractured,"[14] and mostly "inorganic," as the composer is led by "dissatisfaction, a disgust with the individual in its fortuitousness." Adorno sums up by saying, "Herein lies the relationship of the late style to *death*."[15] Lin Xingqian is among the prominent critics to examine the ways in which alienation, privation, illness, skin disease, and even hair loss help frame Eileen Chang's late style.

Jianhua Chen and Zidong Xu are among the most notable Chinese critics in our time who have employed such a concept in their secondary elaborations of Eileen Chang's late novels, to follow up on Leo Oufan Lee's seminal work on the fiction writer's composite style of "desolation" and "sophistication." As we have noted, the notion of "late style," of being unpredictably experimental and disjunctive, has been propounded by Theodor Adorno and Edward Said, among others, to explain Beethoven's late string quartets. It remains a convenient term to discuss sudden stylistic change in face of death. However, it also presupposes rupture and discontinuity rather than evolution and transformation. Su Weizhen has succinctly used Eileen Chang's own concept of "interlocking hinges" to describe Chang's late works as interesting cases of intertextuality, in which she rewrites early novels and film scripts to provide new perspectives and produce new meanings, to look back at the past while trying to make sense of her new existential predicaments in the US. We can actually push her argument one step further to suggest that, because of the new demanding life situations in the US, Chang is forced to develop her potential as a Sinophone writer in attempting to reach out to the Anglophone world in spite of a profound sense of being

---

12. Theodor W. Adorno, *Beethoven: The Philosophy of Music* (London: Polity, 1998), 124.
13. Adorno, *Beethoven*, 146.
14. Adorno, *Beethoven*, 161.
15. Adorno, *Beethoven*, 161.

deserted and estranged: what matters are her discoveries, her travels across time and space. Therefore, Chang tried her hand at new genres and media, at writing film scripts, at appropriating Hollywood comedies and musicals, and readjusted her textual strategies in response to the demands of the film industry.

However, as many recent studies of Beethoven have pointed out, the composer did not in fact cultivate his "late" style in response to aging or death. As Jan Swafford and Edward Dusinberre have recently illustrated in their remarkable studies of Beethoven, it may be more productive to trace the gradual and significant change in light of travel and arrival in a new environment, on top of finding different sources of financial support, negotiating with dissemination networks, and so on which contribute to the discursive practice of composition and publication. Jan Swafford's biography (*Beethoven: Anguish and Triumph*) meticulously documents the patronages, collaboration networks, commissions and subscriptions, among many interpersonal transactions and conflicts, that went into music making in Beethoven's life and works, suggesting a continuous struggle to define identity and style as demanded by new life situations, particularly after the composer moved to Vienna. Edward Dusinberre, the first violinist of the Takacs Quartet, has also shed light on the ways he came to appreciate Beethoven's music and time through performances and rehearsals. Beethoven's travel experience, complicated by his sense of alienation, worries over financial income, unstable family and friendship ties, and so forth, contribute to the fluid and evolving process of his musical composition. Middle or late period is hence elusive. Using a story as told by Karl Holz, Dusinberre illustrates how Beethoven might have developed "the gradual but significant change in music-making practice in the thirty years" since his arrival in Vienna: "Whereas Beethoven's most significant early career developments were overseen by the Viennese nobility, by the end of his life publishers—and to a lesser extent subscribers through their purchase of concert tickets—provided Beethoven with a more significant if at times frustrating source of income."[16]

If we read closely correspondences between Eileen Chang and her friends during her stay in the US, we can certainly encounter similar comments made in relation to financial burden and the real issues over whether her novels in English would be accepted for publication. In other words, it may be more fruitful to consider Chang's writings done in the US other than just "late style," in which extremes and catastrophes are forced together, to produce moments of friction and dissonance. We could be better off probing these topics further by examining Chang's exile and creativity in light of her migration and displacement experiences, so that we might better comprehend the ways in which she wrote in critical response to the new unsettling diasporic predicaments and

---

16. Edward Dusinberre, *Beethoven for a Later Age* (Chicago: University of Chicago Press, 2016), 219.

challenging life situations introduced by travels away from home—first to Hong Kong and then to the US.

Rather than viewing her late work as "regressive," "redundant," or on a more positive note, "feminist," "disruptive," and even "innovative," I would like to suggest here that we could use her film scripts as examples of cross-cultural pollination, of a resilient encounter between the Anglophone and the Sinophone. In many respects, I think Beethoven's arrival in Vienna and his transformation henceforth could be illuminating in our discussion of Eileen Chang's writing across languages and cultures.

It seems to me that Chinese or Sinophone scholars tend to highlight the personal (instead of interpersonal) attributes, the regional (Shanghai) or national (Chinese) rather than trans-regional, transnational, and translational aspects that actually contributed to Eileen Chang's works in response to her diaspora years (up to forty years in the US, compared with thirty-five split between Shanghai and Hong Kong) and her experience away from home. That is to say, they have neglected to heed ways in which she moves beyond the Sinophone world in expanding horizons, so as to innovate about Chinese language and literary traditions as an intrinsic given. In her letters she revealed dissatisfactions with American public culture in the 1950s, which appeared to her as at least not yet brought into a clash with civilizations elsewhere that did not want to recognize or register Chinese as a mode of modern expression except through the lens of American Orientalism and Cold-War anti-Communism, or more disparagingly and even favorably on a superficial level, of an Asian-American model minority discourse to give expressions to ways the Chinese immigrants may react to the cultural policies of assimilation and racial discrimination. Along her line of argument, I propose to examine the translational components in Chang's diaspora experience and her struggle to reach out to new publication agencies and even friends in the US to relaunch a literary career. It could be more productive to consider her late work according to transformative stylistic features as brought about by her choice of a different language, media genre, and gender politics. In other words, Chang's travel experience across borders and genres helps shape her film scripts and late novels, in many ways quite similar to what Beethoven accomplishes when he leaves home (Bonn) for Vienna, in making new friends, undertaking commissions, doing experiments, and responding to new demanding environments.

To make such a point, let us consider a film script by Eileen Chang, titled *Father Takes a Bride* (小兒女 Little Children, 1963). Consisting of scenes about complicated human relationships, misunderstandings, weird adventures, and strange weather, the zany romantic comedy focuses not so much on Mr. Wang Hongshen, a widowed father with three children and hence a convenient patriarch in traditional Chinese drama, as on his older daughter, Wang Jinghui, (aged

22), a young woman of strong determination, who tries in every means possible to prevent her father from bringing in a new woman to the family as her stepmother. The melodrama opens with a ludicrous episode of crabs bought by Sun Chuan incidentally snapping on our female protagonist, Jinghui, on the bus and thereby providing a zany occasion for the two old classmates to get reacquainted. In an apologetic gesture, Sun Chuan offers his crabs as dinner to the Wang family and on such an occasion gets to know Jinghui better. Jinghui's anxiety and fear of her father contemplating a second marriage gradually unfolds over the dinner conversation, as we hear from her an awful story of a neighbor's little girl mistreated by her stepmother. Apparently, she does not want her younger siblings (Jingfang, 8, Jingzheng, 7) to suffer like Xiaofeng, whose life testifies to the misery of her father's second marriage to an evil woman. It suffices to say that the film is in many ways conventional in plot and ideology, but the daughter's role in interfering and in influencing the father's decision-making is rather radical, if not marking a new departure from the Sinophone world system or Chinese feudal ideological apparatuses. A young woman of strong will setting out to protect her much younger brothers, Jinghui slowly takes on a vital role that reminds us of those enacted by Katherine Hepburn in her Hollywood screwball comedies, especially in *Bringing Up Baby* and *The Philadelphia Story*. As William Tay indicates, Eileen Chang saw these movies with her American husband and was drawn to them intimately. As a research fellow at Bonnie Institute of Harvard, Chang was well read in works in Anglo-American feminism, in particular essays and fiction by writers such as Virginia Woolf. It is always through the charm and intelligence of female protagonists played by Hepburn that movies like *Bringing Up Baby* are able to make it to the great film list in spite of their seemingly ludicrous plots, light-hearted surprises, and superfluous coincidences.

Father Takes a Bride is among the more successful box office hits in Hong Kong;[17] it highlights the role of a dutiful and caring daughter, a rare case in contrast to the other seven film scripts by Eileen Chang on romances between men and women in the time of crisis—*Love in the Fallen City* or *Lust, Caution*, for example. Over the years, scholars have turned their sole attention to Chang's screwball comedies that cherish women's manipulative roles (Zhang) or to films with perplexing reconfigurations of "playboy-traitor" or "returnee" lovers in response to the author's real-life experience with Hu Lancheng, who is her first husband (Louie; Lee). But I would argue here that *Father Takes a Bride* is a significant text in rethinking ways in which Eileen Chang attempts to rewrite her family scenario by introducing a strong daughter and by bringing forth a comedy on such themes as love and reconciliation. More importantly, this film constitutes a relatively unique transcultural literary production in which Hepburn's

---

17. Tay, *Zhang Aileen de shijie*, 38.

movies and her "strong woman" images prevail to inspire and to re-vision a different family saga. The films may also gain meaning if we should position them intertextually to Ang Lee's films such as *Eat Drink Man Woman* (1994) and *Crouching Tiger, Hidden Dragon* (2000) in which father-daughter relations become prominent. For it is through powerful (albeit aggressive) characters like the young princess (played by Zhang Ziyi) in *Crouching Tiger, Hidden Dragon* that we better comprehend the gaps between the old (altruistic, spiritual) and new (self-serving and anti-traditional) China. At the end of Lee Ang's *Eat Drink Man Woman*, the father not only takes a young bride but also regains his taste, on top of fathering another child, providing an interesting supplement and follow-up to Eileen Chang's script. It is as if Ang Lee literally fulfills Eileen Chang's fantasy of the father taking a bride, whimsical and far-fetched thought it may first sound. However, if we look closely, the Hepburn-Chang connection might have been the missing link in the Sinophone articulation in which the Shanghai fiction writer reached out to Hollywood and a female actor as role model, and that across linguistic borders and media genres. One should just look at the characterization of Wang Jizi in *Lust, Caution* to realize that a passionate female ready to die for love in face of multiple layers of betrayal and deceit, on top of danger and chaos, had been prefigured in the 1963 script, if not in any other work done much earlier.

To sum up then, we should consider the screwball connection. The many layers of misunderstandings and misadventures certainly owe a lot to the Hollywood melodramatic convention in which comic elements abound, not only to confuse but to entertain. After all, life is full of pleasant and unpleasant surprises, as films like *Sabrina*, *Vertigo*, and many others reveal. Eileen Chang uses the cemetery scene as a turning point in which the little children get rescued by their teacher. The film ends with a happy family union and a marriage proposal. The story and the title are very much adapted from *Father Takes a Wife* (1941, dir. Jack Hively), but with the honeymoon innuendo and boat journey cut, so that the concentration is on the family relations, Jinghui as the protagonist to single-handedly make things happen in the name of maternal and sisterly love. It is of interest to note how Eileen Chang should revise the story of the Hollywood screwball comedy and turn it into a more than modern Chinese family morality play: the ideal mother is the one who has to be found to be able to nurture and to heal, and after the reconfirmation the little children reciprocate with filial piety.

At the second and perhaps more personal level, Eileen Chang revisions her family romance in which her dandy father took a new wife while he was divorcing Chang's biological mother. In real life, Chang was reticent and passive, but in the film and film script she is able to assume a role like Hepburn on the screen to dominate and to make a difference, rendering the choice of a stepmother as rational or at least morally (if not emotionally) justifiable.

Thirdly, this "Sinophone" rearticulation actually brings out American feminist and Anglophone perspectives that are not found in the Chinese society, in which patriarchal values predominate. In the film, it is the female teacher who wins over the heart of her future stepdaughter by proving herself to be worthy of parenthood and capable of bringing the family together. Their deeds of reaffirmation and reconciliation move beyond what the Sinophone system of social signification advocates for individual right and love. The new women voice their power and support of each other, so as to overcome misunderstandings and obstacles. Wang Jinghui is at center stage all the way, raising questions of Confucian moral order in light of affective affinity, emotion, and memory: she embraces new ethical practices of freedom, individuality, and worth. It is in this regard that the film departs from many novels by the author herself back in Shanghai and Hong Kong. Not only are the characters more vibrant and compassionate, they are no longer constrained by traditional Confucian moral codes such as obeying one's parents, saving face, honoring elders, and conforming to collective values. Employing a figure like Wang Jinghui as inspired by Katherine Hepburn, Eileen Chang carves out here an alternate transcultural space in portraying a new woman in her twenties to be every bit uncompromising while always ready to love and to forgive. She is such an extraordinary character that we run into her in the likes of Wang Jizi in *Lust, Caution* or the young and impetuous princess in *Crouching Tiger, Hidden Dragon*.

With this in mind, we may be better off not to place Eileen Chang's works as simply stories from modern Shanghai or writings falling into the repertoire of the Sinophone. As many of her letters to Hsia and Soong demonstrate, Chang was tortured after arrival in the US and had difficulty publishing her novels in English; and even if she eventually accomplished that, the reception was lukewarm. She attempted to push friends to help her get admitted to the American republic of letters, eager to translate her novels into English and to try many channels, such as Knopf and Norton. Her exposure to Hollywood film culture with the guidance of her American husband enabled her to appreciate strong female casts and to internalize the fantastic and funny screwball narratives, on top of learning ways to cope with teams of collaborators such as actors, directors, fashion designers, and multimedia artists. It may be inappropriate to venture that Chang might have turned turmoil to triumph during her stay in the US, as Swaffer has suggested about Beethoven's life and work. However, as more and more scholars begin to be attentive to Eileen Chang's late works, we can be sure that they will garner notice in fields not limited to modern Chinese literature or Sinophone discourse.

9
The Frontier of Sinophone Literature in Syaman Rapongan's Translational Writing

Yu-lin Lee

Introduction

Using the Taiwanese indigenous writer 夏曼藍波安 Syaman Rapongan's translational writing as an example, this chapter describes a frontier that exists within Sinophone literature. First, it notes the encounter between sound and script in Syaman's writing. If Sinophone writing, as Jing Tsu has pointed out, always draws attention to the permanent and irreducible tension that exists between sound and script, it follows then that Syaman's writing no doubt intensifies that tension and pushes it even further to the extreme. Furthermore, as Syaman's writing demonstrates, the tension between sound and script exists not only within the domain of Sinophone articulation but also extends outside its specific territory.

The term "Sinophone literature" is commonly used to indicate a body of writing that uses the Sinitic languages of the Chinese ethnic people and is circulated within the Chinese community both inside and outside China. Therefore, the term "Sinophone" bears not simply a linguistic indication, but it also contains geopolitical, ethnic, and cultural connotations. Syaman's writing, however, further complicates the case. Just as the Tao people are an Austronesian ethnic group that is definitely not of Chinese ethnicity, so the Tao language belongs to the family of the Austronesian languages and has little to do with Sinitic languages. However, as a minority writer, Syaman is forced to use Chinese as his writing vehicle for many reasons, and consequently, his writing experiences an inevitable process of translation and thus produces a special form of Sinophone literature wherein the Tao oral tradition plays a vital role.

Accordingly, this aforementioned encounter between sound and script in Syaman's translational writing becomes one that uses both Tao articulation and Chinese transcription. More precisely, Syaman has channeled Tao sounds into the Chinese writing system, resulting in a linguistic transformation that is inaugurated by the incorporation of foreign sounds into Chinese scripts. Thus, a continuous line of linguistic variation induced by the Tao language, mostly its sounds, cuts through Syaman's Chinese writing with a unique speed and rhythm.

Being part of an ethnic minority on the island of Taiwan and using other languages than his native tongue to write has become an inescapable fate for Syaman. Hsinya Huang has pointed out that "[t]he first and foremost problem facing indigenous writers is the writing system."[1] As translation became a necessary means for Syaman to write at all, the problems connected with translation become indispensable in order to examine Syaman's Sinophone literature precisely. It is well known that trans-lingual and transcultural practice has become a trademark in Syaman's writing. It should also be emphasized that such trans-lingual and transcultural practice is in fact an actual act of translation, both linguistically and culturally. However, translation is never a transparent process of simply transporting a linguistic and cultural system from one language into another; it is rather a deliberate manipulation of the two languages that involves both aesthetic valuation and the complex politics of cultural identity.

With these intertwined questions in mind, this chapter first addresses the issues related to Syaman's translational writing with respect to Sinophone studies while also introducing the supplementary concept of Sinoglossia to the paradigm of the Sinophone. Referencing the Bakhtinian idea of heteroglossia, Sinoglossia underscores multilingualism and multiculturalism in the Sinophone practice. Since Syaman's Chinese writing offers an unusual mode of translational writing, the problematics of translation thus are one of the primary inquiries of this chapter. This chapter argues that Syaman's translational writing embodies a minor articulation that inaugurates a linguistic transformation that is immanent within Sinophone articulation. More importantly, it contends that Syaman actually discovers or invents an "orality" that is prior to his written scripts and can be considered an uncharted field that is intersected by both articulation and signification. This uncharted field is what we term the "frontier" of Sinophone literature, as it actually exists within and inside Sinophone articulation rather than outside it. More significantly, with the discovery of this uncharged frontier, Syaman is able to envision a possible territory of existence for himself as well as the entire tribe.

---

1. Hsinya Huang, "Sinophone Indigenous Literature of Taiwan," in *Sinophone Studies: A Critical Reader*, ed. Shu-mei Shih, Chien-hsin Tsai, and Brian Bernards (New York: Columbia University Press, 2013), 252.

Moving from Sinophone to Sinoglossia

Can Syaman's writing be regarded as Sinophone literature and thus be included in Sinophone studies? The term "Sinophone literature," particularly as Shu-mei Shih applies it, designates a body of literature produced "on the margins of China and Chineseness within the geopolitical boundary of China as well as without, in various locations across the world."[2] Further, for Shih, the term "Sinopone" embodies the historical process of various colonial formations, the migrations of Chinese people (*Huajen*), and more importantly, the dissemination of Sinitic languages by will or by force.[3]

In this regard, it seems natural to consider Syaman's writing as an example of Sinophone literature, not simply because Syaman uses Chinese as his writing vehicle but also because he voices a marginal culture that deviates from the very authority and authenticity of so-called Chineseness, not to mention that the culture's geopolitical location is outside China. Clearly, the term "Sinophone" as used here is mainly understood as a broad category of literary and cultural production that relies mostly on Sinitic languages. Its emphasis on marginality and locality, the term "Sinophone" also proposes a discursive and critical framework that promotes "multidirectional critiques" by underscoring its "place-based" cultural production to debunk the idea of Chinese-centrism.[4]

Intriguingly enough, it is also in this same vein that Syaman's writing as an illustration of Sinophone literature challenges the very concept of the Sinophone as a broad literary category and an expression of a minor or minority culture, relative to its Chinese counterpart. If, according to Shih Shu-mei, the discourse of the Sinophone implies a resistance to Chinese authority as well as a deviation from the authenticity of Chineseness, then these tendencies apparently require some modification in Syaman's case. Syaman has written extensively against colonialism and modernity; for him, both colonialism and modernity are evil powers that have damaged the Tao tribal civilization and harmed its society. However, colonialism and modernity are not exclusively Western or Chinese; ironically, the Taiwanese government should be the one blamed for this kind of "invasion" regardless of whether the administrations belonged to the Chinese Nationalist Party or the "nativist" Democratic Progressive Party.

Having connected the practice of the Sinophone to the discourse on colonialism, Shih has provided, in particular, a framework of "settler

---

2. Shu-mei Shih, "Introduction: What Is Sinophone Studies?," in *Sinophone Studies: A Critical Reader*, ed. Shu-mei Shih, Chien-hsin Tsai, and Brian Bernards (New York: Columbia University Press, 2013), 8.
3. Shih, "Introduction: What Is Sinophone Studies?," 8.
4. Shu-mei Shih, *Visuality and Identity: Sinophone Articulations Across the Pacific* (Berkeley: University of California Press, 2007), 190.

colonialism"—instead of Chinese diaspora—in order to expose "the dark historical underside of the so-called diaspora of imperial subjects."[5] This "triangular" power structure of settler colonialism between colonizers, settler colonizers, and the colonized may seem helpful in order to understand the complicated relationship between Han Chinese settlers (Taiwanese) and the aboriginal inhabitants on the island of Taiwan. However, their intertwined relationship appears to be more complicated and cannot be simply reduced to a colonizers-colonized one, particularly when considering this against the backdrop of China. For example, the Taiwanese nativist movement that continues to fight against China constantly seeks alliances with the aborigines despite the fact that the aborigines view the Han settlers on that island as being not much different from the Chinese on the Mainland. It becomes even more complicated and confusing when both the Taiwanese Han people and the aborigines attempt to establish subjectivities of their own as a means to markedly distinguish themselves from the Chinese on the mainland.

This confusion between Chinese and non-Chinese people potentially derives from the assumption that the term "Sino" embraces a single ethnicity and a unified cultural heritage. Despite the fact that the Sinophone discourse constantly denies such a misconception and emphasizes its own multilingual and multiethnic features, the term "Sino" persistently implies a unified ethnicity and a cultural identity albeit invented and imaginary ones. In this regard, Syaman's literature precisely discloses the pitfalls of such an integrated ethnicity and imaginary unified community. The fact that the Tao tribe belongs to the vast Austronesian ethnic and linguistic group evidences the falseness of this assumption. Clearly, the Tao cultural heritage has little to do with Chinese civilization, and therefore it is incongruous to consider the Taiwanese aboriginal civilization from the Sinophone perspective.

If Sinophone constantly signifies China and Chineseness, it follows logically that Syaman's writing should be excluded from Sinophone studies, especially by ethnicity and cultural heritage. Hence, this chapter proposes the different concept of "Sinoglossia" as a supplement to the paradigm of Sinophone studies, to overcome these apparent limitations in its theorization. With its connotations of Bakhtinian heteroglossia and Foucauldian heterotopia, the concept of Sinoglossia focuses more on the language issue that occupies the central concern of Sinophone studies. Nevertheless, the prefix "Sino-," like that in the term "Sinophone," maintains a consistent binding to as well as resistance against the imaginary unity of Chineseness. Therefore, it becomes more productive to regard Sinoglossia as a site for transmedial possibilities and investigation of the various linguistic embodiments of Sinophone articulation and cultural positionalities

---

5. Shih, "Introduction: What Is Sinophone Studies?," 3.

worldwide. In other words, the term "Sinoglossia" offers an alternative critical approach to use for reconsidering the shifting of linguistic boundaries through translation, thereby positioning so-called Chineseness in its own cultural production.

This aspect, as informed by the new concept of Sinoglossia, is fruitful for examining Syaman's writing, which actually embodies a special form of Sinophone literature. As mentioned, Jing Tsu cautioned regarding the irreducible tension between sound and script in the Sinophone practice, and Syaman's translation writing no doubt intensifies that tension as well as further complicates its cultural significance. The mixture of Tao and Sinitic languages inevitably remaps the linguistic territory of the Sinophone and transforms the conventional function of Chinese characters. Further still, Syaman's trans-lingual and transcultural practice also expresses the urgent search for the survival of an indigenous people and its civilization.

The Aporia in Syaman's Translational Writing

Gilles Deleuze and Félix Guattari have described the predicament of Franz Kafka as a minor writer as "the impossibility of not writing, the impossibility of writing in German, and the impossibility of writing otherwise."[6] Being a Jewish descendant living in Prague and writing in German in the early twentieth century, Kafka faced the problem of having to choose German as his writing vehicle. According to Deleuze and Guattari, Kafka's predicament involved the problems related to national consciousness, the survival of a small literature, the writer's psychological distance from his chosen writing vehicle, the relationship between languages and the living community, etc. As a result, Deleuze and Guattari argue that Kafka's German writing, that is, writing in Prague German, can be recognized as a "deterritorialized language," a strange and minor use of German that can be compared to the use of African American or Black English in the American context.[7]

A similar predicament can be found for the indigenous writer Syaman and his Chinese writing in contemporary Taiwan. Syaman has felt obligated to write and has been eager to preserve the Tao language and culture through the art of writing and storytelling. It seems impossible to write in Tao, not because of the lack of a Tao writing system or because of the insurmountable gap between the oral tradition and literary expression, but rather because of the scarce readership for the Tao language. More importantly, similar to Kafka's predicament, it

---

6. Gilles Deleuze and Félix Guattari, *Kafka: Toward a Minor Literature*, trans. Dana Polan (Minneapolis: University of Minnesota Press, 1986), 16.
7. Deleuze and Guattari, *Kafka*, 16–17.

remains impossible for Syaman to write in Chinese. That is not due to Syaman's inadequate command of that language but primarily, following Deleuze and Guattari, that Chinese for Syaman is a "paper language" that is not rooted in the daily lives of the Tao people and the Tao society.

These recognized "impossibilities" of writing and not writing in Chinese for Syaman become the starting point of our investigation. To write in Chinese, Syaman has to rely on translation. However, translation does not simply mean transporting the Tao language and culture into the Chinese context. Translation is never transparent, and no complete translation is ever possible. As a result, one can detect plenty of translational "remainders" still left from the process of translation. These untranslated and untranslatable Tao words and their meanings in turn force the Chinese language to deviate from its usual syntactical structure and grammatical rules. It can be said as well that, through translation, Syaman's Chinese writing has inaugurated a process of linguistic deterritorialization by inducing a continuous transformation immanent within the language itself, to borrow Deleuze and Guattari's terms.

A few examples of translation practice offered here may further explain the concept of linguistic transformation. First of all, it is noticeable that Syaman's writing is filled with a great variety of sound descriptions, including those for the wind, the sea, the woods, the birds, the fish, as well as chants, songs, prayers and the sounds of worship, women's shouts and their murmurs, etc. These natural sounds and human voices are closely tied to the daily lives of the Tao people in the tribal village and, therefore, are vividly recorded in Syaman's writing. What is striking is that these sounds are transcribed mostly by using Chinese characters and are mixed with Chinese syntax. If the Chinese language relies more on its ideo-graphs than on phono-graphs, then these transcriptions of sounds no doubt change the topography of the language itself. This linguistic mixture produces a particular and distinct rhythm that penetrates the sentence structure itself.

The acoustic characteristic of Syaman's Chinese writing is further exemplified by the chanted songs used to pray for a fishing harvest at sea. Many songs of this kind are recorded in Syaman's works like, for example, his early work, "Memories of the Waves." These songs can be regarded as accounts of the daily life of the Tao people and of their culture that depends heavily on the sea. According to the Tao oral tradition, when these songs are performed, the chanters add lyrics to the ancient melodies and exchange the songs to communicate with other performers. Although transcriptions of these original Tao songs are omitted and only provided in Chinese translation in Syaman's early writings, those somewhat awkward Chinese translations give the readers the impression that the author has tried to maintain the tempo and the melodies of the original songs by modifying the Chinese syntax and sentence structure. Clearly, this acoustic effect is not produced solely by translating the Tao oral tradition, nor by a recomposition of Chinese songs; rather, it is brought about through an intensive mixture of the Tao and Chinese languages, including of their syntaxes and sentence structures.

In addition to the various sound transcriptions and song recordings, a great number of the Tao sentences are rendered verbatim in Syaman's writing and only partially translated. In those cases, one or two lines of romanized Tao speech is placed parallel to the Chinese translation. Here are a few examples:

> *Miya sasedka so pacya lologan no makarala*
> 祈禱潮水順流我船，讓勇士們迅速地回到部落的港澳
> [I pray the waves unhindered, may the warriors return swiftly the harbor of our tribe]
> *Miya sasedka so pacya lologan no makarala*
> 祈禱潮水順流我船，讓勇士們迅速地回到部落的港澳
> [I pray the waves unhindered, may the warriors return swiftly the harbor of our tribe]
> *Iyaya . . . o, Iyaya woy yam . . .* 合唱 [sing in chorus]
> *Iyaya . . . o, I . . .* 合唱 [sing in chorus][8]

As shown in these examples, the author provides Chinese translations for the first two lines that are placed parallel to their original Tao lines, followed by two lines of Tao chants without any further translation. They are left untranslated because they are songs to sing together, as indicated in the parentheses at the end of each sentence. The parallel juxtaposition of Tao and Chinese can also draw the reader's attention. Perhaps this very juxtaposition can be regarded as the author's placing an emphasis on the fact that Tao and Chinese are indeed two separate languages with their own distinct syntax and grammar. However, for most Chinese readers, these romanized transcriptions of the Tao language have no significant function and thus have no meaning. The Chinese readers may or may not skip those Tao lines when reading them in the text. And yet, in these hidden unknown meanings, the Tao lines appear as unrecognizable lyrics that occupy textual spaces and present, along with their own particular tempo and rhythm, merely sound vibrations of the letters themselves. Such composition also gives the readers an impression that these unknown signs convey a vibrating rhythm within, albeit a strange unrecognizable one that nevertheless corresponds to their Chinese translations in a mystic way.

However, the Tao language is not always romanized and separated from the terrain of the Chinese language. Often, it appears as a special form of Chinese and is combined with Chinese syntax to produce a sentence. For example, the sentence, 老人的太陽很低了 *laojen de taiyang hen di le* (The sun of the old man

---

8. Rapongan Syaman, *Heise de chibang* 黑色的翅膀 [Black wings] (Taipei: Unitas Publishing, 2009), 36.

falls low) may seem to be Chinese, but it is actually not.⁹ Syaman understands that its meaning may be unclear to the Chinese readers, so he adds a Chinese sentence as an explanation: 歲月催人老，往事不堪回味 *Suiyue cui jenlao, wangshi bukan huiwei* (The passing years make one older, the past is unmemorable).¹⁰ Just as the Chinese syntax here is awkward, the translation that Syaman provides appears imprecise; it is rather an explanation or implication than a translation.

What is significant is not simply the mixture of the two languages in syntactical composition but also the parallel fashion in which the two are arranged in the text. Further, the mixture is not limited to vocabulary and syntax; sometimes it is extended to textual signification and cultural content. For example, there is 我肉體先前的靈魂 *wo ruoti xianchien de linghun* (the previous souls living in my body), which literally means my deceased father and mother, and 釣魚竿碰觸到的夕陽 *diaoyukan pengchu dao de xiyang* (the sunset touched by fishing pole), which refers to the final days of the flesh.¹¹ In these compositions, new Chinese syntax is invented to convey the Tao literary and cultural significance. Yet, due to their ambiguous meanings, these sentences are followed by more "regular" Chinese expressions that then serve as approximate translations. Apparently, the invented syntax and its Chinese translation are also arranged in a parallel fashion, wherein the latter is placed within parentheses. This parallel juxtaposition gives the readers the impression that the Tao and Chinese languages exchange their textual and cultural significations in a contact zone despite the fact that this exchange remains only on the surface level.

In addition to those "surface" exchanges, there are "deeper" exchanges between the two linguistic and cultural systems, which can perhaps be best exemplified by a neologism. For example, the Tao neologism, *mi kongkong si*, takes the sound and meaning of the Chinese term 恭喜 *kongsi* (congratulations), rendering it into the Tao syntax, wherein the *kong* sound is repeated twice and transformed into the passive form. Other neologisms, including *pananazangan* (grocery store), *kokominto* (Kuomintang), and *kyusanto* (the Communist Party), among many others, appear to have a similar construction. The textual and cultural exchange in these neologisms is "deeper"; however, because they do not simply "translate" words and meaning into a syntactical structure, these neologisms present the appropriation of new terms into the Tao language, along with their notions and ideologies that enter the Tao society.

---

9. Many other examples, such as 被部落裡的家屋之煙火燻的男子 *Bei buluo li de jiawu zhi yenhuo xiu de nanzi* (The man smoked by the fire of the house), appear to have a similar syntactical structure. See Rapongan Syaman, *Hailang de jiyi* 海浪的記憶 [Memories of the waves] (Taipei: Unitas Publishing, 2002), 45.
10. Syaman, *Hailang de jiyi*, 45.
11. Rapongan Syaman, *Hanghaijia de lian* 航海家的臉 [The faces of voyagers] (Taipei: Inke Publishing, 2007), 74.

Another form of expression in Syaman's writing that deserves further attention is the specific form of translingual practice. If the parallel juxtapositions of the Tao and Chinese languages indicate linguistic and cultural exchanges between them, the translingual practice points to a more intense interaction between the two. There appears a hybrid form of linguistic mixture, not simply a mixture of vocabularies and terms, but rather a combination of syntax construction and significations as well. Take, for example, the term 凶悍 *xionghan* (barbaric) in the sentence, "you are not *xionghan* enough."[12] Syaman explains that the expression "not *xionghan*" in the Chinese context can mean "having no guts" or "not barbaric enough"; however, it may have a relatively different meaning in the Tao language. Syaman states that "*xionghan* in the Tao language implies a strong and healthy body that accommodates natural climate and thus can resist illness."[13] Accordingly, the word *xionghan* carries a double linguistic and cultural signification: the Chinese "guts" and the Tao "strong body," both of which then implicitly have the common connotation of "barbarism." What is intriguing about this particular syntactic construction is that the Chinese characters of *xionghan* form a zone of proximity wherein two divergent series of linguistic and cultural significations—Tao and Chinese—converge and cut across each other.

These aforementioned linguistic and cultural exchanges, particularly the parallel juxtaposition of Tao/Chinese syntax and Chinese translation, remain at the surface level. Some are associated with rhetorical expression, and some concern cultural connotations. However, there is a unique kind of exchange here, in which the vibrations of sound penetrate body and things, thereby leading to a very different discursive landscape regarding the encounter of different languages and cultures. A dramatic episode in the novel *The Old Fishermen* (*Laohaijen* 老海人) illustrates just such a complicated encounter.

This particular deliberate episode describes the celebration ceremony in the Tao village on National Day. In the plaza, the Chinese Nationalist military officers and the soldiers, along with the crowd of Tao villagers, are declaiming the slogans that mark the climax of the ceremony: "Long Live the Three Principles; Long Live the Republic of China." The soldiers shout very loudly to create a sincere and stirring atmosphere. However, these acclaimed slogans are nothing but big noise to the ears of the Dawa elders since they have little knowledge of the Chinese language and accordingly barely understand its meaning. They cannot help but burst out: "It's fine for the Nationalist officers and soldiers to shout. Why ask our young men to follow them?"[14] Despite this complaint, the Tao elders try to partake in the celebration ceremony in their own unique way. Having already

---

12. Syaman, *Hanghaijia de lian*, 83.
13. Rapongan Syaman, *Laohaijen* 老海人 [The old fishermen] (Taipei: Inke Publishing, 2009), 17.
14. Syaman, *Laohaijen*, 204.

dressed up in their traditional attire, the Tao elders are shaking their long iron spears in their hands while making loud noises: "Hey, hey, hey!" According to the traditional rituals, these shouts are made to inspire and encourage the tribal warriors to go to war. Not surprisingly, these noises to the ears of the military officers appear hostile and antagonistic, seemingly challenging their authority. In such a scene both the slogans and acclamations lose their significations, and only the voices are left. Since the voices mean nothing to either group, they too become only sound vibrations, floating in the air and yet still confronting each other.

In Syaman's Chinese writing, these shouts are rendered as 鬼叫 *guijiao*, which literally means "ghostly shout" (*gui* as an adjective) or "ghosts shout" (*gui* as a noun), to indicate their already blurred meanings. In the exchange of words between the military officers and the Tao elders, the word "ghostly/ghost" continues to evolve, transforming from an adjective into a noun and even a pronoun, which may signify the Nationalist officers, the crowd of Tao villagers, the aboriginal ancestral spirits, and even actual ghost and demons. What is at stake here is a continuous line of linguistic transformation induced by the sound immanent within the language itself. The sound vibration without any fixed signification simply flows and penetrates the various bodies and things, confronting and fighting, one against the other, each with its own particular speed and rhythm, no matter how high or low, how furiously or gracefully.

In such a scene where language has lost its communication function, the role of translation deserves further attention. Interestingly enough, Syaman depicts a translator situated in between the two argumentative groups, attempting to ease the violent confrontation. In actual practice, it seems that the translator forces the floating sounds to enter into and be fixed in the linguistic territory of the Chinese by rendering to them tentative meanings at the expense of only providing false translations. Syaman depicts the episode in a funny and yet satiric way through which he manages to deliver the opposite message ironically. Despite the fact that such (false) translations may relieve the immediate conflict between different languages and cultures, the battle between them—as represented by the intense confrontations of these sound vibrations—remains very real and seems inevitable.

Orality and the Linguistic Frontier

The previous discussion shows the various forms and strategies of Syaman's writing from the perspective of translation. Among them, including parallel juxtaposition and the hybrid forms of linguistic mixture, the expression of sound is most noticeable and most emphasized. The foregrounding of such sound expression in Syaman's Chinese writing perhaps derived from his primary intention to preserve the Tao language and its tribal civilization in which oral tradition plays a vital role. Furthermore, this sound expression produces an unexpected effect in Syaman's Chinese writing. Often, the Tao sounds remain distinguishable from the Chinese writing system and its significations. In some cases, they are preserved and thus become purely phonic vibrations that contrast with their Chinese counterparts. And yet, sometimes they are combined with a Chinese syntax and are thereby introduced into the fixed territory of Chinese signification.

To a certain extent, Syaman is actually speaking his native Tao tongue while writing in Chinese. This fact is the reason why Syaman's writing undertakes a continuous process of translation from Tao into Chinese. Being a native Tao speaker, Syaman remains a foreigner working on the Chinese linguistic terrain. Or more precisely, being a bilingual writer, Syaman writes Chinese and turns it into a foreign language. It is precisely from this perspective that Syaman's writing can be regarded as an example of "minor literature," according to Deleuze and Guattari's conception of the term. "Minor" and its contrasting term "major" do not specify two different languages but rather different "treatments" of the same language: their different uses and functions. Therefore, minor literature means a minor use of a language, a "becoming-minor" of that language, as characterized by the variation operation.[15] In sum, for both Deleuze and Guattari, the term "minor literature" designates a special form of writing in which a continuous line of linguistic transformation occurs within the language itself; it indicates a movement of linguistic deterritorialization.

In Syaman's Chinese writing, the Tao sound is primarily transcribed using Chinese characters, which emphasizes the sound qualities of those Chinese characters and thus vitalizes the tempo and rhythm immanent within the Chinese language. As for those lines of romanized Tao speech, since they convey no signification to the Chinese readers, they only form a block of phonic vibration without signification, thereby occupying a textual space that is parallel to the Chinese lines with their own unique rhythm and speed. What is more striking is the hybrid form of linguistic mixture that delivers an intensive intersection between the Tao and Chinese languages. The hybrid form of Chinese characters embraces a contact zone wherein previous linguistic territory collapses and brings forth a new linguistic system. As demonstrated by the aforementioned example, the Chinese characters for *xionghan* create a linguistic zone of proximity whereby two divergent linguistic elements are derived from previous distinct signification systems, then converge and wait to be re-composed, just as those intense shouts and acclamations on the plaza during the celebration turn into phonic vibrations that also somehow penetrate each other.

---

15. Gilles Deleuze and Félix Guattari, *A Thousand Plateaus*, trans. Brian Massumi (Minneapolis: University of Minnesota Press, 1987), 104.

These "deterritorialized" sounds mark perhaps the most paramount characteristic of Syaman's translational writing, which can be seen as a special form of "orality." However, to highlight the "orality" in Syaman's writing does not actually provoke an awareness of the Tao oral tradition as distinct from Tao literacy, as distinguished by Walter Ong. Instead, it aims to demonstrate an "orality" that exists within the language and in the writing system as well. The Tao civilization succeeded through inherited oral traditions during its long development of history prior to modern times. This oral tradition is also observable in Syaman's writing, where myths, legends, and stories occupy the vital parts. One may argue that Syaman's foregrounding of the expression of sound may have been influenced by the Tao oral tradition. However, our concern here is more for the "orality" of the language that appears in Syaman's Chinese writing than it is for the Tao oral tradition. Hence, "orality" means less an oral tradition as opposed to writing system than it does the verbal sounds that existed before the script. In other words, orality designates the sounds that exist prior to script and its significance.

The particular orality found in Syaman's writing, therefore, is comparable to what Guattari has described as "machinic orality," which can be understood as an intersection between speech and script.[16] For Guattari, such orality—which is best delivered by performing arts—has the "advantage of drawing out the full implications of this extraction of intensive, a-temporal, a-spatial, a-signifying dimensions from the semiotic net of quotidianity."[17] Noticing the fact that the oral is always over-coded by the scriptural, Guattari provokes the "rediscovery of orality" through a re-composition of the scriptural, such as in the composition of poetry. Therefore, Guattari considers it not necessarily "a return to an originary orality" but instead an invention of new "deterritorialised machinic paths capable of engendering mutant subjectivities."[18] It is in the same vein that Syaman's transformation of Chinese writing by translating Tao sounds into Chinese can be considered a similar rediscovery of orality, which then reveals the full potentiality of the Chinese writing system.

Further still, it is worth noting that these "deterritorialized" oral sounds in Syaman's writing occupy a special space in the overall linguistic terrain. This special space, which is informed mostly by phonic vibration, is what we term the "frontier" of Sinophone literature. However, to describe this special space as a linguistic frontier emphasizes its deterritorialized paths gathered from previous fixed linguistic territories by breaking both syntactical constraints and

---

16. Félix Guattari, *Chaosmosis: An Ethico-Aesthetic Paradigm*, trans. Paul Bains and Julian Pefanis (Bloomington: Indiana University Press, 1995), 88.
17. Guattari, *Chaosmosis*, 90.
18. Guattari, *Chaosmosis*, 90.

grammatical rules. This linguistic frontier may seem to exist outside the Chinese language; however, in fact, that territory exists deep within the language itself, and it is made visible through the operation of variation. Or to put it more precisely, Syaman's minor use of the Chinese language that activates a linguistic transformation immanent within the Chinese helps to create an ambiguous linguistic terrain that belongs neither to the Chinese nor to the Tao language. In other words, Syaman actually is speaking Tao in his Chinese writing and thus makes himself a foreigner operating on the Chinese linguistic terrain but thereby articulating a new voice in an obscure territory where the boundaries between Tao and Chinese do blur.

Becoming-Tao

The rediscovery of "orality" in the Guattarian sense should be regarded as Syaman's most vital invention, and it bears further significance. It is clearly observable that the Tao oral tradition is embedded in Syaman's writing. However, the discovery of this orality comes not so much from the oral tradition itself as from the process of translation. The orality in written language is not the same as that found in the oral tradition, and it should be distinguished from it. Therefore, the discovery of orality does not qualify a revitalization of the Tao oral tradition such as, for example, the production of an oral literature and culture to preserve tribal songs, stories, and legends from the oral past. Instead, this unique innovation seeks an orality through a new composition and arrangement of linguistic elements that actually transgresses both predetermined syntactical constraints and grammar rules.

    Deleuze and Guattari have argued that what is preserved in an artwork is "*a block of sensations*" that is, "*a compound of percepts and affects*."[19] Furthermore, Guattari emphasizes that "affect is not a question of representation and discursivity, but of existence."[20] This perspective is particularly important in order to understand Syaman's discovery of orality through translation, and it is most suitable to link this discovery to the survival of the entire Tao people and their civilization. It is perhaps undeniable that Syaman's determination to write is driven, despite his inevitable use of Chinese as the writing vehicle, by his primary desire and obligation—born out of a national consciousness—to preserve his tribal civilization. Therefore, to use Guattarian terms, the process of writing becomes also a process of "re-singualization" or "subjectification" that seeks to find the

---

19. Gilles Deleuze and Félix Guattari, *What Is Philosophy?*, trans. Hugh Tomlinson and Graham Burchell (New York: Columbia University Press, 1994), 164.
20. Guattari, *Chaosmosis*, 90.

production of subjectivity, also understood as a "Territory of existence."²¹ More significantly, according to Guattari, the production of subjectivity is carried out by an image of becoming other.²² Here, we can characterize the entire process of Syaman's translational writing as a production of the image of "becoming-Tao," in which he seeks a linguistic frontier and a new territory of existence by discovering a new orality in a foreign language where new assemblages of enunciations are thus reinvented.

The aspect of becoming-Tao also leads us back to the questions raised at the very beginning of this chapter on Sinophone studies: (1) how and why Syaman's writing can be regarded as a special form of Sinophone literature, and (2) how Syaman's writing is an example of Sinoglossia, if not Sinophone, and thus demonstrates the limits and potentialities of the Sino-scripts as a writing vehicle.

The previous discussion has suggested recognizing Syaman's writing as a form of Sinophone literature, not simply because of its use of Chinese as the writing vehicle but also because of its articulation of a minority voice. However, what is at stake is the fact that such an articulation of monitory is achieved through the use of a major language, Chinese. Syaman's Chinese writing can, therefore, be compared to what Deleuze and Guattari define as "minor literature," that is, a minor use of a major language, which consequently illustrates a continuous variation within that language itself. Deleuze and Guattari insist that minor literature indicates a treatment of a language and does not specify any literature produced by any minority group. This idea, however, can cause confusion in Syaman's case, since Syaman's writing, along with that of other indigenous authors, is usually labeled "indigenous literature" and included in a broad category of Taiwan literature known as a national literature.²³ Instead of passing judgment on whether Syaman's writing should be recognized as a minor or minority literature, this essay emphasizes the linguistic transformation that occurred in his Chinese writing, which is of course achieved through his continuous process of translation.

Just as the controversial debate over the use of language is often used to define the features of minor and minority literature, so the discussion of Syaman's writing as Sinophone literature by ethnicity is frequently confined by the nature

---

21. Félix Guattari, *The Three Ecologies*, trans. Ian Pindar and Paul Sutton (New York: Continuum, 2000), 35–36.
22. Guattari, *Chaosmosis*, 95.
23. In actual settings, the distinction between so-called minor and minority literatures is sometimes ambiguous and controversial. Shu-mei Shih has consistently called attention to the fact that Sinophone literature does not always make the case for minor literature in the Deleuzo-Guattarian sense. For example, Malaysian Sinophone literature has to be recognized as a minority literature that is opposed to the national literature of Malaysia, despite the fact that the literary works of many Malaysian writers provide a perfect illustration of linguistic transformation that occurs in their Chinese writing. See Shih, "Introduction: What Is Sinophone Studies?," 12–14.

of identity politics. As a matter of fact, to consider Syaman's writing as either minor literature or minority literature leads to two different critical stances and perspectives. The former emphasizes the minor manipulation in the major language that initiates a molecular writing that constitutes an ethico-aesthetic paradigm of variation; the latter seeks a proof of existence through the logic of dialectics. Therefore, the former concerns an aesthetic style of life, while the latter involves identity politics. Guattari has cautioned that the creation of affects in any work of art concerns not the problem of representation but rather one of existence. This perspective may also prevent one from falling into the pitfall of identity that relies too much on the regime of representation and turns the focus onto the production of subjectivity that concerns existence. In other words, Syaman's Chinese writing embraces the other that exists within, thereby creating an image of becoming-other for the sake of existence and survival.

This new territory of existence is made possible by the discovery of the orality present in Syaman's writing through his new assemblages of enunciations. In this regard, Syaman's manipulation of language of the translation of Tao into Chinese challenges the general idea about the mediality of Chinese characters as an expression medium in Sinophone articulation. In those cases where Tao sounds are transcribed by Chinese characters, the sound quality of the Chinese characters is foregrounded. In a similar fashion, those scattered Tao sounds, as presented by either the romanized alphabet or the hybrid form of mixed languages, somewhat intensify the tempos and rhythm existing in Chinese writing.

However, the foregrounding of the sound quality of the Sinoscripts and the rhythm in the Chinese composition may contradict our general ideas about the Chinese language. Chinese characters are usually considered pictographical and ideographical, and their phonic quality is often ignored. Moreover, the Chinese writing system always gives priority to the script and considers the oral to be subordinate due to the variety of regional pronunciations. This fact also leads to the conclusion that the concept of the Sinophone appears insufficient and even inappropriate to use to describe the primary features of Chinese writing. It is precisely these Sinoscripts—the Chinese characters—that maintain and communicate the entire linguistic "family" of Sinophone articulations.

However, I would also argue that the proposal to substitute the concept of "Sinoscript" for that of "Sinophone" is less a dispute based on linguistic principles and language philosophies than a disagreement over cultural ideology. In other words, the confirmation of Sinoscript as a necessary means to sustain the unity and consistency of the Chinese language that is supported by relatively stable characters may further the consolidation of the Chinese linguistic and cultural identity. The concept of the Sinophone, by contrast, resists the dominance of any Chinese authority and its authenticity. In a world now composed of fragmentary differences and not controlled by any unified principle, multiplicity and diversity should be emphasized. This is exactly what Syaman's literary practice clearly demonstrates: what Sinophone literature discloses is precisely the divergent and not the unifying forces already present in society.

10
The Promise and Peril of Translation in the Taiwan Literature Award for Migrants

Tzu-hui Celina Hung*

Introduction: Born-Translated Taiwan Literature

Taiwan's insertion into the global neoliberal economic order since the 1970s and its rapid transformations in various public spheres since the lifting of martial law (1949–1987) have galvanized an academic momentum to see the island-nation anew. In this revisionist history, Taiwan, rather than a mere receptor of world historical events, increasingly features as an active participant connecting human flows and shaping regional politics, particularly across Asia Pacific. In the recent decade, a brewing desire among the humanists for a new paradigm to place Taiwan studies in closer dialogues with societies and intellectual trends worldwide has led to several pathbreaking conferences and publications spearheaded by literary scholars. Among the most notable examples are Shu-mei Shih's conceptualization of Sinophone studies since 2004 and her later volume, *Comparatizing Taiwan* (2015), co-edited with Ping-hui Liao. These works, among other critical aims, emphasize the longstanding tension between the island's Sinitic-language majority populations and its non-Sinitic minorities.[1] In this Sinophone framework, no historically informed accounts of Taiwan literature would be content with the conventional privileging of Taiwan's standardized Sinitic script and Mandarin speech as the analytic standard; instead, they would reckon with the island's ingrained "polyphonic" and "polyscriptic" foundations

---

* I would like to give special thanks to Weixian Pan, Arina Rotaru, and the two anonymous reviewers for their valuable feedback on earlier versions of this chapter.
1. Shu-mei Shih, "Global Literature and the Technologies of Recognition," *PMLA* 119, no. 1 (2004): 16–30; Shu-mei Shih, *Visuality and Identity: Sinophone Articulations across the Pacific* (Berkeley: University of California Press, 2007); Shu-mei Shih, "The Concept of the Sinophone," *PMLA* 126, no. 3 (2011): 709–718; Shu-mei Shih and Ping-hui Liao, eds., *Comparatizing Taiwan* (London: Routledge, 2015).

in and beyond the scope of Sinitic languages.[2] The years since 2012 have seen further scholarly synergies with a similar ambition. For example, the Institute of European and American Studies at Academia Sinica in Taiwan held a workshop—which turned into a special issue in *Chung-Wai Literary Monthly*—on how decades of translation of Euro-American theories and texts have shaped local scholars' perception of the West and, conversely, introspection of Taiwan as an equally active site of knowledge production. Additionally, since the same year, the interdisciplinary Knowledge Taiwan Collective at National Taiwan University has produced a series of workshops and volumes that aim to defamiliarize conventional frameworks for studying Taiwan.[3]

Both academic and popular discourses in the new millennium have been bursting with efforts to see Taiwan from previously untapped angles and vocabulary, especially amid the society-wide development of multicultural discourse. At its core, the demand to rethink Taiwan's history and its relationship with neighboring societies reflects a growing demand for translation—a crucial object and mode of inquiry for literary comparatists. For literary scholars, this trend implies the necessity to examine Taiwan's expanding network of Sinitic and non-Sinitic cultural expressions, as well as the boundary-crossing worldviews carried in these articulations, which together shape the contours of the country's "literary polysystem," to echo Itamar Even-Zohar's term.[4] Further, it requires investigation of the material circumstances and real-life people behind the means, rules, and outcomes of these exchanges. The nature of this intellectual exercise is translational not only because it mediates between different views on Taiwan but also because it anticipates new modes of knowledge production for Taiwan studies and new ways of forming intellectual communities and allies. As such, translation concretizes what Shih's concept of the Sinophone proposes to do: it offers a hands-on analytic method to understand the continuous streams of cultural traffic coming through the island-society, in both linguistic and extralinguistic registers. Translation, in short, sets the Sinophone's heteroglossic feature in action.

This chapter first responds to recent scholarly calls to provide Sinophone studies with a sharper methodological grounding, by considering translation to be an integral action-word of the Sinophone experience. Within the context of Taiwan, a Sinophone studies stronghold, the practice of translation in the face of

---

2. Shih, "Concept of the Sinophone," 716.
3. "Knowledge Taiwan Collective," International Consortium of Critical Theory Programs, https://directory.criticaltheoryconsortium.org/organizations/knowledge-taiwan-collective/.
4. Itamar Even-Zohar, "The Position of Translated Literature within the Literary Polysystem," in *The Princeton Sourcebook in Comparative Literature: From the European Enlightenment to the Global Present*, ed. David Damrosch, Natalie Melas, and Mbongiseni Buthelezi (Princeton, NJ: Princeton University Press, 2009), 240–247.

the current official discourse about multicultural accommodation suggests that the Sinophone concept would yield greater potentials when referring not just to a given linguistic object or destiny—such as the standardized Mandarin or any other specific language spoken in Taiwan—but to a mode of critique and a discursive site for debate. Second, looking at the specific acts of translation on both textual and extratextual levels, my chapter takes up this volume's proposal to expand Sinophone studies' analytic scope and strengthen its theoretical drive, by considering a set of entwined phenomena that our coeditors call Sinoglossia. As the volume's Introduction emphasizes, the Sinoglossic framework draws attention to the layered meanings of the suffix "glossia," which indicates both language and tongue and, therefore, highlights both the text and the human body as active media for producing speech and writing.[5] I argue that this triptych of Sinoglossic emphases on the linguistic, bodily, and medial aspects of language use suggests a powerful way of approaching Taiwan's multilingual literary productions in concrete translational terms. If language occurs through both our writings and bodily acts, then a Sinoglossic analysis of literary and cultural exchanges would require not just identifying examples of linguistic or textual bartering but also interpreting real-life interpersonal relations.

To illustrate how this Sinoglossic condition shapes Taiwan's new-millennial literary market, and how language itself constitutes an important coordinate but not necessarily the sole or foremost factor in the overall tug-of-war of social relations, I examine the troubled politics of translation in the 移民工文學獎 Taiwan Literature Award for Migrants (2014–2020) (TLAM) with a focus on its history, organization, selection process, storytelling patterns, and its implication for community formation.[6] As a unique grassroots literary endeavor, TLAM represents a culminating point from decades of rights movement for Taiwan's Southeast Asian migrant population since the 1990s, and from a growing community of migrant readers and writers whose voices have rarely been heard except in printed venues like the multilingual periodical *Four-Way Voice*, launched in 2006. Every year, TLAM selected awardees from submissions of migrant-themed stories, written within 3,000 words in any style, by Southeast Asians who came to Taiwan for work, marriage, and education, as well as by their Taiwan-born children. The

---

5. See this volume's Introduction, as well as Howard Chiang, "Sinoglossia Incarnate: The Entanglements of Castration across the Pacific," in *East Asian Men: Masculinity, Sexuality and Desire*, ed. Xiaodong Lin, Chris Haywood, and Mairtin Mac an Ghaill (London: Palgrave Macmillan, 2017), 85–105.
6. TLAM's cofounder Cheng Chang announced the closure of this literature award in 2020. On January 6, 2023, however, 英雄旅程股份有限公司 (Monomyth Co. Ltd.) broke the news on Facebook that it was awarded a literature promotion fund of NT$1,000,000 by the Ministry of Culture. With this fund, the company will revive TLAM and organize its eighth edition in 2023. This manuscript went to the copyediting stage when the news came out; therefore, it only focused on TLAM's history from 2014 through 2020.

organizing committee accepted entries in the Vietnamese, Thai, Indonesian, and Filipino languages during the first six years, and it added Burmese in 2020, the same year when it also announced that TLAM would discontinue from the next year onward. While all submissions initially came from the migrants living in Taiwan, in 2019 the call for entries was extended to those residing in Hong Kong, Macao, Singapore, Malaysia, Japan, and South Korea, and in 2020 the scope was broadened to all of Asia.[7] After a board of native-language judges made their initial evaluation, the entries on the shortlist were translated into the Sinitic-language version for final selection by a Sinitic-language jury drawn annually from writers, scholars, journalists, activists, and filmmakers, most of whom were Taiwanese locals. Starting in 2016, each year the organizing board also recruited a group of five youngsters between the ages of fifteen and twenty as part of the final jury. In TLAM's official online postings and annual book collections, both the winning stories and each accompanying "Author's Note" appeared in bilingual prints, showing both the winners' original Southeast Asian versions and their Sinitic translations.

Drawing on a genealogy of literary scholarship concerning the promise and peril of translation, particularly the works of Rita Felski, Lawrence Venuti, and Rebecca Walkowitz, I argue that TLAM's selection and translation of Southeast Asian migrant writings cast light on two intimate terrains of Taiwan's Sinophone literary criticism as it has evolved recently. First, I examine some major contradictions underlying the collective making of TLAM as Taiwan literature, a goal envisioned by the award's cofounders, Cheng Chang and Yun-chang Liao, and Taiwan literature scholar Fang-ming Chen, the jury head in 2014.[8] By collective making, I refer to the mix of professional language-workers and a grassroots network involved in carrying out the award: the migrant writers, translators, native-language judges, Sinitic-language final judges, partnering units in the public sector, and general readers of this translational literary market. Echoing David Damrosch's observation of the dynamic between world literature and

---

7. Cheng Chang 張正, "Yige wenxuejiang de shengyusi: gaobie yimingong wenxuejiang" 一個文學獎的生與死：告別移民工文學獎 [Life and death of a literary award: Farewell to the Taiwan literature award for migrants], *Independent Opinion@CommonWealth*, October 28, 2020, https://opinion.cw.com.tw/blog/profile/91/article/10068.
8. Cheng Chang 張正, "Cong rechaotan dao bowuguan de yimingong wenxuejiang" 從熱炒攤到博物館的移民工文學獎 [From a stir-fry vendor to the museum: The migrant literature award], in *Liu: Yidong de shengmingli, langchaozhong de Taiwan / diyierjie yimingong wenxuejiang zuopinji* 流──移動的生命力，浪潮中的臺灣／第一、二屆移民工文學獎得獎作品集 [Flow: Story collection from the 2014 and 2015 Taiwan literature award for migrants], coauthored by Southeast Asian migrants (New Taipei City: Four Way Publishing, 2015), 288–296; Cheng Chang 張正 and Yun-chang Liao 廖雲章, "Song of Exile, Four-Way Voice: The Blood-and-Sweat Writings of Southeast Asian Migrants in Taiwan," in *The Oxford Handbook of Modern Chinese Literatures*, ed. Carlos Rojas and Andrea Bachner (New York: Oxford University Press, 2016), 440–454.

national literature, I argue that TLAM's relationship with the category of Taiwan literature is both contradictory and complementary.[9] As a product of Southeast Asian migrants' overseas experiences in Taiwan, the award's winning pieces are read mostly in Sinitic-language versions by local readers, who witness these migrant expressions first and foremost as a Taiwanese phenomenon. However, while promoted as part of an emerging Taiwanese genre, the award invites a collective rethinking of Taiwan literature that in many ways undermines the territorial, linguistic, and perspectival boundaries of this increasingly nationalized literary category. Its translingual nature, for example, poses serious questions about the sanctity of the Sinitic script as Taiwan's standard literary language. Seen from this light, translation implies more than the mechanical textual exchange between languages; it entails linguistic and extralinguistic investments by an expansive group of people to picture, conjure, and debate about the previously slighted social reality of migrant life. The award's translational ambition is therefore both literary and social insofar as it serves as a public medium to carry out this embedded educational function; as such, its translational goal exemplifies the tripartite Sinoglossic emphasis on textuality, materiality, and mediality. As cofounders Chang and Liao explain, from the moment of its initial conceptualization, the award is "intended to provide a means" for the migrants to "gain some recognition for their writing" and "offer their 'evaluations' of Taiwan itself"; meanwhile, this socially engaged ambition is joined by their hope that "migrant writings could help enrich Taiwan literature."[10] This suggests that what the award creates, interprets, and transforms is not just certain migrant images but also the meanings of Taiwan literature and society.

This brings us to the second set of questions: what are the target issues, and who are the target audiences, of this large-scale translational project? If the award can be seen as a kind of intervention to ways of seeing or interpreting Taiwan, what assumptions inform its operation, and what are its stakes? These questions are urgent because, as a platform that uses literary competition to mediate between the mutual gazes of Taiwan's migrant and non-migrant populations, TLAM presents an obvious epistemological paradox. For example, its multiculturalist propensity encourages an identity-based staging of selected aspects from the migrants' occupational, religious, emotional, and familial life, and yet, as Chang deliberates in his postscript for the award in 2015, it is also expected to facilitate local Taiwanese readers' self-introspection.[11] This inward-looking drive makes one wonder to what extent the award's multiculturalist staging of

---

9. David Damrosch, "Introduction: World Literature in Theory and Practice," in *World Literature in Theory* (Chichester, UK: Wiley Blackwell, 2014), 1–12.
10. Chang and Liao, "Song of Exile," 452–453.
11. Chang, "Cong rechaotan dao bowuguan," 294; Chang and Liao, "Song of Exile," 454.

migrant voices really facilitates two-way understanding between Taiwan's majority and minority communities, especially since its published pieces are read by Taiwanese readers mostly in the form of translation and, to some extent, veil the direct voices of the migrant storytellers.

TLAM is a perfect example of what Rebecca Walkowitz calls born-translated literature, whose format and goal, as she describes, are designed to be a translated product from the beginning.[12] As she explains, since "translation is not secondary or incidental to these [original] works" but "a condition of their production," what born-translated literature produces is often a work that is "still arriving," a language "on its way from somewhere else," and a "literature produced for other readers."[13] TLAM reflects this feature: the juxtaposition of Southeast Asian languages and their translations has been built from the start as the award's principal form for public display; as such, the bilingual format works effectively to prevent readers of either set of the languages from gaining a proprietary feeling as native-language readers. While the Sinitic-language readers are constantly reminded of the translated and incomplete nature of their reading, the migrant authors and their fellow native-language readers also have to reconcile with a degree of alienation in Taiwan's literary market, where the primary language used for appreciating their works—the Sinitic text—may be foreign to them.

However, in a culture like Taiwan's, where many sociolegal institutions remain unfriendly toward foreign migrants, language itself may not be a bigger barrier than are some of the more deep-seated prejudices, such as classism, racism, sexualization of female migrant workers, and religious intolerance toward Muslim migrants. Furthermore, while the award's bilingual format simultaneously satisfies the curiosity of Taiwanese readers about Southeast Asian migrants and challenges their expectation for a transparent representational access, it also highlights the fantasy of a world-literature community speaking a lingua franca *as* a fantasy with hiccups that can only be slightly ameliorated through translation. In doing so, the award imparts an explicitly foreignizing exercise of translation that promises to alter the readers' relationship with both the original Southeast Asian-language versions and the Sinitic-language translations. This interventionist function harks back to Homi Bhabha's postcolonialist view on cultural translation, which posits that minoritarian voices do not simply pose as cultural samples only to be crudely appropriated for anthropological purposes, a classic critique by Talal Asad and John Dixon, but possess the momentum to occasion structural metamorphosis for both the dominant and marginalized

---

12. Rebecca Walkowitz, "Theory of World Literature Now," in *Born Translated: The Contemporary Novel in an Age of World Literature* (New York: Columbia University Press, 2017), 1–48.
13. Walkowitz, "Theory of World Literature Now," 4–6.

communities.[14] It is in this regard that we may understand TLAM as a broader project of cultural translation.

But the specific ways in which TLAM mediates between the mainstream society and the migrants is far more intricate than Bhabha's idealized interpretation of the function of minoritarian expressions. Bearing this intercultural tension in mind, here below I examine TLAM's cultural translation not to recapitulate the apparent limit of translatability in situations of cross-cultural encounters. Rather, considering translation by its Sinoglossic features as textual, material, and medial practices, I lay out what TLAM's collective labor of translingual mediation produces, in both exciting and cautionary ways: specifically, what organizational energies, intercommunity relations, storytelling techniques, and interpretive risks have emerged, for better or worse. Then, based on this observation of translation's community-building potential, I conclude with its methodological implication for studying Taiwan literature in the new millennium.

Translation as Connection: The Award as a Means to an End

A frequently noted feature of TLAM is its task of translating multiple Southeast Asian source languages. The attention of public eyes to this translingual ambition parallels the predominance of scholarly focus so far on the linguistic register of the Sinophone discourse. Beyond academic conversations, a similar desire for greater access to the languages and cultures of Taiwan's Southeast Asian neighbors can be seen, for example, in President Ing-Wen Tsai's clamorous launch of the New Southbound Policy in 2016, which partly aims to "cultivate more Southeast Asian language experts and regional trade professionals."[15] However, placed in light of Taiwan's settler colonial history and its more recent development into a society increasingly conscious of diversity, calls for language access as such often belie the structural chauvinism underneath what looks like a hospitable multicultural paradigm: for decades, Taiwanese society had systematically excluded migrant, Indigenous, and other minorities from its official history until the state's multicultural rhetoric and policies finally took up speed in the new millennium. If TLAM's cumbersome bilingual format is a glaring telltale of the

---

14. Talal Asad, "The Concept of Cultural Translation in British Social Anthropology," in *Writing Culture: The Poetics and Politics of Ethnography*, ed. J. Clifford and G. E. Marcus (Berkeley: University of California Press, 1986), 141–164; Talal Asad and John Dixon, "Translating Europe's Others," in *Europe and Its Others: Proceedings of the Essex Conference on the Sociology of Literature* (July 1984), ed. Francis Barker et al., vol. 1 (Colchester, UK: University of Essex Press, 1985), 170–193; Homi K. Bhabha, *The Location of Culture* (London: Routledge, 1994); Robert J. C. Young, "The Dislocations of Cultural Translation," *PMLA* 132, no. 1 (2017): 186–197.
15. Office of Trade Negotiations, Executive Yuan, "New Southbound Policy Promotion Plan" (October 3, 2016), https://www.ey.gov.tw/otnen/64C34DCA8893B06/a0e8fd0b-a6ac-4e80-bdd4-16b4cf999b49.

majority population's lack of linguistic literacy, unfortunately this shortcoming is not any more embarrassing than the society's general lack of knowledge about many other aspects of its Southeast Asian neighbors. When Cheng Chang comments that "literature is one of many important forms of cultural expression" and that "this literature award has been a means to an end from the beginning," he refers precisely to the urgency of addressing ignorance not just in language but on a larger structural level.[16] Translation, Lawrence Venuti reminds us, inevitably carries a society's socioeconomic, political, and other agendas, and from this perspective, TLAM reflects not a language-to-language phenomenon only but also an ethnographic venture rooted in decades of grassroots desire to see, read, document, and make intelligible the overseas Southeast Asian experiences in Taiwan.[17] Furthermore, TLAM's embedded educational commitment demands a literary analysis that accounts for the sociology of its textual practice. Therefore, my analysis focuses on both examining the local history of rights activism for migrant labor and explaining how this grassroots history has significantly shaped the award's leading themes and narrative styles, as well as the real-life communities mobilized beyond the text.

While during the 1990s, negative portrayals of marital and labor migrants as social problems abounded in local news reports, the new millennium saw a growing body of print and media productions wherein the migrants exerted greater representational agency. Alongside the continued work from Taiwanese activists, Southeast Asian migrants have directed documentaries, organized labor protests, acted in TV dramas and fiction-feature films, produced photography, and participated in book-borrowing activities through support from the Southeast Asia-themed bookstore called Brilliant Time.[18] Writing between their work shifts, many migrants had submitted native-language poems and essays to the "Taipei, Please Listen to Me!" writing competitions, and since the founding of *Four-Way Voice*, had contributed floods of letters, drawings, poems, and essays to express their longing or laments.[19]

The propitious appearance of TLAM in 2014 represents the convergence of these multisited, multimedia collaborations in bringing Southeast Asian

---

16. Chang, "Cong rechaotan dao bowuguan," 289, 294.
17. Lawrence Venuti, "Translation, Community, Utopia," in *The Princeton Sourcebook in Comparative Literature: From the European Enlightenment to the Global Present*, ed. David Damrosch, Natalie Melas, and Mbongiseni Buthelezi (Princeton, NJ: Princeton University Press, 2009), 358–379; Lawrence Venuti, "Introduction," in *The Translation Studies Reader*, ed. Lawrence Venuti (London: Routledge, 2012), 1–8.
18. Tzu-hui Celina Hung 洪子惠, "Documenting 'Immigrant Brides' in Multicultural Taiwan," in *Asian Video Cultures: In the Penumbra of the Global*, ed. Joshua Neves and Bhaskar Sarkar (New York: Duke University Press, 2017), 158–175; Tzu-hui Celina Hung, "Yixiangren" 譯鄉人 [Translator], *The News Lens*, https://www.thenewslens.com/article/115578.
19. Chang and Liao, "Song of Exile," 447–449.

perspectives to public attention. In the award's annually compiled stories, readers can easily observe frequent overlaps between life writing and fiction, since authors tend to draw inspiration from both their autobiographical experiences and their friends' life, as readers can tell from the "Author's Note" section immediately following each winning piece. Across all styles, the first-person perspective by far dominates all submissions, wherein narrators often elaborate on a range of mixed feelings and thoughts in marriage, at work, with in-laws and employers, with natal families, as participants in Taiwanese society, and as sharp observers of its social problems. The ethnographic taste in these writings is further accentuated by the award's labeling of each migrant awardee by nationality, marital status, and work—caregivers, marital migrants, and students showing the highest frequency among the listed authors.

Just as how these storytelling patterns and biographical information supply Taiwan's majority readers with a surface-level understanding of migrant culture, intellectual discussions of TLAM have been tied, for the most part, to the submissions' ethnographic flavor. Fang-ming Chen, for example, hopes for the award to project a picture of "Southeast Asia within Taiwan."[20] Ironically, this expectation—to write the migrant communities into Taiwan history and literature—is contrasted by few discussions from the award judges of other phenomena of migration to, from, and within Taiwan, or of any existing intellectual genealogies within Taiwan studies devoted to this field of inquiry. The lack is such that, when explaining migrant writings' relevance to Taiwan's literary canon, Chang and other cofounders have to draw points of literary comparison from Anglophone travel and immigrant writings in early twentieth-century Euro-American traditions, particularly from colonial and imperial narratives, like those by Carlos Bulosan, George Orwell, and Pearl Buck.[21] This shows, first, the extent of local intellectuals' lack of ready vocabulary or references for discussing migration even though the country's history illustrates evidence to the contrary, and second, that the award has catalyzed an ambitious intellectual desire to build an open forum whereby migrant and non-migrant communities may brainstorm together what migrant literature can do for Taiwan.

Beyond the text, TLAM exemplifies the extent to which the operation of literary institutions not only relies on support from external organizations and community networks but also encourages direct social engagement at the grassroots level. Likewise, for individual migrant writers, material circumstances at

---

20. Fang-ming Chen 陳芳明, "Taiwan neibu de dongnanya" 台灣內部的東南亞 [Southeast Asia within Taiwan], in *Liu: Yidong de Shengmingli, langchaozhong de Taiwan / diyierjie yimingong wenxuejiang zuopinji* [Flow: Story collection from the 2014 and 2015 Taiwan literature award for migrants], coauthored by Southeast Asian migrants (New Taipei City: Four Way Publishing, 2015), 7.
21. Chang, "Cong rechaotan dao bowuguan," 295.

work and at home are rarely just auxiliary factors but crucial co-determinants behind the possibility of writing and the storytelling patterns, which, in turn, shape the readers' interpretive angles. I believe this extratextual, multi-sited dimension compels us to redirect existing world-literature debates from a focus on problems of untranslatability and objectification within the text—problems rightly identified by scholars like Emily Apter—to one that directly examines the sociality of literary production, that is, its frequently disparaged extratextual fact as an activity reflecting the living conditions of the writers in question.[22] Drawing on Bruno Latour's actor-network theory in *Reassembling the Social*, Rita Felski suggests that this latter focus helps us rethink translation not only with respect to the linguistic "scission or rupture" between texts and thus the need to cross textual barriers but also in relation to the "hybrid and heterogeneous constellations of texts, persons, and things" interacting behind the textual product, none of which can be reduced to the secondary role of contexts.[23] Turning now to this community-based social feature of TLAM as a large-scale translation not just between languages but also between people, I hope to highlight that, notwithstanding Taiwan's highly contingent multicultural market, the award has managed to mobilize a constellation of variegated individuals and institutions to think creatively about what literature awards do, how literary communities are formed, and what interpretive tools are available for readers. As such, the award does not simply offer ethnographic snapshots of migrant life but also holds potential to reinvigorate the field of Taiwan literature with new interpretive angles.

First, the longtime grassroots network cultivated by the magazine *Four-Way Voice* among the journalists, writers, translators, and migrant readers shows that, prior to TLAM, Taiwan's Southeast Asian migrants have been sending out both native-language and Sinitic-language submissions of personal letters for publication, frequently in an autobiographical, epistolary form, and sometimes as drawings. Chang and Liao, in fact, had worked as editorial members of *Four-Way Voice* for a long time; when they decided to cofound TLAM, it was this prior experience that lent support to their ambition to make a stage for the migrant writers.[24] As central participants who help to shape the history of these two closely connected publication outlets, they observe several characteristics of those migrant submissions, such as their letter-writing tradition, frequent first-person narrations on themes like flight from workplace injustice, troubled marriage, domestic violence, and how workplace circumstances have turned specific

---

22. Emily Apter, *Against World Literature: On the Politics of Untranslatability* (London: Verso, 2013), 1–27.
23. Rita Felski, "Comparison and Translation: A Perspective from Actor-Network Theory," in *Comparative Literature Studies* 53, no. 4 (2016): 761–762.
24. Chang, "Yige wenxuejiang de shengyusi."

migrant groups into the biggest contributors to this writerly community. On the last point, about why it is caregivers and domestic workers who form the major constituency of letter-writing authors for *Four-Way Voice*—and not marital migrants, foreign students, or others—they offer the following explanation:

> Because they live with their employers in an environment in which the dominant language and culture is foreign (for them) but in which they spend virtually all their time caring for others and are generally not able to communicate over the Internet, letter-writing is the most convenient and economical medium through which to express themselves. Unlike marriage migrants, foreign domestic workers are not regarded as members of the families of their employers . . . One result of this situation, however, is that these domestics are relatively free to continue using their native language, and many of them become active readers of and contributors to native-language periodicals like *Four-Way Voice*.[25]

The annual lists of TLAM's awardees further indicate that domestic helpers and caregivers continue as the primary group of contributing authors who shape the award's overall narrative orientation. A quick survey of TLAM's initial three years reveals the pattern: among the total of twenty-three winning pieces, twelve are either authored by domestic helpers and caregivers or narrated from such perspectives; of these twelve stories, irrespective of fictional or essayist style, all except one employ first-person or (semi-)autobiographical voices. This authorship pattern suggests a rarely discussed two-pronged issue about the award's potential identity politics. To be sure, it is a valid question for literary critics to ask whether, and to what extent, TLAM's predominant first-person narratives by migrant domestics may have over time steered the award's storytelling patterns toward a narrow range of ethnographic and literary clichés. Domestic work, after all, is only one type of migrant labor in Taiwan. However, this text-based observation of authorship will prompt us to ask a very different question if we consider writing not simply as a free textual exercise of an individual's creative intellect at his or her private desk, an exercise equally available to everyone, but as a direct indicator of how migrant workers juggle between their regular paid work and unpaid creative activities. We would ask, instead, what kinds of workplace circumstances allow the migrants to write at all, and how these amateur writers' everyday work-life experiences contribute to their creation of migrant images. Not only does this alternative view on literary authorship push against the conventional imagination that writing is a marker of learnedness, social status, and privatized cultural capital, but it also signals, quite evidently, the problem of a narrow language- and text-based literary criticism. Indeed, when Chang and Liao observe that "the paper on which these letters [submitted to

---

25. Chang and Liao, "Song of Exile," 443.

Four-Way Voice] were written often revealed as much as the text of the letters themselves," they share Rita Felski's call for literary critics to take seriously the physical labor and the material or social circumstances of writing as a central factor to forming literary communities.[26] From this perspective, the behind-the-scenes material condition of Taiwan's Southeast Asian migrant writings puts pressure on Sinophone literary criticism through at least two registers: one concerns the genuine accommodation of Taiwan's growing non-Sinitic voices into its Sinophone literary membership, and another involves questioning the usual text-based framework through which we conduct intercultural interpretation. As it turns out, reading migrant literature is as much about making textual jumps between source and target languages as about, for example, considering all the unusual locations of writing, all the unconventional paper materials used, like "calendar paper, hospital medical record forms, children's parent-teacher contact book, and even obituary notices," and all the editorial labor of receiving, coding, scanning, translating, and archiving the works.[27]

Viewing the labor of writing as both a creative exercise in language and a personal response to the workplace environment leads us to a more socially grounded perspective on TLAM's staging of migrant writings. For example, it turns our attention to the award committee's collaboration with a hybrid network of people and nonliterary organizations. Chang recollects their outreach efforts as follows:

> We came up with the most old-fashioned promotional strategy—sincerity—in pleading support from reputable allies in the migrants' circle. Every year we invited the jury in earnest, considering the jurists' academic expertise, skill sets, and senses of compassion and justice. We collaborated with public sector units that each represent unique social significance, and we held the award ceremony each time at a different location, such as the National Museum of Taiwan Literature in Tainan; the National Taiwan Museum in Taipei; the Formosa Boulevard metro station in Kaohsiung; Chiayi's Alishan National Forest Recreation Area, managed by the Forestry Bureau; and this time [in 2020], the Nanfang'ao Fishing Harbor in Yilan, supervised by the Fisheries Agency.[28]

While each of TLAM's choices of collaborative units highlights a specific area of the migrant communities' contribution to Taiwanese society, it is also worth noting the extent to which grassroots-level civil-service units have permeated the migrants' everyday life and thus become a crucial advertising channel. Nguyen Cam Thuy, a Vietnamese marital migrant who won the 2014 Choice

---

26. Chang and Liao, "Song of Exile," 443.
27. Chang and Liao, "Song of Exile," 443.
28. Chang, "Yige wenxuejiang de shengyusi."

Award, reveals how her work at the immigration agency led her to information about the award:

> Presently I live in Taidong, where I make a living by collecting betel leaves, doing domestic work, and translating for the local immigration agency ... In fact, I had submitted this story to *Four-Way Voice* during the time that TLAM made a call for submissions. Two immigration agency cadres, Peter and Godem, told me about the award and encouraged me to submit; because of this, I mustered courage to give myself a chance.[29]

Similar to Nguyen's experience, a caregiver from Thailand named Mrs. Khemphon Sridongphet, also a Choice Award winner, receives information "from the Department of Labor and a friend working at the nuclear power plant in Linkou."[30] Some authors also mention having previously worked as journalists or editors and having won other literature awards prior to being selected for TLAM. For instance, Nan Tho, another Choice Award winner in 2014, has previously won Taiwan's literature prizes from the Department of Labor, Tunghai University, Kanglin International Corporation, and Radio Taiwan International, among other organizations.[31] The pattern in these authors' biographical notes suggests that, while living overseas, many migrants have strived to cultivate the habit of writing, create personal space for their interest in literature, and explore local resources beyond work.

Power Differentials between the "Domestic Cultural Constituencies"

On a sobering note, while the everyday life of an average migrant is closely managed by civil service departments, institutional resources that help to sustain the development of a migrant literary network are not easy to come by. TLAM's flexible collaborative model each year shows exactly the contingency of their sources of annual support, unlike some of Taiwan's major literary awards with regular funding, such as the United Daily News Grand Literary Award, the Lin

---

29. Cam Thuy Nguyen, "Guanyu zuozhe" 關於作者 [Author's note], in *Liu: Yidong de shengmingli, langchaozhong de Taiwan / diyierjie yimingong wenxuejiang zuopinji* [Flow: Story collection from the 2014 and 2015 Taiwan literature award for migrants], coauthored by Southeast Asian migrants (New Taipei City: Four Way Publishing, 2015), 61.
30. Khemphon Sridongphet, "Guanyu zuozhe" 關於作者 [Author's note], in *Liu: Yidong de shengmingli, langchaozhong de Taiwan / diyierjie yimingong wenxuejiang zuopinji* [Flow: Story collection from the 2014 and 2015 Taiwan literature award for migrants], coauthored by Southeast Asian migrants (New Taipei City: Four Way Publishing, 2015), 94.
31. Nan Tho, "Guanyu zuozhe" 關於作者 [Author's note], in *Liu: Yidong de shengmingli, langchaozhong de Taiwan / diyierjie yimingong wenxuejiang zuopinji* [Flow: Story collection from the 2014 and 2015 Taiwan literature award for migrants], coauthored by Southeast Asian migrants (New Taipei City: Four Way Publishing, 2015), 107.

Rung-San Literary Award, and the Wu San-Lian Literary Award.³² Even with the support from the Ministry of Culture, TLAM remains a relatively marginalized grassroots initiative on the operational level, and the temporary nature of the migrants' work in Taiwan makes it challenging to track their interaction with local literary communities. Further, as the award's entries become translated and thus highly mediated products, the authors' stake of losing representational or interpretive leverage to their Sinitic-language readers becomes hard to neglect. As Venuti notes, "any community that arises around a translation is far from homogeneous in language, identity, or social position" but is a "site of unexpected groups"; although "initially potential," for these communities to metamorphose into concrete, viable social existence, "they depend for their realization on the ensemble of domestic cultural constituencies among which the translation will circulate."³³ Venuti's caution against utopianizing the promise of translation is a hard-hitting reminder that, beyond promoting migrant expressions, it matters who reads, judges, and discusses these translated stories.

This is where Felski's and Venuti's views on translation may be complementary to each other. While the former spotlights translation's capacity to connect people and things and thus the "inescapability of our attachments," the latter adds that social relations formed because of these exchanges always reflect the existing beliefs, standards, biases, and power asymmetries of the society in question.³⁴ TLAM is a perfect example: with the mission to make a broad impact on Taiwan's majority readers, it uses the tool of translation, and the result is that, much more so than the Southeast Asian-language readers, the award's Sinitic-language cofounders, translators, and judges become the ensemble of primary readers and spokespersons, so to speak, who get to voice professional judgments on migrant self-representations.

This power differential is evident not only when Chen and Chang set the tone for the definition and social role of Taiwan's migrant literature but also when Yu-ling Ku, a longtime labor activist-writer and a fellow judge in 2014, makes the self-deprecating comment at a press conference that "this award feels rather disordered."³⁵ As Chang recollects, Ku's joke turns out also to be a fitting assessment of the complicated social reality facing the migrant people. In Ku's view, the award

---

32. Cheng Chang, "Tan yimingong wenxuejiang: 'zheyoubushi you duoda lirun de gongzuo, ji meiyoulirun, jiuyao zuochu yiyi'" 談移民工文學獎:「這又不是有多大利潤的工作, 既沒有利潤, 就要做出意義」 [On the migrant literature award: "This isn't a job with much profit, and it has to be meaningful if it does not make money"], *The News Lens*, September 16, 2016, https://www.thenewslens.com/article/48964/fullpage.
33. Venuti, "Translation, Community, Utopia," 366, 373.
34. Felski, "Comparison and Translation," 763.
35. Chang, "Cong rechaotan dao bowuguan," 292.

is very marginal, real, and disordered in a perfect way. It accommodates submissions in all styles and makes selection by way of voting by both general readers online [in the first round] and language experts [in the second round]. This design retains the quality of otherness, which resonates closely with the social condition of migrant communities.[36]

Chang, Chen, and Ku are all longtime advocates, to be sure. The issue of power asymmetry occurs, nonetheless, when a series of such framing gestures accrue and give off an aura around the award's organizers and judges as the principal interpreters of migrant writings. The effect is a double-edged sword. In the face of the obvious paucity of stable external funding, promoting migrant writings relies on word-of-mouth advocacy and grassroots community outreach for its social recognition and inclusion. On the other hand, the judgment, observation, and taste of the local team become implicit instructional forces that may inadvertently rigidify the Taiwanese-vs.-Southeast Asian, us-vs.-them, and readers-vs.-writers binarism.

For example, each year, TLAM's story collection devotes voluminous pages to comments and prefaces by the Sinitic-language final judges; placed before the main section that showcases the winning pieces, these voices of expertise impart an instructional tone to the readers, either knowingly or unwittingly, regarding what to expect from these stories. While many judges talk about the award as a humbling experience that allows them to see the migrants' sorrow, pain, loneliness, hardship, and so on, their reflections together assume the quality of something like an interpretive paradigm, often emphasizing what Grace Hui-chuan Wu calls the "affective politics of pain and suffering" in the stories.[37] Wu also criticizes that, by thematizing pain and suffering, the award unfortunately replaces the critiques of migrant subjectivities and sociohistorical contexts with a pervasive introspective look at the majority population's own "anxiety" about identification with the Taiwanese nation.[38] Even as some Sinitic-language judges demur to declare an absolute judgment on these writings' literary values on grounds of their own lack of linguistic proficiency, they all appear unwavering in praising these works' long-awaited entrance into the view of Taiwanese readers. These expressions, interestingly, betray a whiff of Taiwanese centrism that treats migrant writings as a curious representational object, and frequently with respect to the writings' service to local readers as affective samplings of other people's angst and pain.

---

36. Chang, "Cong rechaotan dao bowuguan," 292.
37. Grace Hui-chuan Wu, "Literature and Human Rights Imagination: Taiwan Literature Awards for Migrants," *Chung-Wai Literary Monthly* 48, no. 3 (2019): 90.
38. Wu, "Literature and Human Rights Imagination," 109.

This entrenched position of reading is intensified by the contradiction that, while the Sinitic-language judges are introduced in the annual collections based on their literary fame, professional titles, and the memorable catchphrases in their comments, the migrant authors are instead listed without comparable nuances; following their names, the winning authors are ubiquitously introduced as a marital migrant, a foreign student, a certain type of labor migrant, and so on. Whether by intention or by accident, this labeling scheme risks reducing the writers to preconceived identity boxes; indeed, introducing individual migrants in this tokenistic way contradicts the award's more progressive goal to fight stereotypes. Consider, too, the ways in which TLAM publishes the judges' comments across the seven years: in the collection that combines the 2014 and 2015 winners, while renowned Sinitic-language judges like Fang-ming Chen, Zhi-cong Wong, Kim Chew Ng, and Shuo-bin Su were given ample textual space to lament their inability to access the native-language stories and to praise the award for making migrant experiences visible, nowhere did readers see comments from the native-language judges on their encounters with the original submissions. This uneven inclusion of the judges' views was somewhat ameliorated through the expansion of the jury in the third year when, for the first time, the organizing board recruited teenaged judges in the final round and published their comments. The absence of published reflections from native-language experts, however, was not formally addressed until the fifth year, when the collection incorporated six essay reflections by the Southeast Asian-language judges.

Similar irony can be seen from how the award mobilizes its team of translators but also omits their voices. Despite many Sinitic-language judges' ambivalence toward the promises and limitations of translation as an imperfect means of cross-cultural reading, each year there is little scrutiny of the specific ways in which individual translators toil behind this translingual project. For example, the annual collections include no discussions of how the translators perceive their essential role in the award, how their prior translating experiences may have facilitated the current project, from where and whom they draw references when searching for suitable vocabulary, how they work with the award's turnaround time, whether they have communicated with the authors personally, and so on. The absence of the translators' reflections from the collections reveals the implicit biases among many readers of the world literature market. First, readers readily treat the work of literary translation and its human labor as auxiliary to original literary productions and therefore dismissible. Second, by omitting the voices of translators, the award sends out the message, even if unwittingly, that its translingual practice is obstacle-free. Except in rare comments, like those in 2014 and 2017 by judges Kim Chew Ng and Mau-kuei Chang, there are no direct conversations on the losses and gains of translation in the annual collections.³⁹ Curiously, while the organizing board never explains its choice to leave out the comments of translators at the frontline, such absence starkly contrasts the board's profuse display, each year, of the intellectual energies gathered in understanding what migrant literature looks like in Taiwan.

Between Us and Them

The above analysis demonstrates that, in staging heteroglossic expressions from the migrant writers and non-migrant commentators, TLAM takes on a community-building dimension. As many *us* and *them* speak to one another, the award plays out a conversational logic of cultural translation in and outside the featured stories. To scrutinize the dialogic effect of these cacophonous storytelling positions, I now turn to the winning pieces of the first three years, which appear in two collections: 流——移動的生命力，浪潮中的臺灣／第一、二屆移民工文學獎得獎作品集 (*Flow: Story Collection from the 2014 and 2015 Taiwan Literature Award for Migrants*) and 航——破浪而來，逆風中的自由／第三屆移民工文學獎作品集 (*Navigation: Story Collection from the 2016 Taiwan Literature Award for Migrants*).

    Across these two collections, the first-person "I" and "we" voices—vis-à-vis "they"—are the pronouns most conspicuously used in the winning stories and in the Sinitic-language judges' comments. I argue that these speaking voices reflect more than a rigid self-vs.-other or Taiwan-centered modality of picturing the Southeast Asian migrants. Specifically, each of these narrative subjects is portrayed as incomplete and self-knowing, and each reflects a particular social position within the larger transnational labor market binding together the Taiwanese and Southeast Asian populations. The mix of these "I," "we," and "they" perspectives in the award therefore allows us to examine the vociferous and open-ended process of deliberation and cocreation, by an ensemble of people, regarding the thematic and formal trends of migrant writings, as well as this genre's social significance. Furthermore, while over half of these stories employ the "I" perspective to suggest the narrator's individual migrant experience, almost every

---

39. Kim Chew Ng 黃錦樹, "Zai wenxuejiang zhiwai, shibushi haiyou qita women keyi zuodeshi?" 在文學獎之外，是不是還有其他我們可以做的事？ [Besides the literature award, is there something else we can do?], in *Liu: Yidong de shengmingli, langchaozhong de Taiwan / diyierjie yimingong wenxuejiang zuopinji* [Flow: Story collection from the 2014 and 2015 Taiwan literature award for migrants], coauthored by Southeast Asian migrants (New Taipei City: Four Way Publishing, 2015), 14–15; Mau-kuei Chang 張茂桂, "Ai, jiu yu fengkuang: wode duhougan" 愛、疚與瘋狂：我的讀後感 [Love, guilt, and craziness: My reflection after reading], in *Guang: Yi linghun yelian wenzi, zai anchu faliang / disijie yimingong wenxuejiang zuopinji* 光——以靈魂冶煉文字，在暗處發亮／第四屆移民工文學獎作品集 [Light: Story collection from the 2017 Taiwan literature award for migrants], coauthored by Southeast Asian migrants (New Taipei City: Four Way Publishing, 2017), 11–15.

Sinitic-language judge switches between the singular "I" and the plural "we" when discussing their encounters with the stories. In both cases, the personalized "I" and "we" often read like a witness, a spokesperson, or a messenger on behalf of a larger community. For example, in the biographical notes, many authors acknowledge their fellow migrants or themselves as sources of storytelling inspiration, comment on the struggles of their migrant communities, and plead for the society to see them. Similarly, many local judges mention that the award allows them ("I") and the larger Taiwanese readership ("we" and "us") to finally see the experiences and feelings of the migrants ("they" and "them").

Taken together, these pronouns turn TLAM into a dialogic space where the award's migrant awardees, judges, cofounders, professional translators, and readers all take part as either interlocutors or audiences in making migrant life publicly visible. In doing so, one speaking subject follows another in supplying this budding genre with a tentative tone, mood, ethnographic or aesthetic appeal, representational frame, ethical charge, and even market value. Cultural translation practiced in this dialogic way is therefore not a privilege exclusively reserved for just one group of language professionals, Taiwanese readers, or Southeast Asian migrants, and the stories or viewpoints they each contribute is not totally impervious to retorts or external scrutiny. Instead, from the arrangement of contents in both collections—such as the placing of professional comments at the beginning, the bilingual prints of the stories and their authors' notes, Cheng Chang's postscript in *Flow*, and the appended narratives about migrant mothers by their Taiwan-born children at the end of *Navigation*—we see that TLAM encourages a relatively democratic practice of cultural translation through storytelling and essayist reflection. If each migrant representation depends at least on one narrativized "I"-subject, one translator, and numerous judges speaking either Southeast Asian or Sinitic languages to reach out to its wider readers, then the combination of these stories are truly Sinoglossic works in progress, because it is only through these discordant "us" and "them" as storytellers, mediators, and interpreters that migrant literature becomes a visible presence.

When Yu-ling Ku speaks about her migrant story 逃 ("Flight"), which wins the 2005 China Times Literature Award in the category of literary reportage, she notes that the story relies on an inherent structure that uses the pronoun "we" as a collective voice:

> The reason that I extensively use the narrative subject "we" is because our action indeed relies on organizational support ... To record the history of how minorities struggle to speak out is part of what constitutes collective action.[40]

---

40. Yu-ling Ku 顧玉玲, "Tao" 逃 [Flight], in *Ningshi yixiang: yigong sheyingji* 凝視驛鄉：移工攝影集 [Voyage 15840: Photographs by migrant workers], ed. Taiwan International Workers' Association (Taipei: INK, 2008), 201.

Ku's emphasis on "we," and not on herself or any singular "I," as the real authorial and narrative figure of her story, alerts us to the communal and counter-elitist drive of Taiwan's migrant literature—a propensity that TLAM's Southeast Asian writers also demonstrate through the storytelling voices they craft. When later in 2008 Ku publishes the book-length literary reportage 我們：移動與勞動的生命記 (*Our Stories: Migration and Labor in Taiwan*), she complicates the meaning of collectivity by documenting the layered contradictions between the migrant workers and their Taiwanese employers, between individual migrants, and between the migrants and the activists. Here I echo Siao-yun Chen's analysis in arguing that *Our Stories* uses the collective "we" not as one reductive or uniform position but as a constantly evolving assemblage of voices from people whose life experiences cross paths but are open to changes and redefinitions.[41] Further, I believe the collective "we" and "they" in Ku's works and in TLAM suggest a valuable alternative perspective for critiquing the assumption that translation automatically makes a story transparent—a wishful thinking that, as Apter criticizes, tends to misguide advocates of world literature into promoting a commodifying practice of translation with little regard for epistemological and other barriers.[42] While Apter's reservation about what translation can do in the world literary market hinges on her critique of potential literary condescension in the process of translation, it is worth noting that the contributors to Taiwan's migrant literature through TLAM appear to value the use of translation differently. The faith of these contributors resides not in translation's one-to-one textual barter but in the collective roles of "I," "we," and "they" as subjective but active connectors and interpreters of cross-cultural encounters. Secondly, the personal pronouns in Ku's works and in TLAM enact a counter-capitalist mode of literary production; rather than bestowing onto individual authors any privatized literary aura, these conversational "I" and "we" impart the wish for writing to become an explicit group experiment for a non-proprietary purpose, that is, to create public presence and initiate dialogues with the Taiwanese society.

However, the counter-discourse thereby promised—that writing can be collective action and that translation anticipates a democratic negotiation of meanings—does not by itself concretize the goal of intervention. In scrutinizing what makes TLAM's "I" and "we" voices translational, additional questions must be asked. What kind of migrant writings do these voices impress on the readers? Do these witness-like accounts of migrant experience reinforce the existing media

---

41. Siao-yun Chen, "Redefining 'We/Us': The Dialogic Space and the Historical Process of Migrant Workers in *Our Stories: Migration and Labor in Taiwan*," in *Modern Chinese Literature* 32, no. 12 (2017): 67, 70–72.
42. Apter, *Against World Literature*, 3.

stereotypes regarding Southeast Asian migrants, or do they genuinely hybridize the Taiwan-centered mode of knowledge production?

To begin, TLAM's predominant storytelling pattern suggests that these first-person narratives may be more ambivalent than what readers might expect at first glance. While furnishing the stories of marginality with a touch of verisimilitude and authenticity, these pronouns may be politically protestive, thematically stimulating, and self-critical in perspective, but they can also be ideologically predictable and nonconfrontationally sentimental. Take, for example, the winning pieces from the first three years. Of the total of eighteen first-person narratives, most frame dramatic tension directly around familiar issues of migrant struggles at work or with families—issues that also often inform the lens of Taiwan's media coverage. Three narratives, however, stand out for bringing the migrant "I"-observer beyond this immediate focus on the suffering of the self. In writing "Asap Hitam Di Suriah" ("Black Smoke in Syria"), Sri Yanti takes inspiration from a news report she has once read in Taiwan about a fellow Indonesian caregiver who, while working in war-torn Syria, dies tragically in her employer's residence from an air raid. While she uses the "I"-narrator-protagonist as a direct stand-in for the tragic fate of her fellow countryfolk, she frames the story not around Taiwan, as most other stories do, but around the aftermath of Indonesia's involvement in international human trafficking and of the 2011 Syrian civil war, thereby affording the story a unique breadth of cosmopolitan sensibility.[43] Erin Cipta, a two-time TLAM winner, goes one step further by deliberately placing the struggle of her migrant-narrator off-center—a relatively uncommon and refreshing storytelling gesture in comparison to many other stories. In her 2014 entry, "Kisah Ye Feng Dan Carlos" ("The Story of Ye Feng and Carlos"), a migrant caregiver quietly observes the bonding between two frail members of the family she serves—Ye Feng, a twenty-six-year-old man with Down Syndrome, and Carlos, his old dog, who suffers from terminal illnesses. Rather than placing migrant subjectivity on center stage, Cipta configures the migrant "I"-narrator more as a distant storyteller who comes a long way from Indonesia in order to "witness the drama of life" and, through the stories of others, to "learn about friendship, loyalty, sacrifice, prayer, and hope."[44] In her 2015 entry, "Lelaki Pemberani Di Jiangzicui" ("The Hero of Jiangzicui"), Cipta, like Yanti before her,

---

43. Sri Yanti, "Asap Hitam Di Suriah" [Black smoke in Syria], in *Liu: Yidong de shengmingli, langchaozhong de Taiwan / diyierjie yimingong wenxuejiang zuopinji* [Flow: Story collection from the 2014 and 2015 Taiwan literature award for migrants], coauthored by Southeast Asian migrants (New Taipei City: Four Way Publishing, 2015), 121.
44. Erin Cipta, "Guanyu zuozhe" 關於作者 [Author's note], in *Liu: Yidong de shengmingli, langchaozhong de Taiwan / diyierjie yimingong wenxuejiang zuopinji* [Flow: Story collection from the 2014 and 2015 Taiwan literature award for migrants], co-authored by Southeast Asian migrants (New Taipei City: Four Way Publishing, 2015), 77.

reenacts news reports through the fictional form—in this case a news report in 2014 about a tragic stabbing spree directed at random civilians in the Taipei metro near the Jiangzicui station. However, while "Black Smoke in Syria" can be read as an explicit outcry against war and international human trafficking, the otherwise critical edge of "The Hero of Jiangzicui" is tamped down by a familiar overtone of Taiwanese sentimentalism that renders the female migrant caregiver subsidiary to the primary hero of the story—an aging Taiwanese grandfather she looks after. Although horrified by the killing spree, the migrant-narrator is not an active critic of Taiwan or any other society; instead, her "I"-perspective serves chiefly to highlight the bravery of the Taiwanese patriarch, as well as her family-like affection and concern for him.[45]

The above stories illustrate that TLAM's first-person narratives, while carrying an inescapable ethnographic and self-objectifying taste, are not necessarily docile or defiant in tone as the migrant narrators enter dialogues with world affairs in and beyond Taiwan. Potential ambiguities arise, instead, from two sources. First, although the "I" voice promises a degree of candor and access to the psychic world of the migrants, the bilingual format is a perpetual reminder that, far from producing representational transparency, this migrant "I"-narrator speaks about Taiwan through the intermediary voice of the Sinitic-language translator. Translation, in other words, is the primary if not sole access point through which Taiwan's majority readers see and hear the migrants. The award's recruited translators, then, are not just interpreters but co-authors, so to speak, who voice out on behalf of the Southeast Asian first authors. From this perspective, the "I"-subject can be understood as speaking what I call Sinoglossic ventriloquism. Indeed, the double voice of this layered "I"-narrator cannot be fully appreciated without a corresponding critique of the translator's simultaneous role as the story's interpreter and co-author. Second, ambiguity also emerges when these winning stories, by virtue of their first-person narration, seem to allude to the life trajectories of their authors, whose listed identity markers in the collections as domestic helpers, marital migrants, and so on also allude to many migrants of the same categories in the real world. It is likely, therefore, that the first-person voices render these migrant stories intelligible because, even though these "I"-narrators may be fictional, the stories' predominantly realist contents and the authors' own migrant backgrounds in fact encourage an autobiographical reading that directs the readers toward a reductive mode of analysis based on preconceived notions of the migrant writers' sociolegal and occupational

---

45. Erin Cipta, "Lelaki Pemberani Di Jiangzicui" [The hero of Jiangzicui], in *Liu: Yidong de shengmingli, langchaozhong de Taiwan / diyierjie yimingong wenxuejiang zuopinji* [Flow: Story collection from the 2014 and 2015 Taiwan literature award for migrants], coauthored by Southeast Asian migrants (New Taipei City: Four Way Publishing, 2015), 214–234.

statuses. To overcome this reductive framework of interpretation, a reader will have to learn about these migrant authors through separate channels, like watching their interviews and reading feature stories about them. Such is the case with the lesbian-identified Filipina migrant writer Melinda M. Babaran, who becomes the subject of news reports in Taiwan and the Philippines as a two-time TLAM winner, first in 2018, for writing about childhood beatings by her father in the award's first LGBT-themed story, "Latay sa Laman" ("Whip Scar on the Flesh"), and, again in 2019, for crafting the voice of an overseas Filipino worker as he returns home and learns about his wife's extramarital affair in the narrative poem "Kapirasong Papel" ("A Piece of Paper").[46]

Further nuances regarding how first-person voices shape specific intercommunity relations can be seen in the reflections by the Sinitic-language judges and organizers. On the one hand, an apparent tone of ethnographic curiosity permeates the jury members' comparison of perspectives between Taiwan's majority readers ("I" and "we") and the migrant writers ("them"). For example, similar to Chen in expressing his hope for Taiwanese people to see and empathize with the migrants, Wen-chen Tseng writes that, in "allowing us [the writers and readers] to look at each other," the award also "moves us [the readers] closer to the hearts of the migrants," while Shuo-bin Su comments that TLAM "gives me an opportunity to read the viewpoints of the migrant others through their life writings."[47] Their vocabulary indicates that the Sinitic-language judges view the migrant writings less as a discursive arena where literary merits are measured than as one where multicultural recognition is exercised and where the distance between "us" the Taiwanese readers and "them" the Southeast Asian migrants, as Yi-chin Lo notes, may be gradually dissolved.[48] On the other hand, notwithstanding their affirmation of migrant literature's capacity to bridge communities, many Sinitic-language judges express reservation about their own qualifications as jury

---

46. Melinda M. Babaran, "Kapirasong Papel" [A piece of paper], *Independent Opinion@CommonWealth*, September 26, 2019, https://opinion.cw.com.tw/blog/profile/441/article/8539; Melinda M. Babaran, "Latay sa Laman" [Whip scar on the flesh], *Independent Opinion@CommonWealth*, October 22, 2018, https://opinion.cw.com.tw/blog/profile/441/article/7394; CNN Philippines Life Staff, "In Taiwan, a Filipino Factory Worker Wins Prestigious Literary Award," CNN Philippines Life, August 27, 2019, https://www.cnnphilippines.com/life/culture/literature/2019/8/27/filipino-taiwan-writer.html; Ministry of Foreign Affairs, Republic of China (Taiwan), "Stories of Love and Loss Celebrated at Taiwan Literature Award for Migrants," October 1, 2018, https://nspp.mofa.gov.tw/nsppe/news.php?post=142544&unit=400.
47. Southeast Asian Migrants 東南亞移民工, *Liu: Yidong de shengmingli, langchaozhong de Taiwan / diyierjie yimingong wenxuejiang zuopinji* [Flow: Story collection from the 2014 and 2015 Taiwan literature award for migrants] (New Taipei City: Four Way Publishing, 2015), 16, 17.
48. Yi-chin Lo 駱以軍, "Touguo wenxue de yinmi huandu, jindao women limian" 透過文學的隱密換渡，進到我們裡面 [Through literature's secret transmission, they enter our insides], in *Liu: Yidong de shengmingli, langchaozhong de Taiwan / diyierjie yimingong wenxuejiang zuopinji* [Flow: Story collection from the 2014 and 2015 Taiwan literature award for migrants], coauthored by Southeast Asian migrants (New Taipei City: Four Way Publishing, 2015), 11.

members, due to lack of linguistic proficiency, and about TLAM's indiscriminate acceptance of submissions in all styles.[49] Interestingly, as Chang reflects in his 2015 postscript and again in 2020 when he announces TLAM's closure, these self-doubts about the jury's linguistic capabilities and the pervasive use of translation take on a humorous tone that is confessional yet unapologetic. Deliberately likening the award to the Nobel Prize and thus emphasizing untranslatability as a universal conundrum in all world-literature endeavors, Chang turns his comparison into a self-mocking yet forceful defense of TLAM's flawed but realistic translational logic.[50]

From the third year onward, comments from the jury begin to show growing self-reflexivity and meta-critique. For example, many Sinitic-language judges in 2016, such as Rui-teng Lee, A-Po, Ming-yi Wu, Zi-lan Zhuo, Hui-ling Chang, and Ci-yi Lai, note the evolving themes and techniques from the submissions, question their own implicit biases, and ponder ways of creating literary standards for the award.[51] In 2017, Mau-kuei Chang challenges the Taiwanese readers to read concerns for humanity beyond the narrow self-vs.-other, us-vs.-them divide, and beyond the Taiwan-centric framework of multiculturalism.[52] As the award evolves, as the submissions' storytelling patterns accumulate, and as the migrants' personal circumstances change over the years, many fundamental questions about the definition, feature, and use of migrant literature also receive regular scrutiny. For example, in 2017, Yue-an Fu turns critical focus from discussing the common theme of suffering to analyzing what makes good storytelling strategies; Mau-kuei Chang and Shi-ping Tsai mark women's writing as a central feature of that year; Wei-chun Hsiao discusses the implication of uneven numbers of submissions in the styles of fiction, essay, and poetry; and Wan-chi Chiang asks whether the growing visibility of the migrant issue signals inevitable structural changes for TLAM.[53] The judges' deliberations about the

---

49. For example, see Ng, "Zai wenxuejiang zhiwai," 14–15.
50. Chang, "Cong rechaotan dao bowuguan," 294; Chang, "Yige wenxuejiang de shengyusi."
51. Southeast Asian Migrants, *Hang: Polangerlai, nifengzhong de ziyou / disanjie yimingong wenxuejiang zuopinji* 航——破浪而來，逆風中的自由／第三屆移民工文學獎作品集 [Navigation: Story collection from the 2016 Taiwan literature award for migrants] (New Taipei City: Four Way Publishing, 2016).
52. Chang, "Ai, jiu yu fengkuang," 14–15.
53. Chang, "Ai, jiu yu fengkuang," 12; Wan-chi Chiang 江婉琦, "Chuxian gengduo qiansuoweiyou de ticai" 出現更多前所未有的題材 [Many new themes have emerged], in *Guang: Yi linghun yelian wenzi, zai anchu faliang / disijie yimingong wenxuejiang zuopinji* [Light: Story collection from the 2017 Taiwan literature award for migrants], coauthored by Southeast Asian migrants (New Taipei City: Four Way Publishing, 2017), 25; Yue-an Fu 傅月庵, "Haozuopin yidu bianzhi" 好作品一讀便知 [Good storytelling is easy to see at a glance], in *Guang: Yi linghun yelian wenzi, zai anchu faliang / disijie yimingong wenxuejiang zuopinji* [Light: Story collection from the 2017 Taiwan literature award for migrants], coauthored by Southeast Asian migrants (New Taipei City: Four Way Publishing, 2017), 18–19; Wei-chun Hsiao 蕭瑋均, "Meili de shengminggushi chudong xinling" 美麗的生命故事觸動心靈 [Beautiful life stories are heart-touching], in *Guang: Yi linghun yelian*

nature of migrant literature result in even more vigorous debates in 2018 and onward, showing greater maturity in evaluating the strengths and weaknesses of the annual submissions and in gradually untying migrant writings from the binary identitarian question about "us" versus "them." Pei-chia Lan, for example, questions how a writer's migrant or non-migrant status might have an impact on the reader's evaluation of life writing and fiction respectively.[54] Further, the essay reflections from the Filipino-, Indonesian-, and Vietnamese-language judges in the same year offer the most contextualized and theoretically rigorous insights that TLAM's judges have offered. Reading Filipino-language entries, Philippine social activist Myan Lordiane observes the frequent themes of family and sacrifice, as well as numerous idiomatic patterns like the pervasive use of religiously inspired diction, as the basis of analyzing the correlation between migrant writings and the phenomenon of overseas Filipino workers.[55] Framing his discussion around the often slighted category of proletarian literature, Indonesian poet-judge Heru Joni Putra considers literature to be a tool to "keep the resistance movement energetic" if not to "wield immediate change"; in doing so, he challenges readers' presumption that literature should only address universal issues and argues, instead, that writings by labor migrants change the way people read and interpret literature.[56]

---

wenzi, zai anchu faliang / disijie yimingong wenxuejiang zuopinji [Light: Story collection from the 2017 Taiwan literature award for migrants], coauthored by Southeast Asian migrants (New Taipei City: Four Way Publishing, 2017), 33; Shi-ping Tsai 蔡詩萍, "Xiangruyimo de jiemeiqingyi" 相濡以沫的姐妹情誼 [Sisterhood in times of hardship and need], in *Guang: Yi linghun yelian wenzi, zai anchu faliang / disijie yimingong wenxuejiang zuopinji* [Light: Story collection from the 2017 Taiwan literature award for migrants], coauthored by Southeast Asian migrants (New Taipei City: Four Way Publishing, 2017), 22.

54. Pei-chia Lan 藍佩嘉, "Kuayue wenhuachayi de tiyan" 跨越文化差異的體驗 [Experiences that traverse cultural differences], in *Du: Zai xianshi yu xiangwangzhong qiuyong* 渡——在現實與想望中泅泳／第五屆移民工文學獎作品集 [Wading: Story collection from the 2018 Taiwan literature award for migrants], coauthored by Southeast Asian migrants (New Taipei City: Four Way Publishing, 2018), 17.

55. Myan Lordiane, "Leihaili de zhenzhu: 2018 Taiwan yimingong wenxuejiang feilvbin cansaizhe de bijiaofenxi" 淚海裡的珍珠：2018臺灣移民工文學獎菲律賓參賽者的比較分析 [Pearls in the sea of tears: A comparative analysis of Filipino competitors in the 2018 Taiwan literature award for migrants], in *Du: Zai xianshi yu xiangwangzhong qiuyong* [Wading: Story collection from the 2018 Taiwan literature award for migrants], coauthored by Southeast Asian migrants (New Taipei City: Four Way Publishing, 2018), 328–334.

56. Heru Joni Putra, "Yimingong wenxue: you geren zhi tuanjie" 移民工文學：由個人至團結 [Migrant literature: From individual to solidarity], in *Du: Zai xianshi yu xiangwangzhong qiuyong* [Wading: Story collection from the 2018 Taiwan literature award for migrants], coauthored by Southeast Asian migrants (New Taipei City: Four Way Publishing, 2018), 345.

Coda

The seven-year development of TLAM—its pre-history in labor activism, its prominent first-person storytelling mode, and its impact on community imagination beyond the text—lends us a refreshing, contextualized fulcrum for analyzing the entanglement of Taiwan and its Southeast Asian neighbors in the new-millennial scene of Sinophone literary productions. On the one hand, the award's born-translated feature compels the Sinitic-language readers to redirect the discussion of Taiwan literature away from its usual association with Chinese and Sinographic traditions on the East Asian landmass and, instead, toward one that spotlights its sociocultural ties to mainland and maritime Southeast Asia for a different account of the country's multilingual literary history. This southbound, seaward connection adds necessary granularity to the critical frameworks of scholarly conversations on the foundations of Taiwan literature, not along the usual axis of the country's continuous decolonial and nation-building struggles but through examining inter-Asia transactions in an open discursive field where Sinophone studies and the approach of Sinoglossia, in this case, aim not to draw but to accommodate differences and gaps, both in text and in life. On the other hand, the study of writings by Southeast Asian migrants—as a product resulting from Taiwan's growing reliance on foreign migrant populations in the wake of the larger Asia-Pacific neoliberal market shift, and as a grassroots collective response to Taiwan's official multicultural discourse—enables us to ground questions about the promise and peril of translating migrant literature in a concrete, localized context where the host country is eagerly seeking to redefine itself in the throes of massive socioeconomic, geopolitical, and cultural changes.

From this view, the award is only the beginning of an ongoing process of what future critics might call the making of a new literary genealogy and community history. By sampling migrant experiences through writing, the award makes hopeful initial attempts to anthologize Southeast Asian voices as part of Taiwan literature and thereby reconfigure the standards and uses of literary criticism. Even though the award has reached a temporary closure in 2020, over the latest decade a multiplicity of other local movements on issues related to Taiwan's Southeast Asian population have been budding across different platforms: to name just a few, the biennial Migrant Workers Rally beginning in 2003, the 2011 Migration Film Festival organized by Taiwan Women's Film Association, the 2020 Migrant Worker Film Festival, a digital archive for art history projects called 群島資料庫 (*Nusantara Archive*) and its online journal 荒原筆記 (*No Man's Land*), a website thematizing art programs called *SEA Plateaus*, and, as of June 2022, a newly launched magazine discussing the life of Southeast Asian migrants in southern Taiwan called 開外掛 (*Turn On*). If TLAM marks a precious milestone of the grassroots endeavors to record, translate, and promote migrant voices, it remains to be seen where this recent wave of multi-sited local initiatives will take us in further rewriting Taiwan's position amid these inter-Asia flows.

When Chang announced that TLAM would discontinue after the year 2020, he pointed out that future generations of advocates should brainstorm new ways of promoting migrant writings, such as creating new categories of literary competition, calls for entries from other parts of the world, television and theater adaptations, and so on.[57] These born-translated cultural productions will carry new promises and stakes as they place Taiwan in further dialogues with its southern neighbors; however, as this chapter insinuates, translation's apparent limitations are hardly sufficient reasons to oppose its practice, and readers benefit more not by slighting its social role but by maintaining vigilance about where and how it reveals our deepest epistemological gaps and cultural anxiety. The examples from TLAM suggest that positional contradictions are likely to accompany our expressions of self-critique, and this narrative consciousness alone often does not alter the hierarchical relations between the minoritarian writers and the mainstream readers, or between the language of literary creation and that of literary criticism. Instead, what these introspective "I"- and "we"-narrators share, or project, is perhaps an aspirational position that views the literary competition as a favorable platform for articulating the intricate dynamic between these phenomena: migration from, to, and around Asia; Taiwan as a site of transit or destination for inter-Asia flows; and the crossroads of Taiwan's Sinitic and non-Sinitic cultural expressions. These Sinoglossic crossroads, in turn, provide the soil to birth a new generation of Sinophone literary culture.

---

57. Chang, "Yige wenxuejiang de shengyusi."

Part IV

Conclusions: Theoretical Interventions

11
Sinophone States of Exception

David Der-wei Wang

This chapter seeks to engage with the concept of Sinoglossia by stressing the dynamics of history and changeability in Sino-spheres. The current paradigm of Sinophone studies is largely based on theories from postcolonialism to empire critique, with an emphasis on the politics of voice. Implied in the paradigm is a dualistic mapping of geopolitics such as assimilation versus diaspora, resistance versus hegemony, and Sinophobia versus Sinophilia. Resonating with the provocation of Sinoglossia which stresses embodied mediation, circulation of sound and script, and transculturation within and without Sino-spheres, this chapter offers three conceptual interventions: the "xenophone" (*yi* 夷) or the foreign as that which is always already embedded in the invocation of China (hua 華) since ancient times; "postloyalism" as the phantasmal factor that haunts the platform of Sinophone postcolonialism; and the "state of exception" as a tactic through which Sinophone subjectivity continuously refashions itself.

Sinophone and Xenophone Changeabilities

"Sinophone" is arguably the most provocative keyword of Chinese literary studies since the turn of the new millennium. Although the term has been used since the 1990s in select contexts, it was not made popular until 2007, when Shu-mei Shih published *Visuality and Identity: Sinophone Articulations across the Pacific*.[1] In her book, Shih invokes the "Sinophone" as a language-based critical perspective from which to engage the linguistic, cultural, ethnic, and political dynamics in China, as well as Chinese-speaking communities worldwide.[2] In opposition

---

1. Shu-mei Shih, *Visuality and Identity: Sinophone Articulations across the Pacific* (Berkeley: University of California Press), 2007.
2. Shu-mei Shih, "The Concept of the Sinophone," *PMLA* 126, no. 3 (2011): 709–718; Shu-mei Shih, "Global Literature and the Technologies of Recognition," *PMLA* 119, no. 1 (2004): 16–30; Shu-mei Shih, "Theory, Asia and the Sinophone," *Postcolonial Studies* 13, no. 4 (2010): 465–484.

to conventional references to "China" as a homogenized entity, she argues that the dispersal of the Chinese people across the world needs to be reconceptualized in relation to vibrant or vanishing communities of Sinitic-language cultures rather than of ethnicity and nationality. Sinophone literature seeks to reconsider Chinese literature by projecting a sphere where multiple Chinese language literatures are being produced, circulated, and contested. Shih derives her definition of the "Sinophone" from the Sinitic language family, an immense network comprising more than 400 topolects, dialects, and ethnic languages.[3] While recognizing the dominant position of the Han Chinese, Shih stresses that the "Chinese" language is a multitude of Han and non-Han, regional and ethnic utterances of the Sinitic language family. To this we should also add the multitude of utterances in various social, gender, and class communities. Thus, when studied from a Sinophone perspective, Chinese literature appears to be a kaleidoscopic constellation of soundings, spaces, and identities, as opposed to the enclosed, homogenized corpus upheld by the national apparatus.

Such a Sinophone vision opens up new terrain for studying Chinese literature. At its most dynamic, "Sinophone" amounts to nothing less than a realm of Bakhtinian "heteroglossia," in which the centripetal and centrifugal sources and forces of languages interact with each other.

But beyond this shared recognition of plural soundings of the Chinese language, critics of Sinophone studies are taking different approaches to the questions raised above. For instance, Shih emphasizes the oppositional potential of the Sinophone vis-à-vis the imperialist hegemony of China, thus echoing the tenor of postcolonialism and empire studies. Jing Tsu contends that "Sinophone governance" is a nebulous process of negotiation through which Chinese-speaking regions and cultures form a communicative network. Between these positions, one observes a spectrum of proposals addressing the affective, cultural, semiotic and political terms of Sinophone articulations. These stances compel us to understand modern Chinese literature not as a fixed field but as a flux of practices and imaginaries.

Both Shih and Tsu have made enormous contributions to Sinophone studies, in particular their discovery of the manifold individual voices, regional soundings, dialectical accents, local expressions—alternative "native tongues"—that are in constant negotiation with the standardized, official national language. Meanwhile, their approaches also point to areas where additional critical efforts are desired. I would suggest that, despite their interventional efforts, neither Shih nor Tsu goes far enough to confront the most polemical dimension of Sinophone

---

3. Shih, "The Concept of the Sinophone," 709–718. See also Victor Mair, "What Is a Chinese 'Dialect/Topolect'? Reflections on Some Key Sino-English Linguistic Terms," *Sino-Plantonic Papers* 29 (1991): 2–52.

studies. In my view, for a Sinophone project to exert its critical potential, one must not engage merely with the domain of conventional overseas Chinese literature plus ethnic literature on the mainland. Rather, one should test its power *within* the nation-state of China. In light of the translingual dynamics on a global scale, we need to reimagine the cartography of the Chinese center versus the peripheries so as to enact a new linguistic and literary arena of contestations. As a matter of fact, to truly subvert the foundations of Chinese national literature, we should no longer consider it apart from the Sinophone literary system.

My proposal may sound self-contradictory because, as defined by Shih and Tsu, the Sinophone is invoked in the first place to deal with the literary and cultural production outside China proper. Nevertheless, I argue that while a Sinophone scholar can divert his or her attention from Chinese national literature for various reasons in praxis, he or she must reject the temptation of a dichotomized logic of the Chinese versus the Sinophone. If "Chinese" is not a homogenized entity but a constellation of Sinitic utterances amid a flux of historical changes, a Sinophone scholar can conclude that even the official Han language, however standardized by the state, comprises complex soundings and transformations and is therefore subject to a rhizomatic tapestry or Sinoglossia. Chinese national literature, just like overseas Chinese literature, consists of a *processual flux* of expressions and experimentations in both script and sound. Thus, Sinophone studies cannot eschew the figure of China as both a political entity and a cultural heritage. Particularly at a time when "China is rising" and Chinese literature is commanding more and more attention worldwide, the invocation of the Sinophone should serve as not merely a critique but also a form of agency, helping triangulate the literary paradigm of the Chinese nation and the world.

This would not constitute a new Sinophone "obsession with China" akin to that which C. T. Hsia (1921–2013) diagnosed in 1971 in order to describe the ambivalent attitude of modern Chinese literati toward the challenges of Chinese modernity: a masochistic mentality among Chinese intellectuals to see any given social or political malaise as a sickness unique to China, and thus grapple with Chinese modernity only negatively, by denouncing it.[4] Instead of a new national parochialism, such a redefinition of the Sinophone, as a "Sinophone intervention with China," follows in Hsia's footsteps—though without his fixation on Euro-American culture—to propose a world-literary view of Sinophone literature. By countering both an "obsession with China" and what has surfaced in some strains of Sinophone critique, an "obsession against China," such a Sinophone intervention provides a critical interface through which to rethink the configuration of (Chinese) national literature and Sinophone literature vis-à-vis world literature.

---

4. C. T. Hsia, "Obsession with China: The Moral Burden of Modern Chinese Literature," appendix 1 in *A History of Modern Chinese Fiction* (New Haven, CT: Yale University, 1971), 533–554.

In my view, for a Sinophone project to exert its critical potential, one must not engage merely with the domain of conventional overseas Chinese cultures plus ethnic minorities on the mainland. In light of the transcultural dynamics on the global scale as well as the intricate ethnic histories of premodern China, one needs to reimagine the cartography of the Chinese center versus the periphery so as to enact a new linguistic and literary arena of contestations. In an effort to understand China as not merely a modern polity but also a historical flux of multiple Sinophone civilizations, I call for a critical—and creative—inquiry into the genealogical implications of Sinophone discourse.[5] I have tackled elsewhere the premodern discourse of *hua-yi zhibian* 華夷之辨 (Sino–barbarian distinction) and translated it with respect to "Sinophone/xenophone distinction."[6]

Historians have observed that the valence of the "distinction between *hua* and *yi*" fluctuated in relation to the vicissitudes of Han and non-Han powers throughout medieval China. Whereas the Six Dynasties saw the first major migration of Han Chinese to the south as the north was occupied by the barbarians, the Tang dynasty thrived on its multicultural vitality and ethnic hybridity. It was in the Song dynasty that the "distinction between *hua* and *yi*" gained an increased political thrust partially because of the barbarian threat from the north, which prompted an ethnic and territorial awareness suggestive of the incipient mode of nationhood,[7] and partially because of the holistic view of Confucian orthodoxy. The fall of the Northern Song to the Jurchens and the fall of the Southern Song to the Mongols gave rise to a discourse of loyalty, martyrdom, and consequently loyalism (*yimin* 遺民) on behalf of authentic Han Chinese civilization.[8]

If the conventional discourse of *hua* vs. *yi* stresses distinction or *bian* 辨, which is oriented more to a spatial verification of inside, center, and orthodoxy in opposition to outside, margin, and heterogeneity, the late Ming–early Qing cases suggest the possibility of *bian* 變, which foregrounds the change and changeability of *hua* versus *yi* over time. This happened when the Japanese commercial translators-*cum*-Confucian scholars Hayashi Gahō 林春勝 (1618–1680) and

---

5. For a detailed description of postloyalism, see my book in Chinese *Houyimin xiezuo: shijian yu jiyi de zhengzhixue* 後遺民寫作：時間與記憶的政治學 [Postloyalist writing: The politics of time and memory] (Taipei: Ryefield Publications, 2007), particularly the first chapter, 23–70.
6. David Der-wei Wang 王德威, "Huayi zhibian: huayu yuxiyanjiu de xinshijie" 華夷之變：華語語系研究的新視界 [Sinophone/xenophone changeability], *Zhongguo xiandai wenxue* 中國現代文學 [Modern Chinese literature] 34 (December 2018): 13.
7. Zhaoguang Ge 葛兆光, *Zhaizi Zhongguo: Chongjian youguan Zhongguo de lishi lunshu* 宅茲中國：重建有關中國的歷史論述 [Here resides China: Reconstructing discourses about China] (Taipei: Linking, 2011).
8. Hence, "being loyal to the emperor not only concerned one's external behaviors determined and regulated by a hierarchical order; being loyal to the emperor had become a moral principle of self-regulation that the intellectuals self-consciously enforced." Xuan Li 李瑄, *Ming yimin qunti xintai yu wenxue sixiang yanjiu* 明遺民群體心態與文學思想研究 [Research on the collective mentality and thought of Ming loyalism] (Chengdu: Bashu chubanshe, 2009), 37.

Hayashi Hōkō 林信篤 (1644–1732) came up with *The Altered State of China and the Barbarian* (*Kai hentai* 華夷變態), a compilation of records that describe the changes of Han-Chinese culture in China in the aftermath of the Manchu conquest. All has been turned upside down, as the Japanese observers noted—hence the "altered state of *hua* and *yi*." The Japanese scholars conclude by stating that Japan, not China, turned out to be the civilization that carries on the Chinese legacy at its most authentic. In a similar logic, the eighteenth-century Korean envoy Kim Chonghu 金鐘厚 (1721–1780) famously stated, "There is no China after the fall of the Ming" (mingchaohou wuzhongguo 明朝後無中國).[9] Korea, the *yi*, is entitled to replace *hua*.

I argue that the "changeability of *hua* versus *yi*" emerged in late imperial China to signal the epistemological shakeup of the relationships between China and the world in multiple terms. If the "distinction between *hua* and *yi*" helps define the world of China as a self-contained polity which oversees the taxonomy of Han Chinese versus barbarians, the "changeability between *hua* versus *yi*" informs a China entering the world with expanding horizons, ethnically and otherwise, beyond the purview of the old civilization. It may not be a coincidence that *yi* takes on bifurcated connotations at this juncture. Whereas the *yi* within the conventional geopolitical mapping of China undertook the new designation in relation to "ethnicity," to be contained, assimilated, and eventually naturalized into the Chinese nation, the *yi* from the world outside of China represents the agents of modernity, ever ready to be emulated or contested. The national narratives of the Republic of China and the People's Republic of China, from "there is only one China" to "the homogeneous body of multiple ethnicities,"[10] testify to the continued entanglement with modern ramifications of *hua* and *yi*.

The rise of Sinophone discourse, accordingly, may be understood as a most recent impulse to renegotiate the definition of China vis à vis the changing world. However resistant they may be to China's impact in post–Cold War dynamics, critics in the vein of Shih may actually gain rather than lose critical force if they took a few historical lessons about China in relation to ethnicities and regional cultures in premodern times. It also prods us to rethink the linguistic model of extant Sinophone studies. As Shih indicates, language in regional, dialectical, and spoken terms serves as the last common denominator of Sinophone communities. Such a "Sinophone articulation" is also said to be a barometer by which a Sinophone subject gauges the degree of her Chinese identity, and Sinophone articulation after all is destined to dissipate in a xenophone community as time

---

9. Li, *Ming yimin qunti xintai yu wenxue sixiang yanjiu*, 37.
10. "There is only one China" is a statement by the historian Gu Jiegang 顧頡剛 (1893–1980) on the eve of the Second Sino-Japanese War; China as a "homogeneous body of multiple ethnicities" was a phrase coined by the sociologist Fei Xiaotong 費孝通 (1910–2005) in the late 1980s. See my discussion in "Huayi zhibian."

passes. While Shih may have empirical grounding in making such an observation, she betrays no less a flirtation with phonocentrism, treating vocal articulation as the sole indicator to verify her agenda of "against diaspora."

By historicizing the question of Sinophone and xenophone through the lens of the *longue durée* of *hua/yi* mutations, a Sinophone scholar will hopefully become less susceptible to either Sinocentric or Sinophobic preconception of what *wen* 文 (script, literature, culture) has to be but more willing to observe the changes and (dis)continuities of its pattern—the primordial meaning of *wen*—in a specific time and space.

Between Postcolonialism and Postloyalism

It was amid inquiries into "China" as a *problematique* that Shih Shu-mei's Sinophone discourse appeared on the horizon. A coinage in the vein of terms such as Anglophone, Francophone, and Hispanophone, "Sinophone" was first used in the late twentieth century to refer to the condition of "speaking Chinese" or to a "Chinese-speaking person." Shih brought to the fore the term's colonial undertone, thus igniting its critical power. For Shih, "Sinophone studies takes as its objects of study the Sinitic-language communities and cultures outside China as well as ethnic minority communities and cultures within China where Mandarin is adopted or imposed."[11] She contends that, just as is the case with Anglophone, Francophone, or Hispanophone articulations, Sinophone brings to mind the colonizing and colonized conditions in greater China in military, economic, and cultural terms. Shih's endeavor draws from a complex of theoretical approaches, from postcolonial criticism to minority studies, from humanist Marxism to multiculturalism. Of these theories, postcolonialism stands out as her main stake.

But, the issue of continental colonialism aside, the spread of the Chinese language overseas in the modern period had less to do with China's colonial expansion and coercion than with waves of Chinese people's travel, emigration, and diaspora. That is, when Chinese travelers, emigrants, and refugees relocated to the new places of settlement for economic and political reasons, they kept the Chinese language—often in dialects and topolects—and script system as the linkage to their homeland (but not necessarily their home country). Chinese served less as a vehicle to overpower indigenous languages and cultures than as a linguistic register—and an affective index—to sustain the cultural legacy and ethnic bonding among the Chinese themselves. The result is a hybrid linguistic culture fraught with both naturalized foreignness and alienated nativity, both Sinophone utterance and cacophonous reverberations.

---

11. Shih, *The Sinophone Reader*, 11.

In addition, a postcolonial perspective also implies that the Sinophone is treated as a modern phenomenon, resulting from the fragmentation of China when challenged by modern forces. While acknowledging the importance of issues from immigration to diaspora, colonialism to nationalism, I call for a more serious inquiry into the historical implications of Sinophone discourse. Instead of the postcolonial model, which stresses spatiality, I introduce postloyalism as a way of teasing out the historical bearings of Sinophone discourse, thereby calling forth its inherent politics of temporality.[12] It is in this context that I propose the concept of postloyalism as a supplement to a postcolonial critique. Postloyalism is a coinage derived from a critical reflection on loyalism, or *yimin* 遺民, a unique political and cultural discourse in Chinese history. The term *yimin* originally meant "one who remains loyal to a former dynasty and is ashamed to serve a new dynasty when a change in state power occurs."[13] In Chinese, it is a compound of *yi* 遺—to leave behind or the leftover—and *min* 民—people or subjects. Sinologists have translated *yimin* either as remnant subject or loyalist. The translations point to subtle differences. The former refers to those who survived a dynastic fall, therefore connoting passivity and even eremitism; the later refers to those who willfully rejected the new political order after the downfall of the old one, therefore connoting non-conformism and even combative resistance.[14] Either case, however, presupposes individual allegiance to a bygone imperial authority as well as a political, ethical, or intellectual heritage.

Yi suggests losing something (*yishi* 遺失) while at the same time it means the leaving of something (*canyi* 殘遺); the former points to a total loss, the latter to a leftover or a remnant. But *yi* also means giving or bequeathing (*yiliu* 遺留), implying leaving someone a thing or a gift. The three meanings of *yi* speak to the complex historical and affective syndrome that is loyalism: thrown into the abysmal condition of dynastic cataclysm, a political subject feels entrenched in an irrecoverable loss of his affiliations while cherishing all the more his identity as a survivor, a remnant of the loss; more engagingly, he is compelled to preserve the loss as a legacy, a gift from the past into the future despite the historical fact that suggests otherwise. Loyalism is a discourse premised on the politics of anachrony and displacement, when a political subject of the ancient times insists on retaining his sense of bereavement vis-à-vis a fallen dynasty or a lost culture

---

12. For a detailed description of postloyalism, see my book *Houyimin xiezuo: shijian yu jiyi de zhengzhixue*, particularly the first chapter, 23–70. An abridged version in English translation, by Professor Brian Bernards, is included in Shih, Bernards, and Tsai's *Sinophone Reader*. Partial wording of my argument here is derived from the English version, and I acknowledge Bernards's translation.
13. Zhengguang Xie 謝正光, *Qingchu shiwen yu shiren jiaoyou kao* 清初詩文與士人交遊考 [A study of poetry and literati circles in the early Qing] (Nanjing: Nanjing University Press, 2001), 6.
14. I choose "loyalist" to translate *yimin* because it stays close to the Confucian doctrine on loyalty. Unless specified, whenever I mention loyalist, I also gesture toward "remnant," and vice versa.

against all odds. Loyalism is thus based on a paradox: it derives its claim to legitimacy, be it political, cultural, emotional, or ethical, from a reluctant awareness of the loss of that very legitimacy. In other words, loyalism gestures toward the belatedness of time and yet gains an unlikely future agency in the hope of restoring that which is forever lost. Caught between the desire for the past to be realized in the future and the future to be restored to the past, loyalism plays out a unique politics of multiply folded time.

Post-loyalism adds layers of complexity. Literally, postloyalism refers to that which happens, in conceptual, affective, and political terms, *after* loyalism. But insofar as loyalism already implies temporal posteriority and a resultant sense of mourning and nostalgia, the "post" of postloyalism doubles the temporal and psychological complexity inherent in loyalism. It is either that which breaks with or that which inherits from loyalism. In line with the postmodern subversion of the causal sequence of time, "postloyalism" points to an anticipatory re-visioning of the past on behalf of the future, therefore implying a reopening of the pastness of the past: it implies a (renewed) beginning rather than the ending of a desired history. If loyalism is a thought or an act predicated on anachronistic desire, to turn back the clock so as to return to the primal state of nationhood and selfhood, postloyalism is an exercise that "anachronizes" anachronism. It is aimed to alter or displace a timeline that is already irrecoverably altered or displaced. As such, postloyalism intensifies the precarious nature of loyalism as it seeks to upset—delegitimize—what has already been delegitimized. Like Pandora's box, postloyalism unleashes multiple demons, wreaking havoc with the politics of recognition and loyalty.

As a critical supplement to postcolonialism, postloyalism can help us better understand the polemics of Sinophone literature. Despite incessant foreign encroachments, which amount to a colonial threat, since the early nineteenth century, China was not colonized—with the exception of Taiwan, Hong Kong, and, in part, Manchukuo. Nor can one describe China as a colonial power unless one expands the definition of colonialism to cover all hegemonic systems from the empire to the totalitarian regime. One should also look into the fact that, during the colonial periods of Taiwan and Hong Kong, where Japanese and English were mandated as the official language, Chinese, especially in dialectal forms, appeared to retain its firm grip on the society at large. That the Chinese people under the colonial rule were still capable of preserving their linguistic and cultural habitus, however hybrid in practice, may have to do with either the colonizer's language policy or merely the duration of colonial rule. Still, these cases compel us to think beyond the model of (post)colonialism. One sees a wide range of responses to the use of the Chinese language—and its denial—on the levels of both sound and script, both cognitive recognition and affective negotiation. This is where the Sinophone becomes an arena between postcolonialism and postloyalism. Sinophone literature benefits from a postcolonial perspective that unveils the linkage between Chinese-language literature and global geopolitics. But postcolonialism cannot fully address the intricate mapping of the Sinitic world. It is too grounded in the geopolitical dialectics of the modern times and cannot address the historical intricacies of the Chinese/Sinitic world.

It is at this juncture that Pheng Cheah's emphasis on worlding as a "process of time" becomes especially illuminating. In *What Is a World: On Postcolonial Literature as World Literature* (2016), Cheah offers a critical reappraisal of world literature by rethinking postcolonial literature. Despite the cosmopolitan attempts of theorists of world literature, such as David Damrosch or Pascale Casanova, to break away from a Eurocentric model, as Cheah contends, these scholars derive their concept of world literature from a global imaginary predicated on the circulation of cultural capitals without critically considering their notion of "world." Above all, they imagine the world in spatial terms, instead of taking literature's world-making power into consideration as a temporal process.[15] For Cheah, literature can serve "as an active power in the making of the worlds, that is, both a site of processes of worlding and an agent that participates and intervenes in the processes."[16] While projecting alternative temporalities which unfold along with the opening of the world, as analyzed in postcolonial fiction, Cheah calls attention to historical contingencies and structural interferences (such as global capitalism) that underlie postcolonial imaginations.

In the context of Sinophone and Chinese literatures, Cheah's postcolonial intervention can be enriched by postloyalism. Postloyalist imagination, as the nexus for Sinophone hetero-temporalities, opens a window onto the future as well as onto the past. Through the postloyalist prism, one realizes that Sinophone inscriptions take issue with questions ranging from linguistic (national) sovereignty to enunciative subjectivity, from dynastic allegiance to diasporic imaginaries, thereby directing us toward alternative modernities and alternative histories. A world-literary perspective on the Sinophone activates the complex constellations of meanings of postloyalism: China, not only as the "lost" or "abandoned" heritage, nor as an "incomplete" or "remaining" legacy, but as a cultural "bequest." A postloyalist perspective transforms "Chinese literature" into a worlding process of Sinophone literature.

---

15. Pheng Cheah, "Introduction," in *What Is a World: On Postcolonial Literature as World Literature* (Durham, NC: Duke University Press, 2016).
16. Cheah, *What Is a World*, 16.

Sinophone as a State of Exception

To be sure, when expanding the Sinophone sphere to include China, when proposing postloyalism as a supplement to postcolonialism, one risks being absorbed—co-opted—by the master narrative of "world Chinese literature" as concocted by the Chinese state. This provides one more reason to exercise the dialectic of Sinophone resistance and governance with care. In addition to resistance and governance—*pace* Shi and Tsu respectively—however, I propose something equally polemical: the Sinophone state of "exception." Such an approach helps further the dialectic embedded in the debate between Shih and Tsu. Whereas Shih's resistance model tends to "exclude" China in such a way as to downplay the mutual implications between the state of exception and that of assimilation, Tsu's governance model tends to "include" Sinophone cacophonies with regard to China in such a way as to mitigate the treacherous politics of exception. A strategy of "exception" in the context of the Sinophone relies on a complex scenario. Inspired by, and yet counter to, Giorgio Agamben's definition of a state of exception, one must approach Chinese national literature as an "exception" with regard to the broadly defined world of Sinophone literature.

In practice, we may bracket Chinese national literature only insofar as its prescribed absence facilitates one's recognition of Sinoglossia at large. This constitutes a paradoxical reversal of the current paradigm of Chinese literature versus overseas Chinese literature. Whereas the mainstream discourse of Chinese literature treats overseas literature as an "exceptional case," one that is isolated so as to authenticate the orthodoxy of Chinese national literature, a Sinophone scholar turns the tables by taking exception to such a "state of exception" and treats Chinese national literature as an exception to world Sinophone literature.[17] What is emphasized here is nevertheless a Sinophone scholar's capacity to engage with Chinese language literature by means of a critical philology and an imagined "non-community." Critical philology opens up the genealogical roots and ramifications of Chinese-language literature in its historical flux; imagined "non-community" points to the arbitrary interference and contingent "short circuit" in the differentiation and assimilation of national literature.

To put such a strategy into a literary, and Sinophone, context, we might learn from Eileen Chang's perplexing phrase *baokuo zai wai* 包括在外 (to include something or someone to its or his/her exclusion). If Agamben's approach defines the state of exception in light of the Foucauldian condition of power networks and public governance, Chang's exclusion/inclusion dialectic stresses a Sinophone subject's playful undertaking of defamiliarization—or more

---

17. Giorgio Agamben, *The State of Exception*, trans. Kevin Attell (Chicago: University of Chicago Press, 2005).

polemically, extraterritorialization—with regard to the micropolitics of everyday practice. In a similar vein, a Sinophone scholar seeks out the endlessly exceptional situations wherever exception is least expected both within and without Chinese national literature. He or she is aware of the mercurial state of linguistic transmutations, thus calling forth the dialogic of inclusion by means of exclusion and exclusion by means of inclusion.[18] As both an informed outsider and an estranged insider, a Sinophone subject creates layered "folds," folding inside forces from the outside and vice versa.[19]

What I have proposed here constitutes an attempt to broaden the scope and methodology for studying modern Chinese-language literature. It does not seek to overwrite the extant imaginary of "China" or of the various notions of the Sinophone but rather to tease out the complexity and intricate connections of both. In order to do so, we must replace not only an "obsession with China" but also an "obsession against China" with a "Sinophone intervention with China," one that precariously includes China as an exception. In addition, we have to temper postcolonial critique with a postloyalist approach. Is it not a paradox that critics can subscribe to a "politics of marginality" and pontificate about a "clash of empires" and "global contextualization," all the while rigidly marginalizing forms of Chinese/Sinophone modernity and historicity that do not emerge within some preconceived mainstream? If one of the most important lessons one can learn from modern Chinese literature and history is the tortuous nature of Chinese writers' attempt to grapple with a polymorphous reality, then this knowledge can be appreciated in full only through a criticism and literary history equally exempt from formulaic dogma and geopolitical blindness. I argue that one must genuinely believe that Chinese and Sinophone writers have been, and still are, capable of complex and creative thought, constructing and deconstructing the nation and the world in the literary domain and beyond. From "obsession with China" to Sinophone "intervention with China," from postcolonialism to postloyalism, any critical endeavor in the name of Sinophone literature must be unafraid to look squarely at this historical reality—a reality made up by slippery national and linguistic boundary lines and contested modernities.

---

18. Eileen Chang 張愛玲, "Bawo baokuo zaiwai" 把我包括在外 [Include me out], in *Wangranji: Zhang Ailing sanwenji II* 枉然記：張愛玲散文集II [Failed expectations: Eileen Chang II] (Taipei: Huangguan, 2010). Chang drew her quote from the Hollywood producer Samuel Goldwyn, who reportedly played with the paradoxical implication of the phrase "include me out" on a social occasion.
19. Gilles Deleuze, *The Fold: Leibniz and the Baroque*, trans. Tom Conley (Minneapolis: University of Minnesota Press, 1993).

12
The Inherent Contradiction of Sinoglossia

Ien Ang

China's increasingly assertive global presence and power has spawned a world in which it is increasingly difficult to eschew things "Chinese." As China's influence grows worldwide, the specter of cultural "Sinicization" looms large, in the same way that propositions of "Americanization" or "Japanization" were evoked in previous episodes of contestations over global hegemony.[1] But if the world is ostensibly becoming more "Chinese," what does "Chineseness" mean? When, how, and in which circumstances does the label "Chinese" apply? What does it mean to call something or someone "Chinese"?

In introducing the concept of "Sinoglossia," this book proposes to address such questions by problematizing absolutist and essentialist understandings of Chineseness and advancing "a more flexible conceptualization of Chinese culture as an array of polyphonic, multi-discursive, and multilingual articulations," as the editors pronounce in the Introduction.[2] In today's global context this is an urgent agenda, the relevance of which spans the wide landscape of the humanities and social sciences. In this short commentary essay, I draw on some of my own work on the cultural politics of Chineseness to reflect on the theoretical affordances that the notion of Sinoglossia promises, while at the same time pointing to the necessary tensions implied in the very prefix of "Sino"—tensions from which only partial escape is ultimately possible and which the pairing of "Sino" and "glossia" usefully underscores.

The editors present Sinoglossia as a supplement to the paradigm of Sinophone studies, which has been an influential approach in literary and cultural studies for some time. Shu-mei Shih defines Sinophone studies as "[the] study [of] the Sinitic-language communities and cultures outside China as well as ethnic

---

1. See Peter J. Katzenstein, ed., *Sinicization and the Rise of China: Civilizational Processes Beyond East and West* (London: Routledge, 2012).
2. See "Introduction" in this volume.

minority communities and cultures within China where Mandarin Chinese is adopted or imposed."[3] What this definition divulges is the focus on language, or more particularly, on Sinitic or Chinese languages used by communities inside and outside China and the ways in which they not only deviate from, but actively disrupt, the centrality of Mandarin Chinese as the official Chinese language. My work is not in literary studies, nor is it concerned centrally with language. Indeed, I would argue that the focus on language and on Sinitic-language communities and cultures represents a narrowing of the field opened up by Sinophone studies. In this regard, I welcome the intervention that the idea of Sinoglossia brings to the Sinophone studies paradigm, in that it extends the analysis of "Chineseness" to material and cultural phenomena that lie beyond the strict realm of language, vastly expanding the interdisciplinary reach of this emerging field of inquiry.

Both the Sinophone and the Sinoglossic privilege the epistemic status of multiplicity and heterogeneity, even as the prefix "Sino" raises the specter of homogeneity. The aim is to decenter "any assumed equivalence between 'China' and Sino-representation."[4] This is a conceptual move of great political and intellectual significance, especially in the global context of an increasingly powerful China. China's increasingly imposing presence on the global stage has led to a situation where Mandarin Chinese is now the hegemonic Chinese language and where the provenance of "Chineseness" as such tends to be equated exclusively with mainland China. To articulate the polyphonic and heterogeneous nature of Sinitic languages spoken and written in diverse locations around the world, as Sinophone studies has done, is to contest this China-centric hegemony and to recognize the distinctiveness of diasporic Chinese subjectivities, whose creative productions are generated without or beyond China as their reference point, indeed, by highlighting emphatically that they are "not made in China." The notion of Sinoglossia enables the expansion of this decentering move toward many other diasporic cultural formations and practices that transcend the focus on Sinitic languages.

I use the term "diasporic" deliberately here, to signal that I am skeptical about the claim that Sinophone studies represents a break with the diaspora paradigm, as argued by Shih and others. It is true, of course, that talk of diaspora—the "Chinese diaspora" in particular—has been used predominantly as a way of homogenizing overseas Chinese communities, underscoring their common identities, despite their dispersal, as determined by their origins in China.[5] Here,

---

3. Shu-mei Shih, "What Is Sinophone Studies?," in *Sinophone Studies: A Critical Reader*, ed. Shu-mei Shih, Chien-hsin Tsai, and Brian Bernards (New York: Columbia University Press, 2013), 11.
4. See "Introduction" in this volume.
5. For an authoritative critique, see Gungwu Wang, "A Single Chinese Diaspora?," in *Diasporic Chinese Ventures: The Life and Work of Wang Gungwu*, ed. Gregor Benton and Hong Liu (London: Routledge Curzon, 2004), 157–177.

diaspora is associated with "roots": with the presumably inescapable link of the diasporic subject with the ancestral homeland and with some kind of primordial, originary "Chineseness." In this context, the diasporic subject is perilously positioned in a relation of passive subjection to the singular, archetypical Chineseness of the putative ancestral homeland, with no agency of his or her own. It is this homeland-centric and hierarchical notion of diaspora that Sinophone studies is directed against, as epitomized by Shih's paper "Against Diaspora."[6]

However, since the 1990s a more critical understanding of "diaspora" has emerged in cultural studies, one that stresses not "roots" but "routes": the trajectories of migration—including Chinese migrations—through which diasporic identities and subjectivities are shaped, are conceived as inevitably hybrid, mixed-up, multifocal. This critical conception of diaspora has been elaborated particularly by theorists such as Homi Bhabha, Avtar Brah, James Clifford, Stuart Hall, and Paul Gilroy, who have emphasized hybridity as central to the diasporic condition, creating a "third space" that emerges out of the entanglement of "where you're from" and "where you're at," belonging and unbelonging, sameness and difference.[7] Diasporic subjects occupy this in-between, diasporic cultural space. Importantly, as Hall describes in his memoir, *Familiar Stranger*, this is the space where new, hybrid identities are constructed, articulating new modes of creativity and forms of cultural empowerment. For Hall, what is central to the diasporic experience are the generative dynamics and processes of displacement, producing a constant sense of ambivalence, incongruity, and contingency in the imagination of "home" and "homeland." As he puts it: "The diasporic is the moment of the double inscription, of creolization and multiple belongings."[8]

My book, *On Not Speaking Chinese*, has been informed by this understanding of the diasporic experience.[9] In the book I emphasize the flexible indeterminacy and contestability of "Chineseness" as a signifier for identity in diasporic contexts. I also stress the possibility that the salience of Chineseness—as a category of identification—can be undone or cancelled out, for example whenever the boundaries between "Chinese" and "non-Chinese" become blurred or nonsensical as a consequence of pervasive hybridization or assimilation. More strongly, I have also entertained the possibility of *refusal* of identification

---

6. Shu-mei Shih, "Against Diaspora: The Sinophone as Places of Cultural Production," in *Sinophone Studies: A Critical Reader*, ed. Shih, Tsai, and Bernards, 25–42.
7. Homi Bhabha, *The Location of Culture* (London: Routledge, 1994); Avtar Brah, *Cartographies of Diaspora: Contesting Identities* (London: Routledge, 1996); James Clifford, *Routes: Travel and Translation in the Late Twentieth Century* (Cambridge, MA: Harvard University Press, 1997); Paul Gilroy, *The Black Atlantic: Modernity and Double Consciousness* (London: Verso, 1993); Stuart Hall, "Cultural Identity and Diaspora," in *Identity: Community, Culture, Difference*, ed. Jonathan Rutherford (London: Lawrence & Wishart, 1990), 222–237.
8. Stuart Hall, *Familiar Stranger: A Life Between Two Islands* (London: Allen Lane, 2017), 144.
9. Ien Ang, *On Not Speaking Chinese: Living Between Asia and the West* (London: Routledge, 2001).

with "being Chinese," as suggested in the title of my essay "Can One Say No to Chineseness?"[10] It is fitting that this was the one essay of mine included in the seminal anthology *Sinophone Studies: A Critical Reader*, given that it attempted to "push the limits of the diasporic paradigm."[11] In this regard, my project has a strong overlap with Shih's, in that it problematizes the perpetuity of the diasporic condition. Why would someone who is of Chinese descent but has never lived in China and does not even speak Chinese still have to be tied to a "Chinese" identity? Why would one not be able to stop being diasporic Chinese, that is, to be "no longer Chinese," as I have suggested elsewhere?[12] These questions tally with Shih's contention that there should be an expiry date on the idea of diaspora: "one cannot say one is diasporic after three hundred years, and everyone should be given a chance to become a local."[13]

Unfortunately, however, historical and political conditions have shown that untangling oneself from the diasporic condition is easier said than done. This is more than a question of language: (not) speaking Chinese is by no means a sufficient criterion for Chinese identification (or not), on the contrary. One can be out of China for hundreds of years and no longer have any competence in any Sinitic language but still be identified, by choice or by force, as "Chinese". This is the case, for example, for the "Chinese" in Indonesia, who, despite being thoroughly Indonesianized after decades of assimilation policies, have not been allowed to "forget" their Chinese ancestral origins. Here, Chineseness is reduced to its status as a "race": all Chinese-identified subjects are presumed to be bound by blood as the collective descendants of the Yellow Emperor.[14] This racialized conception of Chineseness has also been exploited by the modern Chinese state, past and present, which has appealed strongly to their diasporic subjects everywhere to show loyalty to the "motherland" and embrace their inherited "Chineseness."[15] Diasporic status, here, is imposed on them, whether they like it or not: they are simply not given the chance unconditionally to be a local. Rather than declaring diaspora out-of-date, in other words, I think it is both analytically and politically important to retain the notion of the diasporic, not so much to

---

10. Ien Ang, "Can One Say No to Chineseness? Pushing the Limits of the Diasporic Paradigm," *boundary 2: International Journal of Literature and Culture*, 25, no. 3 (1998): 223–242.
11. Shu-mei Shih, Chien-hsin Tsai and Brian Bernards, eds., *Sinophone Studies: A Critical Reader* (New York: Columbia University Press, 2013).
12. Ien Ang, "No Longer Chinese? Residual Chineseness after the Rise of China," in *Diasporic Chineseness after the Rise of China: Community, Culture and Communication*, ed. Julia Kuehn, Kam Louie, and David Pomfret (Vancouver: University of British Columbia Press, 2013), 17–31.
13. Shu-mei Shih, "The Concept of the Sinophone," *PMLA* 126, no. 3 (May 2011): 704.
14. See, for example, Lynn Pan, *Sons of the Yellow Emperor: The Story of the Overseas Chinese* (London: Mandarin, 1990).
15. See Ien Ang, "On the Perils of Racialized Chineseness: Race, Nation and Entangled Racisms in China and South Asia," *Ethnic and Racial Studies* 45, no. 4 (2022): 757–777.

affirm an actual link with the "homeland" but to highlight the tensions created in the ambiguous in-between space which diasporic subjects occupy, by virtue of their racialization, their minority status, or even through the intergenerational reproduction of the memory of migration in families and communities.[16] At the same time, it is important to uncouple "Chineseness" from "China": the ancestral homeland—China—is decentred as the normative, absolute source of Chineseness and displaced by highly variable and historically specific, localized, and hybridized articulations of diasporic "Chinese" identity. This, indeed, is the terrain of Sinoglossia, encompassing not just linguistic practices but affect and comportment, imaginaries of belonging and identity, as well as everyday practices and rituals. Nevertheless, although "China" the imagined ancestral homeland is no longer central, it cannot be considered completely irrelevant: indeed, it continues to haunt the diasporic subject, psychically, symbolically, politically, or otherwise. In other words, "roots" and "routes" are deeply entangled, locked in unremitting tension with each other. This fundamental diasporic tension is reflected in the inherent tension between "Sino" and "glossia": the frictional push and pull that is highlighted by linking "Sino" and "glossia" together.

This friction is especially palpable in the current historical period of the so-called "rise of China." As China is becoming an increasingly powerful global nation, diasporic Chinese communities everywhere are being compelled to recalibrate their putative links with the ancestral homeland, even if these links have been weakened or rendered non-existent by the passing of time outside "China proper." Significant geo-cultural and geopolitical factors are at play in the redefinitions and reconsiderations of the meaning of Chineseness in different parts of the world, but inevitably with "China" as an enforced reference point to respond to. In places such as Taiwan and Hong Kong, for example, active *dis*identification with Chineseness is occurring, in favor of assertions of Taiwaneseness and Hongkongness, as a defiant declaration of independence from an increasingly threatening People's Republic of China. They are, in other words, saying "no" to Chineseness as a political act. In other, more far-flung, diasporic spaces, the destabilization of Chineseness as a result of the rise of China is undergoing different, sometimes contradictory, trajectories, ranging from resistance to China's new hegemony and disavowals of notions of a shared Chineseness, to a rush to embrace China's ascendancy as a new source of pride, advantage, and opportunity, invigorating renewed modes of (re)Sinicization and strengthening actual homeland links.[17] These varied and shifting positionalities can be seen

---

16. See, for example, Lingchei Letty Chen, "When Does 'Diaspora' End and 'Sinophone' Begin?" *Postcolonial Studies* 18, no. 1 (2015): 52–66.
17. See, for example, Hong Liu, "Opportunities and Anxieties for the Chinese Diaspora in Southeast Asia," *Current History* 115, no. 784 (November 2016): 312–318.

as manifestations of the inherent contradiction that animates the conceptual heart of Sinoglossia: the tension between the homogenizing draw of the prefix "Sino," on the one hand, and the heterogeneity and multiplicity associated with the term "glossia," on the other. This inherent contradiction, as Howard Chiang suggests in this book's Introduction, "represents the most theoretically powerful and promising aspect of Sinoglossic inquiries."[18]

To exemplify the interdisciplinary reach and potential of the Sinoglossic approach, let us look at the evolution of so-called Chinatowns in many cities around the world. Chinatowns are material cultural formations the analysis of which takes us beyond the humanities fields of literary and cultural studies and into more social science-inflected fields such as sociology, cultural geography, and urban studies, even economics and international relations.

Since the early twentieth century, "Chinatown" has been the name customarily given to city enclaves where Chinese immigrants were concentrated, segregated from the surrounding host society. In Western eyes, these areas were the no-go zones of the Oriental other: Chinatown was seen as the material embodiment of a quintessential, despised Chineseness in their midst. More than 100 years later, traditional Chinatowns still exist, but their meaning and role has been transformed, as they became tourist destinations in increasingly cosmopolitan global cities. In this context Chinatown is imbued with a commodified and highly contrived Chineseness, often through Orientalized, stereotypical "Chinese" architectural and design motifs such as Chinatown gates or *paifang* (牌坊), red lanterns, and green-tiled upturned roofs. At the same time, many Chinese immigrants and their descendants moved out into the suburbs as they increasingly became part of mainstream society. Some traditional Chinatowns went into decline as they were subjected to the forces of gentrification, while others were revitalized by the influx of new migrant arrivals and influences, including from mainland China. Sydney's Chinatown, for example, used to be populated mainly by migrants from Southern China but has today become a highly hybridized, multi-Asian precinct, where the influx of Southeast Asian, Hong Kong, Korean and, especially, mainland Chinese new migrants, students, investors, tourists, shops, restaurants, and businesses have made a particularly strong impact.[19]

By the early twenty-first century, as China's rise became an irrefutably palpable reality, many more diasporic Chinese subjects had begun to say a more emphatic "yes," not just to "Chineseness" but to "China," for sentimental reasons

---

18. See "Introduction" in this volume.
19. Kay Anderson, Ien Ang, Andrea Del Bono, Donald McNeill, and Alexandra Wong, *Chinatown Unbound: Trans-Asian Urbanism in the Age of China* (London: Rowman & Littlefield, 2019).

(think, for example, of the increased popularity of homeland tours to China)[20] or for economic reasons (where capitalizing on one's diasporic connections with the ancestral homeland has proved to be highly lucrative).[21] Indeed, this economic rationale has driven the emergence of a whole range of new Chinatowns in cities around the world, where transnational Chinese entrepreneurs and local politicians have been eager to take advantage of the opportunities promised by the rise of China in the globalized economy. "Chinatown" here operates as a neoliberal urban "brand," conjuring up essentialized "Chinese" precincts whose key function is to make the city attractive for capital investment, trade, and tourism from China.[22] Las Vegas, for example, has prided itself on having built "America's first master-planned Chinatown."[23] Similarly, South Korea recently experienced a "Chinatown fever" where, following the government's establishment of the country's first official Chinatown in Incheon, numerous local governments embarked on Chinatown-making projects of their own in a bid to connect local sites to Chinese capital circuits.[24] In Dubai, which now has a Chinese migrant population of several hundred thousand, a new Chinatown was announced in 2018, on the eve of President Xi Xinping's visit to the United Arab Emirates, said to become "the largest Chinatown in the Middle East" and explicitly designed to galvanize business links between the two countries.[25] In such aspirational instances, Chinatown and its associated Chineseness are perceived as an urban asset. However, while some cities have adopted the Chinatown idea for economic benefit, others—such as Lisbon and Auckland—have rejected it because they associate Chinatown more with the threat posed by China's rise, or object to the exoticization of Chineseness encompassed in the concept of Chinatown.[26] Yet other cities have pursued Chinatown-making projects that ultimately failed. One of the most interesting cases is that of San José, the capital of Costa Rica. In 2012, the city's mayor decided to build a new Chinatown to materialize the visibility of the city's burgeoning ties with China, erecting a Tang dynasty–inspired archway in collaboration with the city of Beijing. However, soon after the grand opening the project proved to be a failure, with buildings remaining vacant,

---

20. See, for example, Andrea Louie, *Chineseness Across Borders: Renegotiating Chinese Identities in China and the United States* (Durham, NC: Duke University Press, 2004).
21. See, for example, Constance Lever-Tracy, David Ip, and Noel Tracy, *The Chinese Diaspora and Mainland China* (London: Palgrave Macmillan, 1996).
22. Ien Ang, "Chinatowns and the Rise of China," *Modern Asian Studies* 54, no. 4 (2020): 1367–1393.
23. Bonnie Tsui, *American Chinatown: A People's History of Five Neighbourhoods* (New York: Free Press, 2010), 214.
24. Sujin Eom, "Traveling Chinatowns: Mobility of Urban Forms and 'Asia' in Circulation," *positions: asia critique* 25, no. 4 (2017): 709.
25. Darragh Murphey, "Dubai Is Getting the Middle East's 'Largest Chinatown,'" *Time Out Dubai*, July 19, 2018, https://www.timeoutdubai.com/things-to-do/things-to-do-news/84635-dubai-is-getting-the-middle-easts-largest-chinatown.
26. Ang, "Chinatowns and the Rise of China," 1367–1393.

sparse visitation, and few shops trading Chinese cultural fare. More importantly, this new, artificial Chinatown was completely disconnected from the city's ethnic Chinese population, who were spread throughout the city and articulated quite different, locally inflected senses of hybridized Chineseness.[27]

"Chinatown," as these divergent examples illuminate, is a globally significant Sinoglossic phenomenon. As a pre-set urban form materialized in vastly different contexts around the world, it displays the inherent contradiction that the concept of Sinoglossia aims to highlight: on the one hand, all actually existing Chinatowns evince a shared reference to "Sino" (otherwise they wouldn't be Chinatown), but on the other hand, each Chinatown is inevitably shaped by a "glossia" of heterogeneous realities and relationships on the ground. In today's proliferation of Chinatowns, "China" looms large, ever more so as China's growing global clout has become an inexorable attractor. At the same time, China's rise seems to have only heightened the contested, resistant, and variable articulations of Chineseness in dispersed diasporic contexts. This inescapable contradiction marks the central conceptual power of Sinoglossia.

---

27. Monica Dehart, "Costa Rica's Chinatown: The Art of Being Global in the Age of China," *City and Society* 27, no. 2 (2015): 183–207.

13
Kingston beyond Orientalism

Colleen Lye

Foundational to the emergence of Asian American literature as a self-conscious field of writing in the 1970s and 1980s was a quarrel over the Orientalism of the most commercially successful Asian American writers, many of whom came under attack for supplying exoticized depictions of Asia and Asians. Kicking off that quarrel and for a long time guaranteeing that the question of Orientalism would define the terms of critical debate about this emerging literary field, Maxine Hong Kingston's *The Woman Warrior* (1976) will be the subject of my reflection here on the affordances of the concept of Sinoglossia for the study of Asian American literature.

The history of *The Woman Warrior*'s reception reflects more than the growing pains of emerging ethnic literatures in general. It reflects a historical conjuncture when the authority of contemporary representations of the People's Republic of China (PRC) were being called into question by the release of new, or newly available, accounts of revolutionary betrayals and the PRC government's about-face verdict on the Cultural Revolution after the death of Mao. Asian American literature's persistent shadowing by suspicions of an endemic Orientalism—and the fact that the accused authors tended to be and to write about Chinese Americans—suggest the salience of this particular international context to the discourse about the emerging minority field.

To be clear, Kingston was by no means a sympathizer of the Chinese Communist revolution. Indeed, *The Woman Warrior* registers a blatant skepticism of the 1950s land reform policies enacted by the CCP after taking power, which are reported in the text to have victimized Kingston's relatives. Moreover, Kingston's involvement in the US peace movement means that her activist opposition to the Vietnam War stemmed from a commitment to principles of nonviolence rather than from a revolutionary nationalist position, much less a critique of the political economy grounding US military involvement in Vietnam. At the same time, *The Woman Warrior*'s identification with the cause of Chinese women's liberation necessarily orients the text's presumption that twentieth-century revolution's attack on the traditional family form had fundamentally improved women's status.

Central to Chinese socialism was the tenet that gender equality measured socialist progress. Western sympathizers who visited the PRC often thematized in their reports examples of women's collective organizing about questions of sexual violence, domestic abuse, divorce rights, and land redistribution. Though a work of fictionalized autobiography by a US-born author who had never visited China before writing it, *The Woman Warrior*'s treatment of the topic of Chinese women made it of intense interest to feminists across the political spectrum of the Second Wave. The book's feminist value granted Kingston a racial crossover audience who read her for a *theoretical* import in a way unprecedented for a US Asian literary writer. But by the same token, Kingston could not escape the charge of Orientalism that after 1976 potentially clung to all those whose writing about contemporary China had been accorded an epistemological authority.

We can best situate the rising influence of Orientalism as a critical mode after 1980, by noting that when Kingston's reputation was eventually secured against the charge of having exaggerated the sexism of Chinese culture, the Kingston defense was built not so much upon the justice of her feminist critique as upon the ethnic fictionist's right to ethnic improvisation. Indeed, so central was Kingston to larger literary debates in the 1980s about ethnic essentialism that she came to represent a central piece of evidence for the more general postmodern conceptualization of ethnicity as a kind of fiction.[1] Within the specialist confines of the Asian American literary field, Asian American feminist critics' lament at having to choose between cultural nationalism and feminism was symptomatic of the broader theoretical impasse that came to characterize the state of feminist debate after the waning of international feminism and the rise of intersectional feminism. Tellingly, readings of *The Woman Warrior* tended to diverge depending on whether the text's Orientalism was used to critique the limits of its feminism, or its feminism was used to critique the (masculinist) cultural nationalism animating the critique of Orientalism. This bifurcation between Orientalist and feminist readings of Kingston indicated the erosion of Third World (or revolutionary nationalist) feminism as a politically credible or even legible position, a phenomenon linked to the recession of left-wing internationalism in general.

The experience of Chinese socialism had presented the potential for the renewal of a Marxist internationalism alert to the pitfalls of Eurocentrism in the years running from the 1950s to the 1970s, both in peripheral societies and

---

1. Michael Fischer, "Ethnicity and the Post-Modern Arts of Memory," in *Writing Culture: The Poetics and Politics of Ethnography*, ed. James Clifford and George Marcus (Berkeley: University of California Press, 1986), 195–233.

in the metropolitan core. As is well known, Edward Said's 1979 publication of *Orientalism* generated the critical vocabulary for postcolonial studies' sensitivity to the colonial complicities of Enlightenment universalisms, including Marxism.[2] Though Said's particular focus was the Middle East, his adaptation of Foucault to the question of imperialism—or more precisely to the question of colonialism in place of imperialism—had a generalizing power in part because of leftist embarrassment over exposés of the actual abuses of the Great Proletarian Cultural Revolution. The concept of Orientalism found ready application to examples of Euro-American discourse about and domination over other regions of the "East," including East Asia, and beyond Asia itself. The era since the demise of left internationalisms has been one in which a liberal framework of human rights adjudicated by Atlantic powers holds unrivaled claim to a realistic internationalism,[3] while positive recollections of past Afro-Asian solidarities remain constrained by the label of Orientalism—representing at best a positive case of cultural appropriation.[4]

Recent recoveries of twentieth-century Asian Marxisms reflect a growing intuition that their histories may offer some clues for how to think universality without homogeneity and humanness beyond Eurocentrism—an intellectual labor that internationalist politics or a broadly inclusive emancipatory politics may not be able to do without.[5] How might the concept of Sinoglossia aid in this effort, by providing a perceptual opening beyond the enclosing suspicion that all the world's an Orientalist stage?

As a limited exercise, and returning to the case of Kingston's *The Woman Warrior*, let us consider what it might mean to read the text not as example of Orientalist feminism but as an example of Sinoglossic feminism. In the former instance, our emphasis would be on the inescapability of Orientalist discourse, including for the US ethnic writer whose performance of ethnicity we would either condemn for a derivative mimesis (or replication) of Orientalism or praise for an innovative mimicry (or critique) of it. In the former instance, attention to questions of colonialism, imperialism, and racism, and attention to gender are

---

2. Aamir Mufti, *Forget English! Orientalisms and World Literatures* (Cambridge, MA: Harvard University Press, 2016).
3. Samuel Moyn, *The Last Utopia: Human Rights in History* (Cambridge, MA: Harvard University Press, 2012).
4. Bill Mullen, *Afro-Orientalism* (Minneapolis: University of Minnesota Press, 2004); Judy Wu, *Radicals on the Road: Internationalism, Orientalism, and Feminism during the Vietnam Era* (Ithaca, NY: Cornell University Press, 2013).
5. Harry Harootunian, *Marx after Marx: History and Time in the Expansion of Capitalism* (New York: Columbia University Press, 2015); Rebecca Karl, *The Magic of Concepts: History and the Economic in Twentieth-Century China* (Durham, NC: Duke University Press, 2017); Petrus Liu, *Queer Marxism in Two Chinas* (Durham, NC: Duke University Press, 2015); Shu-mei Shih, "Is the Post- in Postsocialism the Post- in Posthumanism?," *Social Text* 30, no. 1 (2012): 27–50.

likely to be pitted against each other, such that each defines the methodological limit upon the other's claim to a sufficient analysis. Reading *The Woman Warrior* as a case of Sinoglossic feminism, alternatively, we might be able to take seriously Kingston's text as a translation of the historical experience of Chinese feminism, a project in which the quest for anti-imperial liberation and the quest for women's emancipation went hand in hand. Reading the text in this way would allow us to appreciate not only how the text's desires align with the politics of Third World feminism but how it was the very strength of that alignment that also allowed *The Woman Warrior* to function as a key transitional object in US feminism's passage from the period of Third Worldism's heyday to the period when intersectionality emerged to define US feminism's leading edge, wherein the ongoing struggle is the antinomy of difference and coalition.

To make a case for *The Woman Warrior* as a Sinoglossic *feminist* text, we would have to begin by noting that the stories that the narrator tells about legendary women and female kin are embellishments and mash-ups of received popular folk narratives and Kingston's personal family history. Though set in mythic and historical times before the establishment of the PRC in 1949, the stories reflect the influence of communist reworkings of traditional folk narratives and suggest that the "revolution and its narratives" circulated in the various forms of Chinese mass media in the diaspora.[6] The red flag-flying peasant army led by Mulan in search of redistributive justice and the symbolization of the narrator's mother as a kind of "barefoot doctor" administering traditional medicine in rural villages are just two of the most obvious examples of how *The Woman Warrior*, though composed in the still–Cold War years of limited contact between China and the diaspora, can be counted as a record of the "continuing revolution" faced by Chinese feminism after the formal advent of socialism.

The Woman Warrior might be seen as a *Sinoglossic* feminist text because the text roots the quest for a Chinese American female voice in the problem of having to navigate various textual mediations of the transnational reception of Chinese women's heroism. As such, the preoccupying theme of the speaking subject's identity was formally routed through the question of whether language itself was inimical to the representation of women. While the language of cinema, specifically Chinese martial arts films, was a source of empowering imagery in which "we saw swordswomen jump over houses from a standstill," written language is often freighted with the ideology of a Poundian Orientalism representing an ambiguous inheritance for the Anglophone Chinese female writer.[7] The English "I" is read or, rather, looked at, as an ideograph or a silent sign, an image

---

6. Xiang Cai, *Revolution and Its Narratives: China's Socialist Literary and Cultural Imaginaries, 1949–1966*, trans. Rebecca Karl and Xueping Zhong (Durham, NC: Duke University Press, 2016).
7. Maxine Hong Kingston, *The Woman Warrior* (New York: Vintage, 1989), 19.

so dissimilar from the Chinese character for "I" (我) that the narrator "forgot to pronounce it."[8] The Poundian notion of Chinese as a natural language provides Kingston with the poetic image for Mulan's martial arts training, in which superpowers are attained by molding the human body simultaneously into the likeness of language and of nature. Lest her readers take for granted this naturalistic idea of Chinese writing, Kingston transitions us into the alternate world of Mulan by having us trail the first-person narrator who—*Alice in Wonderland*-like—steps into a Chinese painting, which helps us keep in mind that the ancient-China setting to follow is ultimately an aesthetic construction.

It is easy to make a formalist case for the self-reflexivity of *The Woman Warrior*'s uses of Orientalism. Much harder but more interesting would be to try to make the case that it provides a historical record of Chinese feminism in translation. A full demonstration of this would require filling in the details of its intertextual dialogue with communist revolutionary narratives that were in contemporary diasporic circulation in Kingston's childhood. It would require showing how the Anglophone specificity of *The Woman Warrior*'s innovation upon those narratives involved building a self-reflexive critique of Orientalism into a representation of an anti-imperialist feminism informed by Chinese socialist feminism. Expanding from there, it might then become possible to compare Asian American feminist texts with other Western feminist writings of the long global 1960s, such as Julia Kristeva's *About Chinese Women*. In that peculiar ethnography, Kristeva, though writing in a different language (French) but with comparable self-awareness, sought to reverse the Orientalist eye by trying to write from the standpoint of the object of Chinese women's gaze. The seriousness of the respect Kingston and Kristeva accorded Chinese feminism—their shared concern with how to assess its historical significance for feminist struggles beyond the PRC—is rendered as a formal problem of translation, which led to textual innovation on multiple levels, including that of genre.[9] A judgment on the value of Kristeva's literary achievement from this specific angle is beyond the capacity of this chapter to venture. In Kingston's case, it is safe to say that the result was the discovery that the responsible way of representing Asian American identity was as and through literary fiction.

---

8. Kingston, *The Woman Warrior*, 167.
9. Julia Kristeva, *About Chinese Woman*, trans. Anita Barrows (New York: Marion Boyars, 1986).

14
Demolishing Script
China and 拆那 *(Chai-na)*

Carlos Rojas

The neologism 拆那 (pronounced *chai-na* in Mandarin)—a nickname for China that has recently begun to gain popularity—is a catachresis, a misnomer that brings into sharp relief a set of fissures at the heart of China's contemporary identity, its history, and even the language(s) with which it is closely associated. Whereas the concept of Sinoglossia takes as its starting point the heterogenous foundation of both China and the Chinese language(s), the term *chai-na* gestures instead to the violent processes of disjunction, demolition, dispossession, and uncanny return that have played a critical role in constituting China and the Chinese language(s) as we see them today.

Composed of the characters 拆 (*chai*), a verb meaning "to demolish," and 那 (*na*), a pronoun meaning "that," *chai-na* literally means "demolish that," and gestures to the rapid process of urbanization that is currently transforming the nation. As the speed of China's urban reconstruction and expansion has accelerated, it has become increasingly common to see the character 拆 written on the outer walls of structures slated for demolition, and the term *chai-na* ironically parses the contextualized meaning of the character in combination with the edifice on which it is inscribed: "demolish that [structure]."

At the same time, the neologism *Chai-na* also gestures to the process by which not only buildings but also entire Chinese metropolises are literally being torn down and rebuilt. As urban areas are transformed into vast construction zones, visitors often remark that the cities themselves often become virtually unrecognizable after only a few years. Moreover, although the speed and scale of contemporary China's urban reconstruction is certainly unusual, the underlying phenomenon is not new, and throughout history Chinese cities have been repeatedly razed, rebuilt, renamed, and radically reimagined. Indeed, a similar point could be made about the nation as a whole—in that although China is frequently viewed as a civilization with a continuous history dating back thousands of years, in actuality the nation has undergone repeated ruptures and transformations. In fact, the geographic region corresponding to contemporary China has been ruled by a number of distinct regimes at different periods and has been repeatedly fractured and reconstituted. Although there are indeed some sociocultural and institutional elements that have persisted over time in the region, it is also true that many of these same elements were also adopted in other states positioned along the region's periphery—states that could be viewed as falling under a Chinese cultural sphere but are rarely viewed as being part of China itself. It would be reasonable to ask, accordingly, whether there is *any* necessary and sufficient criterion that delimits our understanding of China as a transhistorical entity.

For instance, it is often claimed that a key factor in helping anchor China's civilizational identity over time has been the relative stability of its writing system[1]—though in reality this writing system, like China itself, has been repeatedly revised and transformed, to the point that early versions of the script are virtually unintelligible to contemporary readers without specialized training. In addition, there have also been many variants of the script, including character sets corresponding to different regional dialects (such as Cantonese and Shanghainese), adaptations used to write other languages (including Japanese *kanji*, Korean *hanja*, and Vietnamese *chữ nôm*, as well as historical languages from the Chinese periphery, such as Tangut, Khitan, and Yi), adaptations to create character-based syllabaries (including Japanese *kana* syllabaries, the Chinese *zhuyin* syllabary, and the *nüshu* "women's writing" syllabary), and even contemporary variants that have come to achieve a life of their own thanks to the internet (such as the so-called Martian script).

As a product of a complicated set of translingual transformations, the neologism *Chai-na* is symptomatic of the radical dynamism that has always characterized the Chinese script, while simultaneously symbolizing the common *belief* that it is precisely the relative stability of the Chinese script that has helped anchor the transhistorical cohesion of the Chinese nation. To begin with, there is the irony that the ability of the term *Chai-na* to signify "China" relies on an aural similarity between a Chinese phrase (as pronounced in Mandarin) and the nation's contemporary name in English (and several other Western languages). Moreover, even as the neologism *Chai-na* reappropriates a foreign term for the Chinese nation and transliterates it back into Chinese characters, there is also evidence that the English word *China* can itself be traced to the name of China's first unified dynasty, the Qin 秦 (pronounced "ch'in"; 221–206 BCE). As early as

---

1. See the conclusion of my chapter, "Chinese Writing, Heptapod B, and Martian Script," in this volume.

the first and second centuries CE, apparent cognates like *Thinai*, *Sinai*, and *Cīna* had begun appearing in Greek, Roman, and Sanskrit texts as terms for China, though by this point the short-lived Qin dynasty had already collapsed and been replaced by the Han, and *Qin* itself was no longer being used to refer to what we view as China within the geographic region corresponding to "China" itself.

In fact, apart from a set of Chinese transliterations of the Sanskrit term *Cīna*, which were used in specifically Buddhist contexts, a version of this term (and, by extension, of the character Qin 秦, from which it appears to be derived) did not reemerge as a name for China *in Chinese* until the early twentieth century. The term in question was *Zhina* (支那), which had been one of several Chinese transliterations of the Sanskrit term *Cīna* चीन, but in this case it was being reintroduced into China as a translingual borrowing from the Japanese term *Shina* (支那), which had been adopted as a name for China in the late Edo period (as a result of a process by which the Japanese used an existing binome to transliterate the contemporary Western-language name for *China*). Both the early twentieth-century term *Zhina* (支那) and the early twenty-first-century term *Chai-na* (拆那), accordingly, may be seen as examples of a belated and mediated reentry into Chinese of a proper name (Qin 秦) that originated from the first unified Chinese dynasty more than 2,000 years ago. In other words, a term that originally meant (something akin to) "China" in Chinese, was transliterated from Chinese into early alphabetic scripts in Greek, Roman, and Sanskrit texts, and was eventually re-transliterated back into Chinese using characters completely unrelated to the original one. One important difference between *Zhina* and *Chai-na*, however, is that whereas *Zhina* quickly fell into disfavor among Chinese after the second Sino-Japanese War (because it was perceived as carrying connotations of Japanese prejudicial attitudes toward China), *Chai-na*, by contrast, has been embraced within China, where it is often treated as an ironic commentary on the nation's overheated urbanization.

To the extent that the contemporary neologism *Chai-na* (like *Zhina* before it) uses a transliteration of a foreign word to refer to China, it emblematizes a tension that has haunted the Chinese writing system from its earliest (imagined) origins. A popular legend about the origins of Chinese writing—as recounted, for instance, in the postface to one of China's earliest dictionaries, the *Shuowen jiezi* [Explanation of simple and compound graphs], composed by Xu Shen around 100 CE—holds that abstract "patterns on the plumage of birds and the pelts of animals," together with "tracks left by the feet of birds and animals," provided the inspiration for both the divinatory hexagrams found in the *Book of Changes*, as well as the Chinese writing system itself. The implication, accordingly, is that linguistic meaning was grafted onto a non-linguistic graphic system, thereby positioning the birth of the Chinese writing system within a process of translation from meaninglessness into meaning.

In the *Shuowen jiezi* passage, the same character, *wen* 文, is used to refer both to actual Chinese characters as well as to the abstract patterns on bird plumage and animal pelts that helped inspire them.² Although it is now conventional to use the homophonous variant *wen* 紋 to refer to non-linguistic patterns, this graphic distinction is merely a retrospect attribution, and originally the same character, 文, was used to refer to writing, non-textual markings, as well as the process of differentiating between the two. The irony, accordingly, is that at the heart of this influential legend about the origins of the Chinese writing system *as a semiotic system that seeks to differentiate human communication from patterns produced by nature*, we find a site of linguistic indeterminacy where the same character can be used to refer both to human writing as well as to its precise opposite. There is a similar tension in the neologism *Chai-na*, in that as a homonym for *China* it functions to distinguish China from its conceptual opposite (non-China), even as the term itself relies on that same conceptual opposite (non-Chinese terms for China) for its very meaning. Moreover, while China's locus of identity is often believed to be anchored in the transhistorical continuity and stability of the Chinese written script, the neologism *Chai-na* underscores the script's inherent instability and fungibility. Accordingly, the translingual origins of the term *Chai-na* capture in miniature a broader process whereby Chinese characters have been repeatedly transliterated and transformed, even as elements from foreign languages have been repeatedly transliterated back into the Chinese script itself.

Therefore, to say that the neologism *Chai-na* is a catachresis is correct, but only to the extent that the Chinese language—and, indeed, *all* language—is a product of a set of catachrestic processes wherein the language is constantly changing and adapting, and non-meaning is constantly being translated into new forms of linguistic expression.

---

2. For a more detailed discussion of this point, see Carlos Rojas, "Humanity at the Interstices of Language and Translation," *Chinese Literature Today* 2, no. 2 (2012): 62–67.

15
Sinotopias

Andrea Bachner

The rise of Sinophone studies has been accompanied by a flood of neologisms. Is this phenomenon just a fad? Just proof of an exaggerated bid for newness or some theoretical sheen that allows us to brush up the image and standing of our discipline in the field of the humanities at large? Perhaps, not all of these terms are doing equally interesting work. But there is, after all, a power to naming. And there is also, I would claim, a power in the proliferation of names. In fact, the sheer multiplicity of terms could be interpreted as the sign of a certain unease with the boundaries, definitions, and terminologies of the discipline that I will still call—for now—Chinese studies. The recent flock of terms would thus mark a creative line of flight from the disciplinary status quo, an invitation to rethink the ways in which our discipline works and indeed to renegotiate our definition of the field.

But if we take these terminological interventions seriously, they lead us to conceptual questions in and beyond the field of Chinese and Sinophone studies. No matter whether these new terms follow and elaborate upon the term "Sinophone," such as "Sinophonics" or "Sinophonia" or switch from "phone" to "graph," such as "Sinographies" or "Sinographia," "Sino-" remains their signature component. Even in coinages that pun through homophony, such as Rey Chow's "xenophone" or my own "si(g)nology," nothing can rid us of the redounding echo of "Sino-" even as we discover its avatars in new graphic shapes and endow them with new meanings. The term around which critical approaches to the paradigm of the "Sinophone" rally in this volume, "Sinoglossia"—originally Chien-hsin Tsai's felicitous invention—is no exception. Its second component, "glossia," gives body to the matter of language (from "glotta," "language" but also "tongue") as well as pointing to a critical meta-level, a way of reflecting on and constructing, or indeed, glossing, its companion, "Sino-". Meanwhile, the term's purported claim to openness, flexibility, or hybridity in and beyond the confines of that which pertains to "China" (of the Sino-proper or as Sino-property) is staked almost entirely on its resonance with Mikhail Bakhtin's term "heteroglossia." But it remains unclear whether the terminological assonance at play infuses "Sino-" with critical energy or reterritorializes "hetero-" by repositioning it in a specific cultural and linguistic context. In spite of all our critical efforts, maybe "Sino-" still marks a stubborn remainder of territorial boundaries and ethnic identity politics. Maybe it is still a reminder also of fantasies of the other—"Sino-" in its Latinate form (from Latin "Sinae," Greek "Sinai," possibly Arabic "Sin") is, after all, derived from terms coined by non-Chinese cultures even though it might have originated from "Qin." More simply put, what is the valence of "Sino-"? And what are the conceptual, political, and disciplinary stakes of remaining attached to "Sino-" even as we attempt to contest the violence of concepts based on national, ethnic, and cultural identity?

Shu-mei Shi's notion of the "Sinophone" (while she did not invent the term, she gave it its current critical thrust) is meant to evade the ethnocentric construction of Chineseness in two interrelated moves. Firstly, the term "Sinophone" updates Chinese studies by contesting its Han-centric perspective. In other words, its "Sino-" component marks a difference between an ethnic denominator with its rigidly policed identity politics and a hybrid constellation of cultural and linguistic Chineseness. Secondly, Shih uses the term as an intervention in diaspora studies. To contest models that imagine Chinese culture as circles of weakening cultural authenticity arranged around a center or origin, Shih insists on an expiration date of diasporic cultures.[1] If we combine these two movements, "Sino-" (in its combination with "phone") has the power to destabilize ethnocentric and nationalistic models of Chineseness precisely because it includes, in some cases even warrants, its own disappearance. As Sino-articulations circulate globally, they might lose the very label of "Sino-."

In fact, many "Sinophone" articulations fit the category "Sino-" only precariously. Some of them might not feature Chinese language material (either orally or graphically) at all; and to call them "Chinese" or "Sinophone" merely highlights the problematic practice of determining the cultural belonging of an aesthetic object by the creator's ethnic look or passport or else by its context or place of production—"made in China" or in spaces read as Chinese. "Sino-" there becomes a topos, a common place. But Shih's emphasis on the temporal boundedness of "Sino-" (and "Sinophone") marks an escape route also from insistently lingering Sino-topoi like authorial ethnic profiling or the tendency to equate place (of production) with cultural identity. Instead, because they sport remnants of Sino-identity politics, in the form of conventional attachments or labels, her examples show the precariousness of just such practices of naming and

---

1. An example of such an approach to the Chinese diaspora is Tu Weiming, ed. *The Living Tree: The Changing Meaning of Being Chinese* (Stanford, CA: Stanford University Press, 1994).

defining. Their Chineseness exists under erasure—in evidence precisely because it has been consigned to negation and disappearance.² "Sino-" there exists in the twilight zone of what will have been lost, or rather, sloughed off—after all, this is not a loss to be mourned but a horizon of new possible attachments and alliances gained. Nevertheless, even as a category under erasure, "Sino-" persists. This paradox is common to conceptual movements that destabilize naturalized categories: in every deconstruction of "Sino-" there lurks a tiny reaffirmation of "Sino-"—albeit only in the form of a construction, by marking "Sino-" as a strategically constructed category that is subject to being constructed differently. As long as we do not cease to reactivate "Sino-" in this critical way, we can keep its essentializing thrust at bay. And yet, we can never entirely rely on the resistant power of terms that sport the component "Sino-". Instead, we have to work constantly at imbuing them with the energy to disrupt identity politics and conceptual violence. Thus, we will neither fall prey to turning Sinophone, or indeed, Sinoglossic, approaches into Sino-topoi (naturalized commonplaces of Chineseness) nor indulging in Sino-topia (the tendency to infuse terms such as "Sinophone" or "Sinoglossia" with utopian desires).

The productive, spectral glimmering that Shih's work proposes, however, is not the only avatar of "Sino-" in Sinophone studies. As a discipline,

> Sinophone studies disrupts the chain of equivalence established, since the rise of nation-states, among language, culture, ethnicity, and nationality and explores the protean, kaleidoscopic, creative, and overlapping margins of China and Chineseness, America and Americanness, Malaysia and Malaysianness, Taiwan and Taiwanness, and so on, by a consideration of specific, local Sinophone texts, cultures, and practices produced in and from these margins.³

But this conceptual intervention, this disruption of essentializing concatenations comes from a specific place or *topos*. The political and cultural resistance embodied in the term "Sinophone" remains tied to the flexibility, even instability, of its very definition, or, more radically, to the possibility of its own expiration date. As such, it is based on its links to specific temporal and spatial contexts. And these need an overarching category, even if only in the form of a label under which we group a diverse array of individual scenarios. As an approach that insists on "difficulty, difference, and heterogeneity" and "frustrates easy suturing," Sinophone

---

2. Here, I use the Derridean notion of "under erasure" ("sous rature," originally Heidegger's term "Durchkreuzung") to think through critical uses of the category "Sino-". Inspired by Heidegger, Derrida uses the notion to destabilize "being." See Jacques Derrida, *La dissémination* (Paris: Seuil, 1972); Jacques Derrida, *Dissemination*, trans. Barbara Johnson (Chicago: University of Chicago Press, 1981).
3. Shu-mei Shih, "The Concept of the Sinophone," *PMLA* 127, no. 3 (May 2011): 709–718, quotation at 710–711.

studies cannot divest itself of the component "Sino-."[4] To destabilize the calcified identity politics of Han- and Sinocentrism means to revisit their commonplaces (topoi) but also to inhabit their space and place (topos), albeit differently.

The assertion that Sinophone studies is a Sino-topos, in that it is tied to particular linguistic and cultural categories, is itself a commonplace. One that warrants further analysis like so many other commonplaces, since they tend to naturalize connections and occlude the fact that they are wired in a certain way for a reason. Sinophone studies is a field of inquiry defined by a specific set of objects. But unlike area studies, Sinophone studies claims to be a method, a specific type of inquiry. What is the relationship between content and method? Is this method circumscribed by its content in that it can only apply to a certain set of objects but not to others? Or have specific objects forged a methodology that can be translated to other objects? Can Sinophone studies apply there where only part of the material is Sinophone, or, even more radically, in cases in which no Sinophone material is under analysis? The question of a Sinophone methodology pertains to a second-order problem with "Sino-." This is no longer a problem concerning the definition of "Sino-," of the potentially problematic inclusionary politics and essentializing force of this label. Rather, it is one of the conceptual limitations attached to an approach that situates itself in a specific cultural context (in this case via its objects of study).

But is this a problem with "Sino-" (and Sinophone) per se, or a problem with academic practices and assumptions instead? Certainly the latter. After all, the politics of exemplarity differ widely depending on cultural situatedness. Whereas Euro-American case studies often make for universal exemplars—examples that are proffered with a view to generalization—non-Euro-American examples only illustrate the discreteness of their own cultural context. This difference is so deeply ingrained that a direct critique seems of little or no avail. In fact, it seems to persist stubbornly in academic practice even though intellectual thought has repeatedly censured it. The current proliferation of approaches of the type "x as method" or "x (作)為方法" is a symptom of this problem as well as an attempt at circumventing the Euro-American monopoly of methodology. Usually, the "x" in "x as method" is something outside of Europe or the US, for instance, Asia, China, or Hong Kong, or in slightly different formulations, Taiwan or the Sinophone.[5] These approaches are reactions against Western-centrism,

---

4. Shu-mei Shih, *Visuality and Identity: Sinophone Articulations Across the Pacific* (Berkeley: University of California Press, 20017), 5.
5. See Chen Kuan-hsing, *Asia as Method: Toward Deimperialization* (Durham, NC: Duke University Press, 2010), inspired by Yuzo Mizoguchi's 溝口雄三 *China as Method* (方法としての中国). For "Hong Kong as method," see the description of a conference at the University of Hong Kong in 2014, https://www.smlc.hku.hk/news/detail.php?id=571. For an approach close to "Taiwan as method," see Shu-mei Shih and Ping-hui Liao, eds., *Comparatizing Taiwan* (London: Routledge,

especially of a US-style area studies for which the West provides theories and methodologies for the study of the rest—which means, of course, that the rest is being relegated to the realm of mere objects. The "x-as-method" paradigm usually attempts to counter such unequal distributions of theories and objects by taking what was formerly described as mere objects and turning them into the basis for a methodology. This means, however, to tie theoretical thought to a specific set of phenomena, to assign it a particular place. The challenge here is to reformulate the link between the particular and the universal; as Pheng Cheah states, "neither to denigrate the universal nor to claim an alternative and usually antagonistic modularity, but for Asian studies [or Chinese or Sinophone studies] to claim that their subject is a part of the universal, not just a check to a preformulated universal, but as something that actively shares in and partakes of the universal in a specific way."[6]

Different challenges come to the fore here. The problem lies not with the link between the specific and the general per se, nor with the presupposition that located particulars can become the ground for a more generally valid theoretical thought. In fact, this is precisely the case with all methodologies or theories, that they spring from specific phenomena and emerge in specific contexts and from specific positionalities. And yet, in most cases, this very link is being forgotten or strategically erased, mostly on the basis of the assumption that singularities of one type of culture—Western culture—are representatives of the norm rather than contingent and culturally specific expressions only. When we claim the status of method or of grounds for a method for non-Western phenomena, however, we cannot put the "x" of method under erasure in the same way. By contrast, nobody needs to posit something like "the West as method," since it is always already presupposed that the unnamed "x" in method is the West to begin with. This twisted logic lies at the heart of our challenge.

Let us bracket for a moment the very crucial differences in the various recent "x-as-method" constructions—the problems of power differentials (for example, China versus Taiwan), of perspective (China as method from a Japanese vantage point versus Hong Kong as method from a Hong Kong perspective) or definition (Asia as method involves the ideological baggage of a Western definition of Asia).[7] Let us assume that we are looking at something like "Sinophone as method." What is the "as" or, not completely equivalent, "（作）為" in this

---

2015). "Sinophone as method" is implied in most of Shih's writings on the Sinophone. For a reflection on this paradigm, see also Carlos Rojas, "Method as Method," *Prism* 16, no. 2 (2019): 211–220.
6. Pheng Cheah, "Universal Areas: Asian Studies in a World in Motion," in *Postcolonial and the Global*, ed. Revathi Krishnaswamy and John C. Hawley (Minneapolis: University of Minnesota Press, 2007), 54–68, quotation at 62.
7. For a critique of the Western construction of "Asia," see Gayatri Chakravorty Spivak, *Other Asias* (Malden, MA: Blackwell, 2008), 208–214.

constellation? What does this structure imply—one a potential, strategic analogy or likeness (taking something as something else), one a slightly more active equation, making something into something? How can we extend the impact of a Sinophone-studies approach, so that it does not remain circumscribed by pertaining only to phenomena understood as related to the Sinosphere (however protean in shape)? And how can we maintain its critical potential that is tied to its positionality? Or, in other words: How can we think the Sinophone beyond the Sinophone—as method that can be potentially detached from its content—while at the same time keeping the Sinophone in Sinophone actively at work?

In order to move beyond its focus on content—Sinophone studies understood as concerned with Sinophone phenomena—and to develop it into a methodology beyond the cultural and linguistic purview of its subjects, we have to rethink its relationship with other disciplines in the humanities and beyond. This implies taking up the challenges that a comparative methodology poses to Sinophone studies, as well as to acknowledge the provocations that Sinophone studies approaches can posit for an ethically responsible way of intercultural work. Here are two ways in which Sinophone studies takes up the challenges of comparison:

1. Sinophone Studies Helps Us Rethink Center-Margin Dichotomies as a Multiply Shifting, Scalar Constellation

The very strife about the definition of what counts as Sinophone embodies the quandary about centers and margins in a way that is integral to this critical approach. Does the Sinophone encompass all works in one of the many Chinese languages, or does it only designate articulations that are off-center vis-à-vis a Sino- or Han-centric tradition? The first approach, while inclusive, also threatens to default to using the term "Sinophone" as just another equivalent of "Chinese-language" works, unless we incessantly reactivate its critical potential. The second approach, however, threatens to exclude what has traditionally been perceived as the center, thus potentially blocking the possibility of critically unworking the center from within the center. If we want to keep the productivity of a Sinophone approach alive, we need not resolve this definitional quandary. In fact, both approaches are in a symbiotic relationship because one constantly needs the other's frictional energy for its critical thrust.[8] Before Sinophone studies work can begin, it has to come to terms with the question of centers and margins and to do so flexibly, critically, and always anew. It has to scrutinize its own distinction of centers and margins constantly and can never settle down into certainty about its

---

8. For a reflection on different definitions of the boundaries of the "Sinophone," see David Der-wei Wang's "Sinophone States of Exception" in this volume.

own definition of what counts as Sinophone and what does not. Sinophone work can both decenter and recenter, even as works in Chinese languages can be both central and marginal, depending on the perspective we espouse.

2. Sinophone Studies Allows Us to Recuperate Mediality as a Lens for Comparison and Intercultural Work

Coined in analogy to terms such as "Anglophone" and "Francophone," the term "Sinophone" does not normally function as a mere indicator of language. While we could (and maybe should) read "Anglophone" and "Francophone" as labels designating all works written in a specific language, either English or French, the uses of these terms are in fact much more specific as well as problematic. Usually, these denominations exclude works (in English or French) produced at the cultural centers that are also colonial or neocolonial centers of power. The terms "Anglophone" or "Francophone" encompass only the margins of postcolonial structures, whereas the term "Sinophone" constantly sparks debates about its inclusivity or exclusivity. The analogy between "Anglophone" etc. and "Sinophone," however, works only precariously for another reason. More importantly, "Sinophone" as a linguistic marker, pertaining to script traditions that are not based on phonetic but on logographic writing systems, implies a question of mediality. To take the medium of literary expression seriously—for instance speech versus writing, alphabetic versus non-alphabetic scripts—allows for a different perspective on interculturality. Rather than confining our analyses to texts that we define as Sinophone, a Sinophone approach can allow us to scrutinize different media politics across cultures.

These two sets of insights—derived from quandaries that lie at the heart of Sinophone work—are only two examples of the ways in which the paradigm of the Sinophone can contribute to transcultural reflections also beyond its purview and comfort zone. Rather than curtailing critical work (for instance, by insisting on exclusively Sinophone objects as grounds of analysis, however inclusively or flexibly we might want to construe them), Sinophone studies can challenge and enrich cultural comparison when we recuperate its conceptual contributions and provocations. This implies, however, that the term "Sinophone" as a conceptual, methodological impulse might well have an end date. For it to have an impact on the ways in which we think transculturally, for it to help us map global circulations and cross-cultural comparisons in politically responsible ways, it will have to leave behind its culturally and linguistically specific references.

This does not mean that a comparative Sinophone methodology will eventually become like Euro- or Western-centric paradigms that have dominated comparative thinking—in the form of unthinking universalization, while maintaining a limited and limiting perspective based on an extrapolation of culturally specific values and interests. In fact, the culturally and interculturally specific position that is the inception point of Sinophone studies matters as a reminder that a radically global thought can only start from a specific point, marked by a specific positionality. It does mean, however, that the tether between content and methodology has to be loosened eventually. Otherwise, Sinophone will simply remain confined to its cultural and regional ghettos. Instead, insights gained thanks to Sinophone-specific objects and the concomitant methodological advances will have to be translated onto other cultural and linguistic phenomena, so that the term "Sinophone" will merely resonate as the superseded place where some conceptual and methodological insights started.

And yet, such an end date of the Sinophone might also be only temporary. After all, as Sinophone phenomena, work with them, and our understanding of what this means undergo constant changes, new methodological impulses will continue to radiate outward from one cultural specificity to other culturally and interculturally specific scenarios and structures. Since the problem of a Sinophone theory and methodology beyond Sinophone material is that of a productive linking and delinking of content and method, it also harbors more general insights—especially if we replace "Sino-" or "Sinophone" with other cultural, regional, ethnic, or linguistic markers, that we have to keep the link between "Sinophone" and "method"—the "as" or "為"—critically open. In the same way, the relation between "Sino-" and its cultural and conceptual contexts, its topoi, has to remain flexible, subject to de- and reconstruction. As long as we do not take these connections for granted but continue to put pressure on these nexus, as well as on our constructions of the specific and the general, Sino-work can radiate outward in productive ways beyond the narrow confines of area studies or identity politics. This volume and its titular neologism of "Sinoglossia" take first steps in this direction, showing ways of engaging with Sinotopias in the plural instead of reiterating Sino-topoi or Sino-topia.

Bibliography

1Malaysia. http://www.1malaysia.com.my/en.
Adorno, Theodor W. *Beethoven: The Philosophy of Music*. London: Polity, 1998.
Agamben, Giorgio. *The State of Exception*. Translated by Kevin Attell. Chicago: University of Chicago Press, 2005.
Anderson, Kay, Ien Ang, Andrea Del Bono, Donald McNeill, and Alexandra Wong. *Chinatown Unbound: Trans-Asian Urbanism in the Age of China*. London: Rowman & Littlefield, 2019.
Ang, Ien. "Can One Say No to Chineseness? Pushing the Limits of the Diasporic Paradigm." *boundary 2: International Journal of Literature and Culture* 25, no. 3 (1998): 223–242.
Ang, Ien. "Chinatowns and the Rise of China." *Modern Asian Studies* 54, no. 4 (2020): 1367–1393.
Ang, Ien. "No Longer Chinese? Residual Chineseness after the Rise of China." In *Diasporic Chineseness after the Rise of China: Community, Culture and Communication*, edited by Julia Kuehn, Kam Louie, and David Pomfret, 17–31. Vancouver: University of British Columbia Press, 2013.
Ang, Ien. *On Not Speaking Chinese. Living Between Asia and the West*. London: Routledge, 2001.
Ang, Ien. "On the Perils of Racialized Chineseness: Race, Nation and Entangled Racisms in China and South Asia." *Ethnic and Racial Studies* 45, no. 4 (2022): 757–777.
Appleton, Vivia B. *A Doctor's Letters from China Fifty Years Ago*. Honolulu [publisher not identified], 1976.
Apter, Emily. *Against World Literature: On the Politics of Untranslatability*. London: Verso, 2013.
Asad, Talal. "The Concept of Cultural Translation in British Social Anthropology." In *Writing Culture: The Poetics and Politics of Ethnography*, edited by J. Clifford and G. E. Marcus, 141–164. Berkeley: University of California Press, 1986.
Asad, Talal, and John Dixon. "Translating Europe's Others." In *Europe and Its Others: Proceedings of the Essex Conference on the Sociology of Literature* (July 1984), edited by Francis Barker et al., vol. 1, 170–193. Colchester, UK: University of Essex Press, 1985.
Babaran, Melinda M. "Kapirasong Papel" [A piece of paper]. *Independent Opinion@CommonWealth*, September 26, 2019. https://opinion.cw.com.tw/blog/profile/441/article/8539.

Babaran, Melinda M. "Latay sa Laman" [Whip scar on the flesh]. *Independent Opinion@CommonWealth*, October 22, 2018. https://opinion.cw.com.tw/blog/profile/441/article/7394.

Bachner, Andrea. *Beyond Sinology: Chinese Writing and the Scripts of Culture*. New York: Columbia University Press, 2013.

Bai, Limin. *Shaping the Ideal Child: Children and Their Primers in Late Imperial China*. Hong Kong: Chinese University Press, 2005.

Banham, Martin. *The Cambridge Guide to Theatre*. Cambridge: Cambridge University Press, 2000.

Bao, Qicheng 包起成. "*Lushan lian* waijing paishe diandi" 《廬山戀》外景拍攝點滴 [Shooting on location *Romance on Lushan Mountain*, bit by bit]. *Dianying pinglun* 電影評論 (May 1980): 14.

Bao, Qicheng 包起成. "Renzao yunwu he dongyong—*Lushan lian* shezhi shiling" 人造雲霧和冬泳——《廬山戀》攝製拾零 [Artificial fog and winter swimming—tidbits on the production of *Love on Lushan*]. *Dazhong dianying* 大眾電影 (June 1980): 26.

Bao, Weihong. *Fiery Cinema: The Emergence of an Affective Medium in China, 1915–1945*. Minneapolis: University of Minnesota Press, 2015.

Barlow, Tani, and Gary J. Bjorge, eds. *I Myself Am a Woman: Selected Writings of Ding Ling*. Boston, MA: Beacon Press, 1989.

Barnard, Timothy P., ed. *Contesting Malayness: Malay Identity Across Boundaries*. Singapore: National University Press, 2004.

Berry, Chris. *Postsocialist Cinema in Post-Mao China: The Cultural Revolution after the Cultural Revolution*. London: Routledge, 2008.

Berry, Chris, and Mary Farquhar. *China on Screen: Cinema and Nation*. New York: Columbia University Press, 2006.

Bhabha, Homi. *The Location of Culture*. New York: Routledge, 1994.

Boltz, William. "Literacy and the Emergence of Writing in China." *Writing and Literacy in Early China: Studies from the Columbia Early China Seminar*. Edited by Li Feng and David Branner. Seattle: University of Washington Press, 2011.

Braester, Yomi. *Witness against History: Literature, Film, and Public Discourse in Twentieth-Century China*. Stanford, CA: Stanford University Press, 2003.

Brah, Avtar. *Cartographies of Diaspora: Contesting Identities*. London: Routledge, 1996.

Bray, Francesca. *Technology and Gender: Fabrics of Power in Late Imperial China*. Berkeley: University of California Press, 1997.

Bu, Liping. "Cultural Communication in Picturing Health: W. W. Peter and Public Health Campaigns in China, 1912–1926." In *Imagining Illness: Public Health and Visual Culture*, edited by David Serlin, 24–39. Minneapolis: University of Minnesota Press, 2010.

Bu, Liping. "Public Health and Modernization: The First Campaigns in China, 1915–1916." *Social History of Medicine* 22, no. 2 (2009): 306–307.

Byrnes, Corey. *Fixing Landscape. A Techno-Poetic History of China's Three Gorges*. New York: Columbia University Press, 2018.

Cadbury, W. W. "Height, Weight, and Chest Measurements of the Chinese." *National Medical Journal of China* 8 (1922): 158.

Chang, Carsun. *The Development of Neo-Confucian Thought.* New Haven, CT: College and University Press, 1963.

Chang, Cheng 張正. "Cong rechaotan dao bowuguan de yimingong wenxuejiang" 從熱炒攤到博物館的移民工文學獎 [From a stir-fry vendor to the museum: The migrant literature award]. In *Liu: Yidong de shengmingli, langchaozhong de Taiwan / diyierjie yimingong wenxuejiang zuopinji* 流──移動的生命力，浪潮中的臺灣／第一、二屆移民工文學獎得獎作品集 [Flow: Story collection from the 2014 and 2015 Taiwan literature award for migrants], coauthored by Southeast Asian migrants, 288–296. New Taipei City: Four Way Publishing, 2015.

Chang, Cheng 張正. "Tan yimingong wenxuejiang: 'zheyoubushi you duoda lirun de gongzuo, ji meiyoulirun, jiuyao zuochu yiyi'" 談移民工文學獎：「這又不是有多大利潤的工作，既沒有利潤，就要做出意義」 [On the migrant literature award: "This isn't a job with much profit, and it has to be meaningful if it does not make money"]. *The News Lens*, September 16, 2016. https://www.thenewslens.com/article/48964/fullpage.

Chang, Cheng 張正. "Yige wenxuejiang de shengyusi: gaobie yimingong wenxuejiang" 一個文學獎的生與死：告別移民工文學獎 [Life and death of a literary award: Farewell to the Taiwan literature award for migrants]. *Independent Opinion@CommonWealth*, October 28, 2020. https://opinion.cw.com.tw/blog/profile/91/article/10068.

Chang, Cheng 張正, and Yun-chang Liao 廖雲章. "Song of Exile, Four-Way Voice: The Blood-and-Sweat Writings of Southeast Asian Migrants in Taiwan." In *The Oxford Handbook of Modern Chinese Literatures*, edited by Carlos Rojas and Andrea Bachner, 440–454. New York: Oxford University Press, 2016.

Chang, Eileen 張愛玲. "Bawo baokuo zaiwai" 把我包括在外 [Include me out]. In *Wangranji: Zhang Ailing sanwenji II* 枉然記：張愛玲散文集II [Failed expectations: Eileen Chang II]. Taipei: Huangguan, 2010.

Chang, Eileen 張愛玲. *Zhang Ailing diancang quanji* 張愛玲典藏全集 [Complete works of Eileen Chang]. Taipei: Huangguan, 2001.

Chang, Eileen 張愛玲 [Zhang Ailing], Song Qi, and Song Kuang Wenmei. *Zhang Ailing siyu lu* 張愛玲私語錄 [Private correspondences with Eileen Chang]. Edited by Song Yilang 宋以朗. Taipei: Huangguan, 2001.

Chang, Mau-kuei 張茂桂. "Ai, jiu yu fengkuang: wode duhougan" 愛、疚與瘋狂：我的讀後感 [Love, guilt, and craziness: My reflection after reading]. In *Guang: Yi linghun yelian wenzi, zai anchu faliang / disijie yimingong wenxuejiang zuopinji* 光──以靈魂冶煉文字，在暗處發亮／第四屆移民工文學獎作品集 [Light: Story collection from the 2017 Taiwan literature award for migrants], coauthored by Southeast Asian migrants, 11–15. New Taipei City: Four Way Publishing, 2017.

Cheah, Pheng. "Universal Areas: Asian Studies in a World in Motion." In *Postcolonial and the Global*. Edited by Revathi Krishnaswamy and John C. Hawley. Minneapolis: University of Minnesota Press, 2007.

Cheah, Pheng. *What Is a World: On Postcolonial Literature as World Literature*. Durham, NC: Duke University Press, 2016.

Chen, C. T. 沈家楨. *Shen Jiazhen jushi yanjiang ji* 沈家楨居士演講集 [Collection of lectures by C. T. Chen]. New Taipei City: Dharma Drum Institute of Liberal Arts, 2017.

Chen, Fang-ming 陳芳明. "Taiwan neibu de dongnanya" 台灣內部的東南亞 [Southeast Asia within Taiwan]. In *Liu: Yidong de shengmingli, langchaozhong de Taiwan / diyierjie yimingong wenxuejiang zuopinji* 流——移動的生命力，浪潮中的臺灣／第一、二屆移民工文學獎得獎作品集 [Flow: Story collection from the 2014 and 2015 Taiwan literature award for migrants], coauthored by Southeast Asian migrants, 6–8. New Taipei City: Four Way Publishing, 2015.

Chen, Kuan-hsing. *Asia as Method: Toward Deimperialization*. Durham, NC: Duke University Press, 2010.

Chen, Lingchei Letty. "When Does 'Diaspora' End and 'Sinophone' Begin?" *Postcolonial Studies* 18, no. 1 (2015): 52–66.

Chen, Qiying 陳其英. "Lushan mianmu xin renshi" 廬山面目新認識 [Knowing Lushan anew]. *Lüxing zazhi* 旅行雜誌 (July 1947): 43.

Chen, Siao-yun. "Redefining 'We/Us': The Dialogic Space and the Historical Process of Migrant Workers in *Our Stories: Migration and Labor in Taiwan*." *Modern Chinese Literature* 32, no. 12 (2017): 59–74.

Chen, Zheng 陳政, ed. *Lushan lao xiangce, 1895–1987* 廬山老相冊, 1895–1987 [Old photos of Lushan, 1895–1987], Vol. 2. Nanchang: Jiangxi meishu chubanshe, 2003.

Chiang, Howard. *After Eunuchs: Science, Medicine, and the Transformation of Sex in Modern China*. New York: Columbia University Press, 2018.

Chiang, Howard. "Contested Minds Across Time: Perspectives from Chinese History and Culture." *Integrative Psychological and Behavioral Science* 56, no. 2 (2022): 420–425.

Chiang, Howard. "Sinoglossia Incarnate: The Entanglements of Castration across the Pacific." In *East Asian Men: Masculinity, Sexuality and Desire*, edited by Xiaodong Lin, Chris Haywood, and Mairtin Mac an Ghaill, 85–105. London: Palgrave Macmillan, 2017.

Chiang, Howard. "Translators of the Soul: Bingham Dai, Pow-Meng Yap, and the Making of Transcultural Psychoanalysis in the Asia Pacific." *Psychoanalysis and History* 23, no. 2 (2021): 161–185.

Chiang, Howard. *Transtopia in the Sinophone Pacific*. New York: Columbia University Press, 2021.

Chiang, Howard, and Yin Wang, eds. *Perverse Taiwan*. London: Routledge, 2016.

Chiang, Ted. "Bad Character." *The New Yorker*. May 16, 2016, https://www.newyorker.com/magazine/2016/05/16/if-chinese-were-phonetic.

Chiang, Ted. "Story of Your Life." In *Stories of Your Life and Others*. New York: Vintage, 2016.

Chiang, Wan-chi 江婉琦. "Chuxian gengduo qiansuoweiyou de ticai" 出現更多前所未有的題材 [Many new themes have emerged]. In *Guang: Yi linghun yelian wenzi, zai anchu faliang / disijie yimingong wenxuejiang zuopinji* 光——以靈魂冶煉文字，在暗處發亮／第四屆移民工文學獎作品集 [Light: Story collection from the 2017 Taiwan literature award for migrants], coauthored by Southeast Asian migrants, 24–25. New Taipei City: Four Way Publishing, 2017.

Chion, Michel. *Guide to Sound Objects*. Translated by John Dack and Christine North. London: Monoskop, 2009.

Chion, Michel. "The Three Listening Modes." In *Audio-Vision: Sound on Screen*. New York: Columbia University Press, 1994.

Chion, Michel. *Words on Screen*. Edited and translated by Claudia Gorbman. New York: Columbia University Press, 2017.
Chiu, Kuei-fen 邱貴芬. "Fanyi qudongli xia de Taiwan wenxue shengchan" 翻譯驅動力下的台灣文學生產 [Taiwanese literary production driven by translation]. In *Taiwan xiaoshuo shi lun* 台灣小說史論 [Taiwan literary history], edited by Hu Jin-lun 胡金倫, 197–273. Taipei: Rye Field Publishing, 2007.
Chow, Rey. "A Phantom Discipline," *PMLA* 116, no. 5 (Oct. 2001): 1386–1395.
Chua, Beng Huat. "Pop Culture China." *Singapore Journal of Tropical Geography* 22, no. 2 (2001): 113–121.
Chua, Beng Huat. *Structure, Audience and Soft Power in East Asian Pop Culture*. Hong Kong: Hong Kong University Press, 2012.
Chung, Ming-der 鍾明德. *Taiwan xiaojutuan yundongshi 1980–89: Xunzhao linglei meixue yu zhengzhi* 台灣小劇團運動史1980–89：尋找另類美學與政治 [The little theater movement of Taiwan (1980–89): In search of alternative aesthetics and politics]. Taipei: Yang-Chih Book Co., 1999.
Cipta, Erin. "Guanyu zuozhe" 關於作者 [Author's note]. In *Liu: Yidong de shengmingli, langchaozhong de Taiwan / diyierjie yimingong wenxuejiang zuopinji* 流──移動的生命力，浪潮中的臺灣／第一、二屆移民工文學獎得獎作品集 [Flow: Story collection from the 2014 and 2015 Taiwan literature award for migrants], coauthored by Southeast Asian migrants, 77. New Taipei City: Four Way Publishing, 2015.
Cipta, Erin. "Kisah Ye Feng Dan Carlos" [The story of Ye Feng and Carlos]. In *Liu: Yidong de shengmingli, langchaozhong de TAIWAN / diyierjie yimingong wenxuejiang zuopinji* 流──移動的生命力，浪潮中的臺灣／第一、二屆移民工文學獎得獎作品集 [Flow: Story collection from the 2014 and 2015 Taiwan literature award for migrants], coauthored by Southeast Asian migrants, 70–87. New Taipei City: Four Way Publishing, 2015.
Cipta, Erin. "Lelaki Pemberani Di Jiangzicui" [The hero of Jiangzicui]. In *Liu: Yidong de shengmingli, langchaozhong de Taiwan / diyierjie yimingong wenxuejiang zuopinji* 流──移動的生命力，浪潮中的臺灣／第一、二屆移民工文學獎得獎作品集 [Flow: Story collection from the 2014 and 2015 Taiwan literature award for migrants], coauthored by Southeast Asian migrants, 214–234. New Taipei City: Four Way Publishing, 2015.
Clifford, James. *Routes: Travel and Translation in the Late Twentieth Century*. Cambridge, MA: Harvard University Press, 1997.
CNN Philippines Life Staff. "In Taiwan, a Filipino Factory Worker Wins Prestigious Literary Award." CNN Philippines Life, August 27, 2019. https://www.cnnphilippines.com/life/culture/literature/2019/8/27/filipino-taiwan-writer.html.
Conley, Tom. *Film Hieroglyphs (With a New Introduction)*. Minneapolis: Minnesota University Press, 1991.
Cumings, Bruce. "Boundary Displacement: Area Studies and International Studies during and after the Cold War." *Bulletin of Concerned Asian Scholars* 29, no. 1 (1997): 6–26.
Cunningham, Maura. "Shanghai's Wandering Ones: Child Welfare in a Global City, 1900–1953." PhD diss., University of California, Irvine, 2014.
Damrosch, David. "Introduction: World Literature in Theory and Practice." In *World Literature in Theory*, 1–12. Chichester, UK: Wiley Blackwell, 2014.

Dehart, Monica. "Costa Rica's Chinatown: The Art of Being Global in the Age of China." *City and Society* 27, no. 2 (2015): 183–207.
Deleuze, Gilles. *The Fold: Leibniz and the Baroque*. Translated by Tom Conley. Minneapolis: University of Minnesota Press, 1993.
Deleuze, Gilles, and Félix Guattari. *Kafka: Toward a Minor Literature*. Translated by Dana Polan. Minneapolis: University of Minnesota Press, 1986.
Deleuze, Gilles, and Félix Guattari. *A Thousand Plateaus*. Translated by Brian Massumi. Minneapolis: University of Minnesota Press, 1987.
Deleuze, Gilles, and Félix Guattari. *What Is Philosophy?* Translated by Hugh Tomlinson and Graham Burchell III. New York: Columbia University Press, 1994.
Derrida, Jacques. *Dissemination*. Translated by Barbara Johnson. Chicago: University of Chicago Press, 1981.
Derrida, Jacques. *La dissémination*. Paris: Seuil, 1972.
Derrida, Jacques. *Of Grammatology*. Translated by Gayatri Spivak. Baltimore, MD: Johns Hopkins University Press, 1998.
Ďurovičová, Nataša, and Kathleen E. Newman, eds. *World Cinemas, Transnational Perspectives*. New York: Routledge, 2010.
Dusiberre, Edward. *Beethoven for a Later Age*. Chicago: University of Chicago Press, 2016.
Elkins, James. *The Domain of Images*. Ithaca, NY: Cornell University Press, 2001.
Elman, Benjamin. *On Their Own Terms: Science in China, 1550–1900*. Cambridge, MA: Harvard University Press, 2005.
El Shakry, Omnia. *The Arabic Freud: Psychoanalysis and Islam in Modern Egypt*. Princeton, NJ: Princeton University Press, 2017.
Eom, Sujin. "Traveling Chinatowns: Mobility of Urban Forms and 'Asia' in Circulation." *positions: asia critique* 25, no. 4 (2017): 693–716.
Even-Zohar, Itamar. "The Position of Translated Literature within the Literary Polysystem." In *The Princeton Sourcebook in Comparative Literature: From the European Enlightenment to the Global Present*, edited by David Damrosch, Natalie Melas, and Mbongiseni Buthelezi, 240–247. Princeton, NJ: Princeton University Press, 2009.
Fan, Victor. *Cinema Approaching Reality: Locating Chinese Film Theory*. Minneapolis: University of Minnesota Press, 2015.
Fang, Fang 方方. *Zhongguo jilupian fazhang shi* 中國紀錄片發展史 [Historical development of the Chinese documentary]. Beijing: Xiju chubanshe, 2003.
Fang, Qing. "Lun tige jiancha zhi biyao" 論體格檢查之必要 [On the necessity for physical examinations]. *Yiyao xuebao* 醫藥學報 [*Medicine*] 3 (1914): 1.
Farquhar, Judith. *A Way of Life: Thing, Thought, Action in Chinese Medicine*. New Haven, CT: Yale University Press, 2020.
Felski, Rita. "Comparison and Translation: A Perspective from Actor-Network Theory." *Comparative Literature Studies* 53, no. 4 (2016): 747–765.
Fernsebner, Susan R. "A People's Playthings: Toys, Childhood, and Chinese Identity, 1909–1933." *Postcolonial Studies* 6, no. 3 (2003): 269–293.
Fischer, Michael. "Ethnicity and the Post-Modern Arts of Memory." In *Writing Culture: The Poetics and Politics of Ethnography*, edited by James Clifford and George Marcus, 195–233. Berkeley: University of California Press, 1986.

Fissell, Mary. "The Disappearance of the Patient's Narrative and the Invention of Hospital Medicine." In *British Medicine in an Age of Reform*, edited by Roger French and Andrew Weir, 92–109. London: Routledge, 1991.

Forrester, John. *Thinking in Cases*. Cambridge, UK: Polity, 2017.

Foucault, Michel. *The Birth of the Clinic*. Translated by A. Smith. New York: Vintage, 1975.

Foucault, Michel. *The Hermeneutics of the Subject: Lectures at the Collège de France, 1981–1982*. Edited by Frédéric Gros. Translated by Graham Burchell. New York: Picador, 2005.

Foucault, Michel. *The History of Sexuality, Vol. 1: An Introduction*. Translated by Robert Hurley. New York: Vintage, 1990.

Foucault, Michel. *The Order of Things: An Archaeology of the Human Sciences*. New York: Vintage, 1994 (1966).

Fu, Jia-Chen. "Measuring Up: Anthropometrics and the Chinese Body in Republican Period China." *Bulletin of the History of Medicine* 90 (2016): 643–671.

Fu, Yue-an 傅月庵. "Haozuopin yidu bianzhi" 好作品一讀便知 [Good storytelling is easy to see at a glance]. In *Guang: Yi linghun yelian wenzi, zai anchu faliang / disijie yimingong wenxuejiang zuopinji* 光──以靈魂冶煉文字，在暗處發亮／第四屆移民工文學獎作品集 [Light: Story collection from the 2017 Taiwan literature award for migrants], coauthored by Southeast Asian migrants, 18–19. New Taipei City: Four Way Publishing, 2017.

Furth, Charlotte. "Concepts of Pregnancy, Childbirth, and Infancy in Ch'ing Dynasty China." *Journal of Asian Studies* 46, no. 1 (1987): 7–34.

Furth, Charlotte. *A Flourishing Yin: Gender in Chinese Medical History, 950–1665*. Berkeley: University of California Press, 1999.

Furth, Charlotte. "From Birth to Birth: The Growing Body in Chinese Medicine." In *Chinese Views of Childhood*, edited by Anne Behnke Kinney, 157–191. Honolulu: University of Hawai'i Press, 1995.

Gallo, Ruben. *Freud's Mexico: Into the Wilds of Psychoanalysis*. Cambridge, MA: MIT Press, 2010.

Ge, Zhaoguang 葛兆光. *Zhaizi Zhongguo: Chongjian youguan Zhongguo de lishi lunshu* 宅茲中國：重建有關中國的歷史論述 [Here resides China: Reconstructing discourses about China]. Taipei: Linking, 2011.

Gillis, Jonathan. "The History of the Patient History since 1850." *Bulletin of the History of Medicine* 80, no. 3 (Fall 2006): 490–512.

Gilroy, Paul. *The Black Atlantic: Modernity and Double Consciousness*. London: Verso, 1993.

Gladston, Iago. "Diagnosis in Historical Perspective." *Bulletin of the History of Medicine* 9, no. 4 (April 1941): 367–384.

Godfrey-Smith, Peter. "The Mind of an Octopus." *Scientific American* (blog), January 1, 2017. https://www.scientificamerican.com/article/the-mind-of-an-octopus/.

Gong, Jow-Jun 龔卓軍. "Roushen gongxiang: Hou Chun-Ming de seqing haofei yu jianchi zhuji" 肉身共享：侯俊明的色情耗費與賤斥註記 [Sharing the flesh: Hou Chun-Ming's pornographic consumption and abject notations]. *Modern Arts* 144 (2009): 38–51.

Guattari, Félix. *Chaosmosis: An Ethico-Aesthetic Paradigm*. Translated by Paul Bains and Julian Pefanis. Bloomington: Indiana University Press, 1995.

Guattari, Félix. *The Three Ecologies*. Translated by Ian Pindar and Paul Sutton. New York: Continuum, 2000.

Gunning, Tom. "Towards a Minor Cinema: Fonoroff, Herwitz, Ahwesh, Klahr and Solomon." *Motion Picture* 3 no. 1/2 (Winter 1989–90): 2–5.

Guo, Moruo 郭沫若. "Taohuayuan li ke gengtian—Du Mao zhuxi xin fabiao de shici 'Qi Lu: Deng Lushan'" 桃花源裡可耕田──讀毛主席新發表的詩詞〈七律・登廬山〉 [Plowing in Peach Blossom Spring: Reading Chairman Mao's new poem "Climbing Lushan"]. *Renmin ribao* 人民日報, February 2, 1964.

Guo, Moruo 郭沫若. "Wuxian fengguang zai xianfeng—Du Mao zhuxi 'Qi jue: Wei Li Jin tongzhi ti suo she Lushan xianrendong zhao'" 無限風光在險峰──讀毛主席〈七絕・為李進同志題所攝廬山仙人洞照〉 [Boundless beauty among perilous peaks: Reading Chairman Mao's poem "On a Photograph of the Fairy Cave Taken by Comrade Li Jin"]. *Renmin ribao* 人民日報, April 11, 1964.

Gupta, Charu. "Vernacular Sexology from the Margins: A Woman and a Shudra." *South Asia: Journal of South Asian Studies* 43, no. 6 (2020): 1105–1127.

Hagman, George. *The Artist's Mind: A Psychoanalytic Perspective on Creativity, Modern Art, and Modern Artists*. New York: Routledge, 2010.

Hall, Stuart. "Cultural Identity and Diaspora." In *Identity: Community, Culture, Difference*, edited by Jonathan Rutherford, 222–237. London: Lawrence & Wishart, 1990.

Hall, Stuart. *Familiar Stranger. A Life Between Two Islands*. London: Allen Lane, 2017.

Hall, Stuart. *The Fateful Triangle: Race, Ethnicity, Nation*. Cambridge, MA: Harvard University Press, 2017.

Harmon, Katherine. "Octopuses Gain Consciousness." *Scientific American* (blog), August 21, 2012. https://blogs.scientificamerican.com/octopus-chronicles/octopuses-gain-consciousness-according-to-scientists-declaration/.

Harootunian, Harry. *Marx after Marx: History and Time in the Expansion of Capitalism*. New York: Columbia University Press, 2015.

Harrist, Robert E. Jr. *The Landscape of Words: Stone Inscriptions from Early and Medieval China*. Seattle: Washington University Press, 2008.

He, Wei 賀偉, ed. *Shike li de gushi* 石刻裡的故事 [Stories in stone inscriptions]. Nanchang: Jiangxi jiaoyu chubanshe, 2016.

Heidegger, Martin. *The Question Concerning Technology and Other Essays*. Translated by William Lovitt. New York: Garland Publishing, 2013.

Heinrich, Ari Larissa. *The Afterlife of Images: Translating the Pathological Body between China and the West*. Durham, NC: Duke University Press, 2008.

Heinrich, Ari Larissa. *Chinese Surplus: Biopolitical Aesthetics and the Medically Commodified Body*. Durham, NC: Duke University Press, 2018.

Herzog, Dagmar. *Cold War Freud: Psychoanalysis in an Age of Catastrophe*. Cambridge: Cambridge University Press, 2017.

"Hong Kong as Method." Conference description at the University of Hong Kong. 2014. https://www.smlc.hku.hk/news/detail.php?id=571.

Hou, Chun-Ming 侯俊明. *Shentitu fangtan chuangzuo: 2014–2017* 身體圖訪談創作：2014–2017 [Male hole: 2014–2017]. Unpublished pamphlet in Mandarin Chinese.

Hou, Chun-Ming 侯俊明. *Soushenji* 搜神記 [Anecdotes about spirits and immortals]. Taipei: China Times, 1994.

Hou, Chun-Ming 侯俊明. *Yazhouren de fuqin: Hengbin* 亞洲人的父親：橫濱 [Asian fathers: Yokohama]. Taipei: L'Orangerie International Arts Consultant, 2008.

Hou, Chun-Ming 侯俊明. *Yazhouren de fuqin: Taiwan* 亞洲人的父親：臺灣 [Asian fathers: Taiwan]. Taipei: L'Orangerie International Arts Consultant, 2009.

Hsia, C. T. "Obsession with China: The Moral Burden of Modern Chinese Literature." Appendix 1 in *A History of Modern Chinese Fiction*, 533–554. New Haven, CT: Yale University, 1971.

Hsia, C. T. 夏志清. *Zhang Ailing gei wo de xinjian* 張愛玲給我的信件 [Letters from Eileen Chang]. Taipei: Unitas, 2012.

Hsiao, Wei-chun 蕭瑋均. "Meili de shengminggushi chudong xinling" 美麗的生命故事觸動心靈 [Beautiful life stories are heart-touching]. In *Guang: Yi linghun yelian wenzi, zai anchu faliang / disijie yimingong wenxuejiang zuopinji* 光——以靈魂冶煉文字，在暗處發亮／第四屆移民工文學獎作品集 [Light: Story collection from the 2017 Taiwan literature award for migrants], coauthored by Southeast Asian migrants, 33. New Taipei City: Four Way Publishing, 2017.

Hsu, Chi-Lin 許綺玲. "Chutan Hou Chun-Ming yishu zuopin zhong de wenben shengcheng lichen" 初探侯俊明藝術作品中的文本生成歷程 [A preliminary genetic observation of texts in the art works of Hou Chun-Ming]. *Sun Yat-sen Journal of Humanities*, no. 37 (2014): 133–160.

Hu, Shih 胡適. "Wenxue jinhua gainian yu ju gailiang" 文學進化觀念與戲劇改良 [Concepts of literature evolution and transformation of drama]. *Xin Qingnian* 新青年 [New youth] 5, vol. 4 (1918): 313–314.

Huang, Hsinya. "Sinophone Indigenous Literature of Taiwan." In *Sinophone Studies: A Critical Reader*, edited by Shu-mei Shih, Chien-hsin Tsai, and Brian Bernards, 242–254. New York: Columbia University Press, 2013.

Huang, Lei 黃蕾, and Feng Ming 馮明. "Zhang Yu: 30 nian hou zaixu Lushan lian" 張瑜：30年後再續廬山戀 [Zhang Yu: Remaking *Romance on Lushan Mountain* thirty years later]. *Shenzhen wanbao* 深圳晚報, September 28, 2012. http://www.zgnfys.com/a/nfrw-9380.shtml.

Huang, Nicole. "Late Mao Soundscapes: Auditory Culture and Daily Practice in 1970s China." Unpublished manuscript.

Huang, Pujiang 黃浦江. "Xin Zhongguo diyi bu wenxi *Lushan lian*" 新中國第一部吻戲《廬山戀》 [New China's first movie with a kiss scene, *Romance on Lushan Mountain*], *Jiangxi yule wang* 江西娛樂網, November 17, 2008. http://ent.jxnews.com.cn/system/2008/11/17/010000160.shtml.

Hung, Tzu-hui Celina. "Documenting 'Immigrant Brides' in Multicultural Taiwan." In *Asian Video Cultures: In the Penumbra of the Global*, edited by Joshua Neves and Bhaskar Sarkar, 158–175. New York: Duke University Press, 2017.

Hung, Tzu-hui Celina. "Yixiangren" 譯鄉人 [Translator]. *The News Lens*. https://www.thenewslens.com/article/115578.

Ibrahim, Anis, and Elvina Fernandez. "Rapper to Sing 1Malaysia Principles." *New Straits Times*, December 10, 2010.

International Consortium of Critical Theory Programs. "Knowledge Taiwan Collective." https://directory.criticaltheoryconsortium.org/organizations/knowledge-taiwan-collective/.

Ji, Weiran 紀蔚然. "Tansuo yu guibi zhijian: Dangdai Taiwan xiaojuchang de xiexu fengmao" 探索與規避之間：當代台灣小劇場的些許風貌 [Between exploration and evasion: On recent developments of Taiwan's little theater]. *Chung wai literary quarterly* 中外文學 31, no. 6 (2002): 41–58.

Jia, Ruzhong, Wei Huimin, and Liu Guiyu. "Ertong jie jinian de qingxing ji banfa" 兒童節紀念的情形及辦法 [A commemoration of Children's Day]. *Shida yuekan* 師大月刊 13 (1934): 187–255.

Jin, Shijie 金士傑. *Jin Shijie juben* 金士傑劇本 [Scripts of Jin Shijie]. Taipei: Yuan-liou Publishing, 2003.

Jin, Wen. *Pluralist Universalism: An Asian Americanist Critique of U.S. and Chinese Multiculturalisms*. Columbus: The Ohio State University Press, 2012.

Johnson, Matthew. "Regional Cultural Enterprises and Cultural Markets in Early Republican China: The Motion Picture as Case Study." *Cross-Currents: East Asian History and Culture Review E-Journal*, no. 16 (September 2015): 103–138.

Jones, Andrew F. *Developmental Fairy Tales: Evolutionary Thinking and Modern Chinese Culture*. Cambridge, MA: Harvard University Press, 2011.

Jones, Andrew F. *Like a Knife: Ideology and Genre in Contemporary Chinese Popular Music*. Ithaca, NY: Cornell University Press, 1992.

Jones, Andrew F. *Yellow Music: Media Culture and Colonial Modernity in the Chinese Jazz Age*. Durham, NC: Duke University Press, 2001.

Jung, Carl G. *Practice of Psychotherapy*, 2nd ed. Translated by R. F. C. Hull. Princeton, NJ: Princeton University Press, 1966.

Kahan, Benjamin. *The Book of Minor Perverts: Sexology, Etiology, and the Emergences of Sexuality*. Chicago: University of Chicago Press, 2019.

Kai, Sheng 盛鎧. "Visual Archive and Dialogical Aesthetics in Chun-Ming Hou's *The Asian Fathers Interview Project*." [In Chinese]. *Journal of Art Studies* 14 (2014): 99–158.

Kane, Brian. *Sound Unseen: Acousmatic Sound in Theory and Practice*. New York: Oxford University Press, 2014.

Karl, Rebecca. *The Magic of Concepts: History and the Economic in Twentieth-Century China*. Durham, NC: Duke University Press, 2017.

Katzenstein, Peter J., ed. *Sinicization and the Rise of China: Civilizational Processes Beyond East and West*. London: Routledge, 2012.

Ke, Pin-Wen 柯品文. "Shentitu de zhaohuan yu jiushu: Lun Hou Chun-Ming 'Nandong' shenti yuwang de keneng zhishe" 「身體圖」的招換與救贖：論侯俊明《男洞》身體慾望的可能指涉 [The summon and redemption of "Body Images": Possible references to bodily desire in Hou Chun-Ming's *Male Hole*]. *Taiwan Fine Arts* 112 (2018): 55–72.

Kingston, Maxine Hong. *The Woman Warrior*. New York: Vintage, 1989.

Kristeva, Julia. *About Chinese Woman*. Translated by Anita Barrows. New York: Marion Boyars, 1986.

Ku, Yu-ling 顧玉玲. "Tao" 逃 [Flight]. In *Ningshi yixiang: yigong sheyingji* 凝視驛鄉：移工攝影集 [Voyage 15840: Photographs by migrant workers], edited by Taiwan International Workers' Association, 192–201. Taipei: INK, 2008.

Ku, Yu-ling 顧玉玲. *Women: yigong yu laodong de shengming jishi* 我們：移動與勞動的生命記事 [Our stories: Migration and labor in Taiwan]. New Taipei City: INK, 2008.

Kuriyama, Shigehisa. *The Expressiveness of the Body and Divergence of Greek and Chinese Medicine*. New York: Zone Books, 1999.

LaMaMa. "Mission+History" (2018). *LaMaMa*. http://lamama.org/about/mission-history/.

Lan, Pei-chia 藍佩嘉. "Kuayue wenhuachayi de tiyan" 跨越文化差異的體驗 [Experiences that traverse cultural differences]. In *Du: Zai xianshi yu xiangwangzhong qiuyong / diwujie yimingong wenxuejiang zuopinji* 渡——在現實與想望中泅泳／第五屆移民工文學獎作品集 [Wading: Story collection from the 2018 Taiwan literature award for migrants], coauthored by Southeast Asian migrants, 17. New Taipei City: Four Way Publishing, 2018.

Latour, Bruno. *Reassembling the Social: An Introduction to Actor-Network-Theory*. Oxford: Oxford University Press, 2005.

"Laws of Malaysia: Act 15—Sedition Act 1948." *Malaysia: The Commissioner of Law Revision and Malayan Law Journal*, 2006.

Lee, Yu-lin 李育霖. *Nizao xindiqiu* 擬造新地球 [The fabulation of a new earth]. Taipei: Taiwan University Press. 2015.

Lever-Tracy, Constance, David Ip, and Noel Tracy. *The Chinese Diaspora and Mainland China*. London: Palgrave Macmillan, 1996.

Li, Jingyang 李景陽. "Aiqing zenme xie—dianying *Lushan Lian* gei women de qishi" 愛情怎樣寫——電影《廬山戀》給我們的啟示 [How to represent love: Lessons from *Romance on Lushan Mountain*]. *Dianying pingjie* 電影評介 (December 1980): 18.

Li, Xigeng 李錫賡. "Ping *Lushan lian* suo xie de aiqing" 評《廬山戀》所寫的愛情 [On love in *Romance on Lushan Mountain*]. *Dianying yishu* 電影藝術 (October 1980): 16–19.

Li, Xuan 李瑄. *Ming yimin qunti xintai yu wenxue sixiang yanjiu* 明遺民群體心態與文學思想研究 [Research on the collective mentality and thought of Ming loyalism]. Chengdu: Bashu chubanshe, 2009.

Lim, Song Hwee, and Julian Ward, eds. *The Chinese Cinema Book*. London: Palgrave MacMillan on behalf of the British Film Institute, 2011.

Lin, Xingqian 林幸謙, ed. *Zhang Ailig: chuanqi, xingbie, xipu* 張愛玲：傳奇・性別・系譜 [Eileen Chang: Legend, gender, genealogy]. Taipei: Lienching, 2012.

Liu, Hong. "Opportunities and Anxieties for the Chinese Diaspora in Southeast Asia." *Current History* 115, no. 784 (November 2016): 312–318.

Liu, Petrus. *Queer Marxism in Two Chinas*. Durham, NC: Duke University Press, 2015.

Lo, Yi-chin 駱以軍. "Touguo wenxue de yinmi huandu, jindao women limian" 透過文學的隱密換渡，進到我們裡面 [Through literature's secret transmission, they enter our insides]. In *Liu: Yidong de shengmingli, langchaozhong de Taiwan / diyierjie yimingong wenxuejiang zuopinji* 流——移動的生命力，浪潮中的臺灣／第一、二

屆移民工文學獎得獎作品集 [Flow: Story collection from the 2014 and 2015 Taiwan literature award for migrants], coauthored by Southeast Asian migrants, 10–11. New Taipei City: Four Way Publishing, 2015.

Loh, Deborah. "Student May Face Music Over 'Negaraku' Rap Video." *New Straits Times*, August 8, 2007.

Lordiane, Myan. "Leihaili de zhenzhu: 2018 Taiwan yimingong wenxuejiang feilvbin cansaizhe de bijiaofenxi" 淚海裡的珍珠：2018臺灣移民工文學獎菲律賓參賽者的比較分析 [Pearls in the sea of tears: A comparative analysis of Filipino competitors in the 2018 Taiwan literature award for migrants]. In *Du: Zai xianshi yu xiangwangzhong qiuyong / diwujie yimingong wenxuejiang zuopinji* 渡——在現實與想望中泅泳／第五屆移民工文學獎作品集 [Wading: Story collection from the 2018 Taiwan literature award for migrants], coauthored by Southeast Asian migrants, 328–334. New Taipei City: Four Way Publishing, 2018.

Louie, Andrea. *Chineseness Across Borders: Renegotiating Chinese Identities in China and the United States*. Durham, NC: Duke University Press, 2004.

Louie, Kam, ed. *Eileen Chang: Romancing Languages, Cultures and Genres*. Hong Kong: Hong Kong University Press, 2012.

Lu, Danlin 陸丹林. "Lushan zhenmian" 廬山真面 [The true face of Lushan]. *Lüxing zazhi* 旅行雜誌 (August 1950): 55.

Lu, Sheldon Hsiao-peng, ed. *Transnational Chinese Cinemas: Identity, Nationhood, Gender*. Honolulu: University of Hawai'i Press, 1997.

Luk, Charles, trans. *The Surangama Sutra*. London: Rider, 1966.

Lushan youcheng: Zhong-ying duizhao 廬山遊程：中英對照 [Lushan Tours/Kuling through traffic: In English and Chinese]. Shanghai: Zhongguo luxingshe, 1936. Microfilm, National Library of China.

Ma, Jean. *Sounding the Modern Woman: The Songstress in Chinese Cinema*. Durham, NC: Duke University Press, 2015.

Ma, Sen 馬森. *Zhongguo xiandai xiju de liangdu xichao* 中國現代戲劇的兩度西潮 [The two Western tides in Chinese modern theatre]. Taipei: UNITAS Publishing, 2006.

MacFarquhar, Roderick. *The Origins of the Cultural Revolution: Volume II, the Great Leap Forward 1958–1960*. New York: Columbia University Press, 1983.

Madson, Richard. "The Public Sphere, Civil Society, and Moral Community: A Research Agenda for Contemporary China Studies." *Modern China* 19, no. 2 (1993): 183–198.

Mair, Victor. "What Is a Chinese 'Dialect/Topolect'? Reflections on Some Key Sino-English Linguistic Terms," *Sino-Plantonic Papers* 29 (1991): 2–52.

Maitra, Ani, and Rey Chow. "What's 'In'? Disaggregating Asia through New Media Actants." In *Routledge Handbook of New Media in Asia*, edited by Larissa Hjorth and Olivia Khoo, 29–39. London: Routledge, 2015.

Makari, George. *Revolution in Mind: The Creation of Psychoanalysis*. New York: HarperCollins, 2008.

Martin, Fran, and Ari Larissa Heinrich, eds. *Embodied Modernities: Corporeality, Representation, and Chinese Cultures*. Honolulu: University of Hawai'i Press, 2006.

McGrath, Jason. *Chinese Film: Realism and Convention from the Silent Era to the Digital Age*. Minneapolis: University of Minnesota Press, 2022.

McKim, Kristi. *Cinema as Weather: Stylistic Screens and Atmospheric Change*. London: Routledge, 2013.

Menon, Sheela Jane. "Rakyat Malaysia: Contesting Nationalism and Exceptional Multiculturalism." PhD diss., University of Texas at Austin, 2016.

Merrins, E. M. "Anthropometry of Chinese Students." *China Medical Journal* 24 (1910): 318–324.

Ministry of Foreign Affairs, Republic of China (Taiwan). "Stories of Love and Loss Celebrated at Taiwan Literature Award for Migrants." October 1, 2018. https://nspp.mofa.gov.tw/nsppe/news.php?post=142544&unit=400.

Mitchell, W. J. T., and Mark B. N. Hansen, eds. *Critical Terms for Media Studies*. Chicago: University of Chicago Press, 2010.

Mo, Yajun. *Touring China: A History of Travel Culture, 1912–1949*. Ithaca, NY: Cornell University Press, 2021.

Morris, Andrew. *Marrow of the Nation: A History of Sport and Physical Culture in Republican China*. Berkeley: University of California Press, 2004.

Moyn, Samuel. The Last Utopia: Human Rights in History. Cambridge, MA: Harvard University Press, 2012.

Mufti, Aamir. *Forget English! Orientalisms and World Literatures*. Cambridge, MA: Harvard University Press, 2016.

Mullen, Bill. *Afro-Orientalism*. Minneapolis: University of Minnesota Press, 2004.

Murphey, Darragh. "Dubai Is Getting the Middle East's 'Largest Chinatown.'" *Time Out Dubai*, July 19, 2018. https://www.timeoutdubai.com/things-to-do/things-to-do-news/84635-dubai-is-getting-the-middle-easts-largest-chinatown.

Nakajima, Chieko. *Body, Society, and Nation: The Creation of Public Health and Urban Culture in Shanghai*. Cambridge, MA: Harvard University Asia Center, 2018.

Nakayama, Izumi. "Posturing for Modernity: Mishima Michiyoshi and School Hygiene in Meiji Japan." *East Asian Science, Technology, and Society* 6 (2012): 355–378.

Namewee. *Asia Most Wanted* 亞洲通緝. Warner Music Taiwan, 2013, Apple Music.

Namewee. *Ho Ho Yeah* 好好野. Prodigee Media PDG 2010A, 2010, compact disc.

Namewee. "Mapo de qingge" 麻坡的情歌 [Muar love song]. Track 11 on *Asia Most Wanted* 亞洲通緝. Warner Music Taiwan, 2013.

Namewee. "Namewee 黃明志 1st Music Video on YouTube [Muar Mandarin 麻坡的華語] @明志同名EP 2007." Directed by Namewee. March 8, 2007. Music video, 4:27. https://youtu.be/6M8fnjPLx6k.

Namewee. "Namewee 黃明志 Controversial Song [Negarakuku 我愛我的國家] @2007." Directed by Namewee. December 22, 2015. Music video, 5:45. https://youtu.be/g0moet-jLw8.

Namewee, director. *Nasi Lemak 2.0*. Prodigee Media, 2011. 1 hr., 8 min. DVD.

Namewee. "Piao xiang beifang" 漂向北方 [Stranger in the north]. Track 2 on 亞洲通車 *Cross Over Asia*. Avex Trax, 2016. Apple Music.

Namewee. "R-18! Namewee 黃明志 [Geebai People 擊敗人] @亞洲通吃 2017 All Eat Asia." Directed by Namewee. July 1, 2017. Music video, 7:10. https://youtu.be/yL1lr2gxRn4.

Namewee. "Rasa Sayang 2.0." Track 12 on *Asia Most Wanted* 亞洲通緝. Warner Music Taiwan, 2013. Apple Music.

Namewee. "Wo hai shi wo" 我還是我 [I am who I am]. Track 1 on *Asia Most Wanted* 亞洲通緝. Warner Music Taiwan, 2013. Apple Music.

Namewee. "Zhe jitian yinwei 'jibairen' zhe shouge, wo bei malaixiya zhuliu meiti diantai baozhi zhengzhi renwu he yulequan de ren lunliu hongzha le yifan" 這幾天因為「擊敗人」這首歌，我被馬來西亞主流媒體電台報紙政治人物和娛樂圈的人輪流轟炸了一番 [Because of my Song "Geebai People," I have been repeatedly bombarded by Malaysian mainstream media, politicians, and celebrities]. Facebook, July 28, 2017. https://www.facebook.com/namewee/posts/10155189586673429.

Neurath, Otto. "Protocol Sentences." In *Logical Positivism*. Edited by A. J. Ayer. Translated by George Schick. New York: The Free Press, 1959.

Newson, J. D. "The Disappearance of the Sick-Man from Medical Cosmology, 1770–1870." *Sociology* 10 (1976): 225–244.

Ng, Kim Chew 黃錦樹. "Zai wenxuejiang zhiwai, shibushi haiyou qita women keyi zuodeshi?" 在文學獎之外，是不是還有其他我們可以做的事？ [Besides the literature award, is there something else we can do?]. In *Liu: Yidong de shengmingli, langchaozhong de Taiwan / diyierjie yimingong wenxuejiang zuopinji* 流——移動的生命力，浪潮中的臺灣／第一、二屆移民工文學獎得獎作品集 [Flow: Story collection from the 2014 and 2015 Taiwan literature award for migrants], coauthored by Southeast Asian migrants, 14–15. New Taipei City: Four Way Publishing, 2015.

Nguyen, Cam Thuy. "Guanyu zuozhe" 關於作者 [Author's note]. In *Liu: Yidong de shengmingli, langchaozhong de Taiwan / diyierjie yimingong wenxuejiang zuopinji* 流——移動的生命力，浪潮中的臺灣／第一、二屆移民工文學獎得獎作品集 [Flow: Story collection from the 2014 and 2015 Taiwan literature award for migrants], coauthored by Southeast Asian migrants, 61. New Taipei City: Four Way Publishing, 2015.

Ni, Xiying 倪錫英. "Jinri zhi ertong shengli weisheng shishi" 今日之兒童生理衛生實施 [A health plan for today's children]. In *Jinri zhi ertong* 今日之兒童 [Today's children], 198. Shanghai: Shenghuo shudian, 1936.

Nicolson, Malcolm. "The Introduction of Percussion and Stethoscopy to Early Nineteenth-Century Edinburgh." In *Medicine and the Five Senses*, edited by W. F. Bynum and Roy Porter, 134–153. Cambridge: Cambridge University Press, 1993.

Nield, Robert. *China's Foreign Places: The Foreign Presence in China in the Treaty Port Era, 1840–1943*. New York: Columbia University Press, 2015.

Office of Trade Negotiations, Executive Yuan. "New Southbound Policy Promotion Plan" (October 3, 2016). https://www.ey.gov.tw/otnen/64C34DCA8893B06/a0e8fd0b-a6ac-4e80-bdd4-16b4cf999b49.

Ong, Walter J. *Orality and Literacy: The Technologizing of the World*. London: Routledge, 1982.

Pan, Lynn. *Sons of the Yellow Emperor: The Story of the Overseas Chinese*. London: Mandarin, 1990.

"Perkasa Disrupts Rapper's Do." *New Straits Times*, September 29, 2010.

Pflugfelder, Gregory M. *Cartographies of Desire: Male-Male Sexuality in Japanese Discourse, 1600–1950*. Berkeley: University of California Press, 1999.

Plotkin, Mariano Ben. *Freud in the Pampas: The Emergence and Development of a Psychoanalytic Culture in Argentina*. Stanford, CA: Stanford University Press, 2002.

Plum, M. Colette. "Orphans in the Family: Family Reform and Children's Citizenship during the Anti-Japanese War, 1937–45." In *Beyond Suffering: Recounting War in Modern China*, edited by James A. Flath and Norman Smith, 186–208. Vancouver: UBC Press, 2011.

Plum, M. Colette. "Unlikely Heirs: War Orphans During the Second Sino-Japanese War, 1937–1945." PhD diss., Stanford University, 2006.

Porter, Roy. "The Rise of Physical Examination." In *Medicine and the Five Senses*, edited by W. F. Bynum and Roy Porter, 179–197. Cambridge: Cambridge University Press, 1993.

Putra, Heru Joni. "Yimingong wenxue: you geren zhi tuanjie" 移民工文學：由個人至團結 [Migrant literature: From individual to solidarity]. In *Du: Zai xianshi yu xiangwangzhong qiuyong / diwujie yimingong wenxuejiang zuopinji* 渡──在現實與想望中泅泳／第五屆移民工文學獎作品集 [Wading: Story collection from the 2018 Taiwan literature award for migrants], coauthored by Southeast Asian migrants, 339–345. New Taipei City: Four Way Publishing, 2018.

Qiu, Zhijie 邱志杰. "Zhongguo fasheng" 中國發聲 [Sounding China]. *ArtLinkArt*. http://www.artlinkart.com/cn/artist/txt_ge/3a3avz/319hAxm.

Quine, Willard van Orman. *Word and Object*. Cambridge, MA: MIT Press, 1960.

Razak, Najib. "The 1Malaysia Concept Part 1." Najib Razak. June 15, 2009. https://najibrazak.com/the-1malaysia-concept-part-1/.

Rhodes, John David, and Elena Gorfinkel, eds. *Taking Place: Location and the Moving Image*. Minneapolis: University of Minnesota Press, 2011.

Rieser, Judith Ellen. "The American Avant-Garde Ensemble Theaters of the Sixties in the Historical and Cultural Context." PhD diss., Northwestern University, 1982.

Robinson, Douglas. "Translating the Nonhuman: Towards a Sustainable Theory of Translation, or a Translational Theory of Sustainability." Unpublished manuscript.

Rocha, Leon Antonio. "Scientia sexualis and ars erotica: Foucault, van Gulik, Needham." *Studies in History and Philosophy of Biological and Biomedical Sciences* 42 (2011): 328–343.

Rogaski, Ruth. *Hygienic Modernity: Meanings of Health and Disease in Treaty-Port China*. Berkeley: University of California Press, 2004.

Rojas, Carlos. "Chinese Writing, Heptapod B, and Martian Script." In this volume.

Rojas, Carlos. "Danger in the Voice: Alai and the Sinophone." In *Sinophone Studies: A Critical Reader*, edited by Shu-Mei Shih, 296–303. New York: Columbia University Press, 2013.

Rojas, Carlos. "Humanity at the Interstices of Language and Translation." *Chinese Literature Today* 2, no. 2 (2012): 62–67.

Rojas, Carlos. "Method as Method." *Prism* 16, no. 2 (2019): 211–220.

Rorty, Richard. "Solidarity or Objectivity." In *Post-Analytic Philosophy*, edited by John Rajchman and Cornel West. 3-19. New York: Columbia University Press, 1986.

Rosenberg, Charles E. "The Tyranny of Diagnosis: Specific Entities and Individual Experience." *The Milbank Quarterly* 80, no. 2 (2002): 237–260.

Said, Edward. *Culture and Imperialism*. London: Vintage, 1993.

Said, Edward W. *On Late Style*. New York: Vintage, 2007.

Sakai, Naoki. *Translation and Subjectivity: On "Japan" and Cultural Nationalism*. Minneapolis: University of Minnesota Press, 1997.

Sampson, Geoffrey. *Writing Systems*. 2nd ed. Sheffield: Equinox Publishing, 2015.

Sasaki, Motoe. *Redemption and Revolution: American and Chinese New Women in the Early Twentieth Century*. Ithaca, NY: Cornell University Press, 2016.

Scheel, David, et al. "A Second Site Occupied by *Octopus tetricus* at High Densities, with Notes on Their Ecology and Behavior." *Marine and Freshwater Behavior and Physiology* 50, no. 4 (September 2017): 285–291. http://www.tandfonline.com/eprint/SuKqGmXPA8zJdrkjkSRE/full.

Scheel, David, Peter Godfrey-Smith, and Matthew Lawrence. "Signal Use by Octopuses in Agonistic Interactions." *Current Biology* 26, no. 3 (February 2016): 377–382.

SETN.com 三立新聞網. "Huang Mingzhi xingge 'jibai ren' geci neiyou xuanji dianji xunshu po baiwan" 黃明志新歌《擊敗人》歌詞內有玄機點擊迅速破百萬 [Hidden messages in Wee Meng Chee's New Song, "Geebai People." Music Video reached a Million Views]. http://www.setn.com/News.aspx?NewsID=268795.

Shan, Lianguo 單聯國. "Zhuazhu 'jiaohua' zuo wenzhang—*Lushan lian* sheying xinde" 抓住"交化"做文章——《廬山戀》攝影心得 [Fussing over capturing "change"—What I learned from shooting *Romance on Lushan Mountain*]. *Dianying yishu* 電影藝術 (March 1981): 52–58, 61.

Shan, Te-hsing 單德興. *Fanyi yu mailuo* 翻譯與脈絡 [Translations and contexts]. Taipei: Bookman Books Co., Ltd., 2013.

Shank, Theodore. *American Alternative Theatre*. London: Macmillan, 1982.

Sheng, Kai 盛鎧. "Fansixing zhuti de fansi: Hou Chun-Ming zuopin zhong de zaixian celuë zhutiguan yu shehui pipan" 反思性主體的反思：侯俊明作品中的再現策略、主體觀與社會批判 [Reflection on reflexive subjectivity: The representational strategy, subjective view, and social critique in Chun-Ming Hou's work]. *Journal of Art Studies* 7 (2010): 213–250.

Sheng, Kai 盛鎧. "Hou Chun-Ming Yazhouren de fuqing zhong de dang'an yishu yu duihua meixue" 侯俊明《亞洲人的父親》中的檔案藝術與對話美學 [Visual archive and dialogical aesthetics in Chun-Ming Hou's *The Asian Fathers Interview Project*]. *Journal of Art Studies* 14 (2014): 99–158.

Shih, Mei-ling 石美玲. "Xingtian fuhao bianyan: Taiwan huajia Hou Chun-Ming xifang huafeng shilun" 刑天符號變衍：台灣畫家侯俊明戲仿畫風試論 [Transformation of the symbol of Xing Tian: On Taiwanese artist Hou Chun-Ming's parody style]. *Chung Hsing Journal of Humanities* 48 (2012): 187–210.

Shih, Shu-mei. "Against Diaspora: The Sinophone as Places of Cultural Production." In *Global Chinese Literature*, edited by David Wang and Jing Tsu, 29–48. Boston, MA: Brill, 2010.

Shih, Shu-mei, "Against Diaspora: The Sinophone as Places of Cultural Production." In *Sinophone Studies: A Critical Reader*, edited by Shu-mei Shih, Chien-hsin Tsai, and Brian Bernards, 25–42. New York: Columbia University Press, 2013.

Shih, Shu-mei. "The Concept of the Sinophone." *PMLA* 126, no. 3 (May 2011): 709–718.

Shih, Shu-mei. "Global Literature and the Technologies of Recognition." *PMLA* 119, no. 1 (2004): 16–30.

Shih, Shu-mei. "Introduction: What Is Sinophone Studies?" *Sinophone Studies: A Critical Reader*, edited by Shu-mei Shih, Chien-hsin Tsai, and Brian Bernards, 1–16. New York: Columbia University Press, 2013.

Shih, Shu-mei. "Is the Post- in Postsocialism the Post- in Posthumanism?" *Social Text* 30, no. 1 (2012): 27–50.

Shih, Shu-mei. "The Sinophone Redistribution of the Audible." In *Sinophone Cinemas*, edited by Audrey Yue and Olivia Khoo, vii–xi. New York: Palgrave Macmillan, 2014.

Shih, Shu-mei. "Theory, Asia and the Sinophone." *Postcolonial Studies* 13, no. 4 (2010): 465–484.

Shih, Shu-mei. *Visuality and Identity: Sinophone Articulations across the Pacific*. Berkeley: University of California Press, 2007.

Shih, Shu-mei, and Ping-hui Liao, eds. *Comparatizing Taiwan*. London and New York: Routledge, 2015.

Shih, Shu-mei, Chien-hsin Tsai, and Brian Bernards, eds. *Sinophone Studies: A Critical Reader*. New York: Columbia University Press, 2013.

Shorter, Edward. *Bedside Manners: The Troubled History of Doctors and Patients*. Harmondsworth, UK: Viking, 1986.

Siegert, Bernhard. *Cultural Techniques: Grids, Filters, Doors, and Other Articulations of the Real*. Translated by Geoffrey Winthrop-Young. New York: Fordham University Press, 2015.

Southeast Asian Migrants *Du: Zai xianshi yu xiangwangzhong qiuyong / diwujie yimingong wenxuejiang zuopinji* 渡——在現實與想望中泅泳／第五屆移民工文學獎作品集 [Wading: Story collection from the 2018 Taiwan literature award for migrants]. New Taipei City: Four Way Publishing, 2018.

Southeast Asian Migrants. *Guang: Yi linghun yelian wenzi, zai anchu faliang / disijie yimingong wenxuejiang zuopinji* 光——以靈魂冶煉文字，在暗處發亮／第四屆移民工文學獎作品集 [Light: Story collection from the 2017 Taiwan literature award for migrants]. New Taipei City: Four Way Publishing, 2017.

Southeast Asian Migrants. *Hang: Polangerlai, nifengzhong de ziyou / disanjie yimingong wenxuejiang zuopinji* 航——破浪而來，逆風中的自由／第三屆移民工文學獎作品集 [Navigation: Story collection from the 2016 Taiwan literature award for migrants]. New Taipei City: Four Way Publishing, 2016.

Southeast Asian Migrants. *Liu: Yidong de shengmingli, langchaozhong de Taiwan / diyierjie yimingong wenxuejiang zuopinji* 流——移動的生命力，浪潮中的臺灣／第一、二屆移民工文學獎得獎作品集 [Flow: Story collection from the 2014 and 2015 Taiwan literature award for migrants]. New Taipei City: Four Way Publishing, 2015.

Spivak, Gayatri Chakravorty. *Other Asias*. Malden, MA: Wiley-Blackwell, 2008.

Sridongphet, Khemphon. "Guanyu zuozhe" 關於作者 [Author's note]. In *Liu: Yidong de shengmingli, langchaozhong de Taiwan / diyierjie yimingong wenxuejiang zuopinji* 流——移動的生命力，浪潮中的臺灣／第一、二屆移民工文學獎得獎作品集 [Flow: Story collection from the 2014 and 2015 Taiwan literature award for migrants], coauthored by Southeast Asian migrants, 94. New Taipei City: Four Way Publishing, 2015.

Sterne, Jonathan. *The Audible Past: Cultural Origins of Sound Reproduction*. Durham, NC: Duke University Press, 2003.

Su, Shuo-bin 蘇碩斌. "Yinwei tamen er kaifang ziji" 因為他們而開放自己 [Opening oneself because of them]. In *Liu: Yidong de shengmingli, langchaozhong de Taiwan / diyierjie yimingong wenxuejiang zuopinji* 流──移動的生命力，浪潮中的臺灣／第一、二屆移民工文學獎得獎作品集 [Flow: Story collection from the 2014 and 2015 Taiwan literature award for migrants], coauthored by Southeast Asian migrants, 17. New Taipei City: Four Way Publishing, 2015.

Su, Weizhen 蘇偉貞. "Lianhuan tao: Zhang Ailing de chuban meixue yanyi: yi yijiujiuwu nian yihou chutu zhuzuo wei wenben" 連環套：張愛玲的出版美學演繹：以一九九五年以後出土著作為文本 [Interlocking hinges], in *Zhang Ailing: chuanqi, xingbie xipu*, edited by Lin Xingqian, 719–751. Taipei: Lienching, 2012.

Swafford, Jan. *Beethoven: Anguish and Triumph*. New York: Harcourt, 2014.

Syaman, Rapongan 夏曼藍波安. *Hailang de jihi* 海浪的記憶 [Memories of the waves]. Taipei: Unitas Publishing, 2002.

Syaman, Rapongan 夏曼藍波安. *Hanghaijia de lian* [The faces of voyagers]. Taipei: Inke Publishing, 2007.

Syaman, Rapongan 夏曼藍波安. *Heise de chibang* 黑色的翅膀 [Black wings]. Taipei: Unitas Publishing, 2009.

Syaman, Rapongan 夏曼藍波安. *Laohaijen* 老海人 [The old fishermen]. Taipei: Inke Publishing, 2009.

Taiwan.com.au. "Martian Language Banned in Taiwanese College Entrance Exam." https://web.archive.org/web/20091024125942/http://www.taiwan.com.au/Scitech/Internet/Trends/20060306.html.

"Taking an Inventory of Health." *Weisheng* 衛生 [Health] 1, no. 1 (1924): 11.

Tan, Ruqian 潭汝謙, ed. *Zhongguo yi Riben shu zonghe mulu* 中國譯日本書綜合目錄 [Comprehensive catalog of Japanese books translated into Chinese]. Hong Kong: Zhongwen daxue chubanshe, 1980.

Tang, Min 唐民. "Wei Zhongguo jiaoyu xunmi shuguang: renmin jiaoyujia, Tao Xingzhi" 為中國教育尋覓曙光：人民教育家，陶行知 [Seeking the dawn for education in China: People's educator, Tao Xingzhi]. In *Minguo Nanjing: Xueshu renwu zhuan* 民國南京：學術人物傳 [Republican Nanjing: biographies of learned persons], edited by Zhang Xianwen 張憲文, 371–385. Nanjing: Nanjing daxue chubanshe, 2005.

Tang, Xiaobing. "Radio, Sound Cinema, and Community Singing: The Making of a New Sonic Culture in Modern China." *Twentieth-Century China* 45, no. 1 (2020): 3–24.

Tao, Xingzhi 陶行知. "Ertong de shijie" 兒童的世界 [The world of children]. In *Jinri zhi ertong* 今日之兒童 [Today's children]. Shanghai: Shenghuo shudian, 1936.

Tao, Yongqing 陶勇清. *Lushan lidai shike* 廬山歷代石刻 [Lushan stone inscriptions through the centuries]. Nanchang: Jiangxi meishu chubanshe, 2010.

Tay, William, ed. 張愛玲的世界 *Zhang Ailing de shijie* [The world of Eileen Chang]. Taipei: Yunchen, 1990.

Taylor, Jeremy. *Rethinking Transnational Chinese Cinemas: The Amoy-Dialect Film Industry in Cold War Asia*. London: Routledge, 2013.

Tho, Nan. "Guanyu zuozhe" 關於作者 [Author's note]. In *Liu: Yidong de shengmingli, langchaozhong de Taiwan / diyierjie yimingong wenxuejiang zuopinji* 流──移動的生命力，浪潮中的臺灣／第一、二屆移民工文學獎得獎作品集 [Flow: Story collection from the 2014 and 2015 Taiwan literature award for migrants], coauthored by Southeast Asian migrants, 107. New Taipei City: Four Way Publishing, 2015.

Tian, Yao-nong 田耀農. "Lun Ji Kang de shengwu aile" 論嵇康的聲無哀樂 [Analyzing Jikang's "music being irrelevant to grief or joy"]. *Zhongguo yinyue xue* 中國音樂學, no. 4 (2013): 20–24.

Tillman, Margaret Mih. "Measuring Up: Better Baby Contests in China, 1917–1945." *Modern Asian Studies* 54, no. 6 (2020): 1749–1786.

Tillman, Margaret Mih. *Raising China's Revolutionaries: Modernizing Childhood for Cosmopolitan Nationalists and Liberated Comrades, 1920s–1950s*. New York: Columbia University Press, 2018.

Tsai, Chien-hsin. *A Passage to China: Literature, Loyalism, and Colonial Taiwan*. Cambridge, MA: Harvard University Press, 2017.

Tsai, Shi-ping 蔡詩萍. "Xiangruyimo de jiemeiqingyi" 相濡以沫的姐妹情誼 [Sisterhood in times of hardship and need]. In *Guang: Yi linghun yelian wenzi, zai anchu faliang / disijie yimingong wenxuejiang zuopinji* 光——以靈魂冶煉文字，在暗處發亮／第四屆移民工文學獎作品集 [Light: Story collection from the 2017 Taiwan literature award for migrants], coauthored by Southeast Asian migrants, 22. New Taipei City: Four Way Publishing, 2017.

Tseng, Wen-chen 曾文珍. "Taxiang yu guxiang" 他鄉與故鄉 [Foreign land and homeland]. In *Liu: Yidong de shengmingli, langchaozhong de Taiwan / diyierjie yimingong wenxuejiang zuopinji* 流——移動的生命力，浪潮中的臺灣／第一、二屆移民工文學獎得獎作品集 [Flow: Story collection from the 2014 and 2015 Taiwan literature award for migrants], coauthored by Southeast Asian migrants, 16. New Taipei City: Four Way Publishing, 2015.

Tsu, Jing. *Failure, Nationalism, and Literature: The Making of Modern Chinese Identity, 1895–1937*. Stanford, CA: Stanford University Press, 2005.

Tsu, Jing. *Sound and Script in Chinese Diaspora*. Cambridge, MA: Harvard University Press, 2010.

Tsu, Jing, and David Der-wei Wang, eds. *Chinese Global Literature: Critical Essays*. Leiden: Brill, 2010.

Tsui, Bonnie. *American Chinatown: A People's History of Five Neighborhoods*. New York: Free Press, 2010.

Tu, Wei-ming. "Cultural China: The Periphery at the Center." *Daedalus* 120, no. 2 (1991): 1–32.

Tu, Weiming, ed. *The Living Tree: The Changing Meaning of Being Chinese*. Stanford, CA: Stanford University Press, 1994.

Venuti, Lawrence. "Introduction." In *The Translation Studies Reader*, edited by Lawrence Venuti, 1–8. London: Routledge, 2012.

Venuti, Lawrence. "Translation, Community, Utopia." In *The Princeton Sourcebook in Comparative Literature: From the European Enlightenment to the Global Present*, edited by David Damrosch, Natalie Melas, and Mbongiseni Buthelezi, 358–379. Princeton, NJ: Princeton University Press, 2009.

Walkowitz, Rebecca. "Theory of World Literature Now." In *Born Translated: The Contemporary Novel in an Age of World Literature*, 1–48. New York: Columbia University Press, 2017.

Wang, Ban. "The Cold War, Imperial Aesthetics, and Area Studies." *Social Text* 20, no. 3 (2002): 45–65.

Wang, David Der-wei. "Foreword." In *Rouge of the North*, by Eileen Chang, vii–xxx. Berkeley: University of California Press, 1998.

Wang, David Der-wei 王德威. "Huayi zhibian: huayu yuxiyanjiu de xinshijie" 華夷之變：華語語系研究的新視界 [Sinophone/xenophone changeability]. *Zhongguo xiandai wenxue* 中國現代文學 [Modern Chinese literature] 34 (December 2018): 13.

Wang, David Der-wei 王德威. *Houyimin xiezuo: shijian yu jiyi de zhengzhixue* 後遺民寫作：時間與記憶的政治學 [Postloyalist writing: The politics of time and memory]. Taipei: Ryefield Publications, 2007.

Wang, David Der-wei. "Sinophone States of Exception." In this volume.

Wang, Gungwu. "A Single Chinese Diaspora?" In *Diasporic Chinese Ventures: The Life and Work of Wang Gungwu*, edited by Gregor Benton and Hong Liu, 157–177. London: Routledge Curzon, 2004.

Wang, Helen. *Chairman Mao Badges: Symbols and Slogans of the Cultural Revolution*. London: British Museum Press, 2008.

Wang, Jianlang. *Unequal Treaties and China*, Vol. 1. Honolulu, HI: Enrich Professional Publishing, 2015.

Wang, Jing. "Affective Listening as a Mode of Coexistence: The Case of China's Sound Practice." *Representations* 136, no. 1 (November 1, 2016): 112–131.

Wang, Jing. "To Make Sounds inside a 'Big Can': Proposing a Proper Space for Works of Sound Art." *Leonardo* 49, no. 1 (July 7, 2014): 38–47.

Wang, Min'an 汪民安. "Lun xiyiji" 論洗衣機 [On washing machine]. *Sub Jam* (blog). April 19, 2014. http://subjam.org/blog/28.

Wang, Mo-lin 王墨林. *Dushi juchang yu shenti* 都市劇場與身體 [Urban theater and the body]. Taipei: Dao-xiang Publishing Ltd., 1992.

Wang, Suhong 王素紅. "Tan Zhou Yun de fuzhuang bianhua" 談周筠的服裝變化 [On Zhou Yun's change of clothes]. *Dianying pingjie* 電影評介 (February 1981): 20.

Wang, Xiaojue. 2013. *Modernity with a Cold War Face: Reimagining the Nation in Chinese Literature across the 1949 Divide*. Cambridge, MA: Harvard University Asia Center.

Wang, Xi-liang 王錫蓮. "Hezhu xinpei" 荷珠新配 [Hezhu's new match]. In *Lanling jufang de chubu shiyan* 蘭陵劇坊的初步實驗 [The first experiment of Lan-ling Theater Workshop], edited by Jing-jyi Wu 吳靜吉, 135–137. Taipei: Yuan-liou Publishing, 1982.

Wells, H. G. *War of the Worlds*. Oxford: Oxford University Press, 2017.

Whyte, G. D. "Height, Weight, and Chest Measurements of Healthy Chinese." *China Medical Journal* 32 (1918): 210–216, 322–328.

Wilcox, Christie. "The Scientific Explanation for why Humans Are So Convinced that Aliens Look like Octopuses." *Quartz*. December 8, 2016. https://qz.com/857377/the-aliens-in-arrival-look-like-octopuses-because-humans-think-cephalopods-are-both-scary-and-smart/.

Wu, Grace Hui-chuan. "Literature and Human Rights Imagination: Taiwan Literature Awards for Migrants." *Chung-Wai Literary Monthly* 48, no. 3 (2019): 89–132.

Wu, Jing-jyi 吳靜吉, ed. *Lanling jufang de chubu shiyan* 蘭陵劇坊的初步實驗 [The first experiment of Lan-ling Theater Workshop]. Taipei: Yuan-liou Publishing, 1982.

Wu, Judy. *Radicals on the Road: Internationalism, Orientalism, and Feminism during the Vietnam Era*. Ithaca, NY: Cornell University Press, 2013.

Wu, Yi-Li. "Ghost Fetuses, False Pregnancies, and the Parameters of Medical Uncertainty in Classical Chinese Gynecology." *Nan Nü* 4, no. 2 (2002): 170–206.

Xiang, Cai. *Revolution and Its Narratives: China's Socialist Literary and Cultural Imaginaries, 1949–1966*. Translated by Rebecca Karl and Xueping Zhong. Durham, NC: Duke University Press, 2016.

Xiao, Ming 曉銘. "Zenyang tuchu 'lian'—*Lushan lian* de yishu tese" 怎樣突出"戀"——《廬山戀》的藝術特色 [How to foreground love: The artistic characteristics of *Romance on Lushan Mountain*]. *Dianying pingjie* 電影評介 (February 1981): 20.

Xie, Zhengguang 謝正光. *Qingchu shiwen yu shiren jiaoyou kao* 清初詩文與士人交遊考 [A study of poetry and literati circles in the early Qing]. Nanjing: Nanjing University Press, 2001.

Xu, Bing. *Book from the Ground: From Point to Point*. Boston, MA: MIT Press, 2014.

Yan, Jun. "Lao Yang, Untitled." *Sub Jam* (blog). May 6, 2013. http://www.subjam.org/archives/2528.

Yan, Jun. "The Laundromat by the Sea." https://yanjun.org/archives/1286.

Yan, Jun. *The Only Authentic Work: Fragments, for Lionel Marchetti's 23 Formes En Elastique*. Beijing: Sub Jam, 2003.

Yan, Jun 顏峻, and Hsia Yu 夏宇. *Qishou shi he yixie erming* 七首詩和一些耳鳴 [7 Poems and some tinnitus]. Beijing: Sub Jam, 2016.

Yang, Gang 楊崗. "Wo zhande laoyuan laoyuan de kan ni—cong *Lushan Lian* de aiqing miaoxie tanqi" 我站得老遠老遠地看你——從《廬山戀》的愛情描寫談起 [I look at you from very far away: Starting from the depiction of love in *Romance on Lushan Mountain*]. *Dianying pingjie* 電影評介 (February 1981): 21.

Yang, Ming-E 楊明鍔. "Yongbao zhizhuo: Hou Chun-Ming de mili huanjing" 擁抱執著：侯俊明的迷離幻境 [Embracing perseverance: Hou Chun-Ming's blurred fantasy]. *Modern Arts* 115 (2004): 46–55.

Yanti, Sri. "Asap Hitam Di Suriah" [Black smoke in Syria]. In *Liu: Yidong de shengmingli, langchaozhong de Taiwan / diyierjie yimingong wenxuejiang zuopinji* 流——移動的生命力，浪潮中的臺灣／第一、二屆移民工文學獎得獎作品集 [Flow: Story collection from the 2014 and 2015 Taiwan literature award for migrants], coauthored by Southeast Asian migrants, 114–129. New Taipei City: Four Way Publishing, 2015.

Yao, Dajuin. "Revolutions Per Minute: Sound Art China." School of Creative Media, City University of Hong Kong. https://www.scm.cityu.edu.hk/event/37.

Yap, Bryan. "Stand Up and Speak Up If You're Malaysian." *New Straits Times*, August 15, 2007.

Ye, Zhaoyan 葉兆言. "Weicheng li de xiaosheng" 圍城裡的笑聲 [Laughter in the fortress besieged]. *Shouhuo* 收穫 4 (2000): 141–150.

Yeow, David. "Namewee: I Did Not Mean to Insult Malays." *New Straits Times*, August 10, 2007.

Yip, Ka-Che. "Health and Society in China: Public Health Education for the Community, 1912–1937." *Social Science & Medicine* 16 (1982): 1197–1205.

Young, Robert J. C. "The Dislocations of Cultural Translation." *PMLA* 132, no. 1 (2017): 186–197.

Young, Samson. "The Possibility of Authenticity: Sounding the Socialist China in FM3's Buddha Machine." In *Contemporary Music in East Asia*, edited by Hee Sook Oh, 267–283. Seoul: Seoul University Press, 2014.

Yu, Sun. "Tige jiancha fa" 體格檢查法 [How to conduct a physical examination]. *Zhonghua jiaoyu jie* 中華教育界 [Chinese educational world] 5, no. 10 (1916): 1–6.

Yue, Audrey, and Olivia Khoo, eds. *Sinophone Cinemas*. London: Palgrave Macmillan, 2014.

Zakarin, Jordan. "Arrival Invented a New, Insanely Complicated Alien Language." *Inverse*. Last modified November 2, 2016. https://www.inverse.com/article/23159-arrival-invented-new-complicated-alien-language.

Zaretsky, Eli. *Political Freud: A History*. New York: Columbia University Press, 2015.

Zhang, Danhong 張丹紅, and Zhang Sumeng 張蘇萌. "19 Shiji houye 20 shiji qianye Zhongguo de xuexiao jiankang jiaoyu" 19世紀後葉20世紀前葉中國的學校健康教育 [Health education in Chinese schools during the late nineteenth century and early twentieth century]. *Zhonghua yishi zazhi* 中華醫史雜誌 [Chinese journal of medical history] 29, no. 3 (July 1999): 168–170.

Zhang, Jiehou 張介候. "Buliang shaonian tige jiancha shang zhi zhuyidian" 不良少年體格檢查上之注意點 [Key points to pay attention to when making a physical examination of a no-good youth]. *Zhongxi yixue bao* 中西醫學報 [Journal of Chinese and Western medicine] 4, no. 9 (April 1914): 1–5.

Zhang, Longxi. "The True Face of Mount Lu: On the Significance of Perspectives and Paradigms." *History and Theory* 49, no. 1 (February 2010): 58–70.

Zhang, Renhua 張任華, ed. *Ertong zhi weisheng* 兒童之衛生 [Child health and hygiene]. Shanghai: Shangwu yinshuguan, 1924.

Zhang, Yingjin. *Cinema, Space, and Polylocality in a Globalizing China*. Honolulu: University of Hawai'i Press, 2010.

Zhang, Yingjin. "Gender, Genre, and the Performance in Eileen Chang's Films." In *Chinese Women's Cinema: Transnational Contexts*, edited by Lingzhen Wang, 55–73. New York: Columbia University Press, 2011.

Zhang, Yingjin, ed. *A Companion to Chinese Cinema*. Hoboken, NJ: Wiley-Blackwell, 2012.

Zhang, Zhongmin 張仲民. "Wan Qing chuban de shengli weisheng shuji ji qi duzhe" 晚清出版的生理衛生書籍及其讀者 [Books of physiology published in the late Qing dynasty and their readers]. *Shilin* 史林 4 (2009): 20–36.

Zhou, Shang 周尚. *Ertong baojian yu jiaoshi* 兒童保健與教師 [The care and education of children]. Shanghai: Shangwu, 1939.

Zhu, Mingji 朱明基. "Guanyu shengwu aile lun zhong sheng de biaoshu fangshi tantao" 關於〈聲無哀樂論〉中"聲"的表述方式探討 [A discussion on the expressions of "sound" in "on the absence of emotions in sound"]. *Yinyue tansuo* 音樂探索, no. 4 (1999): 39–42.

Zhuo, Ming 卓明. "Dang women zaiyiqi: Jieshao Lanling jufang de peitai gengxin shiyan jutuan" 當我們在一起：介紹蘭陵劇坊的胚胎耕莘實驗劇團 [When we are together: Introduction to an experimental embryo troupe Lan-ling Theater Workshop]. In *Lanling jufang de chubu shiyan* 蘭陵劇坊的初步實驗 [The first experiment of Lan-ling Theater Workshop], edited by Jing-jyi Wu, 19–26. Taipei: Yuan-liou Publishing, 1982.

Zito, Angela, and Tani Barlow, eds. *Body, Subject, and Power in China*. Chicago: University of Chicago Press, 1994.

Index

actor-network theory, 182
Adorno, Theodor W., 151
affective listening, 132–136
Agamben, Giorgio, 210
Americanization, 64
Anglophone: intersection with the Sinophone, 147–156, 206; usage of term, 235–236; *The Woman Warrior* (Kingston), 224
Appleton, Vivia B., 27–28
Apter, Emily, 182
Arrival (Villeneuve): alterity, 127; language and community, 122–126; language and meaning, 113–119; language and time, 119–122
art: labeling deviance, 42–51; *Male Hole* (Hou), 40–54; psychoanalytic turn, 38–39, 52; therapeutic instrumentation of art, 51–54
Asian American literature, 220–224
Asian Tigers, 64
attentive listening, 128–129
avant-garde theater, 64–66

Bakhtin, Mikhail, 6–7, 230
Beethoven, Ludwig van, 151, 152, 153
Berry, Michael, 79, 82–83
Bhabha, Homi, 178
bodies, in theater performance, 55–58; American avant-garde theater and Taiwan, 64–66; cultural materialism, 62–64; epistemology of area studies, 66–69; *Hezhu xinpei*, 57, 60–62, 68; stage performance techniques, 58–62
bodily metrics: as part of child health education, 23–35; physical examination in Republican China, 9, 19–36
body-subjectivity connectivity, 20
born-translated literature, 178. *See also* Taiwan Literature Award for Migrants (TLAM)
Bray, Francesca, 21–22

Cage, John, 132, 137, 138
Cantopop, 95, 109
center-margin dichotomies, 234–235
Chai-na (neologism), 225–228
Chang, Cheng, 177–178, 180–187, 190, 195, 198
Chang, Eileen, 13, 147–156, 210–211
Chang, Mau-kuei, 195
Cheah, Pheng, 209, 233
Chen, Fang-ming, 181, 186–187, 194
Chen, Jianhua, 151
Chiang, Howard, 10
Chiang, Ted, 112–113, 121–122. *See also* "Story of Your Life" (Chiang)
children: National Children's Day, 29, 30; physical examination and child health education, 19–36
Chin, Shih-chieh, 57, 60–62
China, global influence of, 212, 216–218
Chinatowns, 217–219
Chinese as label, 1, 3
Chinese history, 3–4

Chineseness, 1, 6; absolutist and essentialist understandings, 212–219; bodily metrics, 20–21, 36; in cinema studies, 73–76; debates in Chinese cultural studies, 73; ethnocentric and nationalistic models, 230–231; as landscape, 12, 79–82; linguistic boundaries, 160–161; mediality, 11–12; pluralistic experience of being Chinese, 98; race and ethnicity, 8–9; Sinoglossic approach, 7; Sinopop music, 94
Chinese sound. *See* sound in Chinese languages
Chinese writing systems, 111–113; adrift on Neurath's ship, 126–127; *Chai-na* (neologism), 227–228; language and community, 122–126; language and meaning, 113–119; language and time, 119–122; linguistic boundaries, 171–172; "Martian script," 123–126; phonetic values, 111–112, 120–121
Chion, Michel, 133, 136
Chiu, Kuei-fen, 56
Christian missionaries, 26
Chua, Beng Huat, 95–96
cinema studies: in China, 73–76; landscape of words, 82–89; *Romance on Lushan Mountain*, 78–89
civil rights movement, 65
clinical transference, 52–54
Cold War, 10–11, 62–64, 65, 67, 150
colonialism, 159–160
Communist Party, China: Chinese landscape, 82; Cold War, 63; physical examination, 9
community, ethnocentric bases of language, 122–126
concrete ethics, 22
Confucianism, 95–96
contrapuntal culture, 56–57
corporeality, 8–11
counter-transference, 52–54
Crouching Tiger, Hidden Dragon (Lee), 98, 143, 155, 156

cultural context: Euro-American and non-Euro-American, 232; Eurocentrism, 209, 221–222; the particular and the universal, 233, 235–236; Sinoglossia, 5–7
cultural materialism, 57, 62–64, 68
cultural stability, technology, 21–22
cultural translation, 56, 178–179, 189, 190

degeneracy, physical examination in Republican China, 25–26
Deleuze, Gilles, 6, 74–75, 161–162, 167, 169–171
delimitation, Sinoglossia as, 90
democracy: Cold War, 63–64; openness in theater, 65; for Taiwan, 63
Derrida, Jacques, 110–111, 112, 126–127
deviance, *Male Hole* artwork, 42–51
diaspora in Sinophone studies, 97–98, 153, 213–219
diasporic attachment, 76
Dusinberre, Edward, 152

Eat Drink Man Woman (Lee), 155
ethnicity: Chineseness, 8–9; portrayals in Sinopop music, 92–94, 107–108; "Sino," 160; Syaman Rapongan's writing, 158, 167–172
ethnocentric bases of language, 12–13; adrift on Neurath's ship, 126–127; Chinese writing, 111–113; *Of Grammatology* (Derrida), 110–111; language and community, 122–126; language and meaning, 113–119; language and time, 119–122
Eurocentrism, 209, 221–222. *See also* Western cultural context
Even-Zohar, Itamar, 174

Fang, Qing, 25–26
Father Takes a Bride (Chang), 153–155
Felski, Rita, 182, 184, 186
feminism, *The Woman Warrior* (Kingston), 220–224
Foucault, Michel, 222

Four-Way Voice, 182–184
Francophone, 235–236
Fu, Jia-Chen, 9
Fu, Yue-an, 195

gender equality, Chinese socialism, 220–224
geopolitics, 62–64
gloss, etymological meaning, 4
glossia: meaning of, 2, 3, 4–5; as method, 6
glottographic writing systems, 114–115
Of Grammatology (Derrida), 110–111, 126–127
Guattari, Félix, 6, 74–75, 161–162, 167, 169–171

Hall, Stuart, 76–77, 214
health, physical examination in Republican China, 19–36
Heisserer, Eric, 115–116
"Heptapod B," 113–119
heteroglossia, 6–7, 160, 189, 230
heterotopia, 160
Hezhu xinpei, 57, 60–62, 68
historical context: Chinese history, 3–4, 86–88, 90; Malaysia, 99–102; physical examination in biomedicine, 21, 22–24; Sinophone studies, 4; sound art, 132–133, 135; Taiwan, 173–174, 179–180, 181, 187
Hokkien, 102, 104, 107
Hongkongness, 216–217
Hou, Chun-Ming, 10, 37–41; labeling deviance, 42–51; psychoanalytic turn, 38–39; therapeutic instrumentation of art, 51–54
Hsiao, Wei-chun, 195–196
Hsia, Yu, 128–129, 139–140
Huang, Junting, 13
Hung, Tzu-hui Celina, 14

identities: pluralistic experience of being Chinese, 98; "Pop Culture China," 95–97, 98; portrayals in Sinopop music, 92–94; "Sino," 160; Taiwanese, 160, 187. *See also* Chineseness
infant mortality, 28
Iovene, Paola, 12
Islam, portrayal in "Negarakuku," 91–92

Japan, child health education, 24–25
Japanese writing, 111–112
Ji, Kang, 142
Jibai ren, 104, 106–107
Jin, Wen, 101
Jingju drama, 68

Kafka, Franz, 161
Kingston, Maxine Hong, 220–224
Ku, Yu-ling, 186–187, 190–191

landscape: Chineseness as, 12, 79–82; *Romance on Lushan Mountain*, 79–82, 90; of words, 73, 82–89
language. *See* ethnocentric bases of language; glossia
Lan-ling theater, 56–59
Latour, Bruno, 182
Lee, Ang, 98, 155
Lee, Leo Oufan, 148
Lee, Yu-lin, 14
Liao, Ping-hui, 13
Liao, Yun-chang, 182–184
linguistic context, Sinoglossia, 5–7
listening skills, 13; attentive listening, 128–129; reduced and affective listening, 132–136; "techne of listening," 130–131; towards a theory of Chinese sound, 139–144. *See also* sound in Chinese languages
literary polysystem, 174
logocentrism, 110–111, 112, 115, 117, 127
Louie, Kam, 149–150
loyalism, 207–209

Malaysianness, 93–94
Malaysian society: linguistic pluralism, 102–104; postcolonialism, 104–108;

Wee Meng Chee's work, 93–94, 99–104
Male Hole (Hou), 40–54; labeling deviance, 42–51; therapeutic instrumentation of art, 51–54
Mandarin Chinese, 213
Mandopop, 95, 108, 109. *See also* Sinopop music
"Martian script," 123–126
materiality, 9
media, 11–13
mediality, 11–12, 235–236
migrants, Taiwan Literature Award for Migrants (TLAM), 175–198. *See also* translation
minor literatures, 2, 6; Chinese cinema, 74–75; Syaman's writing, 167, 170–172
"Muar Love Song," 102–103
"Muar Mandarin," 103–104, 107
multiculturalism: Sinopop music, 94–95, 101–104; Taiwan, 174, 177–178
music. *See* Sinopop music

Namewee. *See* Wee, Meng Chee
narcissism, *Male Hole* (Hou), 46–47
national anthems, 91
National Children's Day, 29, 30
National Child Welfare Association (NWCA), 30
Nationalist Party, China, 29–30, 82, 159
"Negarakuku," 91–94, 102
neologism, *Chai-na*, 225–228
neutrality, 142
Ni, Xiying, 33

ontology of sound, 129, 139. *See also* sound in Chinese languages
oral tradition, 166–172
Orientalism, 220–224

patriarchal values, 149–150, 156
People's Republic of China (PRC), 220–224

phonetic writing systems, 111–112, 120–121
physical examination in Republican China, 9, 19–36
"Pop Culture China," 95–97, 98
pop music. *See* Sinopop music
postcolonialism: Sinophone discourse, 206–209; Sinopop music, 104–108
postloyalism, 206–209
power differential, experienced by migrants, 185–189
psychoanalytic turn, art, 38–39, 52

Qiu, Zhijie, 137–138
Quine, W.W.O., 118–119, 127

race: bodily metrics, 20–21; Chineseness, 8–9; in Malaysia, 99–101
Rancière, Jacques, 143
rap music, in "Negarakuku," 91–94
"Rasa Sayang," 101–102
reduced listening, 132–136
Reyher, Ferdinand, 149
Rojas, Carlos, 12–13
Romance on Lushan Mountain: delimitations of Sinoglossia, 90; landscape of words, 82–89; love and the landscape, 78–82

Said, Edward, 56–57, 151, 222
Schaeffer, Pierre, 133, 136, 137
semasiographic writing systems, 114
settler colonialism, 159–160
sex industry, Taiwan, 49–51
sexism, and gender equality, 221
sexual deviance, 42–51. *See also Male Hole* (Hou)
Shan, Te-hsing, 63
Shih, Shu-mei, 97–98, 103, 143–144, 159–160, 212–215, 230–231
Shorter, Edward, 22–23
"Sinicization," 212
Sinitic language, 2
Sino-body, 57

Sinoglossia: and Chinese history, 3–4; cultural/linguistic contexts, 5–7; as delimitation, 90; distinction from Sinophone, 2; as inherent contradiction, 212–219; linguistic boundaries, 160–161; objects and methodologies, 7–8; as term, 2–3, 4–5, 76–77
"Sino" identity, 160
Sinophone literature: frontier of, 157, 166–169; orality, 167–169; Syaman Rapongan's writing, 157–172; as term, 157, 159
Sinophone studies: Chinese sound, 143–144; history and changeability in Sino-spheres, 201–206; intersection with Anglophone, 147–156; mediality, 11; as term, 1, 6; translation, 13–14
Sinophonicity, 104–108
Sinopop music, 12, 91–94; as concept, 94–99; distinction from Mandopop and Cantopop, 95, 109; "Negarakuku," 91–94, 102; postcolonialism, 104–108; Wee Meng Chee's work as, 99–104
Sinotopias, 229–236
socialism, 220–224
sound in Chinese languages, 13, 128–131; reduced and affective listening, 132–136; Sinophone studies, 143–144; technological mediation, 136–139; towards a theory of Chinese sound, 139–142
sound in Tao, 157–158, 161–163, 167–172
Sridongphet, Khemphon, 185
Sterne, Jonathan, 136
"Story of Your Life" (Chiang): language and community, 122–126; language and meaning, 113–119; language and time, 119–122
storytelling, Taiwan Literature Award for Migrants, 189–194
Swafford, Jan, 152
Syaman, Rapongan, 157–172

Taiwan: identity as Taiwanese, 160, 187; Syaman's writing, 157–172
Taiwaneseness, 216–217
Taiwan Literature Award for Migrants (TLAM), 175–198
Tan, E. K., 12
Tao sounds, Syaman Rapongan's writing, 157–158, 161–163, 167–172
Tao, Xingzhi, 31–32
Tay, William, 150
"techne of listening," 130–131; reduced and affective listening, 132–136; Sinophone studies, 143–144; technological mediation, 136–139; towards a theory of Chinese sound, 139–142
technology: cultural stability, 21–22; sound production, 136–139
theater, 55–57; American avant-garde and Taiwan, 64–66; cultural materialism, 62–64; *Hezhu xinpei*, 57, 60–62, 68; Lan-ling, 56–59; Wu's stage performance techniques, 58–62
therapeutic humanism, 51–54
Tho, Nan, 185
Thuy, Nguyen Cam, 184–185
transference (therapeutic instrumentation), 52–54
translation, 13–14; born-translated Taiwan literature, 173–179; Syaman's writing, 157–172; Taiwan Literature Award for Migrants (TLAM), 175–198
translingual practice: Syaman's writing, 165; Taiwan Literature Award for Migrants (TLAM), 177
Tseng, Wen-chen, 194–195

Venuti, Lawrence, 180, 186
Vermette, Patrice, 116
Villeneuve, Denis, 113. *See also Arrival* (Villeneuve)

Walkowitz, Rebecca, 178
Wang, Ban, 66–67
Wang, Chun-yen, 10

Wang, David Der-wei, 148
Wang, Jing, 132–133, 134–135
Wee, Meng Chee: controversies in "Negarakuku," 91–94, 105–108; the media and postcolonialism, 104–108; Sinopop music, 99–104
Wells, H. G., 124
Western-centrism, 5
Western cultural context, 5; alphabetic scripts, 111; Americanization, 64; avant-garde theater, 64–66; child health education, 27; Eurocentrism, 209, 221–222; intersection of the Sinophone and the Anglophone, 147–156; sound, 132–133
Wilcox, Christie, 124–125
The Woman Warrior (Kingston), 220–224
Wu, Jing-jyi, 55–62, 67–69

"x as method," 232–233
xenophone, 201–206
xionghan, 165
xiqu, 59
Xu, Zidong, 151

Yan, Jun, 128–129, 139–142
Ye, Zhaoyan, 147–148

Zhang, Ailing. *See* Chang, Eileen
Zhang, Jiehou, 25
Zhang, Yingjin, 150–151
Zhao, Wang, 61–62
Zhina, 227
Zhou, Shang, 32–35